THE TALE OF GENJI THROUGH CONTEMPORARY *MANGA*

SOAS Studies in Modern and Contemporary Japan

SERIES EDITOR:
Christopher Gerteis (SOAS, University of London, UK)

EDITORIAL BOARD:
Stephen Dodd (SOAS, University of London, UK)
Andrew Gerstle (SOAS, University of London, UK)
Janet Hunter (London School of Economics, UK)
Barak Kushner (University of Cambridge, UK)
Helen Macnaughtan (SOAS, University of London, UK)
Aaron W Moore (University of Edinburgh, UK)
Timon Screech (SOAS, University of London, UK)
Naoko Shimazu (NUS-Yale College, Singapore)

Published in association with the Japan Research Centre at the School of Oriental and African Studies, University of London, UK.

SOAS Studies in Modern and Contemporary Japan features scholarly books on modern and contemporary Japan, showcasing new research monographs as well as translations of scholarship not previously available in English. Its goal is to ensure that current, high quality research on Japan, its history, politics and culture, is made available to an English speaking audience.

Published:
Women and Democracy in Cold War Japan, Jan Bardsley
Christianity and Imperialism in Modern Japan, Emily Anderson
The China Problem in Postwar Japan, Robert Hoppens
Media, Propaganda and Politics in 20th Century Japan, The Asahi Shimbun Company (translated by Barak Kushner)
Contemporary Sino-Japanese Relations on Screen, Griseldis Kirsch
Debating Otaku in Contemporary Japan, edited by Patrick W. Galbraith, Thiam Huat Kam and Björn-Ole Kamm
Politics and Power in 20th-Century Japan, Mikuriya Takashi and Nakamura Takafusa (translated by Timothy S. George)
Japanese Taiwan, edited by Andrew Morris
Japan's Postwar Military and Civil Society, Tomoyuki Sasaki
The History of Japanese Psychology, Brian J. McVeigh

Postwar Emigration to South America from Japan and the Ryukyu Islands, Pedro Iacobelli
The Uses of Literature in Modern Japan, Sari Kawana
Post-Fascist Japan, Laura Hein
Mass Media, Consumerism and National Identity in Postwar Japan, Martyn David Smith
Japan's Occupation of Java in the Second World War, Ethan Mark
Gathering for Tea in Modern Japan, Taka Oshikiri
Engineering Asia, Hiromi Mizuno, Aaron S. Moore and John DiMoia
Automobility and the City in Japan and Britain, c. 1955–1990, Simon Gunn and Susan Townsend
The Origins of Modern Japanese Bureaucracy, Yuichiro Shimizu (translated by Amin Ghadimi)
Kenkoku University and the Experience of Pan-Asianism, Yuka Hiruma Kishida
Overcoming Empire in Post-Imperial East Asia, Barak Kushner and Sherzod Muminov
Imperial Japan and Defeat in the Second World War, Peter Wetzler
Gender, Culture, and Disaster in Post-3.11 Japan, Mire Koikari
Empire and Constitution in Modern Japan, Junji Banno (translated by Arthur Stockwin)
A History of Economic Thought in Japan, Hiroshi Kawaguchi and Sumiyo Ishii (translated by Ayuko Tanaka and Tadashi Anno)
Transwar Asia, edited by Reto Hoffman and Max Ward
Haruki Murakami and the Search for Self-Therapy, Jonathan Dil
Japan's Empire of Birds, Annika A. Culver
Chronicling Westerners in Nineteenth-Century East Asia, edited by Robert S. G. Fletcher and Robert Hellyer
The Translocal Island of Okinawa: Anti-Base Activism and Grassroots Regionalism, Shinnosuke Takahashi
Contesting Memorial Spaces of Japan's Empire, edited by Edward Boyle and Steven Ivings

THE TALE OF GENJI THROUGH CONTEMPORARY *MANGA*

Challenging Gender and Sexuality in Japan

Lynne K. Miyake

BLOOMSBURY ACADEMIC
LONDON • NEW YORK • OXFORD • NEW DELHI • SYDNEY

BLOOMSBURY ACADEMIC
Bloomsbury Publishing Plc, 50 Bedford Square, London, WC1B 3DP, UK
Bloomsbury Publishing Inc, 1359 Broadway, New York, NY 10018, USA
Bloomsbury Publishing Ireland, 29 Earlsfort Terrace, Dublin 2, D02 AY28, Ireland

BLOOMSBURY, BLOOMSBURY ACADEMIC and the Diana logo are trademarks of
Bloomsbury Publishing Plc

First published in Great Britain 2024
Paperback edition published 2026

Copyright © Lynne K. Miyake, 2024

Lynne K. Miyake has asserted her right under the Copyright, Designs and Patents Act,
1988, to be identified as Author of this work.

For legal purposes the Acknowledgments on pp. xvi–xxi constitute an extension
of this copyright page.

Cover image: Ide Chikae, *The Tale of Genji: Elegant Dissolution*, 1:98.
Copyright © Ide Chikae 2008

All rights reserved. No part of this publication may be: i) reproduced or transmitted in
any form, electronic or mechanical, including photocopying, recording or by means of
any information storage or retrieval system without prior permission in writing from the
publishers; or ii) used or reproduced in any way for the training, development or operation
of artificial intelligence (AI) technologies, including generative AI technologies. The rights
holders expressly reserve this publication from the text and data mining exception as per
Article 4(3) of the Digital Single Market Directive (EU) 2019/790.

Bloomsbury Publishing Plc does not have any control over, or responsibility for, any
third-party websites referred to or in this book. All internet addresses given in this
book were correct at the time of going to press. The author and publisher regret any
inconvenience caused if addresses have changed or sites have ceased to exist,
but can accept no responsibility for any such changes.

A catalogue record for this book is available from the British Library.

A catalog record for this book is available from the Library of Congress.

ISBN: HB: 978-1-3504-2493-7
PB: 978-1-3504-2496-8
ePDF: 978-1-3504-2494-4
eBook: 978-1-3504-2492-0

Series: SOAS Studies in Modern and Contemporary Japan

Typeset by Newgen KnowledgeWorks Pvt. Ltd., Chennai, India

For product safety related questions contact productsafety@bloomsbury.com.

To find out more about our authors and books visit www.bloomsbury.com
and sign up for our newsletters.

For Dennis
And my parents Francis and Shigeko Miyake

CONTENTS

List of Illustrations — xi
Preface: Why *The Tales of Genji Manga*? — xiii
Acknowledgments — xvi
Notes on Japanese Terms — xxii
List of Characters in *The Tale of Genji* — xxiii

Introduction — 1

Part I
MURASAKI SHIKIBU'S *THE TALE OF GENJI*

Chapter 1
CONTEXTUALIZING *THE TALE OF GENJI*: THE STORY, THE PERIOD, AND THE CONSUMER PRODUCERS — 19

Chapter 2
THE TALE OF GENJI THROUGH THE AGES: TRANSPOSITIONS, TRANSLATIONS, CULTURAL CAPITAL, AND INTERPRETATIVE COMMUNITIES — 35

Part II
MANGA'S MANY TALES OF MANY GENJIS

Chapter 3
SHŌJO GIRLS *MANGA*: OBJECTS OF WHOSE DESIRE? — 51

Chapter 4
BOYS LOVE *MANGA*: APPROPRIATING, (CHILD) PORN-ING, AND QUEERING MALE–MALE ROMANCES? — 73

Chapter 5
LADIES COMICS: SUBJECTS OF CONSUMPTION, PRODUCTION, AND DESIRE — 93

Chapter 6
SHŌNEN BOYS/*SEINEN* YOUNG MEN *MANGA*: MALE PERSPECTIVES
REFRACTED   117

Chapter 7
EDUCATION FOR SOFT POWER, NATIONAL PRIDE, AND FEMINIST
CRITIQUE: *GENJI* IN *JŌHŌ* INFORMATIONAL *MANGA*   139

Chapter 8
CONCLUSION: THE CULTURAL DNA OF *THE (MANGA) TALES OF GENJI*   163

Notes   173
Bibliography   197
Index   217

ILLUSTRATIONS

3.1	Niou and Kaoru ardently pursue Ukifune	52
3.2	Genji and Fujitsubo consummate their relationship	55
3.3	On a stormy night Genji is caught in Oborozukiyo's rooms by her father	60
3.4	Genji is attacked by an assassin sent to kill him, but he dispatches the assassin instead	66
3.5	As the male figure, Fujitsubo initiates the lovemaking with Genji, who is gender-flipped into a young girl	70
4.1	Hanachirusato comforting and teaching Genji the ways of love	77
4.2	Rokujō taunts Genji that his pleas to stop belie the pleasure he is experiencing from Rokujō's ministrations	80
5.1	Fujitsubo is captured at the height of her sexual pleasure with a solicitous Genji looking on	97
5.2	A vibrant peoplescape of carpenters at work on Genji's fabled Rokujō Mansion, filled with their lively discussion about Genji's plans for his new abode and two of its future inhabitants in the foreground	99
5.3	On the right page Aoi walks in procession to the teahouse as a top-ranking courtesan in full regalia, and on the left page she catches the eye of Gen, the Genji stand-in and most sought-after man of Yoshiwara	107
5.4	On the right page the ladies from Shikibu's world are talking when there is a sudden shift to Genji's world in the last frame on the lower left. The young Murasaki's grandmother worries about Murasaki after her death, and Genji in the top three frames on the left gallantly says he will take care of Murasaki, only to put her in a cage in the bottom frame	113
6.1	Iyami Genji gets his first glimpse of the red-nosed princess and reacts in exaggerated fashion, his face shattering in surprise	119
6.2	Koizumi succinctly depicts the first chapter of the tale "Kiritsubo" in eight frames	121
6.3	Tomi embellishes in graphic fashion Genji's mother tumbling to her death, as an illness, perpetrated by the harassment she suffers at court, gets the better of her	125
6.4	Unbeknownst to Yū, Terumi spies on her lifting her top to cool off. Fan-service close-up of her breasts is very much on display, but on the left page we also see Terumi's sense of shame at being a "peeping Tom"	130

7.1	In the transposed English version, the left-hand page (page 26) depicts Genji looking at himself walking down the corridor	148
7.2	In the Japanese version, page 26 is on the right and is situated so that Genji is looking across to page 27 (on the left) at Fujitsubo	149
7.3	As he sets the scene for Genji's seduction of the provincial governor's wife, Hasegawa details the material culture of a Heian mansion	153
7.4	Empress Kokiden sprouts horns, revealing the ferocity of her jealousy over Fujitsubo's promotion to empress and giving birth to a son who becomes crown prince, despite the biological father being Genji and not the emperor	155
7.5	Murasaki is overwhelmed by the power and prestige of her new rival for Genji's love, the Third Princess, as she "invades" Rokujō-in with her army of ladies-in-waiting	158

PREFACE

Why The Tales of Genji Manga?

"What do you think about making a presentation at the National Institute of Japanese Literature? It's a conference on 'Visuality and Verbal Expression,'" a friend emailed me early in the new millennium. "I don't do film or painting or visuals, but would a *Tale of Genji manga* work?" I replied. *Manga* at such an elite conference would definitely be off the beaten track, but the Institute very graciously accepted my proposal. In 2000 I arrived in Tokyo to give my first ever *manga* presentation on artist Tsuboi Koh's *The Illustrated Tale of Genji: A Classic Japanese Romance*. The conference attendees, intrigued by the topic, offered questions and comments—one male professor confessed that he was so captivated by artist Yamato Waki's reworking of the *Genji, Fleeting Dreams*, that in the 1980s he went to buy each new volume as it hit the bookstores but always under the guise that it was for his daughter. On the plane home, I reflected upon the comments and the special mention the conference organizer made of my presentation in his closing remarks and realized that the topic held great promise. My journey to explore the *Genji manga* began.

My first order of business was coming up to speed in the field of *manga*, their history and criticism. I began by reading other *Genji manga* and *manga* more widely. At the same time, I pursued the history of *manga* genres/categories, the ins and outs of the boys, girls, ladies, young men, and informational *manga* categories, and the tenets of visual culture production. To delve deeper into the subject, I launched a class on Japanese *manga* in 2006. I ended up teaching it every other year, but in truth, the students were teaching me. Reading comics since childhood, they were born and bred in *manga* literacy. True, they tended to favor one or the other categories, but were excited to discuss *manga* titles from all categories, helping us develop a broad understanding of the field. All in all, I learned a lot, as we discussed and engaged the *manga*, and critiqued the comics, *manga*, and visual culture theory that we read in class. My study captures many of the topics and issues we discussed, and it shares so much of what I learned in those wonderful classes!

To the great delight and envy of my students, I was also able to travel to Japan to visit many *mangaka* artist museums all over Japan and, of course, to explore *anime* director Miyazaki Hayao's offerings at his Ghibli Museum. In 2009 I joined 500,000 fans in Tokyo at the greatest comic conventions of them all, Comiket (Comic Market), where artists and fanzine artists sell their wares and cosplayers strut their stuff very much in the fashion of Comic-Con in San Diego (which I had the pleasure of attending in 2010). For several years I scoured used bookstores to buy volumes of *manga*, past and present, and on one research semester abroad, I sent twenty-seven boxes of *manga* home to California. To broaden my understanding of how *The Tale of Genji* was adapted into other media and came to be *manga*, I toured exhibitions of the twelfth-century *Tale of Genji* scrolls at the Gotoh Museum in Tokyo and the Tokugawa Art Museum in Nagoya, viewed Tokugawa woodblock prints of the tale here in Claremont through shows that my colleague at Scripps College, Bruce Coats, and his students staged, purchased art history books on the tale, and read studies of the tale's transformation into poetic and then later nativist commentary lauding *The Tale of Genji* as the essence of Japanese culture. I searched websites for modern iterations of the tale and discovered such gems as the 2,000-yen bill with an image from the *Genji* scroll on it, the Murasaki Shikibu MP3 bot that recited parts of the *Genji*, an opera with English librettos, and even a symphony, the *Genji Monogatari Illusion Symphony Picture Scroll*, whose premiere I attended in 1999 in Pasadena. (More new things keep popping up. I just found notice of a ballet "Genji" that premiered in Houston on March 24, 2023!)

A total of 24,000 pages and forty plus *Genji manga* (perused much more slowly than the 3.75 seconds per page speed of boys-comics readers!) later, *The Tale of Genji through Contemporary Manga: Challenging Gender and Sexuality in Japan* came to fruition. It explores girls, ladies, boys, young men, and informational *manga* comics adaptations of the venerable old tale. It showcases the ways in which these iterations make visual gender, sexuality, and desire that challenge perceptions of reading and readership, morality and ethics, and what is translatable from one culture to another. The forty *manga Genjis*, which I examine, visually and narratively rework (fe)male gazes, gently inject humor, eroticize, gender flip, queer, and simultaneously reinscribe and challenge heteronormative gender norms. The first full-length study of *Genji manga*, *The Tale of Genji through Contemporary Manga* examines these adaptations within *manga* studies and the historical and cultural moments that fashioned and sustained them. However, this book also interrogates the circumscribed, in-group aristocratic society and the consumer and production practices of the Heian society that formed the basis of the eleventh-century tale. My study utilizes western queer, feminist, sexuality, and gender theory and Japanese cultural and narrative practices to illuminate the ways in which the tale redeploys itself. But I also give much needed context and explanation regarding the charges of appropriation of prepubescent (fe)male and gay bodies and the utilization of (sexual) violence mounted against *manga* and *anime* once they went global, implicating the *Genji manga* as well.

Genji manga iterations continue to be produced—a testament to the tale's viability in the twenty-first century and beyond. Writing a book, however, I had to stop somewhere. It took me some time to sort through the *Genji manga* that were being produced, to locate those out of print, and to wait for some to complete their series. In the end I chose forty *Genji manga* published between 1974 and 2019, focusing on thirty-four of them. I took care to select several from each of the five mainstream categories and also from the informational *manga* category. I chose those deemed iconic, pioneers in the field, or representative of their categories.

These selections also showcase the rich variety and expanse of the adaptations—and are great fun to boot! I hope you agree!

Manga studies, too, is an ever-evolving, fast-moving field, and deciding on which theoretical studies to include has been challenging. In the end, I selected studies that worked best with my assessment of *manga* and *Genji manga* in particular. These include Japanese and English works that explore gender, sexuality, visual culture, and the imaginary as well as informative studies on *manga* history, media literacy, and *manga* consumer practice. I also utilized my own rendering of in-group, collaborative, participatory, and performative reading practices that grew out of an exploration of Heian reading practices that, I argue, have come full circle in contemporary *manga*.

My own engagement with *The Tale of Genji* and *manga* over thirty years also informs my study. A distillation of teaching and presentations before academic and community audiences, *The Tale of Genji through Contemporary Manga* makes theory accessible, condenses centuries of the *Genji*'s consumer practices, and introduces *manga* in topical chapters that dovetail one with the other. I hope my study will provide a window not just into *The Tale of Genji* and the field of *manga* but also into contemporary Japanese society, examining age- and gender-targeted audiences enacting and challenging their fantasies, hopes, and desires. Forty *Genji manga* stand ready to show you the way.

ACKNOWLEDGMENTS

My study of *The Tale of Genji Manga* brought together my love of Heian literature and my passion for popular culture steeped in superhero comics, *Star Trek, Star Wars,* and *Snoopy*. It has taken me on a journey that spans both sides of the Pacific, time periods separated by a thousand years; differing cultural, social, and theoretical frames of references; and all the marvelous people who taught me, challenged me, and fought for me and my project. Where to start to thank them all? Of course, it should begin with my profound gratitude to Christopher Gerteis, series editor of the SOAS Studies in Modern and Contemporary Japan at Bloomsbury Publishing, for encouraging and enabling the publication of my study. Senior editor Rhodri Mogford patiently shepherded me through thick and thin, answering all my queries and keeping me on track—for which I am most grateful! They say that the devil is in the details, and it is so true, and I thank editorial assistant Gabriella Cox for sorting them out. I most appreciate the attention that production editor Emma Tranter and production manager Amy Brownbridge devoted to this project, the meticulous and thorough copyediting by K. S. Latha, and the invaluable suggestions and kind and steadfast support provided by project manager Sam Augustin Durai.

Immeasurable thanks must be given to Jan Bardsley who believed in me and my project. She constantly pulled me back from the brink as I wondered if my study would ever see the light of day. A beacon of boundless light and energy, she responded to my queries with johnny-on-the-spot articles, links, examples, incisive advice, anything I needed and always with great cheer. She read through drafts of chapters (some pretty ponderous), wrote to editors on my behalf, edited proposals, advised me on how publishing worked and how to put my best foot forward. I cannot thank her enough!!

A heartfelt thank you must be extended to Udagawa Yoshie, Kamimura Tarō, and Kitajima Ayumi for obtaining copyright permissions for the images in my study. No small feat, they cajoled publishers to fill in request forms, combed social platforms to find artists, and exhibited profound patience and fortitude in contacting and recontacting publishers and artists. Special thanks to Yoshie for assembling this wonderful team and setting things up, and to Ayumi and Yoshie for polishing the translations of sections of my book that artists requested to see. Without the dedication and resilience of this team, there would not be a single image and the maxim that a picture is worth a thousand words never realized.

In yet another border crossing, I profited greatly from my colleagues in French and Spanish at Pomona College who renewed my faith in a comparative literature approach to literary studies. To Jack Abecassis who was always ready to discuss Japan, film, and literature at 6:00 a.m. on any Tuesday or Thursday, I owe much gratitude for helping me encapsulate the cultural, moral, and narrative DNA of *The Tale of Genji* and its importance in the configuration of the *Genji manga* and Japanese literary practices. José Cartegena-Calderón, the other 6:00 a.m. regular, expanded my reading of gender, sexuality, and queer studies and how they played out in the tale and *manga* providing insightful observations, readings, and resources—thank you José! Paul Cahill has been there from the beginning: engaging in hours of discussion, he encouraged me to include the differently configured production and consumption practices of *The Tale of Genji* and helped me formulate my arguments and even format the text properly, for which I am eternally grateful. Thanks must also be extended to Livi Yoshioka-Maxwell, who so carefully read many of my early drafts and kept reading and discussing them with me even after taking a position in Minnesota!

I am indebted to art historian and unflagging supporter of things *Genji*, Bruce Coats who directed me to Utagawa Kunisada's *Genji* prints and more. I thank Samuel Yamashita, too, for seeking out publishers and garnering invitations for me to speak on *Genji manga*. My gratitude as well to Adan Gallardo who helped me solve many a computer-based mess-up and who, as an avid *manga* reader, provided sage advice on how to present challenging topics and much more. I am also most grateful to Akiko Otsu for helping me get to the Comiket *manga* convention and a smaller version in her hometown. I would be remiss not to express my gratitude to Stanleigh Jones who gifted me with Tsuboi's *Genji manga*—inspiring me to teach it in class and make my first *Genji manga* presentation.

To cross over to another time and place, I am most grateful to all in Japan who provided me with the in-depth knowledge, appreciation, and understanding of Japanese literature and *The Tale of Genji*. I must first thank my mentor from Tohoku University, Kikuta Shigeo, who invited me as a Monbusho Ministry of Education (now the Ministry of Education, Culture, Sports, Science, and Technology [MEXT]) Scholar while I was in graduate school. His careful tutelage and infinite passion, he will be glad to know, has produced the *Genji manga* study you have before you. I also thank those affiliated with the Kokugo Japanese Literature Department at Tohoku University: Suzuki Norio and Kureha Susumu, second- and third-in-command who ensured that the department operated as a well-oiled intellectual entity; Kikuchi Yasuhiko who taught me so much about Japanese poetry; and Nitta Takako who patiently worked with me through my dissertation text and provided amazing direction on Heian literature and culture. My thanks, too, to my fellow classmate Kojima Yukiko who was my tutor and comrade in arms at the time and who continues to be a good friend and invaluable resource to this day. She along with Ishikawa Hidemi helped me make my way at the university. All welcomed me into their midst and taught me the tools of the trade. My studies were further expanded during another stint in Japan, this time several decades later at Hirosaki University as a Japan Foundation Fellow. First and foremost, I thank Itoh Moriyuki for sponsoring my stay, and especially Satoh Kazuyuki for introducing me to colleagues who provided eye-opening revelations and engaging me in thoughtful discussions on the Japanese language and conventions that continue to this day. My thanks to Victor Carpenter in this regard as well.

Other wonderful scholars and artists whom I must thank: Kinko Ito has been a wealth of information on ladies comics, a very careful reader of my manuscript, and a provocative speaker at a *manga* symposium I mounted. She also put me in contact with scholars in Japan and orchestrated my visit with artist Ide Chikae who provided a stunningly instructive, behind-the-scenes look into the workings of a *manga* artist. She generously fielded my questions, explaining how she outlines, draws, and produces her *manga*, and invited me to her studio to witness the nuts and bolts of getting a *manga* to press. I am grateful, too, to Sonja Arntzen for writing numerous letters supporting my grant proposals and for introducing me to two premodern scholars. Iwasa Miyoko served as a child companion to the present Japanese emperor's aunt and was instrumental in providing rare insight into how the ladies-in-waiting of old served their imperial mistresses. Imazeki Toshiko encouraged me to make my first *manga* presentation at the National Institute of Japanese Literature conference and the rest is history. I am indebted as well to Ronald Stewart for his expert advice on copyright laws and the positionality of *manga* artists. Rachel Thorn has also been most supportive through e-mail exchanges and especially for her stewardship of est em (whose work I discuss) and numerous *manga* students at Kyoto Seika University's Graduate School of Manga. I also want to acknowledge and thank Victoria R. M. Scott who did an amazing job copyediting my manuscript not just polishing the text but pinpointing areas that needed further clarification and reworking.

Over the years I have been blessed by amazing students to whom I am most grateful: Rachel Davidson kindly read early drafts of my chapters; Ben Liu enabled treks to the Ghibli Museum, *manga* artist museums, and *manga* and *anime* exhibitions and the like in Japan; and Adrienne Johnson (now a professor in Japan!) introduced me to invaluable research sources. The research assistants I have had over the years at Pomona College have been astounding: Jorge Rodriguez, Xin Wang, Brandon Tran, Eli Fessler, Dylan Mendoza, Jason Yoo, Alana Mori, Chihiro Tamashiro, and Yuki Numata to name a few scoured the internet for information on *manga* and *manga* studies, located *manga* statistics, perused *manga*, and two, Jorge and Xin, even did original research which I use in my study. I am indebted as well to the students who took my *manga*, Japanese and Japanese American women writers, and autobiography classes: they helped me hone my readings of *The Tale of Genji*, premodern Japanese narratives, and modern *manga* and Japanese texts and kept me honest and on track!

For permission to use images from their publications, I thank the artists and publishers of Bunkasha, Chūō Kōron, Geibunsha, Gentōsha, Heibonsha, Homesha, Kadokawa, Kōdansha, Shōgakukan, and Shūeisha. Special thanks to Ide Chikae for her captivating image of Genji and Fujitsubo and for permission to use another for the book cover; to agent Kawai Minori and Atelier Eiko Co. for Hanamura Eiko's wonderful two-page spread; to Fujio Productions for Akatsuka Fujio's humorous Genji; to Maki Miyako/Leijisha for the slice-of-life look at Heian society; to Kyōto Minpōsha Newspaper for Takenaka Ranko's 1998 serialization; and to Saotome

Ageha for her riveting image. Without all these exquisitely rendered illustrations my study would be all the poorer. The publisher and I would also be grateful to hear from any copyright holder who is not hereby acknowledged and promise to rectify any errors or omissions in proper credits in future editions of the book. (Every effort was made to trace the copyright holder of one image but to no avail, and it has been included under the Japanese copyright law [Article 32, Section 1] and "fair use"/"reasonable effort" protocols that allow for copyrighted images to be quoted like text without permission in academic publications.)

Generous intuitional support from the Monbusho Ministry of Education (now MEXT) Scholarship, the National Endowment of the Humanities Fellowship, five National Endowment for the Humanities Supplemental Sabbatical Fellowships, Japan Foundation Grants to do research in Japan and to mount symposia ("Marauding Rabbits, Starry-Eyed Girls, Battling Boys, 'Ordinary Ladies': Japanese [American] *Manga* in Review" and another on humor), and two Hirosaki University Investigative Grant provided invaluable opportunities to conduct research as well as meet with experts in Japan and bring specialists to Pomona College.

Pomona College has supported my research, teaching, and academic development for three decades for which I am most grateful. I received numerous grants to do research and visit museums and exhibitions, and to acquire *manga* volumes and materials on *manga* and *The Tale of Genji* in libraries and bookstores in Japan. I am most thankful for the Sontag Fellowship that funded the completion of my manuscript. I am grateful as well for the monies I raised from departments and programs at the Claremont Colleges to host Kayono, a Japanese girls-comics artist; Carl Horn, Manga editor of Dark Horse Comics; Stan Sakai, creator of the Japanese American comics, *Usagi Yojimbo*; and Christine Yano, author of *Pink Globalization* and the rise of Hello Kitty. Wig Curriculum Development Grants provided funds to mount my *manga* class, while a Technology and Hahn Gift Fund grant enabled me to post on my website the original *manga*, virtual novels, *manga* translations, and papers that my students produced. You should check them out!! Special thanks must go to Margaret Starbucks, Rosie Narasaki (a former student!!), and the Boston Court Pasadena for inviting me to serve as a dramaturg for the world premiere of Rosie's play *Unrivaled*, which features Murasaki Shikibu and "rival" lady-in-waiting Sei Shōnagon of *Pillow Book* fame. Amazing performances and an even more amazing experience!

Making presentations and engaging with community, student, and faculty audiences has enriched my understanding of *The Tale of Genji* and *Genji manga*. Of special honor has been speaking at community venues like the Michelle Berton Memorial Lectures on Japanese Art at the Los Angeles County Museum, Los Angeles, California; the Minneapolis Institute of Art-mounted "*The Tale of Genji* in Japanese Art," Minneapolis, Minnesota; the Japan Society, San Francisco, California; the Japanese American Cultural Center with the Annenberg Foundation, Los Angeles, California; the Ministry of Foreign Affairs, Japan Foundation Center for Global Partnership, Los Angeles, California; and the Nibei Lecture Series, Nibei Foundation, Los Angeles, California—my gratitude to all for their kind invitations. I am also especially thankful for being interviewed on *On Point with Tom Ashbrook*, for the *Ideas with Host Paul Kennedy*, aired by Canadian Broadcasting Corporation, and for the "Invitation World Literature: *The Tale of Genji*" on the Annenberg Media website.

Much gratitude is extended to my colleagues in the field who have invited me to present at academic venues such as the San Jose State University Kazuki Fukuda-Abe Endowed Lecture Series in Contemporary Japanese Arts, San Jose, California; the Middlebury College Museum Exhibit on Narrative Art, Middlebury, Vermont; The Ohio State University Libraries and the Billy Ireland Cartoon Library and Museum, Columbus, Ohio; and the Canadian Broadcasting Cooperation presentation at the University of British Columbia, Vancouver, Canada. I am also most grateful for the opportunities to speak at the National Institute of Japanese Literature, Tokyo, Japan; the Ferris University International Conference on Japanese Literature, Yokohama, Japan; the International Conference of Asian Scholars, Shanghai, China; Hirosaki University Kommunication Kenkyūkai, Hirosaki, Japan as well as at conferences in Chicago, Illinois; Washington, DC; San Diego and Claremont, California. I thank my colleagues who asked me to make *Genji manga* presentations at Stanford University, Stanford, California; the University of California at Berkeley, Berkeley, California; the University of California at Los Angeles, Los Angeles, California; Lyons College, Batesville, Arkansas; and California State University San Bernardino, San Bernardino, California.

I am also very pleased to announce that my *manga* collection has found great homes at two institutions in the United States. Japanese Studies Librarian Ann Marie Davis and I spent twelve hours over zoom during the pandemic sorting through every *manga* volume I collected over the last twenty-five years selecting those that would be housed at the Ohio State Libraries or the Billy Ireland Cartoon Library and Museum in Columbus, Ohio. I was thrilled that she was excited about the academic tomes on *manga* and *anime* but even more so about my numerous *manga* magazines, original art by artists Ide Chikae and her daughter Kayono, and a cubic foot of ephemera—*anime* and *manga* flyers, brochures, Comiket and Comic-Con conference catalogs, advertisements for *manga* and *anime*, and this and that I had gathered over the years. Equally exciting, Xiuying Zou, head of the Asian Library at The Claremont Colleges Library in Claremont, California, has agreed to provide a dedicated space for my *Genji manga* and other volumes, some of which are out of print and hard to find. Films, Takarazuka all-female musical revue *Genji* performances, a rare production by dollmaker Hori Hiroshi (who made *Genji* dolls, staged, and filmed them) as well as other materials will be included. I am especially pleased that my *Genji manga* stuff will be nearby so I can go visit them. To Xiuying Zhou, Ann Marie Davis, I owe a debt of gratitude for preserving my collection in a day and age where most libraries are no longer interested in obtaining books. It fills me with such joy to know that they will continue to serve as a resource for research and reading enjoyment. Special thanks as well to Louie Kulber who came at 8:00 a.m. most mornings during the summer of 2021 to create spreadsheets of the over one thousand books I owned so that librarians could quickly assess my collection. It is indeed thanks to Louie that I gave away every volume—to five libraries and to students, him included. A dream come true for the ultimate bibliophile.

I would also be remiss in not thanking my very good friends who helped me throughout my journey: Steven Carter whom I have known since graduate school has provided intellectual and much needed support and direction from the very beginning; fellow activists and travelers, Miguel Tinker Salas, Raymond Buriel, and Sidney Lemelle, showed me that battles can be fought and won, helping me wend my way through academia; and, of course, my Asian American cohorts and steadfast friends, Sharon Goto, Linus and Julie Yamane, and Madeline Gosiaco, ensured that I made it through. Perhaps most unusual, I must thank Masao Miyoshi, James Larsen, and Susan Matisoff for directing and signing my Ph.D. dissertation so many decades ago when upheavals in my graduate program threatened to engulf many of us at the time. Without their seeing me through, it would have been all over before it even began.

To my parents and sisters and their families, I owe a thanks for their patience and support. But none more to my husband and BFF Dennis Eggleston who always had the time and energy to cheer me on, pull me out of the dumps, and be my anchor and support. A physicist by training, he is always clear-eyed about how to tackle problems and solve them. His "appreciation" of my silly antics always made me laugh and carried the day! Thank you ever so much and more, Dennis!

Lynne K. Miyake
Pasadena, California
September 30, 2023

NOTES ON JAPANESE TERMS

I italicize words in Japanese and include an annotated list of characters from *The Tale of Genji* at the beginning of the volume to help keep track of the characters in the tale.

Following Japanese custom, I indicate Japanese names providing the surname first followed by the given name, except for authors who publish in English. This may cause confusion in places, because some Japanese authors have published both in Japanese and in English, which are reflected in the different order of their names.

Following *manga* conventions, the images in this study are read utilizing Japanese word order, that is, from right to left and from top to bottom.

I use macrons to indicate long vowel sounds in Japanese except in well-known instances such as place names, Tokyo, Osaka, or Kyoto, and for terms commonly used in English.

All translations from the Japanese are my own unless indicated otherwise.

CHARACTERS IN *THE TALE OF GENJI*

The Akashi Lady/Akashi no ue

The mother of the Akashi Princess, who is one of Genji's children. A storm destroys Genji's residence in Suma while he is in exile, and the Akashi Priest, the lady's father, rescues Genji and his entourage and takes them to his mansion in Akashi, where Genji meets Akashi and has a daughter with her. She comes to the capital but has to give up her daughter to Murasaki to raise.

The Akashi Priest

The Akashi Lady's father, who rescues Genji and his entourage when they are beset by a violent storm. A former provincial governor who has taken the tonsure, he has high hopes for his daughter marrying a courtier and sees his chance when he rescues Genji.

The Akashi Princess (later the Akashi Empress)

The daughter of Genji and the Akashi Lady. She is raised by Murasaki so that she can be groomed as an imperial consort. She becomes empress and is the mother of Niou.

Akikonomu

Reizei's empress and Rokujō's daughter, who first serves as the Ise High Priestess, enabling Rokujō to leave the capital and Genji. Upon Akikonomu's return to the capital, she is sponsored by Genji and is pitted against Tō no Chūjō's daughter, whom she bests at a picture contest, Genji's paintings from Suma winning the day.

Aoi, Lady

Genji's first principal wife, Tō no Chūjō's sister, and the mother of Genji's son Yūgiri. Aoi has dreams of becoming an imperial consort and remains aloof toward Genji, who is several years younger than she, until she gives birth to Yūgiri, only to be killed by Rokujō soon thereafter.

Asagao (Princess Morning Glory)

Genji's cousin, who maintains a chaste correspondence with Genji, effectively evading him for sixteen years. She serves for a period as a high priestess at the Kamo Shrine, where all sexual encounters are eschewed.

Fujitsubo, Lady (later Empress)

Genji's stepmother; empress to Genji's father, Emperor Kiritsubo; the mother of Reizei, who is Genji's son; and Murasaki's aunt. She is Genji's stepmother and his central love interest who is said to resemble his mother. Genji pursues her relentlessly, so after the emperor's death, she takes the tonsure to remove herself from the sexual economy of being courted by men.

Genji

The central protagonist of the tale and the child of the emperor and his favorite consort Kiritsubo, who dies when Genji is three. Genji marries Aoi, the daughter of the powerful Minister of the Left, and is demoted to commoner status to protect him from the Kokiden faction. He is lauded as beautiful, talented, and the consummate eligible man and establishes romantic liaisons with his stepmother Fujitsubo, the love of his life Murasaki, the Akashi Lady, and many others. Although a commoner, he rises to great heights and is even given the title of Honorary Retired Emperor.

Gen no naishi

An older lady-in-waiting who served Genji's father. Forward and not afraid to flirt, she woos Genji into a relationship and draws Tō no Chūjō into a mock competition for her attentions. An altercation occurs where Genji runs off with Tō no Chūjō's sleeve and Tō no Chūjō runs off with Genji's sash, all in fun.

Hanachirusato (Lady of the Orange Blossoms)

The younger sister of one of Genji's father's consort, she has had romantic relations with Genji in the past. Genji later moves her into his fabled Rokujō-in mansion with his other ladies, where she looks after Genji's son Yūgiri until he marries and Yūgao's daughter Tamakazura until she is wed, highlighting her caretaker role.

Kaoru

The son of Genji's second principal wife, the Third Princess, and Kashiwagi. Genji must acknowledge Kaoru as his son even though he is not. An evocative Genji scroll painting depicts Genji viewing the baby Kaoru for the first time. Although Kaoru embodies Genji's kinder, more responsible and caring aspects, he fails to convince Ōigimi that he will not love her and leave her, and after her death he aggressively pursues Ukifune.

Kashiwagi

Tō no Chūjō's oldest son and Yūgiri's good friend. He pines after Genji's second principal wife, the Third Princess, with whom he sires a son, Kaoru, but dies of guilt as a result.

Kiritsubo, Emperor

Genji's father, whose excessive love for Genji's mother, the Kiritsubo no kōi, angers the other consorts and especially the powerful Empress Kokiden. After the Kōi's death, he takes Fujitsubo as his new empress. Unbeknownst to the emperor, Genji and Fujitsubo have a son, Reizei, but the emperor acknowledges him as his own.

Kiritsubo no kōi (the Kiritsubo Consort)

Genji's mother, who is extremely beautiful and who becomes Emperor Kiritsubo's favorite. But because she does not have powerful relatives, she is driven to her death by the other imperial consorts, especially Empress Kokiden.

Kokiden, Empress

Empress to Emperor Kiritsubo and the mother of Suzaku, who becomes emperor after the death of Kiritsubo. Oborozukiyo's sister, Empress Kokiden is the arch enemy of Genji, his mother, and later Fujitsubo, and is instrumental in forcing Genji into self-imposed exile to Suma.

Koremitsu

Koremitsu is the son of Genji's wet nurse and is Genji's foster brother and faithful personal attendant. He does Genji's bidding and arranges for Yūgao's funeral after her untimely death, among other things.

Kumoinokari

Tō no Chūjō's daughter, she marries Yūgiri and has many children with him. She is featured in one of the Genji scroll paintings nursing her baby.

Murasaki

Fujitsubo's niece, whom Genji takes in after the death of her grandmother and raises from the age of ten to be his ideal wife. The love of his life, she marries Genji but never attains the status of his official wife because of her low status. She suffers through Genji's marriages to and liaisons with other women. She never has a child of her own, has to raise the Akashi Lady's daughter, and is finally killed by Rokujō's vengeful spirit.

Naka no kimi (the Middle Princess)

The second of the Uji sisters, she resides with her imperial father, who has left the capital for the hinterlands of Uji in pursuit of Buddhist enlightenment. Her older sister Ōigimi wants Kaoru to marry Naka no kimi, but Kaoru introduces her to Niou instead, who marries Naka no kimi and moves her to his mansion in the city.

Niou

Genji's grandson and the son of the Akashi Empress. He is Murasaki's favorite among Genji's grandchildren but has inherited Genji's womanizing ways. He marries Naka no kimi and is pressured to also take Yūgiri's daughter Roku no kimi as his wife. He is fast friends with Kaoru but becomes involved with Kaoru in a love triangle involving Ukifune.

Oborozukiyo

Empress Kokiden's sister, Oborozukiyo is betrothed to Suzaku, Genji's half-brother, but has an affair with Genji. Genji is discovered in her quarters one rainy night, and is forced to go into self-imposed exile in Suma as a result. Known for her daring personality, Oborozukiyo revels in conducting an affair with her sister's adversary right under her family's noses.

Ochiba no miya

The Third Princess's sister and Kashiwagi's wife. Yūgiri courts and marries Ochiba after Kashiwagi's death.

Ōigimi (the First Princess)

The oldest of the Uji sisters. She becomes Kaoru's primary love interest but wills herself to die so that Kaoru will marry her younger sister, Naka no kimi.

Reizei, Emperor

The son of Genji and Fujitsubo. Genji's father Emperor Kiritsubo claims Reizi as his own son, however, and Reizei succeeds Suzaku as emperor. Reizei is only told of his true paternity later in the tale. He is unable to acknowledge Genji as his father but bestows an honorary title upon him.

Rokujō, Lady

A consort to a crown prince who dies young, Rokujō falls in love with the much younger Genji against her will and becomes so obsessively jealous that, unbeknownst to herself, she turns into a living spirit who kills Yūgao and Aoi and, later, Murasaki. Rokujō makes Genji promise not to take her daughter Akikonomu as a lover but to be her guardian, which he agrees to do.

Suetsumuhana, Princess

The old-fashioned, red-nosed princess who is so nicknamed because she has a long nose whose tip is red from the cold in her unheated mansion. She is a secondary character known for her steadfast loyalty to Genji and appears in almost all the *manga* remediations because of her potential as a comic figure.

Suzaku, Crown Prince and Later Emperor

The son of Emperor Kiritsubo and Empress Kokiden, Suzaku is Genji's half-brother. The emperor demotes Genji to commoner status and makes Suzaku his heir because of the power of the Kokiden family. At the behest of his mother, Suzaku forces Genji into exile, but calls him back to the capital after being reprimanded by his father's ghost. Suzaku later abdicates the throne to Reizei, takes the tonsure, and asks Genji to marry his daughter, the Third Princess, with disastrous results.

Tamakazura

The daughter of Yūgao and Tō no Chūjō, Tamakazura is taken away from the capital by her wet nurse after Yūgao's death. She returns to the capital as a young woman and comes to live with Genji, who pretends to be her father. Genji has designs on her, but she is courted by many men and finally marries one of her suitors, seemingly to avoid Genji's clutches.

The Third Princess

Suzaku's young, naïve daughter, whom he asks Genji to marry. Genji is dazzled by her high rank as an imperial princess and does wed her, to the dismay of Murasaki. Her youth and reticence, plus Murasaki's falling ill, cause Genji to neglect her. She is seduced one night by Kashiwagi and comes to bear him a son, Kaoru.

Tō no Chūjō

Aoi's brother and Genji's brother-in-law, friend, and sometime rival. Tō no Chūjō is the father of Kashiwagi and Kumoinokari. He is married to the fourth daughter of the Minister of the Right who is the sister of Empress Kokiden and Oborozukiyo. Tō no Chūjō tries to best Genji at court by marrying his daughter also named the Kokiden Consort (who is a separate entity from Empress Kokiden, consort to Emperor Kiritsubo) to Emperor Reizei, but fails and initially is against Yūgiri marrying his daughter Kumoinokari. Nonetheless, he remains on good terms with Genji throughout the tale and is the only courtier who visits Genji in exile in Suma, defying his mother-in-law Empress Kokiden.

Ukifune (Princess Floating Boat)

The half-sister of the Uji sisters. She moves away from the capital after her mother remarries and is courted by a suitor who proposes marriage but who withdraws it when he finds out she is a stepdaughter. Ukifune returns to the capital, where she becomes the principal love interest of Kaoru and Niou in the last ten chapters of the tale. Distressed by the attentions of the two men, she nearly drowns in a river but is found by a priest and his nun sister who provide her a safe haven. The tale ends with Kaoru's unsuccessful attempt to win her back, leaving matters ambiguous and unresolved.

Utsusemi

The young wife of the Iyo no kami (the provincial governor of Iyo) whom Genji seduces when he is forced to spend the night at Iyo's mansion because of unfavorable directional taboos. Thereafter honoring her marriage vows to the governor, Utsusemi outsmarts and rebuffs him, making the liaison a "one-night stand," much to Genji's chagrin.

Utsusemi's Stepdaughter

The daughter of the Governor of Iyo on whom Genji spies at her father's mansion playing *go* with her stepmother Utsusemi. That night Genji slips into Utsusemi's rooms, but she evades him, leaving behind her robe. Genji mistakes the stepdaughter for Utsusemi but then proceeds to engage her in sex. The encounter in Egawa's remediation goes on for sixty-eight pages.

Yūgao (Lady of the "Evening Face" Flowers)

Tō no Chūjō's lover and the mother of Tamakazura. Yūgao is driven away by Tō no Chūjō's principal wife and hides out in a rustic house next door to Genji's wet nurse. On a visit to his wet nurse Genji spies Yūgao's ladies-in-waiting and starts up a relationship with Yūgao. One night he takes Yūgao to one of his houses, and there she is killed by Rokujō's living spirit.

Yūgiri

Genji's son with Aoi, Yūgiri rises in power at court. He is known for being reliable and responsible and does not seem to have inherited Genji's *suki* womanizing ways. However, upon Kashiwagi's untimely death he relentlessly pursues Ochiba, Kashiwagi's wife, disrupting his marriage to Kumoinokari and causing anguish to Ochiba and to Kashiwagi's family.

INTRODUCTION

Setting the Stage for Genji Manga

A roly-poly chestnut? A bucktoothed lover wannabe? A bashful boytoy? These are some of the new heroes of the venerable *Tale of Genji* from eleventh-century Japan, but how can that be? Written over a millennium ago by a lady-in-waiting, the tale speaks of an exceptionally beautiful and talented courtier named Genji, born of a union of love between a fictional emperor and his low-ranking consort, and traces his family's ascendency at court through four generations. The full story can be found in Chapter 1, but it begins with Genji's birth and the harassment his mother faces at the hands of the other imperial consorts. After his mother's death, the tale follows Genji, as he establishes himself at court romancing various women along the way: a tryst with his stepmother produces a son who becomes emperor, secret rendezvouses with the sister of his rival at court precipitates a self-imposed exile, and the abduction of a young girl ends with his raising her to become his wife. Genji's later years are marked by the highs of becoming honorary emperor but also the lows of being cuckolded by his son's best friend. The tale continues with the escapades of Genji's oldest son and culminates with the fraught relationships Genji's grandson and a second son (who is not his biological offspring) embark upon with three princesses.

A story for the ages, it is full of court intrigue, political jockeying at court, and life's trials and tribulations couched in romance. It was a "hot bestseller" of its time and has continually captured the hearts of generations of Japanese readers, writers, artists, and performers. Told and retold in verbal, visual, and musical forms not only for pleasure and enjoyment but also to further the political fortunes of those jockeying for power and the right to rule, it has helped establish and sustain the identities of courtiers, warriors, townspeople, women and girls, and even the Japanese government.

No doubt the author Murasaki Shikibu would be surprised to find her peerless hero Genji transformed into a bucktoothed Don Juan lover wannabe, or transmigrated into the body of a contemporary Japanese high schooler, or even gender-flipped into a fetching young woman. But this is what happened when the venerable old tale merged with the pop culture visual/textual Japanese *manga* comics. A fortuitous meeting, in their repurposing of the tale the *manga* showcased the variety, creativity, and richness of their different categories, making concrete the immersive, interactive reading strategies that brought the *Genji*'s courtier reading strategies full circle. The tale in turn highlighted its power to shape ways of thinking, parameters of desires, and even the construction of nation through a new medium. Possessing what I term the literary DNA of Japanese storytelling, *The Tale of Genji* defined how and what kind of narratives would prevail, what characters would be viable and in what ways, and what stories would come to serve as the database of culture, dreams, and desires.

In their retelling, *manga* also contemporize the tale, eroticizing the encounters between lovers and making visual the dreams and desires of their finely calibrated, in-group audiences. In accordance with these conventions, the *Genji manga* provide young girl readers different positionalities, as they search for true love, and offer ladies-comics readers the opportunity to become subjects in control of the production and consumption of their desires. Left without the usual battles and male camaraderie populating boys and some young men comics, the *Genji* male-oriented iterations interrogate male lust—with gentle humor, unrelenting realism, or by turning the male gaze on its head. In contrast, educational *manga* construct the *Genji* as a kind of database of the best of Japanese culture, touting it as a national treasure that pays homage to the nation that conceived it.

The Boys Love (BL) same-sex *Genji manga* create spaces for gender exploration not just for their targeted heterosexual women practitioners but also for straight men, bi/trans, and in-between genders. Once *manga* left Japan and their in-group audiences and went global, however, BL as well as ladies and the soft porn young men adaptation potentially opened up the *Genji manga* and the tale to be viewed as perverse and obscene.[1] In fact *manga* and *anime* encountered pushback in the 1990s and 2014—charged with the appropriation of prepubescent (fe)male and gay bodies and the utilization of (sexual) violence.

I argue, however, that these charges are overdrawn and that an explanation of the development, deployment, and consumption of *manga* and *Genji manga* in specific will help us better understand how *manga*'s narrative and visual conventions push back on the pushback mounted against them.[2] Three critical terms, remediation, its subset repurposing, and transposition, shape my analysis. Broadly speaking, remediation constitutes the adaptation of the content of an artifact (e.g., a novel) into another medium such as film, a musical, or even a computer game, and for our study *manga*. Georgia Institute of Technology scholars Jay David Bolter and Richard Grusin utilize remediation to map the ways in which new digital technologies like computer games, digital photography, and the internet developed from older media (1999, 273, 44–5). They argue that the new forms/remediations attempt to "improve" on a particular medium by making things more reliable (as e-mail does "snail" mail), more "natural" (as virtual reality does film or photography), or "more immediate or authentic" by erasing the medium used to deliver the experience as is found in immersive virtual reality (Bolter and Grusin 1999, 59, 19). Bolter and Grusin identify four types of remediation, but for our purposes, the first type that provides new means to access older media is the most germane.[3] Painters of old illustrated Bible scenes or those from other literary texts and, in doing so, they simply adapted the content into the pictorial medium of painting. This is called repurposing, for the content is "reinterpreted" without any referencing of the textual medium of the Bible (Bolter and Grusin 1999, 44–5).[4] To take a contemporary example, J. K. Rowling's *Harry Potter* novels have been remediated/repurposed into films, action figures, an RPG (Role Playing game) *Hogwarts Legacy* where participants play to save the wizarding world as well as rides at Universal Studios in Hollywood, Orlando, and Japan that simulate different aspects of the books and films. These remediated new forms have some "interplay" with the content of the novels but do not replicate their textual medium.

Remediation then signals the repurposing/reformatting of content (from one medium such as a novel) for use in other media. For *The Tale of Genji*, the tale has been repurposed from a textual-based narrative into pictorial scrolls and *ukiyo-e* paintings, into dramatic *nō* plays, and into new media such as films, all-female musical revues, and *manga* (discussed further in Chapter 2). This repurposing of the textual, courtier discursive content of the tale into differing media is how the tale has remained alive and well since its inception in the eleventh century. But these remediations did not take place only because people in the ensuing eras found the tale scintillating. Rather, they enabled their producers and consumers to use the tale to forge new identities and places in society. Throughout the ages, the tale has morphed from courtly discourse to painting to novel across time, space, and genre, but it has also used these adaptations to position itself within the social, cultural, and artistic landscapes of each new period. I have coined these manifestations "transpositions"—newly configured painterly, dramatic, filmic, musical, material culture that movers and shakers and other groups used to establish their positionalities as the political and cultural brokers of their times.[5]

From the outset then, the tale remediated itself into different media not just to provide better access to *The Tale of Genji* but also to serve as transpositions to help its producers and consumers forge new cultural and social identities and gain political prowess. As we see in Chapter 2, the twelfth-century *Genji* paintings not only remediated the tale into the pictorial but also showcased the power and prestige of the imperial court that created them. In similar fashion the *nō* drama adaptations of *Genji* repurposed the tale into the dramatic medium—but also provided the landed warrior class of the fourteenth and fifteenth centuries with the cultural capital necessary to emerge as the transcendent political force of their times. Even in its inception, the *Genji* was used by Regent Fujiwara no Michinaga to lure the emperor to his daughter's salon to enable the birth of the next emperor under his auspices.

The story of how *manga* and *Genji manga* in specific developed is fascinating, for they not only serve as entertainment and identity-creation venues for in-group readers but also function as repositories of the dreams and desires of their producers and consumers and spaces where these are enacted. In what follows, I examine the repositories of these niched, age- and gender-targeting groups and show that readers only engage these fantasies in the imaginary and other sanctioned spaces. A series of four strategies ensure that it be so and that real beings are not endangered, nor society harmed, as some fear. Rather, these rich and inventive engagements actually serve as safety values and coping mechanisms for the inhabitants of contemporary Japan—and perhaps other communities as well.

Manga *Speak*

The History of Manga: *Situating Gender and Age In-Group Readers*

To begin our study, in Japan *manga* became a viable force in the second half of the twentieth century and now cover almost any topic under the sun.[6] Unlike western comics,[7] they are not just for children but target the youngest readers through the oldest, creating content specifically tailored for their respective demographics, although crossovers and the blurring of boundaries regularly occur.[8] Modern *manga* began in the 1920s and 1930s and took off in postwar Japan as a vibrant, cheap, and innovative form of entertainment. Notwithstanding debates over *manga* stemming from the twelfth-century humorous Animal Scrolls and progressing through eighteenth-century art forms,[9] *manga* as we know them gained inspiration from Japan's premodern art and textual forms; merged these with the narrative techniques, ideas, and formats garnered from western comics; and came into their own as a new genre. According to *manga* critic and activist Nagayama Kaoru, pioneering *manga* artist Tezuka Osamu established a cartoony style in the 1940s and 1950s, but this was countered in the 1950s and 1960s by realism-based *gekiga* dramatic drawings that reflected a "gritty aesthetic, social and political consciousness and focus on reality" (Nagayama 2021, 39n.2, 49–62). Artists began pushing the boundaries of *manga* expression "with gritty sociopolitical commentary and spectacular violence that appealed to young people" (Galbraith and Bauwens-Sugimoto 2021, 25). Developing after the defeat of the movement against the 1951 US-Japan Treaty of Mutual Cooperation and Security that allowed the United States to maintain military bases in Japan, *gekiga* appealed to young men and by the mid-1960s counted university students and young white-collar workers among its readers (Nagayama 2021, 55, 54).

To counter this politicized, ultrarealistic form of *gekiga*,[10] Tezuka Osamu and Ishinomori Shōtarō (another pioneer in the field) responded with cute, cartoony, and entertaining comics that featured male interests in action, camaraderie, valor, and perseverance (Kinsella 2000, 28). Tezuka's pioneering cinematic approach became the perfect format for such storytelling (Gravett 2004, 24),[11] and by the 1960s not only were *manga* targeting young boys a matter of course but those for young men readers came into being, complete with more sophisticated and psychologically complex content and graphic sexual illustrations suited to their interests (see Thorn n.d.1). The sophomoric voyeurism of girls' bodies found in boys comics thus developed into what is known in the field as eye-candy fan service—sexually titillating shots of bosoms and panty bottoms—that raised specters of *manga*'s objectifying of female bodies despite the fact that these images were a part of mainstream advertising at the time.

Shōnen boys and *seinen* young men comics, then, follow the interests and conventions of their respective audiences and constitute what is known in the field as categories.[12] These in effect determine the content, point of view, drawing style, and method of narration of titles within their purview. The last predominantly male-oriented *manga* is called "adult male,"[13] which tends toward the erotic and is also pronounced *seinen* but with different kanji, 成年 (in contrast to 青年 for young men), while children's comics that were not overtly gendered and targeted the youngest of readers formed yet another demographic. Female-produced comics[14] did not make their appearance until the 1960s. Girls *manga* had been around since the 1930s but were drawn mostly by men, and it took a group of gifted young female artists to better represent female perspectives (Thorn n.d.1; Gravett 2004, 76). Dubbed the Nijū-yonen-gumi, or "Fabulous Forty-Niners" (Forty-Niners for short) for Shōwa 24, the year of their birth (1949 by the western calendar), they hit their stride in the 1970s, as Hagio Moto, Ōshima Yumiko, and Takemiya Keiko introduced innovations that became the hallmarks of *shōjo manga*, interrogating traditional notions of gender and sexuality and utilizing boys-comics themes such as science fiction to explore "the weightiest issues of human existence" (Thorn n.d.1). Yamato Waki, creator of the *Genji* remediation *Asaki yume mishi* (*Fleeting Dreams*, 1980–93),[15] utilized many of the Forty-Niners' techniques. Long pensive looks and poignant moments that focused on full-body figures of the heroines in irregularly shaped panels privileged their psychological interiority. The different pace and rhythm of these female-oriented *manga* were roundly criticized by male critics born and bred on fast action (M. Takahashi 2008, 130–2, 122).

Changes in the law, economy, and the feminist movement all shaped notions of women in the 1980s. Ladies comics, or *rediisu komikku* (or *redikomi* for short), also called *josei*, or women comics, which were written by and for women, appeared as a result of several of these forces. First, the Equal Employment Opportunity Law leveled the playing field for women but also created a gendered labor system that placed men in managerial and women in clerical tracks. Nonetheless, it increased the number of women pursuing careers and helped usher in ladies comics to address work/home life balance (Ogi 2003, 782). The passage of the law coincided with the loosening of monetary policy by the Japanese government, resulting in "an abundance of cheap credit" and the advent of a second force, the bubble economy (Christopher Wood, qtd. in Ito 2010, 85). This proved fortuitous for women who now had disposable income and sought goods and services catering to their needs and desires. One such phenomenon was the media attention paid to the rise of highly attractive, socially independent young women whom men vied to chauffeur and provide meals for and upon whom they bestowed gifts—all with no sexual or monetary compensation (Ito 2010, 86). As part of the "era of women," many universities began offering women's studies courses (Kitamura 2008, 345–6), laying the groundwork for a third force, the 1990s feminist movement, which promoted sexual freedom as a way for women to challenge the relegation of their sexuality to roles as good wives and wise mothers.[16] This gave rise to erotic magazines and films targeted at women, and, of course, to ladies comics,[17] some of which also became targets of censorship.

Manga featuring male–male relationships written by and for female practitioners joined in the mix of comics offerings. They are known as *shōnen ai* (boys love), *yaoi* (from the acronym for the expression "*yama nashi, ochi nashi, imi nashi*," meaning "no climax, no point, no meaning" [Schodt 1996, 37]), and *bōizu rabu* (also called Boys Love), or BL for short. Detailed explanations will follow in Chapter 4, but all are same-sex male romance *manga*. First appearing in the 1970s and 1980s, they gained commercial success in the 1990s (McLelland and Welker 2015, 5) and are prominent today. In the 1990s and 2000s gay rights activists and others, however, challenged the depiction of underage protagonists and appropriation of the gay community in their texts.

Pushback against "Harmful Publications"

Concern over the publication of male–male romances and the increase in eroticized adult male and female *manga* titles caused mothers, feminist groups, and politicians in Japan to call for a censure of the industry, which came to a head in the 1990s. Local ordinances against "obscene *manga*" were passed, and some artists, publishers, and bookstore owners arrested. The Publishing Ethics Committee kicked into high gear, calling for the reduction of sexual imagery in *manga*.[18] Texts that did not comply could be discontinued, removed from bookshelves, or relegated to the adult *manga* section, but the most effective approach was the self-censoring enacted by *manga* editors and artists (Kinsella 2000, 150; Zanghellini 2009, 161).

Much of the outcry resulted from the 1988–9 deaths of four preschool girls at the hands of a fan, Miyazaki Tsutomu, whose actions were thought to stem from his fascination with the sexually explicit *rorikon*, or "Lolita Complex," erotic videos, *manga*, and *anime* (Schodt 1996, 45–6; McLelland 2015, 256–7). A sense of panic ensued, and sexually explicit material was dropped from children's magazines, while "adult only" magazines were not sold in most stores or only in cordoned-off adult sections by the end of 1994 (Schodt 1996, 59). Mainstream publishers such as Kōdansha and Shūeisha also ceased publishing sexually explicit ladies comics, although smaller publishers continued to do so (Jones 2005, 98; Schodt 1996, 124). Pushback against what was deemed "harmful publications" began in the mid-1950s and 1960s, even Tezuka's titles being labeled as "unhealthy" and "vulgar" at that time, but Nagayama Kaoru points to the self-censoring by the industry in the 1990s and the establishment of the "Adult comics label" (*seinen komikku māku*) in 1996 as especially devastating not only for erotic *manga* but also for freedom of expression in all categories of *manga* (2021, 53, 95–8). This foreshadowed problems *manga* would face at home and abroad in the new millennium.

In the 1990s (R-rated) ladies comics were demonized as sexually abusing and humiliating to women by US critics such as Nicholas Kristof[19] and came under fire in the United States and elsewhere as performing "stereotypical ideas of male fantasy."[20] This came to a further head in 2014, this time invoking child endangerment, with the passage of the Act to Amend the Act on Punishment of Activities Relating to Child Prostitution and Child Pornography and the

Protection of Children in Japan, which banned possession of child pornography (in photographs, film, video but not in fictional images like *manga, anime*, and computer games). The outcry against this exclusion was swift and powerful—journalists and critics abroad as well as countries charged Japan with perversion and child endangerment and dubbed it the "Empire of Child Porn."[21]

Situating *Manga*: Pushback on the Pushback

Taken at face value, the *manga* portrayals of young (fe)male protagonists can be troubling, but the situation is complex, and situating the narrative and visual conventions that gave rise to the drawing styles found in *manga* as well as examining the guardrails regulating the consumption and production of *manga* are in order. I begin with a historical, legal explanation as to why eroticism came to be portrayed and deployed in *manga* in the ways that they did. I follow with an assessment of four strategies that counter the charge that *manga* are harmful. These include Japan's different reading approaches, the context-specific reading selves deployed to engage *manga*, the separation of fiction and reality that mandates that fantasies remain in the imaginary and in specialized venues, and the societal guardrails put in place to ensure compliance.

The historical, legal reasons for *manga*'s eroticized portrayal of young bodies and the objectification of women protagonists are enlightening. Cultural anthropologist Anne Allison places the blame for these "offensive" portrayals of the sexual at the feet of obscenity laws adopted by Japan in the Meiji (1868–1912) period that specified how sex be visually depicted. Before Japan's entry into the global arena in the mid-1880s, sexually explicit material—namely, pornographic images known as *shunga* (spring pictures)—was a matter of course (Buckley 1991, 165, 168). This all changed when Japan sought recognition from the west: overt sexual materials and public displays of the body in mixed baths and such required eradication (Allison 1996, 163). In response, two laws, Article 175 of the Criminal Code and Article 21 of the Customs Tariffs Law, were enacted in 1907 and 1910, respectively, prohibiting "indecent" exposure of the body. A 1918 ordinance made it clear that the offending body parts were the genitalia, and their anatomical depictions were eschewed (Allison 1996, 164).

Allison argues that, ironically, by mandating the obscuring of the pubis and genitalia, these laws eroticized and transformed these body parts into objects of desire, setting in motion complex workarounds in order to narrate sexual activity visually. As a result, sex and the sexual act came to be represented by other parts of the body (breasts, buttocks, crotches) and by activities such as the "insertion of various objects ... into other bodily orifices." Underaged, prepubescent bodies took center stage, infantilizing women and requiring men to use "phallic weaponry" such as baseball bats, sticks, and guns as replacements for sexual organs. Attempts at obscuring the genitalia (by covering or blocking their view) resulted in hypereroticizing them (Allison 1996, 169). This, Allison argues, gave rise to bare breasts, seminude women, and panty shots appearing on primetime television and in comics and magazines. In Allison's estimation this "[state-]endorsed" sexual economy fostered fetishized body parts, infantilized females by making them (look) prepubescent, and replaced genital copulation and genitalia with voyeurism and sadomasochism (1996, 149–50). Not surprisingly, this imaging is read as "obscene" and "perverse" and is negatively viewed by many western readers, including Allision.[22]

Addressing the Charges

Manga and *anime* have been deemed "harmful," but they play an invaluable role in Japanese society as safety valves and coping mechanisms for the inhabitants of a highly regulated Japanese society.[23] In recent years the long-held ideal of a middle-class lifestyle has given way to more non-regular employment, more women having to balance work and home life, and more segments of the population living in precarious social and financial situations (see Allison *Precarious Japan* for more information on such groups), but the old paradigms that men should be the breadwinners and women the caretakers of home and children remain very much alive and well. These expectations make for very stressful lives and necessitate some form of release. One such coping mechanism is the creation of a rich imaginary populated by dreams and desires. These imaginary venues, however, are not simply given free rein to be enacted at will, but are carefully monitored and channeled in safe ways. As noted above, there are four strategies: the utilization of collaborative, participatory, and performative readers who create specialized in-groups within which fantasies are engaged, the deployment of these reading selves in specialized venues to safely engage the fantasies, the maintenance of fiction and reality as separate, and the placement of societal guardrails to ensure adherence to the above strategies.

The first of these strategies is the creation of collaborative, participatory, and performative readers who in fact replicate *The Tale of Genji*'s in-group production and consumption techniques. Much like the ways in which the tale cultivated and fostered the interests of the Heian-period (794–1185) courtiers, *manga* categories target their niched readers from the youngest readers through the oldest and create content specifically tailored to their respective demographics—although crossover readership and the blurring of boundaries regularly occur. The niched content and drawing styles foster specialized readerly interests and allow like-minded people to safely and fully traffic in characters and scenarios that appeal to them in the imaginary and in prescribed shared spaces. Readerly interactive buy-in is fostered by images of iconic significance that are fully understood only by those in the know. Flowers further signal romantic interest, a nosebleed denotes lustful thoughts, sweat drops betoken anxiety or concern. Possessing the operative visual and narrative codes, boys-comics readers, for example, can scan a page in 3.75 seconds (Schodt 1983, 18)—in effect replicating the strategies employed by readers of *The Tale of Genji*. Heian readers used their knowledge of social and cultural conventions of the period, and the emotional affect of the words and images as regulated by poetic tradition, to connect with the protagonists and fill out the parameters of the tale—essentially serving, as what I have termed elsewhere, "collaborative readers" (Miyake 1993). To enable such reading in *manga*, artists bridge time, space, and setting, creating characters that readers can relate to. Unlike American comics superheroes such as Wonder Woman or Batman, most *manga* characters are regular Joes/Janes with personal fears and foibles who are simply struggling to survive and to do good (or bad) even when the stakes are as high as saving (or destroying) the world. Expertly knowing how much to present, *manga* artists encourage readers to collaborate in the production of meaning by tapping into their own experiences, emotions, and psyche or energy and infusing the narrative with them. A fuller explanation will follow in Chapter 1, but suffice it to say here that *manga* readers function as collaborative, participatory coauthors.

By enabling readerly collaboration, *manga* transform readers into complicit in-groups that are groomed to care about the protagonists and to interact with them as if they are friends or acquaintances like those in real life. This caring is further cultivated by aligning the perspective of the reader with that of a given protagonist, shifting from one protagonist to another and rarely if ever proffering an omniscient point of view. Depicted from the reader's perspective, actions and interactions then gradually unfold frame by frame—skillfully replicating real-life interfacing with peoples, places, and events (Schodt 1983, 21-2) and making them as fully engaging as real life. This "seeing" things through the eyes of the characters allows readers to experience the world of the *manga* in and through the "bodies" of the protagonists, thus empowering readers not simply to peruse but to "participate" in the action. These participatory readers often take things one step further, embodying and "performing" along with, and in the guise of the characters.[24] One manifestation of these "performative readers" is cosplay,[25] in which fans dress up as their favorite characters and enact their transformations, but only in the accepted spaces of comics and *anime* conventions and venues, such as the *manga/anime* mecca Akihabara or Ikebukuro in Japan and Little Tokyo in Los Angeles. In a sense, readers "cosplay" as they peruse the *manga*. By cosplaying the *Genji* characters in their Heian setting, then, modern audiences more fully embody the situations and emotional affect that the *manga* artists go out of the way to make relatable.

More will follow in Chapter 1, but it is the narrative conventions of *The Tale of Genji* that form the ground for *manga* in-groups and their collaborative, participatory, and performative readers. A product of a highly niched, circumscribed Heian-period courtier society, the tale sets the tone for what stories can be told, how, and through what means. It opts for open-ended, fluid narratives that are difficult to parse for the uninitiated and that create characters—selves—who are socially, culturally, and historically context specific. They are interpersonally situated and operate along a continuum of selves appropriate to the moment and the participants involved. I do not mean to be reductive, but, as anthropologists have argued, the authenticity of Japanese selves is less based on continuity over all domains and more on being context- and situation appropriate. So the courtier self appears before the emperor in formal dress and language; the poetic self composes season- and venue-suitable verses when called upon to do so;

the lover self declares his unending devotion in romantic trysts. Tailored to best fit the occasion, these selves are properly and seamlessly executed. And through them, the tale establishes the parameters of Japanese narratives, their moral, erotic, and aesthetic imagination, and in effect serves as a kind of DNA defining Japanese culture.

The context-specific, collaborative, participatory, performative selves found in *The Tale of Genji* are also central in the second strategy that ensures proper engagement of fantasies as well. These reading selves are created to engage in the dreams and desires afforded in the tale. Similarly, *manga* and anime-specific selves are devised to participate in the imaginary world of *manga* and *anime* and they, too, do so within the parameters established for them. But this does not occur only in the engagement of *manga* and *anime*. The practice pervades Japanese life, for the Japanese self is situationally constructed and regulated, in every interpersonal interaction, both by the venue (formal/causal, public/private) and by the status (rank and age) and gender (male/female) of the participants. The Japanese persona remains fluid, shifting and changing to fit the moment.[26] It constantly embodies and sheds context-specific selves, cosplaying different versions of itself. Dorinne Kondo calls this "crafting selves," as we will see in Chapter 1. This cosplaying "change of dress," if you will, is readily apparent in the different words for "I" in Japanese, which are demarcated by gender and status. By no means an exhaustive list, boys and men tend to use "watakushi," "watashi," "boku," and "ore," while girls and women function with the first two and "atashi." For both genders "watakushi" is reserved for the most formal of situations in which the speaker must place him/herself in a lower position vis-à-vis others, showing the utmost respect for those above him/her in age, power, and status. "Watashi" is used by both genders in formal situations such as interviews, conversations with bosses, and the like. "Boku" and "ore" for males, and "atashi" for females, signal more casual interaction with friends, family, or cohort in-groups.[27] In each situation the "I" is configured differently, as appropriate for the particular interaction. The imaginary "I" who participates in fantasies of its own making is just another "I," conceived for that particular time and space and appropriate for that venue. It is as engagingly "real" as any "I" crafted for everyday situations, but it remains operative in the imaginary and would only be deployed there and in prescribed in-group venues.

This rich imaginary life operates in spaces created and maintained by *manga* artists, readers, and society alike and is premised on participants knowing the difference between fiction and reality. This separation of fiction and reality represents the third strategy utilized by *manga* consumers and producers and is based, first, on an acknowledgment that fantasies ranging from innocent dreams of becoming heroes or coveted love interests as well as the less savory ogling of buxom women or the egregious fulfillment of illicit sexual desires are part of life. So rather than denying or suppressing them, artists have created spaces in the imaginary where context-appropriate selves, devised for this purpose, can enact these fantasies. Critic and activist Nagayama Kaoru argues that it is "better to acknowledge and work through fantasies in the open with [like-minded] others than to deny them or, worse, project them onto a deviant and dangerous 'other'"

(Nagayama, paraphrased in Galbraith and Bauwens-Sugimoto 2021, 28). Second, this engagement requires adherence to carefully mapped-out protocols. Through his field work anthropologist and fan culture expert Patrick W. Galbraith found that aficionados of computer games that feature sexualized content go to great lengths to devise ways to interact with the fictional characters from the games but also take great pains to ensure that they and others in their circles adhere to specific protocols of engagement. (See chapter 4 in his *The Ethics of Affect*.) Lastly and most importantly, engagement with *manga/anime* is premised on knowing and maintaining the difference between fiction and reality. Nagayama argues that *manga* readers are clear that "Fiction is fiction." They are also aware that reality cannot be completely kept at bay, but they have become very adept at maintaining a distinction between fiction and reality, for "more pleasure can be gained if reality and fiction are explicitly separated" (Nagayama 2021, 122, 163). Patrick Galbraith and Jessica Bauwens-Sugimoto call this "media literacy," the ability to distinguish between fictional "cartoony characters" and "realism of the natural world," honed by growing up with *anime*, *manga*, and gaming (2021, 28; Galbraith 2021, 6). In his interview of feminist cultural scholar and professor Fujimoto Yukari, Galbraith also calls this literacy *moe*, an "economy of the desire for images," which will be discussed further in Chapters 3 and 4 (2017a, 115; 2009b).

For *manga* readers, as Fujimoto points out, growing up in the "culture of drawing and fantasy," "the desire is for … the fictional character … [and] there is absolutely no connection to reality" (qtd. in Galbraith 2017a, 115). (See Fujimoto 2015; also Galbraith 2021, chapter 4 on how the desire is enacted and kept in check.) The desire is for the two-dimensional world, and, perhaps not always unconnected to reality, the protocols for consumption of *manga* in the real world are, nonetheless, carefully laid out by artists and participants and maintained through in-group interactions at *manga/anime* conventions, online, and other gatherings. The proper "way" to read and participate in these works requires deciphering the visual and textual codes specific to each category and, most importantly, understanding that the narrative, the scenarios, and the bodies that embody them occur in the imaginary and should be engaged there or, as Galbraith and others argue, in prescribed in-group settings. Galbraith is mainly speaking about computer gamers, but he writes that gamers draw a line between fiction and reality and engage in the everyday ethics of *manga* and *anime*, which dictate that these lines be drawn and negotiated and maintained daily in concert with other like-minded aficionados (see 2021, chapters 4 and 5). Thus, underage bodies, violence, and force are viewed as fictional tropes that are to be engaged in the realm of the imaginary and in specialized real-world settings with in-group aficionados who help maintain the line between fiction and reality. Should practitioners actualize fantasies of harming or forcing themselves on women and children, they are reprimanded, otherized, and ostracized by their in-group and even more so by society at large (Galbraith 2021, 183–5; Nagayama 2021, 122).[28]

Even with protocols to ensure that the sexual and erotic scenarios in *manga* are not actualized in the real world, things are not left to chance. Societal guardrails, the last of the strategies deployed, direct publicly permissible and privately deployable behaviors and actions. Anthropologist Jane Bachnik identifies these as "directional vantage points" or *uchi/soto* ("inside"/"outside") and considers them central in defining selves and their interactions with society (1994, 3). These coordinates locate the positionality from which the self is looking/interacting/speaking—that is, the physical, social, and psychic orientation from which the self relates to the world (Backnik 1994, 3). *Uchi* focalizes the self to "me" or "my group" and to selves who should remain private, while *soto* points outward and to selves who are publicly sanctioned.

Other directionals support similar orientations: *ura*, for example, ensures that what is "in back" remains "hidden from others," while the *omote* "surface appearance" can operate freely in public venues. *Honne* ("inner life feelings") and *ninjō* ("world of personal feelings") must remain under wraps, but *tatemae* ("surface world of obligations") and *giri* ("social obligations") need to comply with social expectations.[29] The "self" cluster of *uchi*, *ura*, and *ninjō* presents in personal, intimate, and even illicit feelings that are to remain private and be deployed in the nonpublic world (which includes the imaginary). The "social" cluster of *omote*, *tatemae*, and *giri* represents obligations and responsibilities to the community that are necessary to maintain social order. The Japanese "I," then, has numerous faces: fluid and constantly shifting in dialogue with life situations, and constituting and also being constituted by these negotiations, it is solidly embedded in a collectivity. The Japanese self deploys individually, yet it does not act on a whim but participates in communally agreed-upon patterns of thought and action.

Racially, socially, and culturally homogeneous for the most part and with a population of over 125 million people sharing a country the size of the state of Montana, Japan by necessity has set up a stringent system of rules and regulations delineating what is lawful and permissible behavior in both the public and private domains. These behaviors are reinforced and normalized through a system of education, media, religion, law, and the like, what Louis Althusser calls Ideological State Apparatuses, and enforced by very effective, socially deployed peer group pressure that is much more actively in play than in the United States. Generally speaking, pressure from the public at large governs people in Japan, so the arbiters of what is permissible are those around an individual, "everyone," as Japanese linguist Satoh Kazuyuki once told me, rather than left for the most part to an individual's conscience. Hence in Japan peers keep each other in check. In such a milieu, ardent fans of *manga* known as the *otaku*[30] and *fujoshi* "rotten girls" fans (who traffic in BL comics discussed in Chapter 4), for example, enact their desires in the realm of the imaginary or in-group venues. Any leakage outside their in-group is met with ridicule, censure, and otherizing to such an extent that most fans will not publicly reveal their positionality as *otaku* or *fujoshi*. In society at large they are tagged as "abnormal" and "perverse." *Fujoshi* are even accused of betraying Japanese society by trafficking in male–male sexual interests that deter them from their reproductive sexual responsibilities. Thus, readers are well aware of what they will encounter when they read BL, adult male, or ladies comics and, should they find them not to their tastes or are adversely "triggered" by what they read, they pull away and often say nothing, because just showing interest in such comics invites stigmatization.

Scenarios that can be triggering and threatening to readers[31] may be present in certain categories of *manga*, so *manga* work hard to signal the presence of such content through their system of age- and gender-targeting categories. Labeling a *manga* as adult male or erotic ladies comics alerts readers of their sexually explicit and "R-rated" content and restricts access to adult consumers.[32] Although the internet has made it easier for readers to inadvertently encounter such narratives, readers are forewarned and self-select to avoid sex and violence that supersede their comfort level, much as is found among movie viewers. The high degree of readerly collaboration and participation, required to read comics (discussed above), further makes it imperative that readers agree with the premise as well as the conventions of the *manga* to continue reading. For example, for many years I didn't read Oda Eiichirō's boys comics *One Piece*, which began in 1997 and is the highest selling *manga* ever, because I found the drawing style off-putting. I also avoid girls comics in which the protagonists vie with each other for the attention of a boy and do anything to "win" him, for I view these works as focalizing some of the least desirable traits among women. *Manga* readers, like movie viewers, then self-select and actively choose what they consume.

The fail-safes in place to deter readers who might be traumatized by erotic ladies comics' and adult male comics' depiction of women's bodies, notwithstanding, Allison argues that these portrayals are the height of "gender chauvinism" and a reflection of male dominance not just sexually but in society at large (1996, 63–4, 78).[33] Yet she also proposes that submission, sexual and otherwise, is demanded of both men and women by societal power dynamics that are in play (1996, 78). The complex positioning of the female body in erotic ladies comics discussed in Chapter 5 further shows that readings of bodies are not unilateral or universal but function in different ways for different purposes and, most importantly, for different readers. As we will see in Chapter 6 in our discussion of Egawa Tatsuya's soft porn *Genji manga*, the male gaze is also not monolithic, nor the perspective necessarily predetermined and fixed by gender. All are embedded in race, class, ideology, sexuality, and, in our case, in Japan's very differently configured historical, cultural, and moral expediencies. Cultural border crossings are complex, and much is lost in transition.

Conclusion: Repurposing The Tale of Genji

No doubt *The Tale of Genji* and contemporary *manga* are two unlikely bedfellows, but when they engaged each other something magical happened: hugely funny, romanticized, tragic, gender-flipping remediations of Heian courtier life centered on a dashing hero and his fabulous counterparts came to be. Produced from the 1980s through the new millennium, *The Tale of Genji manga* made the tale accessible to a new stratum of readers in Japan and abroad, garnering goodwill but also opening up both the tale and the *manga* to pushback. The Japanese context-and-venue-specific readers, however, make certain that the eroticism and desire are deployed in appropriate fantasy spaces and prescribed real-world venues. Engagement with the 2D *manga* representations of characters[34] and encounters with heterosexual, queer, nontraditional, and same-sex reading positionalities, and interpretations of love, life, relationships, and multifaceted interaction with literary texts are the goal. The collaborative, participatory, and performative *manga* readers in *The Tale of Genji manga* have much to teach us, as we will see in Part II of my study.

Chapters

My study is divided into two parts. Part I speaks to the tale and Part II to the *Genji manga*. Chapter 1 in Part I provides a summary of *The Tale of Genji* and examines the historical, cultural, and narrative conventions that produced it. I also look at how the highly aristocratic Heian courtier society shaped the DNA of the tale's storytelling, character construction, and in-group reading strategies that come full circle in *manga Genji* over a millennium later. Chapter 2, also in Part II, centers on *The Tale of Genji* and the ways in which it embedded itself in the cultural, social, and political milieu of ensuing periods by transposing into cultural capital for specialized communities as varied as courtiers, warlords, and even the Japanese government. I trace from the twelfth century into the new millennium the pictorial and the textual threads that served as inspirations for the *Genji manga*. Among the most influential are the sumptuous scrolls, black-and-white line drawings, stunning woodblock prints, philosophical treatises, parodies, and the novelization of the tale.

In Part II we will meet many Genjis/*Genjis*—honorable, licentious, difficult, complex—bringing to the fore the richness of *The Tale of Genji* written over a millennium ago. Chapter 3 on girls comics features young female protagonists who stylize themselves as objects of desires in search of true love. In the process they create parallel *Genji* universes, modernize settings, and place Genji into the bodies of a high schooler or a fetching young woman. Provocatively entertaining, the *Genji* girls comics call into question issues of gender, positionality, and desire and provide differing, mixed-messaging positionalities of girlhood for readers. Equally provocative are the BL remediations of the tale that constitute Chapter 4. Here Genji remains a man, but all his ladies from the eleventh-century tale are stunningly handsome young men. This "Heian" world is unlike any that author Murasaki Shikibu may have envisioned: male–male romance reign, all progeny are male, and plot and characterization are eschewed for sensuous kisses and intimate love scenes. Charges of appropriation of gay men and overly determined sexuality have been raised, but the BL remediations also function as liberatory, exploratory spaces for queer/straight, male/female, trans/bi, and in-between genders.

In Chapter 5 girls-comics protagonists give way to more adult female protagonists seeking to be "mistresses" of their own (sexual) destinies. The offerings run the gamut, featuring peoplescapes that bring to life the lives of men, women, and commonfolk of the Heian capital or lay bare the trauma, the hurt, the unrequited love of the women protagonists. The titles include a scathing feminist-leaning critique of Genji and his fellow courtiers in a serialized weekly newspaper, a hard-core erotic remediation, and the Heian world transposed to the seventeenth-century love capital Yoshiwara where the ladies become top courtesans plying their trade.

Chapter 6 features the tale through the lens of boys and young men *manga*. Having to eschew the usual camaraderie, adventure, and battles found in boys comics and to a lesser degree in many young men comics, the *Genji manga* interrogate Genji's lusting after women. The boys-comics remediations turn to humor, lampooning a bucktoothed Genji and his womanizing, while a roly-poly sweet chestnut is gently teased for his very human self-absorbed desires. In contrast, the young men remediations put Genji's lusting after women on full display not only for readerly enjoyment but also to parody in hyperbolic fashion. Genji is further transformed into a naïve, inept college student instructed to bed fourteen formidable, modern women in the name of "research." Varied and inventive, these male-oriented *Genji* comics refashion and challenge notions of masculinity and "hero" creation through hyperbole, slapstick humor, and parody.

In Chapter 7, I examine the lesser known *jōhō* informational comics, which form a substantial portion of *Genji manga* remediations. Still targeting audiences by age and gender, they support hegemonic cultural constructs touting *The Tale of Genji* as a national treasure, a database of the best of Japanese culture, and a literary masterpiece on par with western works. The general "unmarked male" titles laud the Heian period as an exquisitely rich and elegant landscape populated by beautiful people and a kind, thoughtful, and admirable Genji. For those focused on women, the trials and tribulations suffered by the women living in a patriarchal society come to the fore. Not viewing Heian society as the best of Japan, they fulfill a second function of the tale providing life lessons and coping mechanisms that resonate with the healing boom in the new millennium. Informational *manga* "educate" domestic and international audiences on the accomplishments of *The Tale of Genji* not just in terms of literature but politically, culturally, and beyond.

Forty *Genji manga*[35] stand at the ready, and I invite you on a journey to explore these remediations of *The Tale of Genji* as they reconfigure and expand the venerable old tale in ways that entertain and delight many but also cause concern in others. Japan has long relied on a separation of public and private spaces, of fiction and reality. Niched in-groups with their own bodies of knowledge, experiences, and behaviors thrive in private spaces. It is not to say that the Japanese deployment of context-specific selves and parallel but separate existence of different bodies of knowledge and being is better or worse, but unraveling the Japanese way of looking at things will go a long way in understanding Japan, how *manga* and *anime* work, and point us toward new ways for diverse groups with different agendas to coexist.

Part I

MURASAKI SHIKIBU'S *THE TALE OF GENJI*

Chapter 1

CONTEXTUALIZING *THE TALE OF GENJI*: THE STORY, THE PERIOD, AND THE CONSUMER PRODUCERS

Told and retold in verbal, visual, and musical form by different people for different reasons, *The Tale of Genji* (1000–1010) has made a remarkable journey in the last millennium. But its inception and role in the highly literate and circumscribed world of the eleventh-century Heian court are equally noteworthy. Art is rarely ever just for art's sake, and in the Heian courtier circles where the tale was conceived the political stakes were high, for the tale was used to garner power for the Northern Branch of the Fujiwara family. Author Murasaki Shikibu (c. 978–c. 1014) came to court to serve Empress Shōshi (988–1074) because her *Tale of Genji* was the talk of the court, and Shōshi's father Fujiwara no Michinaga (966–1028) utilized the tale to induce Emperor Ichijō (986–1011) to visit his young daughter's salon in the hope that she would produce the next imperial heir—which she did. Shōshi bore the emperor two sons, in fact, and it was through these young heirs and others that Michinaga effectively ruled the country as regent.

Undoubtedly the stakes were high for Shōshi, for she had stiff competition from other well-placed, well-heeled consorts brought to court by her father's competitors. But most aristocratic women of her time were placed in similar situations: to gain access to the throne or to acquire prominence at court, families married their female members to Fujiwara and other high-ranking men to secure lucrative political alliances. To this end, women were trained in the arts and letters to fashion them into suitable mates. These accomplishments were expected of the men as well, but they were vital for the women, who often served as marriage pawns.[1] It was this training in the arts that enabled Murasaki Shikibu and her fellow women writers to become some of the first female literary practitioners in the world, establishing a literary legacy for Japanese women so early in their history that later generations did not have to echo Virginia Woolf's poignant lament that "any woman born with a great gift in the sixteenth century [in England] would have certainly gone crazed, shot herself or ended her days in some lonely cottage outside the village, half witch, half wizard, feared and mocked at" (Woolf 1929, 51).

In this chapter we look at the conventions through which *The Tale of Genji* and other literary works were produced, deployed, and consumed, and also at how these works provided Heian courtiers with cultural, social, and even political capital. We look first at the specialized society that produced the tale, and then at the role that it accorded to the arts. Heian society was highly aristocratic, stratified, and circumscribed, made up of the imperial court, courtiers and their families, and high-ranking clergy. It comprised one-tenth of 1 percent of the population of Japan at the time,[2] yet the members of this small group of aristocrats were the producers, consumers, and even the subject matter of what was written in that period. Moreover, they were all expected to compose poetry, so demarcation between writers/producers and readers/consumers of literature was much diminished, and, as an in-group who shared not just the same values but also the same education, body of knowledge, experience, and social networks, much could be abbreviated and simply alluded to.

This body of knowledge encompassed literature, religion, history, philosophy, and the fine arts, fields that were not separate one from the other. Blending fluidly together, these texts in fact were the means through which power was secured and maintained. The Chinese Tang dynasty (618–907) "Confucian ideal" in vogue at the time accorded the right to rule only to scholar-bureaucrats well versed in official histories and philosophical teachings—that is, to those who had skills in calligraphy, painting, and music, and who, most of all, possessed knowledge and expertise in poetry, the moral compass of the society (McCullough 1968, 17). Not simply for aesthetic and leisure enjoyment, then, poetry formed an integral part of intellectual discourse and social practice. A statesman was deemed suitable to govern only if he exhibited a mastery of poetry and the arts. Of course, there were varying degrees of competency, surrogates could be found to compose poems for others, and poetic ability rarely superseded lineage in importance. Nevertheless, poetic knowledge and the knack to turn an appropriate verse at the appropriate moment were as necessary to a Heian courtier as public-speaking skills are to a present-day politician. Letters and other correspondence were often written in verse, or at the very least contained a poem or two.

Suitable marriages also hinged on poetic appropriateness, if not prowess. Composing a poem with sensitivity to season and the emotional tenor of the occasion was key. But winning the hand of the woman had less to do with love and romance than with forging political alliances with the woman's powerful male relatives. For the woman as well, mastery of poetry, calligraphy, music, painting, sewing, dyeing, and other skills was not just a sign of good breeding but a means of attracting the attention of high-placed men. Although women could inherit land and property, they relied upon their male relatives to operate and maintain them as women were largely restricted to their homes. The gender-based hierarchy was restrictive on another level as well: classical Chinese, like Latin in medieval Europe, was the language of governance, government documents, and edicts. The "party line" was that proficiency in classical Chinese was reserved for men, effectively barring women from participating in governmental affairs. In practice, women such as Murasaki Shikibu and Sei Shōnagon, the author of *Makura no sōshi* (*The Pillow Book*), did learn Chinese and incorporated aspects of it into vernacular Japanese to create a hybrid style.

With women effectively kept out of governance, things might have been exceedingly difficult for women writers had it not been for the marriage politics of the time. The dominance of the Fujiwara family necessitated the marrying of female relatives to high-ranking men. This practice was not a rarity in Japanese history (or in world history); what made it unusual was the convention of educating women in letters and the arts to make them attractive mates—which enabled women, ironically, to create what later came to be recognized as the major literary pieces of the Heian period. This did not, of course, preclude men's literary production, which included poetry in Japanese and classical Chinese, diaries in classical Chinese, and prose tales in Japanese. The last were predecessors to *The Tale of Genji*, but men did not append their names to them because prose tales were considered frivolous writings for the consumption for women. Thus, while the men were occupied with writing in both Japanese and classical Chinese, the women wrote largely in Japanese. Victoria Vernon argues that the keys to these women writers' success were: (1) lineage—the right pedigree to acquire training in the literary arts; (2) language—the freedom to compose in vernacular Japanese; and (3) leisure—the time and space to write, since they were confined to their homes and not saddled with the social and official responsibilities associated with male courtier service (Vernon 1988, 20). Of course, many women writers, including Murasaki Shikibu and Sei Shōnagon, did serve at court, but their duties were limited largely to serving their master or mistress.

The Tale and Its Conventions: Counterpointing the Classic Realist Novel

These unusual circumstances led to the creation of a tale regarded as central to the classical canon of Japan, and even considered to be the world's first "novel." The millennial celebrations of *The Tale of Genji* ran from 2000 to 2008—commemorations warranted not just by its longevity but by the remarkable role the tale has played in the cultural and aesthetic history of Japan, capturing the imaginations of so many and transposing itself so readily to multiple contexts. Comprised of fifty-four chapters, the tale operates as a series of vignettes stitched together by the life story of the central male character, Genji. The tale centers on Genji, an elegant and sought-after romantic hero, and on his progeny, set in a fictionalized, semi-historicized backdrop of tenth-century Japan. The storyline covers four generations: (1) Genji's father, Emperor Kiritsubo, and his consort, Genji's mother; (2) Genji and his ladies, in tandem with Tō no Chūjō, his brother-in-law and rival; (3) Genji's progeny—a daughter with a mistress and two sons, one with his principal wife and the other with his stepmother; and (4) Genji's grandson and a third "son" who is not really his own. Each generation, of course, blends and overlaps with the one preceding and following it. Genji, however, occupies most of the narratives from chapter 1 after his birth until his demise in chapter 41. An alphabetical list of characters is supplied in the front matter of this volume, and Royall Tyler provides a very helpful timeline in his translation of the tale (Tyler 2001a).

The Story: All About So Much

More fully, the first generation centers on the love story between Genji's parents—how the emperor becomes so smitten by Genji's mother that he seeks her company, neglecting his other consorts. Perhaps as a result of such a powerful love union, the peerless Genji is born, and so begins his rise as the ideal, most sought-after male protagonist in the tale. Much of the tale, then, focuses on the second generation: Genji and the women in his life, beginning with his principal wife, Aoi, the daughter of the powerful Minister of the Left. It is Aoi who provides Genji with political support even after his demotion to commoner status makes him ineligible to ascend the throne. Although his relationship with the distant and aloof Aoi is difficult, Genji sires a son, Yūgiri, with her, solidifies the backing of his father-in-law, and embarks upon a friendly and sometimes not-so-friendly rivalry with his brother-in-law Tō no Chūjō. Thus begins Genji's ascendency at court, mapped by associations with several women. Some of these connections form the central narrative, such as his relationship with his young stepmother and father's consort Fujitsubo, who is said to resemble his deceased mother, and with Fujitsubo's niece, the young Murasaki, whom Genji raises to be his ideal wife (and for whom the writer of the tale has been nicknamed), for Fujitsubo bears him a secret son who becomes emperor, and Murasaki represents his "true" love.

Other liaisons that are often considered secondary but still important to the tale lead to jealousy, intrigue, and even exile. The proud older woman Rokujō, who had once been consort to a now deceased crown prince, transforms into a living spirit who attacks her rivals for Genji's affection, killing not only the hapless Yūgao (Lady of the "Evening Face" Flowers) but also Genji's first principal wife Aoi, and also his beloved Murasaki, while Genji's affair with Oborozukiyo, the younger sister of his archenemy at court, leads to his self-imposed exile to Suma and a liaison with the Akashi Lady. This last relationship results in a daughter who later becomes empress. Less prominent, non-main-lineage dalliances with the provincial governor's young wife Utsusemi, the old-fashioned, red-nosed princess Suetsumuhana, and the above-mentioned Yūgao all help to round out Genji's character and advance the plot.

For his association with Oborozukiyo, Genji embarks upon a self-imposed exile to Suma under a cloud (chapter 12) but returns in triumph in the "Picture Contest" (chapter 17), where he wins imperial favor for his ward Akikonomu and his faction by presenting a collection of paintings that are deemed superior to those commissioned by his brother-in-law Tō no Chūjō. In fact it is Genji's own autobiographical renderings of his time in Suma that win the day. Slowly but surely Genji rises in power, building the fabulous Rokujō mansion where he showcases all his women and becomes Honorary Retired Emperor at age thirty-nine (chapters 33 to 41). But as he moves into middle age, Genji loses some of his glamour as an object of desire—the "sketchy," not so gallant side of him comes more and more to the fore, especially in his pursuit of Tamakazura, the long-lost daughter of Yūgao and Tō no Chūjō. He also meets his worst defeat and hastens the death of his beloved Murasaki by wedding the Third Princess, who is the young daughter of his half-brother Emperor Suzaku (chapter 34). Shy and innocent for her age, she is seduced by Tō no Chūjō's son Kashiwagi, their tryst resulting in the birth of a son, Kaoru (chapter 35). And, although the tale never makes clear whether Genji's father knew the true paternity of Reizei, Fujitsubo's son by Genji, Genji is placed in the similar position of having to publicly acknowledge Kaoru as his own.

Meanwhile, overlapping with Genji's middle-age and twilight years, there is the emergence of generation three, as Yūgiri, Genji's son by his principal wife Aoi, and Tō no Chūjō's son Kashiwagi take the stage and enact their stories. Amid much opposition, Yūgiri pursues Tō no Chūjō's daughter Kumoinokari and finally wins her hand (chapter 33), while, as mentioned above, Kashiwagi pursues the Third Princess, sires Kaoru, falls ill from guilt, and passes away (chapter 36). After Kashiwagi's demise, the sensible, staid Yūgiri pursues Kashiwagi's widow Ochiba, the older sister of the Third Princess, causing great discord at home, but he persists and marries her (chapter 39).

As we move on to the fourth and last generation, we see the last of Genji (chapter 41). Chapters 42 through 44 serve as an interlude before the last ten chapters, often called the "Uji Chapters," which center on Genji's presumed son Kaoru and his grandson Niou and their associations with three beautiful princesses: Ōigimi, Naka no kimi, and Ukifune (literally, First Princess, Middle Princess, and Floating Boat).[3] Here the narrative becomes markedly darker, both literally and figuratively, as the setting moves away from the grandeur of the court to a secluded retreat of a displaced prince in the mountains, aptly named Uji ("Melancholy"). Stunningly beautiful princesses remain the objects of desire, but much goes fatally awry, the main players suffering untoward and tragic consequences. Death visits the women in the earlier part of the tale, but here the First Princess wills herself to death in order to thwart Kaoru's advances. Genji is no longer in the picture, but he is replaced by two "heroes" who embody different aspects of his character: Kaoru represents the kinder, gentler Genji (who looked after women), but Kaoru is so pensive and self-reflective that it immobilizes him. In contrast, Genji's grandson Niou embodies the wilder, *suki* unbridled amorous, woman-seeking side of Genji. Many say that this focalization to fewer characters, more in-depth portrayals, and the delineation of grander issues of religious salvation are indicative of the maturation of Murasaki Shikibu's writing skills, moving her away from the older, less "realistic" depictions to a more psychologically consistent narrative—more in line with that of the modern novel. It is for this reason that the last ten chapters have been heralded as more compelling and even superior by some scholars.

Although a summary of the tale delineates the events, these plot moments serve primarily as foils for the complex themes and ideas that the tale addresses. For one, they obscure the political implications of the tale. Genji's siring of Emperor Reizei does not just add excitement and intrigue to the story but also represents a covert challenge to the sanctity of the imperial line, mounted by a deposed prince, Genji, who cannot inherit the throne. Political struggles to gain ascendency at court are disguised as romantic liaisons (Genji's marriage to Aoi provides him with political alliances, his seducing of the younger sister of his rival at court challenges their hegemony) or as poetry/painting/archery contests (Genji's Suma exile paintings win favor for the consort he supports). Genji's abducting of the young Murasaki focalizes sexual desire and male privilege, while the sufferings of women living in a polygynous (one man with many wives) society can morph into supernatural spirits to kill off rivals. Exile from the capital, forbidden trysts, the cuckolding of (imperial) fathers, and the (non)discovery of long-lost progeny fill the pages of the tale. Desire to find the elusive perfect man or woman, to seek out substitutes for mothers (and fathers), or to secure spiritual solace by taking the Buddhist tonsure—coupled with hero quest-fulfillment narratives of old[4]—expands the tale in numerous directions, their complexity mapped out in the many remediations found in the much later *Genji manga*.

The Politics of Categorizations

Although the story is complex and multilayered and focuses on the central character Genji, the tale is not a novel in the classic realist sense. This should not come as a surprise, since the tale predates the novel by nine hundred years—its narrative structure not following the conventions of the classic realist novel or even what we might usually expect of a novel. For one, it does not maintain a strict demarcation between poetry and prose. Although the modern novel does not mandate such a divide, for the *Genji* the interlacing of poetry in prose is standard. Thus the tale boasts almost eight hundred poems, and these are not window dressing but play an integral role in moving the tale forward and, more importantly, in highlighting the emotional tenor of the moment.[5] Take, for example, the Suma chapter, in which the hero Genji sets out on a self-imposed exile after an ill-advised liaison with the sister of his political rival at court. As he puts his affairs in order and prepares to leave the capital, Genji marks each farewell with a poem; more poems arrive in letters and through visitations once he reaches Suma, totaling forty-eight poems in a span of fifteen pages in the English translation. In almost every case the prose description leading up to the poetic exchange describes the who and the when, while the poems act as the emotive distillation of the poignancy of the moment. One of the most sorrowful partings occurs between Genji and Murasaki, the young girl whom he raises to be his wife, and it is marked by a short prose description that culminates in the poems exchanged by the two (Tyler 2001b, 1:233).[6] The prose preceding the poems is understated, simply describing Genji selecting a cloak to wear and viewing himself in the mirror. His image in the mirror is what triggers the first poem, and then a response from Murasaki—swiftly bringing the anguish of the parting moment into sharp relief. Only thereafter does the prose give voice to Murasaki's suffering: "She was sitting behind a pillar to hide her weeping" (Tyler 2001b, 1:233).

This merging of poetry and prose was not restricted to the *Genji*: during the Heian period, literature tended to be categorized into prose and poetic works, but border crossings in name and in fact were the norm. Fictional and historical *monogatari* tales were prose- rather than poetry-heavy; poetic tales were centered on poems but used prose to provide the circumstances surrounding the production of the poems. Poetry anthologies, in contrast, were collections of poems, but each poem was still introduced by a short prose contextualization of the circumstances under which it had been composed. This easy merging of poetry and prose came from the brevity of the *tanka* ("short poem," but usually referred to as *waka*, or simply "Japanese poetry"), the most prominent poetic form during the Heian period. Comprised of thirty-one syllables—a little less than twice the length of the more widely known *haiku*—the *tanka* is short, but its brevity conceals a depth not readily discerned by readers who are not steeped in its conventions. Succinctly put, the poem functions on at least two levels: on the surface, it typically references nature in some way—perhaps a snowy day that belies the coming of spring despite what the calendar indicates—but at the same time it comments on the special circumstances of the poet, perhaps standing for the cycle of life and death or providing commentary on the fickleness of the poet's lover. These relatively short poems also expand their meanings by reaching out horizontally to other poems in the tradition. So well known were the poems in the oeuvre that even a word or two would reference a specific poem, and that meaning would thus be seamlessly incorporated into the poem at hand. For example, the mention of orange blossoms and the *uguisu* (bush warbler) would point to a poem in the first imperially commissioned poetry anthology, the *Kokinwakashū* (*Collection of Old and New Japanese Poems*, hereafter *Kokinshū*),[7] eliciting fond and distant memories of a loved one. These techniques were readily adapted into the prose fictional tale, and *The Tale of Genji* is no exception.

Where's the Plot? Differently Configured Narrative Structure

In terms of its plot, here again the *Genji* departs from the classic realist novel and is more akin to the contemporary novel. There is less of a progression through which the story begins, builds up to a climax, and then travels down to a denouement. Rather, the tale tracks the romantic liaisons and goings-on of four generations of Genji's family. As noted above, the first half of the tale recounts Genji's liaisons with centrally important women, such as his stepmother Fujitsubo and his love interest Murasaki, but side trips portraying his dalliances with women such as the red-nosed princess Suetsumuhana and the provincial governor's wife Utsusemi also figure in. Even as the tale closes in chapter 54, readers are left with the sense that the tale could continue, for the fate of Ukifune, the young woman pursued so vigorously by both Genji's reputed son and by his grandson, told in the last ten chapters, is left unfinished. There is no denouement, as would be found in a classic realist novel. The tale simply stops, leaving things unresolved, much in the fashion of many Heian-period works.

Unusual in classic realist novels, this incompleteness can be found not just in Heian and other premodern works but in modern literary examples as well. A case in point would be Kawabata Yasunari's 1968 Nobel Prize–winning *Snow Country*. Written in three increments over twelve years, with long gaps in between, it appeared to be finished on at least two occasions, but more was added, each segment published in different journals at different times. Kawabata then gathered these together into a "single" novel—subsequently garnering the Nobel Prize for Literature. Reading the work in translation, the Nobel Prize judges did not find the incremental additions disruptive or lacking integration. Rather they—and readers—found that the three segments fit together nicely.

Such an amalgamation—or, put another way, tendency to provide structures that invite additions without disruption to a conceivable whole—can be found in Japanese architecture as well. The Katsura Detached Palace in Kyoto began as a small structure in 1616 but incrementally added three more wings, tripling its size (Nishi and Hozumi 1985, 78–9). Yet the villa not only stands as a completed entity but is considered "by Japanese and Western critics alike as the quintessence of Japanese taste" (Nishi and Hozumi 1985, 78). This open-endedness appears to stem from the extensive integration of structures into their surroundings, a blending in with the natural environment to such an extent that boundaries separating inside from outside are fluid or, as sociologist Tanaka Shigeyoshi argues, form *aimai* undifferentiated/undesignated spaces. He finds these features as well in the verandas (*engawa*) around farm and small town homes and in the spaces under the eaves (*hisashi*) that denote not only boundaries but also connections (Tanaka 1995, 17–18). Scholar Mack Horton notes that artistic unity is maintained by a system of "proportional design ... in which each structural member is related by formula to the others through the use of modules thereby ensuring a structural harmony within single buildings and from one building to another in a complex" (Horton 1983, 11)—which is analogous to how I argue *The Tale of Genji* might be viewed as well.

Rewriting Character: Dovetailing Empty Centers

The *Genji*, however, is not just open-ended: its organizing principle replicates an autobiography or a biography as well. Structured along the timeline of its central protagonist Genji and his progeny, the tale faithfully records their age, rank, and court office, and traces their activities and relationships. And because the lives of Genji (and his cohorts) are so enmeshed within the narrative of their society, and its (re)presentation of life, death, love, religion, and other social and political issues of the day, a picture of the period and its mores emerges. Sociologist Takie Sugiyama Lebra once noted that individual life stories told by her modern Japanese subjects were always embedded in the familial, social, and cultural obligations and networks within which they resided, whereas American subjects from a similar period tended to focus largely on personal events from their lives, with little referencing of the historical, even social goings-on that served as the backdrop to their narratives. This, according to anthropologist Dorinne Kondo, is due to the fact that, although both Japanese and Americans are "relationally defined," the construction of the self in American discourse "remains solidly within a linguistic and historical legacy of individualism," while the Japanese self is constructed "as a single thread in a richly textured fabric of relationships ... inextricable from context."[8] The main protagonists of the *Genji*, then, are inextricable from their relationships with family and other people around them and from the specifics of their time—so much so that, along with the classical Chinese diaries by Heian male courtiers, historians treat the *Genji* like a historical document that references the mores of the period.

As a result, the *Genji* narrative neither privileges the individual nor creates well-rounded characters. Rather, it embeds its protagonists into the time and place of the tale and employs two different methods to fill out their contours—through interactions with other characters and through poetic, familial, and natural-object associations. In the first, Genji and his cohorts appear on stage with little more known about them than their names and ranks—and we are only introduced to them incrementally, by what literary scholar Kikuta Shigeo terms "dovetail fitting" with other protagonists,[9] that is, a process through which different aspects of their personalities come to the fore through interaction with other characters. This may be viewed as the literary counterpart of the "contextually constructed, relationally defined selves" so prominent in interpersonal interactions in Japan, already described in the introduction (Kondo 1990, 26). Such selves are not bounded or fixed but are open-ended entities that negotiate the boundaries between themselves and others, constantly "crafting" themselves in relation to different persons and as required by social engagement (Kondo 1990, 26–33).[10]

I would argue that this makes the non-individuated Genji operate like a two-dimensional figure whose contours only begin to take shape in and through his relationships with other characters. When we first meet Genji he is exceedingly handsome and talented, befitting his high aristocratic rank—but we know precious little beyond that. As he grows up and interacts with his young stepmother Fujitsubo, we see that his desires are so powerful that he will satisfy them even at the cost of hurting and betraying those around him—including Fujitsubo and the father who loves and protects him. In his pursuit and abduction of the girl-child Murasaki, Genji reveals a darker, not-very-herolike side of his personality. But interactions with others bring to the fore an infinite kindness. Critics point to his solicitous, lifelong care of the old-fashioned, red-nosed princess Suetsumuhana as such an example.

Genji, the most elegant and sought-after object of desire in the tale, thus functions like an empty center that requires interaction with the women (and other characters) in the tale to fill out the contours of his being. For this reason some writers, such as Setouchi Jakuchō, the novelist-turned-nun who completed the most recent modern Japanese rendering of *The Tale of Genji*, considers the story to be about the women in it rather than about Genji. And indeed, many of the *manga* versions take such a view—the women's grief-stricken and difficult lives in the Heian polygynous society where men have many wives fill their pages, with Genji employed primarily to afford the women stage time. No doubt a central thrust of the tale is to relate the stories of the women, but in the narrative economy of *monogatari* storytelling, just as Genji requires the women to delineate who he is, so the women need Genji and other characters to fill out their contours. Thus what ultimately emerges is a multifaceted look both at Genji and at the women who help transform him from a smart and talented pretty face into a caring lover and an astute, politically successful courtier. Genji, then, is firmly embedded in his times and in his network of relationships with those around him who define and contextualize him—so telling Genji's story results in relating those of his cohorts and of the times as well.

The second method employed in defining the characters in the *Genji* is even more striking, being what I term "surface depth." Like the *honkadori* foundational poems[11] that reach out horizontally to other poems in the tradition and incorporate their meanings into those of the text, the facets of family lineage, position, and rank covertly define the selves of the characters. Eleventh-century readers were aware that, as an imperial offspring, Genji would inevitably be talented, beautiful, and accomplished. A privilege of rank, these attributes reside in Genji's half-brother Suzaku as well: it is just that Genji is exceptionally endowed. Lineage and familial connections also ensure shared personalized traits: even as a little child Murasaki, the niece of Genji's stepmother Fujitsubo, exhibits her aunt's beauty, intelligence, and grace. This connection is made clear by the sobriquet used for both women: the aunt Fujitsubo is Wisteria, while Murasaki (Violet) echoes in a lighter hue a rare dye of the era that presents as purple or a resonant yellow with hints of lavender, depending on the lighting. In poetry, according to translator Royall Tyler, *murasaki* "stands for close relationship and lasting passion" (2001b, 1:81)—an apt description of what Murasaki comes to mean to Genji in the course of the tale.[12] Names, colors, and flowers, then, often delineate specific personality traits. The hapless young woman who is killed by Genji's jealous lover Rokujō is appropriately named Yūgao ("Evening Face" Flowers), after a delicate white flower that blooms for only a short time at dusk, rather than in the glory of the morning sunlight as does Asagao (Morning Glory), the name given to Genji's cousin who boldly eludes Genji's clutches.[13]

Objects used as evocative symbols and images also abound: the young Murasaki's richly abundant hair spreads out like a fan, referencing the white fan upon which Yūgao presents a poem to Genji accompanied by "evening face" flowers, so that the image of a fan comes to signal his amorous interest both in the young woman Yūgao and in Murasaki when she is a girl. Fragrance, natural and otherwise, alludes to sexual and romantic interest and availability. Thus Genji's natural aroma acts much like a man's cologne might today in drawing attention to his presence and amorous allure. This trait is replicated in the names and beings of his grandson Niou and reputed son Kaoru. Kaoru, whose very name means "Fragrance," exudes a natural perfume that wafts from his being and, much as it did for Genji, invites sexual, romantic encounters, though unlike Genji, Kaoru neither wants nor knows how to pursue women to his advantage. In contrast, Niou, whose name also indicates "fragrance" but with connotations "scent" or "smell," both good and bad, does not possess natural perfume and works hard to concoct one to match Kaoru's. In effect Niou represents the unbridled amorous, lustful side of Genji, who seeks what he wants at all costs, while Kaoru is the kind, caring one whose thoughtfulness prevents him from acting on his desires. Genji's male (biological and reputed) progeny thus have similar names but perform two disparate sides of the Genji coin. By populating the narrative with non-individuated subjectivities embedded in the social discourse and entangled with other protagonists, the tale skillfully uses the surface depth of poetic, familial, and natural-object associations and names to color in the contours of its protagonists.

In-Group Reading Strategies: Collaborative, Participatory, Performative

The deployment of the plot and the creation of character in *The Tale of Genji* have much to do with the society that produced and consumed it, namely, the highly circumscribed, highly literate and aristocratic culture of the court. The courtiers—numbering four or five hundred up to a thousand people—were the producers, consumers, and subject matter of the literary and artistic works of the period, constituting insider artists/writers creating for other insider artists/writers, albeit of different competency levels. What this meant was that writings could be brief, highly encoded, and imbued with layers of meaning through association with other poems and texts. Perhaps as a result, many of the works produced at court were short, most prominently the thirty-one-syllable *waka* poem (also known as *tanka*), which can use a single image to serve multiple purposes. A bird, for example, functioned as a bird in a natural scene but also represented the poet, his/her addressee, and even a bird from other poems in the poetic and prose tradition all at the same time. Poets and prose writers such as Murasaki Shikibu thus utilized a shorthand to communicate with their in-group readers and listeners, who were highly conversant in the cultural and textual coding of the times.

In practice, much of the verbal and literary coding required for reading resided in the aforementioned *Kokinshū* and other poetic collections, as well as in Chinese poetry and the Chinese classics (Itoh 2001). Like Alexander Pope and the neoclassicists active from 1600 to 1798, Heian courtiers prized full knowledge of the tradition, so much so that what was considered "innovative" was not daringly new images or diction or "breaking the fetters" but adherence to the rules and conventions of poetry—what many post-neoclassicist proponents would call "derivative," and "flow[ing] from conformity" (Lewis 1967, 4). In other words, the *Genji* and other works from the period require readers to know the poetic, social, and cultural references made in the text, in effect expecting readers to provide the information needed to produce the meaning of the tale. In a previous work I have deemed these readers *collaborative*. It is therefore not surprising that many *Genji* readers today are lost without footnotes explaining cultural objects, courtship interactions, rituals, court positions, and customs, among other things. Replicating the Heian process of reciting and consuming poetry, this reading stance requires readers to "fill in" the gaps and complete the meaning of the text (Miyake 1993, 79).[14]

As Mikhail Bakhtin notes, the process of completing the meaning of the text requires "hooking up" with the everyday events and practices of the world in which the text is produced and consumed (1984, 276, 254). Interpretation is therefore context specific, and for Heian readers this meant invoking real-world utterances of conversations, poetic production, and gossip engendered in interpersonal, social exchanges to complete the meaning of the textual world. As readers consumed diaries, poetic anthologies, and historical tales, they would acknowledge the poet or personage in question, recall the details of his/her life and family, access the gossip surrounding the person, and most likely reference the event/occasion being described. All this would be brought to bear to understand the poem or passage in full. For the fictional *Tale of Genji*, not only covert referencing of historical events and personages but also overt signification and knowledge of rituals and conventions would have been very much in play.

Stanley Fish's notion of "interpretive communities" is instructive in situating Heian-period *Genji* readers. Sharing the same interpretive strategies for producing, consuming, and deploying texts (Fish 1980, 171), the community of Heian readers was already in possession of the specific literary and extraliterary everyday knowledge required to make sense of the texts, by virtue of what Pierre Bourdieu would call the distinction of class—"the status-derived [cultural] capital" of a particular stratum of people (1984, 70)—and this was the only "proof" necessary for membership in the Heian community of consumers (Fish 1980, 173). In fact, readers of *The Tale of Genji* were the ultimate interpretive community,[15] for they were all aristocratic by birth, often related by blood, and shared interpretative strategies learned from a circumscribed set of literary and historical texts during a particular historical moment. So closely aligned were the texts produced in this period to their interpretive community that complicity was a given, not just with content and style but with interpretive strategies as well,[16] for the tale's readers were the producers, readers/consumers, and the subject matter of literary discourse of the time. In contrast, those of us who are not part of that historically specific interpretative community must make accommodations. That is, we must not only actively agree to comply with said values but must bring with us the proper cultural, social, interpersonal knowledge of the society if we are first to *collaborate* in the production of the meaning of the text. Yet because we cannot be part of the specialized Heian-period interpretative community, we must rely on footnotes delineating the conventions of the period, so that we can engage the text more fully and become full-fledged collaborative "coauthors" (Duranti 1986).

Readerly collaboration and full complicity point to a second interpretive strategy utilized by Heian practitioners: *participation* in the represented world. Enacting the oral conversation aspect of *waka* poetry composition and recitation—reminiscent of Bakhtin's dialogic relationship of reader and text—readerly participation embodies the speech act paradigm of a speaker conversing with a recipient about a topic (Searle 1969). In short, the *Genji* text reaches out to readers, addressing them directly, as if the readers were participants in the represented world of the tale. The *Genji* utilizes a narrator, known as the *sōshiji* in *Genji* studies, to draw the reader into the text. The narrator, however, is not a character in the tale (as in Henry James's *The Turn of the Screw*) nor a figure inscribed in the text (like Fyodor Dostoevsky's "Gentlemen" in *Notes from the Underground*). Rather, the narrator reaches out beyond the confines of the text and addresses a "you," the implied reader of the text, who is then pulled into the textual world and becomes conflated with the narratee (i.e., the listener *within* the fictional world to whom the narrator relates the tale; Miyake 1993, 78).[17]

This readerly participation in the fictional world of the *Genji* is marked by the presence of what is termed the topic marker "wa"—a grammatical indicator that posits a speaker-narrator in dialogue with a listener-reader. This provides for a narrator who is not omniscient, and also for readers who are not simply voyeurs invited to look into the fictional world from the outside, as would be the case in realist novels. Rather, this device situates readers inside the text, sharing the same narrative time and space as the narrator and the characters. And as noted above, even though the narrator is inscribed in the represented world of the tale, she remains a narrative presence unnamed, unidentified, and never fully conceived as a character.[18] Despite this ambiguity, the *Genji* narrator appears to be a lady-in-waiting by virtue of the situations she witnesses, the narrative details to which she is privy, and the language of deference she employs vis-à-vis the imperial family, Genji, and high-ranking personages.[19] Although only one narrator is on stage at any one moment and the narrator speaks in a singular voice, "she" in fact represents a series of ladies-in-waiting, because the narrator embodies personages who appear in different times and places over a stretch of four generations—a rather difficult feat for a single persona. (See Miyake 1993 and Bowring 1988 for more information.)

The reader's participation in the represented world of the tale is orchestrated by the direct address of the *sōshiji* narrator and the grammatical necessity of the Japanese language, but it is further enabled by the third function of the reader as *performative*. Simply put, *The Tale of Genji* is not just a narration of past events that are treated as a fait accompli in the fashion of classic realist novels but is a reenactment of a story in process, an unfolding of the action as if it were taking place right before their eyes. In other words, readers do not simply function as third-person viewers of the action but see it through the eyes of the characters themselves. One way that this process is enacted, according to Heian poetry scholar Kikuchi Yasuhiko, is the readers' employment of reading/recitation strategies in their encounters with the *waka* poems in the tale.[20] As will become apparent from the *Tales of Yamato* episode below, the reader assumes the stance of the unbounded, contextually based *waka* persona and participates in the fictive moment as an experiencer or witness of the events recounted (Miyake 1993, 85). The *Tales of Yamato* is a poem tale that dates from around 951–2 and is composed of 173 episodes that focus on the everyday exchange of poetry in the late-ninth- and early-tenth-century Heian court. In Section 147 of *Tales of Yamato*, several female poets from an empress's entourage view a screen painting and compose poems from the perspective of the young woman and her two suitors (Tahara 1980, 93–8). Utilizing the convention of taking up the pose of a persona different from their own in terms of gender as well as positionality, the ladies-in-waiting take advantage of the open-endedness and undifferentiatedness of *waka* personas to "embody" the characters and "perform" as different personas—"becoming" a young woman and even gender crossing as male suitors. (See Miyake 2001, 26–9 for a fuller accounting of this process.)

It is precisely because a *waka* is most often genderless, devoid of rank-distinguishing honorific language, and generally of pronouns that readers can take up the space of the "I" of the poem and "perform the lines" as the character in the fictional world for the duration of thirty-one syllables, hence enacting the third readerly stance, namely, the performative. The reader's performance is somewhat analogous to an actor's "playing" Hamlet. By intoning the verses, the reader "becomes" the character immersing him/herself in—and in a sense living—the unfolding emotion and event for the duration of the "reading" of the poem. This enables the reader to adopt the stance of an experiencer of the emotion, the fluid, non-gender-differentiated multi-persona voice enabling the performance.[21]

What is striking about the *Genji* text is that the reader's performative function is maintained even in the prose descriptions, as a result of what Richard Bowring terms the "covert presence" of the narrator (1988, 58). This is enabled, because there are no grammatical differences between direct and indirect quotes, making the distinction between the narrator and the interiority of the protagonists fluid (Bowring 1988, 63). The narration moves effortlessly between the narrator and the protagonist with little demarcation as to when the switch occurs. A close merger of narrator with character, without the total dissolution of either, comes into play—very different from modern English, which demands a clearer differentiation of grammatical subjects. (See Bowring 1988, 61–7 for further information.) Thus we can conclude that readers take up stances vis-à-vis the dialogic and interiority moments of characters that replicate their performative readings/recitations of *waka*—embodying the character in ways that a *nō* actor internalizes the role that he plays.

Conclusion: Coauthoring Empty Centers

The Tale of Genji was conceived by a lady-in-waiting, Murasaki Shikibu, around the turn of the first millennium, and, because the tale was the "bestseller" of the day, Shikibu was brought to the court of Emperor Ichijō in hopes of drawing the emperor to the salon of the imperial consort whom Shikibu served. In this way we see not only the power and privilege literature held in early-eleventh-century Japan but also the positionality of the women who were used to secure political advantage for their families by producing imperial (and other high-ranking) heirs or serving those who could produce them. To be suitable mates and/or highly regarded ladies-in-waiting, the women had to be trained in the arts, including literature. Used as pawns in high-stake political power grabs, women, ironically, composed many of the major literary pieces of the period, one of which, *The Tale of Genji*, came to be regarded as the world's first novel.

Indeed, *The Tale of Genji* performs more as a contemporary novel than as a traditional classic realist one, for it challenges the structures and practices of the latter. Tracing the life story of Genji and his progeny, the tale eschews the usual plot structure of beginning, middle, and end with a definitive climax and denouement in tow. It has a beginning but no conclusive ending and remains fluid, open-ended, and undifferentiated. No well-rounded characters with psychological depth on the order of Madame Bovary or Anna Karenina are in sight; instead, it is populated with almost two-dimensional characters who require dovetailing with others and allusive associations with poetic, familial, and natural objects to flesh out the contours to their beings. Comprised of fifty-four chapters that operate like vignettes, the tale is a product of a highly circumscribed, highly aristocratic in-group in which Heian courtiers functioned as the producers, consumers, and subject matter of texts. All were generally acquainted with each other, privy to family as well as other details about each other, and trained in the same corpus of (Japanese language-based) knowledge—thus fashioning the strategies for producing, consuming, and deploying texts in particular ways. Texts could operate in shorthand, in effect positioning readers as collaborative, participatory, and performative consumers in senses that are foreign to the more voyeuristic perusal of classic realist novels. Readers could be counted on to bring cultural, social, and historical information to the texts, and as such were well positioned to become a part of the textual world and to experience it in tandem with the characters.

Such embodied participatory reading practices are, in fact, very much in keeping with strategies developed by *manga* artists, who create visual narrative pacts of understanding and communication with their audiences. The targeting of audience by age, gender, category, and to an extent topic or genres allows artists to interact with similar-minded audiences, much like the circumscribed court of Murasaki Shikibu's time, and to participate together as members of in-group interpretive communities that tacitly share bodies of visual and narrative cues. Through well-placed images and phrases, artists can gesture toward a specific meaning or plot development in much the same way that Murasaki Shikibu did, confident that readers possess the information necessary to grasp the intended implications. And just as the presence of orange blossoms or the *uguisu* (bush warbler) evokes shared memories of times past in classical poetry, so flower motifs in a girls comics signal a romantic encounter, or at least romantic interest on the part of the protagonists. Remarkably, the eleventh-century reading techniques have come full circle and have much to say about those of contemporary readers of *Genji manga*. But is understanding how the tale came to be all that is needed to understand the making of the *manga* versions? Perhaps not, as we see in the next chapter.

Chapter 2

THE TALE OF GENJI THROUGH THE AGES: TRANSPOSITIONS, TRANSLATIONS, CULTURAL CAPITAL, AND INTERPRETATIVE COMMUNITIES

A millennium after it was written, the reading strategies of *The Tale of Genji* have come full circle in its *manga* remediations. In that process, the tale has traversed time and space, and has been "translated" into cultural, intellectual, and political capital for differing interpretative communities. It has highlighted the splendor of the court, focalized men and also women, been transposed into non-Heian settings, and evolved into parodies of male lust, rice-paddy art, and all-female musical revues. It has bolstered the fortunes of poetic families, landed warriors, female artists, and townspeople in the premodern age, and functioned as soft power to garner readmittance into the world order and obtain international acclaim for the Japanese government in this century and the last. Generation after generation of Japanese readers, writers, and performers have kept the tale so alive and well that it has become synonymous not only with Japanese literary history but with Japan's cultural history as well.[1] Whether in straightforward, digested, embellished, or even completely rewritten form, *The Tale of Genji* has been transposed into seemingly every new cultural form—literary, painterly, dramatic, filmic, musical. It has been reenvisioned as *ukiyo-e* woodblock prints, film, drama, *anime*, and even a symphony and an opera—and, finally, as *manga*, "multimodal (hybridised visual linguistic) texts" (Bryce et al. 2008, 1).

How did a tale written in a female discourse of a circumscribed courtier society become so conversant with such a global youth culture as *manga*? How successful was its "translation," and what did it capture but also obscure? The answers lie in examining the transpositions—cultural manifestations through which the tale positioned itself and its consumer producers in each period—and in tracing the ways in which they set the stage for the *Genji manga*. As already mentioned, the tale "morphed" into a myriad of cultural forms. Due to space limitations, I focus here on two major threads that have impacted the *manga* versions: the *Genji-e* painting tradition and the tale's textual "translations." In doing so, I discuss two dramatic forms (*nō* and kabuki) and a few filmic and other innovative modern transpositions. Audial/music forms are not featured beyond mention of a few. Generally speaking, I map how specialized interpretative communities used differing visual and textual *Genji* transpositions to create their identities to further their political, social, and cultural agendas. I also look at how these transpositions influenced and fashioned the content, thematic treatment, and drawing styles of the *Genji manga*. The two lines of inquiry—the textual and the visual—will be traced in tandem.

Genji *Transpositions through the Ages*

The transpositions of the tale run the gamut from imperially commissioned, sumptuous paintings to musicals to commemorative coins. They include ladies' "gossip" sessions, novelizations by authors Japanese and otherwise, bombastic, larger-than-life kabuki performances, and even an MP3 RoboMurasaki intoning the tale. The *Genji-e* painterly remediations that served as visual inspirations[2] include (1) the twelfth-century *Genji* scrolls housed in three museums; (2) *hakubyō* black-and-white ink illustrations from the thirteenth century linked to women artists; (3) fifteenth- through nineteenth-century Tosa School paintings that operated as handbooks for illustrating the *Genji*; and (4) kabuki-inspired *ukiyo-e* woodblock prints by artists such as Utagawa Kunisada. Though not reflected in all *Genji manga*, these served as important resources for many practitioners. Black-and-white woodblock prints that emulate Tosa School paintings, for example, influenced *manga* artist Hasegawa Hōsei and others (Shinohara et al. 1988).[3]

In premodern times, digests, commentaries, and character genealogies provided access to the tale. And as the tale became as difficult for later Japanese readers to parse as the mid-seventh-century *Beowulf* was for English readers, it was "translated" into modern Japanese and made available to generations of new consumers. Even the parodies, pastiches, and colorful rewritings from the Tokugawa period (1600–1868) provided inspiration, if not fodder and ideas, for thematic treatment. Throughout, different aspects of the tale were highlighted, embellished, or omitted; specific characters held court or all but disappeared; the tale diversified and actively "translated" itself to fit the agendas of different interpretive communities. But one thing remained constant: the creation of an encoded, in-group-specific text that invited readers/viewers in the know to collaborate and even participate and perform in the fictional world at hand. Tacitly sharing codes of understanding and communication with their audiences, writers and artists brought full circle the reading strategies deployed by Murasaki Shikibu and her courtier readers. It is a tour de force, then, that the tale was subsequently transposed into the very differently situated hybrid texts of word and image in the twentieth- and twenty-first-century *manga* as well.

Medieval (1185–1600) Warrior Genji *Adaptations: Heian Court Nostalgia, Male Warrior Cultural Brokers, Female Voices*

With the rise of the warrior Kamakura and subsequent Ashikaga military governments, the Heian court that had produced *The Tale of Genji* ceased to be a political force, although it continued to exert influence because the ensuing medieval period[4] remained aristocratic in outlook and looked back to the golden age of Heian culture. Thus the tale stood as a talisman of courtier culture and cultural capital, bestowing political and cultural relevancy to varying male- and female-based interpretive communities that produced new literary and art-based "translations" of the tale as their consumer base expanded from courtiers to warriors and even to some high-ranking peasants.

The earliest extant pictorial remediations of the tale are the twelfth-century *Genji* scrolls, which showcase in splendid color the grandeur of the Heian court and, by one account, the power and prestige of the Imperial House to orchestrate such a vast undertaking.[5] Currently owned by the Tokugawa Reimeikai Foundation, the Gotoh Museum, and the Tokyo National Museum, they successfully translate the tale's complex emotions and dovetailing interrelationships in tableau-like images. Like *manga* readers, viewers had to know the *Genji* story and be well versed in the specialized coding of the medium—this time, the painting tradition. "Kashiwagi III," for example, depicts Genji's first encounter with Kaoru, his "son" sired by another man—a highly charged moment illuminated by diagonally placed beams and drapery stands, and robes in disarray. (See Taguchi 2009, 103 for more information.) Centuries later, artist Koizumi Yoshihiro incorporated much of the sumptuous color and magnificence of these paintings in his *Genji manga*.

The individual scroll scenes do translate the grandeur of the court, but not the contiguity of the tale. Rather, they highlight central moments, and also lesser known ones. Art historian Yukio Lippet points to the "Yokobue" ("The Flute") interlude, in which Genji's son Yūgiri watches his wife Kumoinokari nurse their child after being awakened by a ghostly presence. A very unusual, intimate look at domesticity, the scene focuses on a minor character, Kumoinokari, giving her center stage in ways that Murasaki Shikibu's text does not (Lippit 2008, 54–6). Here we see our first example of how the tale was remediated and transposed to serve differing priorities, a strategy used with great latitude in subsequent transpositions and in the *manga* versions as well.

From the fifteenth through the nineteenth centuries, it was the Tosa School that took up the mantle of the *Genji* scrolls, codifying and fragmenting the tale even further. Drawn on *shikishi*, 6- by 5.2-inch sheets, the Tosa School polychrome images were pasted onto large folding screens or collected into albums, the latter comprising an iconography of specific scenes for each *Genji* chapter, mainly featuring romantic relationships, festivals, and ceremonies (McCormick 2008, 103; Murase 1983, 20–1, and 2001, 15). Together with the *Genji* scrolls, the Tosa corpus of more than two hundred images controlled the transmission of polychromatic *Genji* paintings, although the Kanō School paintings gained prominence around 1573–1615.[6] Nonetheless, the Tosa and other *Genji* paintings remained "symbols of elite culture" among the warlords of the period, adorning private rooms in mansions (Nakamachi 2008, 173–4) and later finding their way into *manga* renditions as well.

The Tale of Genji also helped two differently positioned male interpretative communities secure and maintain authority. Displaced politically, descendants of the courtiers such as the poets Fujiwara no Shunzei (1114–1204) and his son Teika

(1162–1241) utilized secret interpretations of *The Tale of Genji* and other Heian texts, which they passed on to heirs and disciples and doled out to members of the warrior class who coveted these teachings as means to acquire their right to rule (Cook 2008, 146, 138–9). In the fourteenth and fifteenth centuries, however, the newly emerging landed warrior lords and shoguns of the Ashikaga military government recreated the *Genji* as *nō* drama to establish their own cultural capital. Surprisingly, the plays did not laud (male) military prowess but harked back to the gentility of the Heian period, featuring female characters such as Genji's wife Aoi, his lover Yūgao, and Ukifune, one of the Uji princesses. The *nō* renditions thus sidestepped Genji and the other men and focalized the women as embodiments of *yūgen*, "a darkly mysterious and sublime elegance" (Brown 2001, 10–11, 33, 31)[7]—serving as inspirations for girls and ladies *Genji manga*.

Female interpretative communities were in operation as well, providing platforms for women's voices through such venues as the so-called *Genji* gossip in the Kamakura period and *Mumyō-zōshi* (*A Nameless Notebook*) in the thirteenth century, where women presented their views (Shirane 2008a, 20).[8] The most influential female remediations for *manga*, however, were *hakubyō* "white drawings." Produced in the thirteenth- through sixteenth-century imperial court salons, they were created by women to entertain their superiors, to enable their participation in poetry and painting events, and to showcase their knowledge of the *Genji* for marriage purposes (McCormick 2008, 110, 117, 112–13). The drawings' luxurious black lines and inked-in black hair spotlit the women and supported their positionalities in times when (male) military prowess prevailed— their delicate beauty invoking the elegance of Yamato Waki's girls comics and Ide Chikae's ladies comics centuries later. Interestingly, at the end of the Kamakura period the *Genji* was labeled sinful, relegating its author to hell for its writing, but it was also deemed suitable for educating women because it displayed "refined and gentle femininity" and cultivated artistic taste (Shirane 2008a, 18–19, 30–1). Here we find some of the first pushback against the tale, a reaction that became more pronounced in its *manga* and *anime* remediations.

The Edo (1600–1868) Explosion: From Woodblock Prints to a Champion of National Identity and Nationalism

The ensuing Edo or Tokugawa period fostered much growth and innovation, despite—or perhaps because of—Japan turning inward and expelling all foreigners during its nearly three hundred years. Anchored by yet another military government, the Tokugawa Bakufu (named for the warrior family who defeated the other warlords), Japan was less a unified country under one polity than a "national coalition of daimyo [landed warrior families]" (Yamashita n.d., 5). The bakufu controlled the country by owning most of the land, forcing the landed lords to alternate their residences between Edo (present-day Tokyo) and their home province, and setting up a rigid hierarchical system with the samurai class at its apex. This political system created urbanized spaces—castle towns and thriving economic centers in the cities of Edo, Kyoto, and Osaka—which, in turn, fostered commercialization and the rise of merchants who were economically powerful despite their low social status falling below that of the samurai, farmers, and even artisans. The merchant townspeople turned to conspicuous consumption and the pursuit of pleasure in entertainment districts, and, together with the artisans, became the cultural brokers of their times, once again translating the *Genji* and other works to serve their own agendas.

The townspeople (and some repurposed samurai) paid homage to the *Genji* but pushed and prodded and stretched the tale, producing heretofore unseen translations: sumptuous woodblock prints, flamboyant, fast-paced narratives, mixed-media texts, philosophical treatises that laid the groundwork for modern statecraft, and larger-than-life kabuki dramatic performances. For instance, the earliest *ukiyo-e* woodblock prints followed the tale in dress and story but later presented in *mitate* visual paintings—highly contemporized remediations of a scene or a figure from a classical or medieval work (Nakamachi 2008, 191–4, 196–7). Hence a print by Chōbunsai Eishi (1756–1829) depicts two women dressed in Edo-period kimonos staring off in the distance, though few viewers without knowledge of the tale and of Tokugawa aesthetics would have recognized the work as a rendition of the famous scene in which the young Murasaki, her grandmother, and a lady-in-waiting watch her pet sparrow wing away, as Genji looks on (Tokugawa Museum 2005, 77).

Creating such visual puzzles is very much alive today in *manga* remediations ranging from Maya Mineo's *Patalliro Tale of Genji!* to Tomi Shinzō's *Genji*. Further inspiration is found in Ihara Saikaku's (1642–93) wonderfully playful *Kōshoku ichidai otoko* (*The Life of an Amorous Man*, 1682)—the hyperbolic tall tale of a sensational Genji-like lover who records almost four thousand sexual relations, the first with his nanny when he is barely four years old. An *ukiyo zōshi*, or floating world tale, *Amorous Man* hypersexualizes and hyperexaggerates male lust in hyperbolic, cheeky fashion. Santo Kyōden's (1761–1816) *kibyōshi* yellow book *Edo umare uwaki no kabayaki* (*Playboy Roasted à la Edo*, 1785)[9] also satirizes the *Genji* by featuring a pug-nosed merchant protagonist who desperately wants to be a Genji ladies' man but can only manage disastrously funny, compromising situations. *Kibyōshi*'s use of narrative explanation and its dialogue sans speech balloons are evocative of modern *manga*—although labeling them a precursor rather than a progenitor of *manga* is advisable, as Adam Kern cautions.[10] Markedly different from other works, *kibyōshi* provide fodder for the parodic treatment of the *Genji* found in the *manga* by Akatsuka Fujio, Koizumi Yoshihiro, and Egawa Tatsuya—bringing to the fore what it is in the *Genji* that is "translated" as the tale is transposed from genre to genre.

Ryūtei Tanehiko's (1783–1842) *Nise murasaki inaka genji* (*A Fraudulent Murasaki's Bumpkin Genji*, 1829–42),[11] accompanied by woodblock illustrations by artist Utagawa Kunisada (1786–1865), employs inventive visual/textual *mitate* puzzles. *Bumpkin Genji* differs so much from the tale in format, content, characterization, and plotline that viewers may well wonder whether it has any ties to the eleventh-century originating text—much as is the case for Maya's *manga* entitled *Patalliro Tale of Genji!* Simultaneously situated in the Edo, Muromachi, and Heian periods, *Bumpkin Genji* "defies easy characterization" and is a tour de force of parody.[12] The startlingly inventive manner in which the illustrations are formatted and the book designed and packaged certainly warranted the excitement its publication generated. Michael Emmerich, however, contends that these are not the only reasons *Bumpkin Genji* was eagerly awaited: Tanehiko was a master at combining "high-class elegance" with a page-turner plot that makes for a scintillating read (Emmerich 2008, 220). As a result, *Bumpkin Genji* became one of the central conduits through which readers in the Edo through early Shōwa (1926–89) periods came to know the *Genji*,[13] anticipating the influence on contemporary *Genji* culture of Yamato's *manga* entitled *Fleeting Dreams* and Tanabe Seiko's modern Japanese translation.

Literary *Genji* transpositions notwithstanding, the tale's translation into statecraft was the most surprising transformation of all. In the late 1800s, nativist scholar Motoori Norinaga (1730–1801) employed the tale to champion his views in the ideological debates of the time. Composing treatises such as *Genji monogatari tama no ogushi* (*Tale of Genji, a Fine Jeweled Comb*, 1796), he eschewed foreign ideas and pressed for a return to Japan's "original," pre-Buddhist and Confucian roots—which in his opinion were best exemplified by the *mono no aware* (pathos of the transience of things) found in the *Genji* (Caddeau 2006, 3). Norinaga questioned the dominance of Buddhist scriptures and Chinese literary and historical works in Japanese intellectual discourse, arguing instead for consideration of the *Genji* as the repository of the "essence" of Japanese culture, and for the placement of the homegrown *waka* poetry and *monogatari* tales at the top of the literary hierarchy. The full import of this reordering did not come to fruition until the Meiji period (1868–1912), when Japan needed a "national language" and "national literature" to establish itself as a modern nation-state (Shirane 2007a, 12–13), but Norinaga's assessment of the *Genji* as a repository of the best of Japanese culture positioned it well to champion national identity and nationalism.

Modernization (1868 Through the Second World War): Modern Japanese "Translations," Novelization, and Nation-Building

The arrival of Commodore Matthew Perry and his black ships in 1857 effectively ended Japan's self-imposed isolation, forcing the Tokugawa government to defend itself against not just American but also French and English guns. Unable to do so, the government was overthrown by a band of samurai in the name of the emperor, forcing Japan to modernize and "catch up" with the west in short order. Often labeled the Meiji Restoration for reinstating the emperorship, the new era thrust Japan into the modern world, a challenge to which the new heads responded by sending its best and its brightest to Europe to learn western ways of governance, military strategy, and education, among other things. But entry into the modern age came at a price. Forced to open its doors to superior firepower, Japan fell victim to unfavorable treaties imposed by the United States, France, and England. New technology from the industrialized west challenged the lifestyle that Japan had known for three hundred years. In terms of the literary arts, Shakespeare, the nineteenth-century novel, and modernization theories arrived simultaneously, pushing aside *The Tale of Genji* and other premodern Japanese texts (Shirane 2008a, 6).

Dealing with western ways would no doubt have sidelined *The Tale of Genji* for many years had not certain forces come into play in the 1880s and 1890s, most notably the desire to join other modern western nation-states (Caddeau 2006, 4; T. Suzuki 2008, 244). As Tomi Suzuki explains, several events set the stage for Japan's foray onto the global stage: first, Japan won the 1904–5 Russo-Japanese War against great odds, giving it confidence to participate in worldwide affairs. (It also beat the Chinese in 1894–5 but this was of lesser concern in the eyes of the west.) Second, in order to join the new world order Japan had to prove that it was a modern nation, and according to Benedict Anderson, this meant solidifying itself as "an imagined political community" through the establishment of a "national print language" and "a national print literature" (T. Suzuki 2008, 244, and 2000, 72; see Anderson 1991, 6, 14). The nation-builders called upon native Japanese poetry and prose, and specifically *The Tale of Genji*, to create Japan's "common language, culture, and history," which dovetailed nicely with the 1880 European literary polemic that the novel rendered a nation civilized (T. Suzuki 2008, 249). Suematsu Kenchō, Japanese legation member and Cambridge University student, produced the first translation of the tale in 1882 as proof that Japan possessed a novel and was "a civilized nation" (T. Suzuki 2008, 244–5, 249).

On the home front from the late 1880s through the 1910s, *The Tale of Genji* encountered resistance as being "effeminate," "upper class," and unsuitable for the modern age (T. Suzuki 2008, 255). The poet Yosano Akiko (1878–1942) came to the rescue in 1912–13, translating the tale into a modern novel (T. Suzuki 2008, 261–3),[14] and Arthur Waley (1889–1966) provided the tale with a global stage, transposing it into English from 1925 to 1933.[15] Together with the Yosano remediations, Waley's translation propelled *Genji* into the modern age, where its translation into *manga* and other popular cultural media further tested what was transferrable across different times and cultures.

Popular Soft Power/Cultural Capital (1950–Present): Film, the Takarazuka Musical Revue, Manga, Anime, *Symphonies, and More*

The novelization of *The Tale of Genji*[16] was a watershed moment, for it propelled the tale into new media—transforming the text-based tale into temporally configured films, *anime*, and all-female revue musicals and providing it with a global popular culture audience through *manga* and *anime*. It also set the stage for three *Genji* booms domestically and globally,[17] and highlighted the ways in which the tale was translated from one medium and one era to another. The first boom, in the 1950s, marked Japan's recasting of its image from bellicose aggressor to civilized, genteel nation, marshaling the *Genji* and other works in the construction of its new look. The second occurred in the 1980s: its postwar woes in the rearview mirror, Japan rode high on its bubble economy that was the envy of the world; women were flexing their social and cultural muscle; Japanese exports had shifted from the traditional arts to high tech and pop culture, replete with Cool Japan soft power "takes" on the *Genji*. The twenty-first century brought the third *Genji* boom, with the inception of the tale being celebrated from 2000 through 2008. After a decade of economic slowdowns, terrorist acts, and political scandals, Japan needed something to celebrate, and what better than a work renowned at home and throughout the world? Each boom was very much a creature of its times, and in all three the tale served as a soft power and/or as cultural capital to promote the agenda of its wielders.

The first *Genji* boom took place in the 1950s as Japan sought to rejoin the global postwar community by moving beyond its defeat and away from its responsibility for wartime atrocities.[18] Japan shed its samurai, *kamikaze* suicide bomber ferocity and returned to its pre-warrior classical, more female *Tale of Genji* roots. Internationally, Edward Fowler argues that a marked shift in the geopolitical landscape—the onset of the Cold War between the Soviet Union and the United States lasting from 1945 to 1997—caused the United States to seek an ally in Asia. Under American Occupation since 1945, Japan was seen as the perfect candidate for this position, and so commenced the joint effort to reconstitute the nation that had relentlessly bombed Pearl Harbor as a gentle, peace-loving country (Fowler 1991, 3, 6).

One little-known strategy in this campaign to refashion Japan as a US ally was the publication in English of Japanese novels that featured emasculated Japanese male protagonists—one series marketed them as weak and ineffectual, another as enthralled with female sexuality, and a third as overcompensating for their "manly" identity. The authors in question are: the 1968 Nobel Prize winner Kawabata Yasunari, the three-time translator of *The Tale of Genji* Tanizaki Jun'ichirō, and, oddly enough, Mishima Yukio, a writer known for the maintenance of his own personal army and for committing *seppuku* (ritualistic disembowelment) in 1970 (Fowler 1991, 8). The male characters at the center of Kawabata's novels are gentle, feminized, emasculated males who—like Genji's reputed son Kaoru in the tale—encounter beautiful women but are unable to seize the moment. In contrast, Tanizaki's male characters are not weak, but his female characters are ultrapowerful femmes fatales, accomplished manipulators, or fetishized beauties under whose spells his male protagonists willingly and enthusiastically fall. Mishima, with his militaristic machismo, is a bit of a mystery. Scholar Earl Jackson, Jr. explains that, although Mishima presented as a macho male in Japan, he had homosexual tendencies, divesting him and Japan of their military teeth and making Japan feminine/female and safe to consume in the eyes of westerners.[19] So successful was this disarming of Japan that, as late as the 1980s, an editor from *Delos* commented, "For the average Western reader, [Kawabata's] *Snow Country* is perhaps what we think of as typically 'Japanese': 'elusive, misty, inconclusive'" (Kizer, qtd. in Fowler 1991, 9).

On both sides of the Pacific, the reconfiguring of Japan as a peaceful nation progressed in force, and the feminine, elegant *Tale of Genji* was marshaled to promote that narrative. The tale was "translated" into modern Japanese by several women authors; it was remediated into new venues (music, radio, television, *manga*, *anime*) and enacted in kabuki performances that centered on Genji in the 1970s, with ten kabuki productions featuring the tale's women protagonists from 1953 to 1979 (Tateishi 2005b, 185–7). The all-female troupe of the Takarazuka musical revue staged its first performance of the tale in 1952, adding more performances in 1966 and 1973 (Tateishi 2005b, 186). The Second World War military narratives were replaced in school curricula with the softer, gentler *Tale of Genji* (T. Suzuki 2008, 276). Japan marked its reentry into the global community by garnering the best cinematography award at the 1951 Cannes Film Festival for a film on the *Genji* that depicts Japan as a compliant, passive, exotic other (Tateishi 2008, 303, 307–8; 2005a, 145–8). In the United States, an image of Japanese literature as feminine and nonthreatening took hold as translations of classical works, largely Heian works by women, appeared in the 1960s and the 1970s (Miyake 2000).

The second *Genji* boom occurred about thirty years later, during the 1980s, following Japan's impressive economic growth in the 1960s and 1970s. By then Japan's global image had shifted from one of traditional Zen-inspired fine arts, the tea ceremony, and woodblock prints to visions of high-tech "Honda Civics and Sony Walkmans" (MacWilliams 2008, 15). This should have put *The Tale of Genji* at a disadvantage, except that the bubble economy had Japan riding high, with other nations seeking its formula for success. Taking a page from Motoori Norinaga's playbook, Japan looked to its past to explain what was quintessentially Japanese about its success, eliciting a resurgence of interest in things classical. Celebrated as a decade of women's advancement, the 1980s also initiated the golden age of girls comics and fostered the inception of ladies comics. Globally, things Japanese soared, with *anime* and *manga* evoking great excitement and attention.

Joining forces with the first girl-oriented, Hello Kitty *kawaii* cute cultural trend, the emphasis on the feminine escalated further, yielding Yamato Waki's pivotal girls comics *Fleeting Dreams* and the institution of ladies comics. Writer-turned-nun Setouchi Jakuchō's novelization of the tale deleted all the male-oriented episodes and gave voice to the sexuality of the female protagonists in "visceral and physical" fashion. By the end of 1999 seventeen million copies of *Fleeting Dreams* had been sold, shaping the transmission of the tale in contemporary Japanese culture.[20] Tateishi Kazuhiro argues that *Fleeting Dreams* and author Tanabe Seiko's *Shin genji monogatari* (*The New Tale of Genji*)[21] formed the new ground-zero resource for contemporary remediations of the *Genji*—translating the tale as sweet and gentle and creating the "mass-produced, mass-consumed [*Genji*] culture" discussed further in Chapter 3 (Tateishi 2008, 303).[22]

On the global front, Cool Japan soft power[23] mesmerized the world with its pop culture music, fashion, *anime*, and, of course, *manga*. It also brought attention to other things Japanese, with *The Tale of Genji* appearing in two prestigious literary series. In 1989 the tale became the only Asian title in the Cambridge *Landmarks of World Literature*. In 1993 *Approaches to the Teaching of Murasaki Shikibu's The Tale of Genji* was published as part of the Modern Language Association's series on world literature. Numbering 213 volumes, the series publishes studies of literary works or writers deemed important for higher education (Modern Language Association n.d.). To date, *The Tale of Genji* remains one of three Asian titles in the series, alongside *Dream of the Red Chamber* and a volume on Indian writer Amitav Ghosh.

As diverse as these venues were, they did not prepare us for the explosion of *Genji* transpositions in the third *Genji* boom, which began in 2000 and brought not only hope but also great trepidation. The bursting of Japan's bubble economy in the 1990s resulted in a severe economic downturn and was accompanied by terrorist acts and political scandals. Japan badly needed something to celebrate— and the one-thousandth year since the inception of a work touted as the world's first novel was just the thing. Once more the *Genji* was enlisted to help Japan cope and regain its footing. The magnitude of the events, activities, foods, and goods produced between 2000 and 2008—the years designated for the celebrations— was unprecedented, ranging from parades, knitting exhibitions, moon viewings, and cosplaying in twelve-layer Heian robes to sweets, free refrigerator magnet giveaways, and even a Heian hairstyle show. By one account more than one thousand events were mounted in 2008 alone (Tyler e-mail), while Michael Emmerich recorded more than two thousand newspaper articles on various celebrations, with one-fourth of Japan's population participating between 2006 and 2009 (2013, 12–13). This extravaganza was capped by *The Tale of Genji* Millennial Anniversary Memorial Ceremony attended by 2,400 people, including the emperor and empress, where the tale was lauded as a "Japanese [and] world classic" and a guide to Japan in "a world in constant fluctuation" (Emmerich 2013, 14, 16; see Chapter 7 for more information).

The millennium also brought new remediations in familiar forms: Dennis Washburn published his English translation in 2015, while a Kindle English edition of Yamato Waki's *manga Fleeting Dreams* made its appearance in 2019–20. Modern Japanese artists created vibrant, exquisite renditions in cutouts (Miyata Masayuki 2001), Tosa-style prints (Ishidori Tatsuya 1999), and flamboyant watercolors (Amano Yoshitaka 2006).[24] In keeping with the Tanabe-Yamato *Genji* culture, a 2009 TV *anime* entitled *Genji monogatari: sen'nen ki* (*The Tale of Genji: A Millennium-Old Journal*) contemporizes and makes more dramatic the anguish of the women in their romantic dealings with Genji. Scenes are added, situations embellished.[25] Equally under the Tanabe-Yamato spell is the 2001 film *Sen'nen no koi: hikaru genji monogatari* (*A Love of a Thousand Years: The Tale of the Shining Genji*), with its wildly creative take on the tale. As will be discussed in Chapter 7, much is added: a singing sprite weaves in and out of the film, and author Murasaki Shikibu and her daughter pull in fishing nets in faraway Echizen province at the end of the film. Most striking of all is the casting of Amami Yuki, a member of the all-female Takarazuka troupe, as Genji. By gender-bending and focalizing the romance and the thoughts and feelings of the characters, the film tracks the world of Tanabe remediations and *Fleeting Dreams*. Even more remarkable is the nationalist, almost colonialist tone in parts of the film (Tateishi 2008, 321). Premiering in Hollywood, it closes touting the *Genji* as the world's greatest novel, and in one telling scene, entourage after entourage of envoys from China, Korea, and the Ryūkyū Islands, laden with lavish gifts, come to pay homage to the Japanese emperor—who is Genji and

Fujitsubo's secret son—in keeping with the nationalistic glorifying of the tale and of the country that produced it.

Kabuki also went all out, staging productions in 2000 and 2001, this time based on author Setouchi Jakuchō's novelization and starring the sensational Ichikawa Shin'nosuke (now known as Ichikawa Ebizo) as Genji.[26] The Takigi Noh troupe (Okochi n.d.) and Takarazuka musical revue (Caddeau 2006, 14–16 for the 2000 performance) staged performances as well. Moreover, Kōdansha Publishing and Fuji Xerox established a "*Genji* college" website (genji-daigaku.com) that contained Jakuchō's novelization of *Genji* and lectures by local scholars, with whom Jakuchō held *Genji* seminars in nine cities in 2000 (Fuji Xerox 2001).[27] Pioneer Electronics also sponsored a world premiere of a *Genji* symphony in Pasadena, California, in May 1999 that I attended. Inspired by Jakuchō's remediation, Tomita Isao composed the symphony and conducted the Pasadena Symphony.[28] Even more remarkable was *The Tale of Genji Opera*, which was commissioned by the St. Louis Opera Company and premiered in St. Louis in June 2000. Miki Minoru composed the music, and Colin Graham wrote the story and libretto—all in English! It debuted in Japan in English the following year (Komesu 2001).

Not to be left behind, the Japanese government produced a two-thousand-yen bill (depicting Fujitsubo's son Reizei intimating to Genji that he knows his true paternity) from the twelfth-century *Genji* scrolls, and a commemorative Kyoto coin. The bill first appeared in July 2000, but few are in circulation, the result perhaps of eager collectors like myself snapping them up. *The Tale of Genji* coins were minted in 2008, in 500- and 1,000-yen denominations, and remain collectors' items (*Japan Times* 1999 and 2008). Two of my favorite tributes to the tale were a *tanbo āto* rice-paddy-art "portrait" of Murasaki Shikibu and a "Murasaki" robot. Near the city of Uji, where the last ten chapters of the tale are set, a fifty-square-meter rice field was planted with red-, purple-, and lavender-colored rice plants to create Murasaki's profile, which appeared in its full glory in mid-June 2008 (Mainichi Shinbun n.d.). The Murasaki-humanoid robot was invented by Takahashi Tomotaka, founder of Kyoto University's Robo-Garage. Dressed in a traditional kimono and with flowing black hair, RoboMurasaki stands 31 centimeters high, weighs 1,500 grams, is made of aluminum and plastic, and recounts *The Tale of Genji* in Japanese via an embedded MP3 player (Hall 2008; Robo-Garage n.d.). She holds a fan that can be drawn into the sleeve of her kimono. Just a prototype, but how cool it would be to have one's very own Murasaki!

Last but not least were the record number of twenty-four *Genji manga* produced from 2001 through 2015. Riding the wave of the millennium Genji boom, the advent of the era of the woman, and the "girl culture" *kawaii* trends, fifteen of these *manga* are girls comics or ladies comics. All twenty-four diversify the setting, characterization, scope, and point of view of the tale. Inspired by other imaginative "translations," many are complete embellishments, no longer contiguously following the chronological order and substance of the tale, or at least choosing at will what they retell and how they retell it. Several are not even set in Heian times, one casts Genji as a chestnut, and another is not really about Genji. Many, however, enact the new Tanabe/Yamato *Genji* cultural poetics. And all bring much to the crossing, marching to their own drumbeat, translating aspects of the tale in their own way—all while reaching out to differing targeted audiences and expanding the reach of the tale in the new millennium. With their global entry, these *manga* remediations also "translate" aspects of the *Genji* and Japanese culture that cause concern in ways that other transpositions do not. Why that is the case, what is untranslatable, and why will occupy Part II of this study.

Conclusion: Transposing Interpretative Communities

Embedding itself into the cultural, social, and political milieu of each ensuing period since its inception a thousand years ago, *The Tale of Genji* has never been just an aesthetic object. Instead, it has been transposed into culturally and politically relevant cultural capital and soft power, thereby providing authority and identity for interpretative communities as various as courtiers, ladies-in-waiting, warlords, townspeople, and even the Japanese government. Morphing from one medium to another, it has translated—highlighted, added, subtracted, reworked—different aspects of the tale at will. At each juncture the tale has proved its resilience, its narrative possibilities, and its ability to speak to and for a variety of in-groups.

The transpositions and translations are numerous, but two in particular—the pictorial and the textual—are pivotal to the tale's manifestations as multimodal, visual-and-linguistic-hybridized *manga*. From the twelfth century to the present day, the tale has been translated into tableau images, riveting orchestral pieces, stylized dramatic performances, and modern Japanese novels. Some of these remediations religiously follow the tale, others mix times and places, and still others produce visual puzzles that provide little clue as to what they are referencing, but all create for in-groups who must have the proper coding to read/understand the production.

We can also say that specialized in-groups enabled the translation of specific aspects of the tale to address the needs and desires of their communities. The twelfth-century *Genji* scrolls, for example, focalized the Heian court that had the leisure to poignantly showcase emotions for a medieval society that was riven by strife and warfare and looking back with nostalgia at more genteel times. The eighteenth-century scholar Motoori Norinaga deemed this underscoring of emotion to be quintessentially Japanese, and after its defeat in the Second World War the Japanese government highlighted this aspect of the tale to present the country as a gentle, refined, non-bellicose entity. During the 1980s bubble economy, the tale stood as a testament of the Japanese-ness that had bested the west economically, while Japan's millennial celebration of the tale as a globally revered classic was aimed at proving to the world that Japan was a great nation.

Women's concerns were represented as well. First appearing as the thirteenth-through sixteenth-century "white drawings" by women, the focus on women expanded exponentially in the modern era, as women gained traction. Poet Yosano Akiko's novelization of the tale set things in motion, but it was the Tanabe/Yamato *Genji kawaii* cute, cultural poetics that established the tone of the woman/

girl-focused transpositions of the tale that translated the desires, hopes and dreams, and trials and tribulations of being female in Japanese society. Girls comics and ladies comics followed in quick succession. The all-female Takarazuka musical revue staged the female point of view of both sides of romantic relationships, while Boys Love comics, discussed in Chapter 5, staged romances between two males.

Male interests were translated into a heroic (male) quest in *Bumpkin Genji*, and turned into playful visual *mitate* puzzles in woodblock prints. Male lust was lampooned in Santo Kyōden's Genji-wanna-be yellow book rendition, and hyperexaggerated and hypersexualized in Ihara Saikaku's *The Life of an Amorous Man*. These threads found their way into boys comics, young men comics, and a soft porn *Genji manga*, all understood within the confines and imaginaries of Japanese society. After going globally, these creations were initially heralded as exciting, different, and innovative, with perhaps a touch of exoticism. In the twenty-first century, however, things began to change as the social and political climates of the nations importing *manga* and *anime* shifted. *Manga*'s moral, ethical, and artistic codes of reference began to run into opposition, as already discussed in the introduction. Can these codes ever be fully translated from one venue, or one culture, to another? Or can some references never be translated—or only be historically displaced and deemed perverse once they leave their country of origin? It is against this backdrop that the chapters in Part II examine five categories of *Genji manga*, beginning in Chapter 3 with a study of the *shōjo* girls comics, which by their sheer numbers and early entry into the field constitute what might be called the "essence" of the *Genji manga* oeuvre.

Part II

MANGA'S MANY TALES OF MANY GENJIS

Chapter 3

SHŌJO GIRLS *MANGA*: OBJECTS OF WHOSE DESIRE?

"Oh, I will be cut into two!"—a young woman protests, as two dazzling young men tug her back-and-forth like a rag doll on the left page in Figure 3.1.

Her hair in disarray, on the right page the young woman is literally wedged in by a triangular close-up of each of the men. Untenable anguish, one would imagine, but the young woman is none other than Ukifune, the heroine of the last ten chapters of *The Tale of Genji*, and the two men are Genji's grandson Niou (pictured in the top two frames) and Genji's reputed son Kaoru (depicted in the fourth frame). Ardently pursued by the "best catches" of the day, Ukifune has been the envy of female readers ever since the twelfth-century author of *Sarashina nikki* (*The Sarashina Diary*) came upon her predicament in a manuscript of *The Tale of Genji*. For the diarist and for contemporary *shōjo manga* readers alike, embodying an Ukifune so passionately desired by to-die-for male leads is a dream come true.

Encouraged to identify with the female characters in such *manga*, girls-comics readers generally twelve to eighteen years old (but young adult women and others as well) can pick and choose among a rich array of love interests—not just to-die-for handsome studs but pretty boys, bashful tweeners, contemporary high schoolers, and dark antiheroes. Readers are also afforded a range of acceptable roles for girls: they can be head over heels in love, find autonomy in a patriarchal society, rescue men through their undying love, or embody transgender characters. Contesting not just the tale but the category itself, the *Genji shōjo manga* also create parallel universes, utilize modernized settings, and introduce scenarios not found in the eleventh-century tale itself. Thus the "fictional" sphere of the tale and the "historical" setting of the author Murasaki Shikibu butt up against each other in uneasy symbiosis; in another instance, an antihero Genji is redeemed by a young Murasaki who transforms him into her object of desire, as she becomes his—making for a feel-good ending premised on the girls comics' notion of "pure" love. Genji can even be a "she" on the hunt for *bishōnen* beautiful young men lovers. Provocatively entertaining, these transformations call into question issues of gender, positionality, and desire. The *shōjo manga* improvise at will, but surprisingly—given how different they are—they all subscribe to the tenets of girls comics, ensuring that their message stays on target and is age-and-category appropriate. Though often viewed as frivolous entertainment for young girls, girls comics have their finger on the pulse of contemporary Japanese society and have

Figure 3.1 Niou and Kaoru ardently pursue Ukifune. Yamato Waki, *Fleeting Dreams*. 13:74–5. Copyright © 1980–93. Courtesy of Yamato Waki and Kōdansha.

much to teach us about the meanings of love, girlhood, and the role of the feminine in the new millennial culture. Above all, they speak to the mixed messaging that girls receive from society at large: seek love, establish your autonomy, but remain good girls who become "good wives and wise mothers" (*ryōsai kenbo*).

So pervasive is this messaging of romantic love—embodied by dashing heroes bedding gorgeous leading ladies—that the progenitor of *Genji* girls comics, Yamato Waki's *Asaki yume mishi* (*Fleeting Dreams* 1980–93), along with Tanabe Seiko's modern Japanese novel remediation of the tale have become the most prominent face of modern *Tale of Genji* culture. Films, *anime*, Takarazuka all-female musical revues, pictorial renditions, and more are now based not on the eleventh-century tale but on *Fleeting Dreams* and Tanabe's novelization. The tale has been reduced to what I term comic book "poetics" that feature "iconic" *Fleeting Dreams* visuals, Tanabe/Yamato dialogue and narration, and a Heian period infused with modernized emotions and concerns.

When did girls-comics poetics become a "thing" in a world where boys comics ruled for so long? *Shōjo manga* have been around since the 1930s; as we will see below, they became a serious enterprise in the 1970s, under the auspices of a vibrant group of female artists nicknamed the Fabulous Forty-Niners (for Shōwa 24, the year of their birth; 1949 by the western calendar). But it was only in the 1980s and

1990s that *shōjo manga* gained prominence, at the height of the bubble economy, when Japanese society had more economic valence to support nonmainstream movements and segments of the culture. The rise of girls comics was accompanied by the *kawaii* cute phenomenon (founded in girls culture), the *otaku* zealous fandom movement, and the over-the-top *moe* passion for cute (often feminized) fictional characters that formed the basis of the *manga/anime* cultural and media literacy.[1] The 1980s and 1990s also touted the betterment and liberation of women and formed the backdrop for the second *Tale of Genji* boom (see Chapter 2) and the serialization of *Fleeting Dreams*. The bursting of the bubble economy slowed things down for the *Genji manga*, but the 2000–8 millennium celebration of the inception of the tale then set in motion the third *Genji* boom and a frenzy of *shōjo* and other *Genji manga* remediations. More followed in the 2010s.

Utilizing what Bolster and Grusin call repurposing remediation—that is, "borrowing" and "reusing," rather than overt referencing of the content, as texts move from one medium to another (1999, 44–5)—the *manga* iterations of *Genji* retell the tale while embedding it in modern times and places. For *Genji* girls comics, "the borrowed content" is refashioned as a search for the perfect object of desire, but that object of desire must be pure, innocent, and not "tainted" by adult concerns or too much realism. Even the most sexually aggressive and graphic *shōjo manga* are premised on love. Accordingly (with the exception of BL or Boys Love renditions, a subcategory of girls comics discussed in Chapter 4), the consummation scenes are demure, so that nudity is kept at bay, depicted with elegance and refinement, or is at least Hello Kitty cute. Be true to your love, even giving up your life for it; stay the course and seek self-fulfillment; be pleasing to male interests but never fail to be pure and innocent—these are the mixed messages in which girls comics (including *Genji shōjo manga*) paradoxically traffic, reflecting a profound ambivalence in society at large.

The Shōjo Genji Manga *Objects of Desire*

Unsurprisingly, then, the focus of the twelve girls comics in the *Genji manga* category is the pursuit of pure-love objects of desire. But they are not uniform in their endeavors and divide into four groupings, with different takes on love, *kawaii* cute, and the imaginary life of the girl. They also encounter different Genjis—from heartthrob to raging, wild-eyed crazy person. Here we examine four in detail, and reference five others, as they remediate—or repurpose—the content of the tale.[2] It is fitting that the first group, "Making *Shōjo Genji Manga*," examines only selections from Yamato's *Fleeting Dreams*, for it was *Fleeting Dreams* that set the tone and established the narrative and visual conventions for all subsequent girls-comics iterations of the tale. As already mentioned, *Fleeting Dreams* has become the twenty-first-century face of *Genji* culture. Published from 1980 through 1993, *Fleeting Dreams* most prominently refashions the tale into high-drama romance, largely eschewing religious, political, and cultural considerations and making overt the emotional angst of its characters. Pursuit of the object of desire takes precedence in *kawaii* cute visuals and styles—with the emotional cost and angst made plain. The selections in the second group, "Doing *Shōjo Manga*," expand on *Fleeting Dreams*' innocent, wide-eyed *kawaii* cuteness, conveying *shōjō*-ness as giving voice to female characters or as depicting shy teeny boppers playing at romance. Those in the third group, "Challenging *Shōjo Manga*," contest the conventions of *The Tale of Genji* and of girls *manga* by blending the "historical" with the "fictional" and highlighting the supernatural and demonic, by displacing the setting to a modern high school, and even by depicting the dark and evil flip side of the tale. The selections in the fourth and last group, "Counterpointing *Shōjo Manga*," operate as outliers of girls comics, playing with the conventions of the tale, *shōjo manga*, *shōjo Genji manga*, and gender normativity. One artist displaces Genji and the tale with his own gag humor *manga* "hero" and story, while another gender flips Genji into a young woman who occupies positionalities that have primarily been the purview of men and that invite transgender possibilities as well.

Making Shōjo Genji Manga: *Yamato Waki's* Asaki yume mishi *(Fleeting Dreams)*

Although Yamato's *Fleeting Dreams* was not the first girls-comics *Genji manga*, it nonetheless benchmarked the tone and style for *shōjo Genji* comics against other iterations well into the new millennium. Its 1980–93 run was situated during the second *Genji* boom (see Chapter 2), a time of conservative social and political policies on the one hand, but of the bubble economy and new opportunities for women on the other. In fact this *manga* boom opened doors for a cadre of female artists known as the Fabulous Forty-Niners (Forty-Niners for short). There is some debate as to whether or not Yamato Waki, the creator of *Fleeting Dreams*, is a Forty-Niner per se. Nevertheless, in *Fleeting Dreams* and other works, she incorporates their innovative techniques that helped transform *shōjo* comics: manipulating the layout of frames, placing dialogues outside of speech balloons, and providing complex stories and detailed psychological depictions.[3] Yamato's serialization of *Fleeting Dreams* in the then-popular girls-comics magazines *mimi*, *Fortnightly mimi*, and *MimiExcellent* contributed to the development of the target audience of upper-elementary-school through high school girl readers.

On the whole, *shōjo manga* conventions stipulate that narratives concentrate on love and romance. The protagonist must be a teenager searching for her one "true" love or object of desire. Wooing and being wooed are depicted in a dramatic, emotionally engaging fashion that highlights the thoughts and feelings of the protagonists. The eleventh-century *Tale of Genji*, however, has other ideas: the storyline is ostensibly about Genji, his male progeny, and their relationships with women, for author Murasaki Shikibu tells the women's stories very much in tandem with those of Genji and the other men. The lead protagonist in girls comics is usually a young girl, yet the tale has only one such candidate, the young Murasaki (who grows up). This means that *Genji manga* must make women the female leads. The convention of the *shōjo* "getting" her one true love also hits the Heian wall because that period's polygynous courtier society enabled men to have many liaisons. Yamato, however, devises ingenious workarounds, using girls-comics conventions to remediate, that is, repurpose, the tale and vice versa, skillfully positioning idealized heterosexual males seeking female objects of desire and female protagonists who willingly become these objects—but as a means to secure their identity and agency.

In accordance with girls-comics conventions, then, Yamato first and foremost makes romantic love central to her *manga*, creating exquisitely handsome *bishōnen* beautiful men wooing stunning *bishōjo* beautiful women with whom girls-comics readers identify. To be swept off their feet by the most sought-after males of their times is a dream come true for female protagonists and readers alike, and Yamato works her magic by featuring Genji as well as his son Yūgiri and their romantic liaisons in the first ten volumes, and Genji's grandson Niou, reputed son Kaoru, and the three Uji sisters in the last three. In one of the most prominent of these remediations, Genji declares his forbidden love for Fujitsubo, his stepmother and the wife of his father Emperor Kiritsubo. The episode opens with Genji's frenzied ride on horseback to Fujitsubo's quarters, the wind and speed lines portraying his urgency (Yamato 1980–93, 1:188–95). Pushing his way past her astonished lady-in-waiting, Genji bursts into Fujitsubo's room, informing her that he has come at great risk. On the right page of Figure 3.2 Fujitsubo protests, but, like a true

Figure 3.2 Genji and Fujitsubo consummate their relationship. Yamato Waki, *Fleeting Dreams*. 1:194–5. Copyright © 1980–93. Courtesy of Yamato Waki and Kōdansha.

girls-comics hero, Genji brushes aside her feeble attempt at rationality and ardently declares his love. The consummation scene is elegant, sweeping, dramatic: white bodies etched against a black background, swirling hair and limbs denoting the passion of the moment (Figure 3.2).

It is the passion of being so loved and desired for which girls-comics readers yearn and which *Fleeting Dreams* delivers. What girl would not want such love? Woman after woman succumbs to Genji's charms, even though a few, such as Genji's cousin Asagao and Rokujō's daughter Akikonomu in Murasaki Shikibu's tale, never give in. Whatever the personal cost, the women are willing conquests, quick to forgive Genji's slights, indiscretions, and betrayal, and even to give their lives, as in the cases of Yūgao and Murasaki, who are both killed by the spirit of Genji's jealous lover Rokujō. On her deathbed Murasaki sums up her life as worthy because she loved Genji and was loved by him (Yamato 1980–93, 10:186–7).

As sincere and heartfelt as the romantic relationships in the tale appear to be, the *shōjo*-esque ideal of a man pledging his everlasting love to one woman has little chance of survival in *Fleeting Dreams*, for Heian men have many love interests and no woman, not even Murasaki, can have Genji all to herself. Yamato alludes to this by adopting for her title the phrase *asaki yume mishi*, from the Heian "Iroha" poem which utilizes all the syllabaries in the old version of the Japanese language. But she does so with a twist, for most commentators of the poem utilize the phrase in its negative, voiced consonant iteration, namely *asaki yume miji*.[4] In accordance with the orthographic conventions of the period, voiced consonants were not identified as such, so the phrase could be *miji* or *mishi*. *Miji* would render the meaning "we/I/someone will not partake in fleeting dreams," resulting in the title "No Fleeting Dreams." Yet the negation of the verb "to see" belies what happens in Yamato's *manga*: the women fully understand the futility of pursuing true love, but nevertheless deem the thrill of consummating their desire for one such as Genji, however briefly, to be worth it. And chase after objects of desire they do—for four generations and thirteen volumes. In effect the women—but Genji and the other men as well—turn the "Iroha" poem on its head indulging in fleeting dreams of love and making the positive rendering of "Fleeting Dreams" most appropriate.

Fleeting Dreams, then, is about seeking objects of desire. Ostensibly the men target the women, but Genji and other men are female objects of desire as well. And although the women are a far cry from Bunny, the schoolgirl with magical powers in Takeuchi Naoko's *Pretty Guardian Sailor Moon*, or the high schooler Teru in Motomi Kyōsuke's *Dengeki Daisy*,[5] they participate in a conventional heterosexual gender economy but do so in a particularly Heian way. Rather than vying to "get the boy," as happens in many girls comics (Thorn 2001, 48), I would argue that the goal here is "being caught by the boy." Placed in a tree like so many nestling birds, the women best epitomize the essence of the first ten volumes of the *manga* (Yamato 1980–93, 10:191–2), for "being caught by the boy," especially if the captor is a man like Genji, is the goal.

Such "capture" has the appearance of passivity; ironically, however, Heian women are empowered by succumbing to the ideally handsome perfection of manhood. Being desired by and being desirable to such a man provides self-affirmation, for according to the mores of the time, female self-fulfillment can be realized only through men.[6] In modern times, much of a woman's success is determined by educational and professional accomplishments, but Heian women were assessed by the caliber of the men who were their mates and of the progeny they produced. We see this reflected time and again in the *manga*—and in the tale. The most striking example is young Murasaki. Shunned by her father's house as the love child of her father's mistress, Murasaki has few options until Genji raises her to be his ideal wife. The Akashi Lady would also have ended her life on the lonely coast of Akashi had she not met Genji and borne him a daughter who becomes empress. Raised in the hinterlands, Tamakazura (the long-lost daughter of Yūgao, Lady of the "Evening Face" Flowers) and Ukifune (the aforementioned Uji princess) would have suffered similar fates had their lives not crossed paths, respectively, with those of Genji and of his reputed son Kaoru and grandson Niou. In Heian times, the man made the woman.

But such a state of being is not without its perils, as seen at the outset of this chapter. Ardently pursued by two men, Ukifune does not fully escape their grasp, though she has the last word and image in Yamato's *Fleeting Dreams*. Many other *Genji manga* end with an image of Genji or Kaoru, but in Yamato's version Ukifune sits copying out a sutra, declaring that she and Kaoru will meet again, but "as disciples of Buddha" (1980–93, 13:213). She confronts the river (which in Murasaki's tale draws her to its depths) and pays homage to its power, likening her/their lives to small boats helplessly adrift upon it (reflecting the meaning of her name, Floating Boat). But she also declares she is no longer afraid of it, for all rivers flow into "a great ocean, bathed in light" (Yamato 1980–93, 13:214–17). Flowing water, (en)lightenment—the *manga* ends on an uplifting note of love and hope, steeped in Buddhist imagery, hinting that Ukifune has found a modicum of peace.[7]

But does the end signal an affirmation of life without men, as Ukifune's Buddhist garb and imagery would indicate? The *manga* is ambiguous, but if we read the shift in pronouns from "we" (Ukifune and Kaoru) to an implied "I" (Ukifune) as Ukifune relinquishes her gendered identity (Yamato 1980–93, 13:213), then perhaps at least one woman in *Fleeting Dreams* finds a fulfillment that does not require a man and will live on as a nun. Without a doubt Ukifune and the other women in the *manga* also engage in conventional heterosexual gender relations, but as women worthy of the attentions of "perfect" heroes like Genji and Kaoru, they attain self-affirmation and even agency, albeit on Heian terms. In the end, as much as the men are idealized and sought after so earnestly by the women in *Fleeting Dreams*, Yamato's *manga* is about the women and their perspectives. The focus is on the emotions, feelings, and relationships based in love, and the women are the prisms through which we view the narrative. Be it Murasaki, the red-nosed Suetsumuhana, or Ukifune, readers are encouraged to engage with the female characters, interact with them, care about them, share with them. Understanding how they feel, what they think, shadowing them to the depths of their anguish and the heights of joy—all this is fostered and supported. We see how Yamato gives full rein to the interiority and complexity of the women as they come to occupy center stage more and more. Her full-body portraits make vivid their thoughts and feelings through body language, undulating hair, and richly expressive eyes, limbs, and faces. Engaging in tandem with the experiences of the female characters, readers gain validation of their own emotional lives and come to understand their complexity as well.

So successful is Yamato's *Fleeting Dreams* at drawing readers in that it became an instant sensation in the 1980s, enabling the *Genji* to be accessible to a wider audience and even displacing the tale itself as the text of choice for students preparing for college entrance exams. Together with Tanabe Seiko's novelization of the tale in 1978–9, *Fleeting Dreams* makes the *Genji* "user friendly," replacing the complex and unfamiliar cultural codes of the Heian period with the interiority of the characters (Tateishi 2005c, 198). The inner thoughts and feelings of Yamato's characters are focalized—the *shōjo-manga*-esque drawings, featuring large, liquid, wide eyes, make explicit their emotional states of mind. Fragile, buffeted by the winds of fate, and oh, so very humanly vulnerable, the men and women come to life in the *manga*'s swooning, swooping lines of swirling hair, irregular frame sizes, diagonal lines, and dark and light shading. All speak to the agony and ecstasy of their lives in this "mass-processed" Heian world, crying out for engagement and an unwavering fan following. Tateishi argues that, as a result, the Tanabe and Yamato remediations of *The Tale of Genji* stand as an aestheticized, sanitized version of the Heian period (Tateishi 2005c, 198).

In fact, just as I pointed out in Chapter 2 the ways in which the Tosa School miniatures created an iconography for the premodern pictorial representations of the *Genji*, so scholar Hijikata Yōichi writes that the Yamato and Tanabe "mass-produced, -consumed, and -processed" *Genji* have come to form the basis of modern remediations of the tale. Storylines and motifs (such as a young noble's search for his mother, forbidden love ending in death, and men and women destined never to be with their beloveds) as well as certain scenes, characterizations, and even language come from *Fleeting Dreams* and Tanabe's texts.[8] Most modern *Genji* remediations are no longer based on the eleventh-century tale but on *Fleeting Dreams* and Tanabe, as they have become the face of films, *anime*, Takarazuka all-female musical revues, and more. The tale has been reduced to a love story with blindingly handsome heroes bedding equally stunning women, all professing their love in extravagantly expressive ways. Comic book "poetics" feature stereotyped characterizations, recycling "iconic" *Genji* imagery and lines from *Fleeting Dreams* and Tanabe Seiko. Much diminished are the complexities and the ambiguities of the story—politically, philosophically, religiously, even interpersonally. Gone, too, are the specificities of the Heian period. Is this a bad thing? The purists would say yes, but if we look to the past, this is no different than the cultural work accomplished by other repurposed remediations. *Fleeting Dreams* is just one of the new ways that the venerable *Tale of Genji* has been transposed into yet another form—that is, embedded in the cultural mores of the time so that it better speaks to and with and of new audiences, in ways that make sense to them and that they can claim as their own. *Fleeting Dreams* does indeed set the stage for *shōjo Genji manga*, but it also invites those that follow to enhance, challenge, and counterpoint its vision of the category as well as of the tale.

Doing Shōjo Manga: *Establishing* Shōjo *Cute*

In this group of remediations, three artists feature the *Fleeting Dreams shōjo manga* template of beautiful women being swept off their feet by their object of desire, and do so following their own muses. Centering this section, Toba Shōko mirrors Yamato's pretty-boy tropes for Genji but gives voice to the women in her 1991 remediation, while the two other artists bring the *shōjo* cute into the new millennium: Sasaki Misuzu bases her 2001 *Genji* on a film by the same name, made to commemorate the thousandth anniversary of the tale; and Miō Serina, in her 2006–9 remediation, shifts the Hello Kitty cute into another register, targeting a younger audience with age-appropriate, innocent, largely nonsexual trysts.[9]

Our first artist, Toba Shōko,[10] published her *Genji monogatari* (*The Tale of Genji*) as part of the *NHK manga de yomu koten* (*NHK Reading the Classics through Manga*) series, which introduces classical literary works in *manga* format.[11] Toba's *manga* is only loosely based on the state-sponsored station television version, and the adaptation is hers.[12] Published under the auspices of NHK, it does have an educational component, but Toba's drawing style, narrative technique, and content all signal girls comics.[13] Her depiction of Genji and other male protagonists, for example, portrays the feminized pretty-boy look in keeping with that of the male heroes in the *shōjo manga* classics *Sailor Moon* and *Fruits Baskets*—and, of course, *Fleeting Dreams*. Toba's women, too, are drawn as wide-eyed innocents in a dreamy, featherlight style. Flower motifs, shiny, dewy, vulnerable looks, and undulating robes and hair prevail, resulting in protagonists possessing a cuteness prized in modern Japanese popular culture. Her drawings exhibit a Hello Kitty cuteness with a sexually alluring and innocent eroticism about them—but with no nudity in sight. Genji does not escape the *shōjo* touch either: in the last panel on the left page in Figure 3.3, he is drawn with very pretty-boy looks and exudes a kind of matching pretty-boy arrogance, standing his ground when he is caught red-handed in the rooms of Oborozukiyo, the sister of Empress Kokiden, his rival at court.

Toba's women, however, are sensitively and less melodramatically portrayed, their love stories told from their perspectives, with a focus on the cost to the other women. Rather than retelling the tale as a whole, Toba organizes her 176-page *manga* around pivotal moments in the lives of the heroines. Each episode operates as a self-contained vignette. Most pointedly, Toba gives voice to the women protagonists. Unlike in the tale itself, the accosting and subsequent demise of Yūgao (Lady of the "Evening Face" Flowers) by Rokujō's living spirit is narrated from Yūgao's perspective. A similar kind of "giving voice" and ascribing of agency occurs for the other women as well. Oborozukiyo, Empress Kokiden's sister, comes across as assertive and daring—a female version of Genji who "hooks up" with him, the illicit thrill and danger enhancing her sexual pleasure. In the episode on Lady Rokujō, her spirit kills Yūgao and Genji's wife Aoi, but, unlike

Figure 3.3 On a stormy night Genji is caught in Oborozukiyo's rooms by her father. Toba Shōko, *NHK Reading the Classics through Manga: The Tale of Genji*, 160–1. Copyright © 2006. Courtesy of Toba Shōko and Homesha.

in many *manga*, Rokujō is not viewed as a vengeful spirit. Rather, Toba portrays her as a beautiful woman so tormented by her love for Genji that she is unaware of her actions until after the fact. Yet in good *shōjo* fashion, it is all about love— Rokujō's pursuit of her object of desire causes the attacks, but, as we saw with Murasaki in *Fleeting Dreams*, a love for one so beautiful and kind as Genji makes life worthwhile. In Toba's hands, such love even has the power to cleanse the most horrific of Rokujō's deeds.

The stories are indeed about the women, but the one who comes out smelling like roses is Genji. Enacting the traditional girls-comics trope, the women declare their love for the wonderfully handsome and kind heartthrob Genji. Blame for the deaths caused by Rokujō's living spirit falls not at his feet but at those of Rokujō and the women who are killed. Even the sexual initiation into wifehood of the young Murasaki is carefully explained away. Toba devotes six pages to Murasaki's shocked reaction (Toba 2006, 102–7), but everything is carefully choreographed so that Murasaki forgives Genji, pledging to become a good wife (2006, 110)!—a bit contrived and too convenient a resolution, but one that carefully removes the specter of rape or any indiscretion on Genji's part. Toba's adaptation reveals its roots in *shōjo manga*, for as in Yamato's *Fleeting Dreams*, the female characters seek self-fulfillment through men. But the lack of nudity of any kind, the non-illustration of essential *shōjo* high points of romantic/sexual consummation, and the avoidance of the explicitly erotic subtly speak to the educational nature of Toba's remediation and to the guiding hand of NHK Television. Under these state-sponsored auspices the *Genji* is a classic to be presented for instruction on TV: even in *manga* form, where the artist supposedly had more freedom, it still bears the NHK "Good Housekeeping" seal of approval.

The decade in which Toba published her *Genji* found a Japanese populace beaten down by eleven years of slow growth, high unemployment, a rapidly aging populace, and other challenges both at home and abroad.[14] On the bright side, the global exportation of Japanese popular culture, fashion, pop music, TV dramas, and venues such as sushi restaurants, karaoke bars, and Hello Kitty stores was expanding (MacWilliams 2008, 13; Yano 2009, 42; see Yano 2013). Things Japanese, including *manga* and *anime*, became hot international commodities, and in that wake Japan mounted an extravagant millennial celebration of its national treasure, *The Tale of Genji*, extending from 2000 through 2008. Activities, events, and material cultural objects commemorating the tale exploded on the scene, albeit largely in Japan.

In this milieu Sasaki Misuzu published her 2001 *A Love of a Thousand Years*, which remediates the film *A Love of a Thousand Years: The Tale of the Shining Genji* into *manga* form. The film debuted in Hollywood on December 15, 2001 (Tateishi 2008, 320, 324). Sasaki was commissioned to release her *manga* version on the same day and completed it by that date, taking just twenty-five days to finish it.[15] Much condensed, Sasaki's *manga* retains the film's innovative "story within a story," utilizing the author Murasaki Shikibu's "historical" times as a narrative frame within which the fictional story of the tale is told. Within this "historical" frame, Shikibu relates *The Tale of Genji* to Shōshi, her mistress and the daughter of Regent Fujiwara no Michinaga. But, more directly than in the film version, Sasaki imagines Shikibu giving mixed messages to Shōshi, educating her to accept her role as an imperial consort but also covertly presenting a life of freedom and self-expression, independent of men, through Shikibu's own example. Sasaki also avoids the "creativity" and political heavy-handedness of the film, which has a strident nationalistic and even imperialistic overlay and offers a saccharine, Takarazuka-esque enactment of the story.[16]

Instead, Sasaki centers on Consort Shōshi's coming to appreciate Genji's value and purpose as an object of desire. Genji's actions then function as the means through which Shōshi finds love/herself and accepts her role as an imperial consort as her own choice and not her father's decision. At the same time, Shikibu herself is depicted as mistress of her own fate. She rejects Michinaga's sexual overtures and leaves the capital for Echizen—a site representing not only romance and domestic tranquility but also danger and new possibilities. Early on in Sasaki's *manga*, Shikibu's husband is brutally killed there, leaving Shikibu a widow but also enabling her to begin "a woman's tale," *The Tale of Genji*, which is what brings her to court. At the end of the *manga*, Echizen affords her an escape from Michinaga, and Nobutaka's violent death can be construed as punishment for planning to exploit his daughter as a marriage pawn. Sasaki allows similar questions to linger about Michinaga and his brother Michitaka, as they use their respective daughters to gain access to the throne. Equally provocative are the objections and concerns that Shōshi raises about Genji's womanizing, his treatment of his lovers, and the plight of women who live in a society where men have many love interests—all of which remain unanswered at the end of Sasaki's *manga*.

The brevity of the *manga* may well account for why Sasaki sidesteps a rigorous critique of patriarchy or of men's utilization of women. Rather, it remains a story of one young girl/woman, Shōshi, who comes to know the power of being loved and thus accepts her role as a marriage pawn and bearer of imperial children. Yet it also speaks of another woman, Murasaki Shikibu, who finds her freedom not through love, as *shōjo manga* require, but through the writing of a story that challenges the deity of the imperial family and who cultivates space in Echizen, away from the patriarchy of men. Which story is the principal tale? Perhaps both, perhaps neither—for the two exist in tandem one to the other.

Our next artist, Miō Serina,[17] produced her *The Tale of Genji manga*, the last title in this grouping, in a further remediation of *shōjo* cute. She takes the unusual step of retaining the twelve- to fourteen-year-old ages of the protagonists in the tale and devising a "love" story that is appropriate for the comparably aged contemporary elementary- and early junior-high students.[18] Colloquial and informal discourse in modern settings take center stage, and unkind or overly sexualized behavior is banished. What results is a story about children who act more like friends than rivals in love and who are the best versions of themselves, because the star Genji (and his father the emperor) are kind, considerate, and very earnest in making themselves into the girls' objects of (innocent) love.

Per the conventions of girls comics, in Miō's remediation "love" is still the name of the game, but its "grown-up" iteration is replaced by innocent, exceedingly adorable Hello Kitty cute romances. Emperors are unbelievably handsome but will not impose themselves on their consorts. Rather, they lie down next to their "ladies" and simply chat, patiently awaiting consent from their consorts (Miō 2007–9, 1:10–12). When impulsive sexuality occasionally erupts, it is extinguished. Young lovers will endure being slapped in the face moments before engaging in "H" (*etchi suru*, *manga* jargon for having sex) and deliver an impassioned plea, confessing their desire to fill their lover's body and soul (Miō 2007–9, 2:116–19)—a bit direct for its young audiences, but very much playing to readerly desire. All the vignettes relate sweet and innocent stories of boy meets girl: the boy is an absolutely perfect gentleman, kind, sensitive, touchingly unsure of himself. Similarly, the girl has adorable luminous eyes and a pure and unadulterated belief in the love of her young suitor—be it Genji's father, Genji, his sons, or his grandson. In all cases the stories center on the romantic, largely nonsexualized love relationships between boy and girl, refashioned for preteen consumption.

What are we to do with a *Genji* that reads like a teenybopper romance, immersed in contemporary and young adult slang and told in the emotional register of junior-high girls?[19] Very much a part of mass-processed *Genji* culture, Miō's *manga* is in keeping with the *shōjo*-esque quality of *Fleeting Dreams*, but shifts it even more toward the cute and to younger audiences. Without a doubt Miō restructured the tale to be age appropriate, but her work—along with Toba's and Sasaki's—definitely enacts *shōjo* cute in standard traditional girls-comics fashion, most assuredly expanding upon Yamato's 1970s style. Miō's contribution is that she pushes it one step backward, if you will, and one rung lower in terms of audience demographic, for she has the *Genji* meet the very youngest Hello Kitty cute. In the process she makes the tale accessible to yet another stratum of *Genji* readers, and although her *manga* may not be "true" to the tale or to the Heian period, it is "true" to its audience and does a good job of stimulating interest in the tale.

Challenging Shōjo Manga: *Hybridized Parallel* Genji *Universes*

Shōjo cute, adult, and not-so-adult romances stand at the center for girls *Genji* comics, and Miyagi Tōko's (2011) *Genji monogatari: sen'nen no nazo* (*The Tale of the Genji: The One-Thousand-Year-Old Riddle*) and Shimaki Ako's (2002–4) *Gekka no kimi* (*The Prince in the Moonlight*) follow suit, but with a twist. Miyagi creates a narrative where the "historical" world in which author Murasaki Shikibu interacts with Fujiwara no Michinaga, the father of the consort Shōshi whom she serves, affects the fictional world of the tale. In turn, Shimaki's *Prince in the Moonlight* displaces the Heian world by reincarnating Genji and Murasaki as contemporary high schoolers. The last *manga* in this grouping, Sakurada Hina's (2015–16) *Kuro genji monogatari: hana to miruramu* (*The Black Tale of Genji: So Like a Flower*) challenges the central tenet of girls comics as premised on love, featuring an evil Genji who is brutal, cruel, abrasive, and self-centered. Sakurada's depiction of her antihero as a "black Genji" (which can be read as a blackface performance that impersonates black people) unfortunately results in perpetuating stereotypes of people of African and black descent as violent or evil—which is not the message of her *manga*. Rather it speaks to the ways in which a pure girls-comics heroine can "save" even the most despicable of souls. Nonetheless, we must take to heart Baye McNeil's plea that "regardless of intent, ... Blackface can and does harm, not only to foreigners of African descent living in Japan but also to Japanese of mixed heritage" (McNeil 2018)[20] and read the *manga* with his injunction in mind.

Looking at the first work in this grouping, we see that Miyagi Tōko's *The Tale of Genji*, subtitled *The One-Thousand-Year-Old Riddle* (or *Enigma*), creates a *Genji* with two parallel worlds that ultimately collide. One is the "fictional" world in which a handsome Genji courts stunningly beautiful women, their tragic stories of unrequited love solicitously related. To the "fictional" is added the "historical" world where Murasaki Shikibu and Fujiwara no Michinaga interact. This world does not function just as a narrative frame but operates in tandem with the fictional world—making the two worlds serve as alternate but parallel universes that influence each other. More accurately, Miyagi frames the occurrences in the fictional realm as signaling dangerous consequences for the "historical" Shikibu/Michinaga world.

Michinaga is introduced early on, conspicuous for his arrogance and self-assurance in capturing Shikibu's heart (Miyagi 2011, 1:52–60), but neither the existence nor the import of the two worlds is apparent at the outset. Miyagi utilizes the historical Yin-Yang *onmyōji* (or *on'yōji*) practitioner Abe no Seimei[21] to tie them together, positioning him to move seamlessly from one world to the other. Paying homage to the 2000 *onmyōji* boom,[22] she also deploys Seimei to protect Michinaga from evil spirits (2011, 1:63–72) and, more importantly, to solve the thousand-year-old enigma alluded to in the title. Seimei begins to suspect that the writing of the *Genji* is invoking the evil spirits that appear around Michinaga's person—and that Shikibu's unrequited love for Michinaga is at the root of this paranormal activity (Miyagi 2011, 1:104–8). The conflation of the "historical" Shikibu and the "fictional" Rokujō, whose living spirit kills Genji's lovers, becomes more and more pronounced.

A darkness hangs over Miyagi's *manga*, as the harsh realities of the unrequited love inhabiting both worlds collide, yet despite the deaths, there is redemption. The story begins with Seimei's comprehension of the depths of Shikibu's sufferings in the historical realm and his allowing Aoi's death in the fictional world, both of which are mirrored in Genji's forgiving Rokujō and her exiting Genji's life to avert further demonic metamorphoses (Miyagi 2011, 2:98–101). Just as Rokujō leaves the capital and Genji to stop the cycle of her harming other women, so Shikibu resolves to do the same (Miyagi 2011, 2:153–5)—well aware that this is the only way she can keep her demons in check and locked within the pages of tale. Seimei lauds Michinaga's good fortune as the parallel universes come to an end—in Miyagi's version of *The Tale of Genji* at least.

Less a story about the romance between Genji and his ladies than a story of the supernatural, Miyagi's *Genji* expands upon the Shikibu/Michinaga relationship and exploits the sexual tension between the two to great advantage, utilizing the Rokujō/Genji relationship as a foil. Setting up two worlds, the fictional and the "historical," as parallel, alternate universes that mirror each other, Miyagi foregrounds two aspects of Genji's personality. He is both the kind, ideal lover who takes care of his women and the irascible womanizer whose actions lead to Rokujō's obsession—with the latter serving as a foil to Michinaga's seduction of Shikibu and her unrequited love for him. First serialized in the *shōjo* magazine *Asuka* from January through October 2011, *The Tale of Genji: The-One-Thousand-Year-Old Riddle* appeared in book form in March and November of the same year. An unusual remediation of the tale and girls comics, but also of the 2001 film and Sasaki's *manga* discussed in the preceding section, its amplification of the supernatural and the demonic in ways not found in other *Genji manga* makes it a fascinating addition to the *Genji manga* oeuvre.

Miyagi's parallel worlds interweave the "fictional" eleventh-century tale with the "historical" time frame of author Murasaki Shikibu, whereas our next work, Shimaki Ako's *The Prince in the Moonlight*, produced ten years earlier, takes the novel approach of transposing the *Genji* to a modern high school setting. Shimaki envisions Genji and Murasaki as reborn one thousand years later as high school students Kunishige Hazuki and Kikuchi Shū, respectively. Both attend a typical Japanese high school, and the seven-volume series revolves around their romantic (mis)adventures as they attempt to develop a relationship in the midst of slowly becoming aware of their lives as reincarnations of Genji and Murasaki. Replete with shy declarations of love, obstacles that impede their relationship, and a cast of supporting actors, *The Prince in the Moonlight* is a typical *shōjo manga*. It features a *bishōnen* tragic hero and his adorably cute and loyal heroine. Shimaki fully utilizes a series of *shōjo*-esque tropes—instant attraction between the central protagonists, the hero's gallant saving and protecting of the heroine, and the heroine's overcoming numerous obstacles that test her love and ultimately enable her to get her guy.[23]

Traditional girls-comics readers, however, find *The Prince Under the Moonlight* unwieldy and unconvincing, for it requires knowledge of the *Genji* to fill in the backstory of Genji and Murasaki, and by extension of Hazuki and Shū, yet it is precisely this collaborative reading that captures the imaginations of readers in the know. Half the fun lies in discovering what aspects of Genji and Murasaki have been incorporated into Hazuki and Shū, and in identifying the modern-day counterparts of other figures or events from the *Genji*. One such example has Hazuki's stepmother announcing that she is Fujitsubo and making advances to Hazuki, rather than vice versa (Shimaki 2002-4, 5:169-70). Genji's self-imposed Suma exile and time in Akashi are transposed into Hazuki's transferring to another high school and being subjected to an arranged marriage (Shimaki 2002-4, 7:29, 53-4). To this inventive narrative Shimaki adds Hiroshi, Hazuki's sidekick/foil, who supports and enables the budding love between Hazuki and Shū not only as a friend but as a diarist of the romance, raising intriguing connections to the *Genji sōshiji* narrator within the tale and even to the author Murasaki Shikibu herself.

Other questions are left unexamined, such as the possibility of the reincarnation of characters in other bodies and the evocation of parallel worlds occupying the same temporal and physical space, though Shimaki employs innovative strategies in depicting Genji and Hazuki residing in the same body at the same time. In the end, however, some might say that the concept of reincarnation and the displacement of the *Genji* story into a high school setting are not convincingly executed. Nevertheless, *The Prince in the Moonlight* remediation is a further example of "repurposing." Shimaki does not just borrow the content of the *Genji*, but self-consciously calls attention to its reenactment in texts within texts. Should we have missed this interplay, Shimaki posits a classical literature teacher invoking the eleventh-century tale, stages it as a play, and reworks it in Hiroshi's diary. By constantly calling attention to the tale from which she "repurposes" her story, Shimaki keeps *The Prince in the Moonlight* in constant dialogue with the eleventh century, albeit on its own terms and in conflation with and in the *shōjo manga*.

Shockingly un-Heian, our last title in this grouping, Sakurada Hina's *The Black Tale of Genji: So Like a Flower*, makes Genji evil, manipulative, and very unheroike. He is beautiful, intelligent, and attractive to women but has a nasty streak about him. As a young boy he shoots an arrow at his half-brother Crown Prince Suzaku, causing Suzaku to fall into a dead faint (Sakurada 2015-16, 1:16-17). Infuriated, Suzaku's mother Empress Kokiden sends an assassin to kill Genji, but a crazed Genji dispatches the killer instead. The two pages depicting the attack are horrific in their blood and gore—more like a boys comics than a girls comics (Figure 3.4).

For most of Sakurada's *manga*, Genji is depicted wild-eyed, his face contorted in a snarl or a scream. His encounters with women are rough and overbearing,

Figure 3.4 Genji is attacked by an assassin sent to kill him, but he dispatches the assassin instead. Sakurada Hina, *The Black Tale of Genji: So Like a Flower*, I: 67–8. Copyright © 2015–16. Courtesy of Sakurada Hina and Shōgakukan.

with little regard for their well-being—a far cry from the genteel, romantic girls-comics ideal lover. In her encounter with Genji, Utsusemi, the young provincial governor's wife, is so aggrieved that she pledges that Genji can take her body but not her soul (Sakurada 2015–16, 2:12–13). Even Genji's profession of love for Fujitsubo is delivered through clenched teeth, in a violent and crazed manner (Sakurada 2015–16, 2:14). The usually gentle Suetsumuhana is transformed into a maker of poisons whose services Genji acquires by promising her the power to crush those who look down on her (Sakurada 2015–16, 2:97–101).

Lecherous, exceedingly arrogant, and manipulative, Genji takes whatever he wants from whomever he wants—making readers wonder what kind of world they have stumbled into. There is very little to like about Genji. I was hard-pressed to finish reading this *manga*, but a strange thing happened about halfway through Volume 2. In a two-page spread, Sakurada introduces an adorably cute girl—wide-eyed (but not crazed), sweet, and innocent, in sharp contrast to the sinister-looking Genji (2015–16, 2:106–7). She happily chats with him when she first meets him, and during a second encounter she weeps and asks Genji if to love someone is a sin (*tsumi*)—which, ironically, stabs Genji in the heart (Sakurada 2015–16, 2:121). Therein begins Genji's transformation. He actually shies away from getting involved with the young girl, but, after the death of her grandmother, he rushes to bring her home—Sakurada noting that this is the first time Genji has done anything for someone else (2015–16, 2:163).

The adorable girl is indeed the young Murasaki, and the cover of Volume 3 signals a much-changed Genji who tenderly looks on at the bubbly, pretty little girl. The nasty, self-centered antihero Genji is transformed into the handsome true love of girls comics, his commitment to Murasaki growing daily. Murasaki, too, proves herself worthy of his love, orchestrating a meeting with Fujitsubo to warn her off Genji. Fujitsubo is taken aback but realizes she has met her match (Sakurada 2015–16, 3:114–21). Unlike in the tale, here the proof that Murasaki has captured Genji's sole affections is made clear when Fujitsubo must resort to blackmailing Genji into siring her son. Genji only accedes to Fujitsubo's demands to protect Murasaki, for Fujitsubo threatens to tell the world of their earlier indiscretion and of Genji's killing the assassin. After reluctantly agreeing to Fujitsubo's request, Genji apologizes to Murasaki (Sakurada 2015–16, 3:80–7).

So goes Sakurada's remaking of the tale: Murasaki grows up and yearns to have their relationship consummated, but Genji is disinclined—not because he does not want to, but because he loves her so much that he fears his passion will overcome him and he will hurt her. Once again, this is a far cry from the cruel, self-centered Genji of the past, for Genji consummates their relationship only after receiving Murasaki's reassurance that this is what she wants. Sakurada's *manga* ends here—heartwarming in girls-comics fashion, and we can almost hear all the sighs of satisfaction and envy from readers. Without a doubt Sakurada's *Genji* successfully challenges the girls-comics category through its very dark and negative portrayal of Genji, which keeps readers guessing and wondering what is going on. But in a tour de force move, Sakurada flips and re-remediates it into a surefire girls comics, replete with a handsome, ideal lover who is true to only one girl/woman—helping to make sense of its subtitle, *So Like a Flower*, be it a reference to the cruel and vindictive Genji-turned-redeemed-lover or to the *manga* itself. Much is refashioned, but Sakurada does a fine job in resurrecting Genji—and her readers—into believing in true love and its power to transform the darkest of souls.

Counterpointing Shōjo Manga *and* The Tale of Genji

In the previous section the remediations challenge the more traditionally conceived *shōjo Genji manga* by melding parallel worlds and even entertaining a dark underbelly version of the tale, whereas the two titles in this section spin yarns that vastly counterpoint the tale and girls comics. Maya Mineo's (2004–8) *Patalliro genji monogatari!* (*Patalliro Tale of Genji!*) in fact incorporates yin-yang masters to such an extent that the *Genji* operates like an excuse for the telling of their story. And it is not even the master Abe Seimei from Miyagi's *manga* who is at the center but Patalliro, the bumbling hero of Maya's *Patalliro* series, who eclipses even Genji. For these reasons, it is more illuminating to examine the second *manga* in this grouping, *The Comics Anthology of the Tale of Genji: Ms. Shining Genji's Hottie Diary*, edited by

Asuka Henshūbu and published in 2011, which gender bends Genji into a fetching young woman, turning the romances from the tale on their heads.

As mentioned earlier, Maya Mineo's five-volume *Patalliro Tale of Genji!* does little to repurpose the tale or *shōjo Genji manga*. Although it opens with the requisite romance between Genji's mother and the emperor, her harassment by her rivals at court, and the birth of the peerless Genji, all bets are off in what follows. Most tellingly, Maya bases his *Genji* on his long-running series *Patalliro!*, presently in its 104th volume and counting. First published in 1979, it stars a ten-year-old king, Patalliro, from the South Seas island of Malynera. Precocious, mischievous, and often thoughtlessly cruel, the boy-king encounters terrorists, space aliens, and the like, requiring the services of a bodyguard named Bancoran and troops called Tamanegi or Onion. For the *Genji* remediation, Maya transposes Patalliro into a yin-yang master who is ostensibly there to help Genji but who interjects himself into the story at Genji's expense—so much so that *Patalliro Genji!* is really about Patalliro engaging in preposterous Heian-style new adventures. As the series progresses, the stories have less and less to do with the *Genji*—in many instances the protagonists from the tale simply act as window dressing for Patalliro's escapades.

In this *manga*, the incidents, the manner in which they are narrated, and the use of slapstick, scatological humor are exaggerated to the extreme. The banana *oden* concocted by Patalliro (and used as the means through which Genji is found in Oborozukiyo's rooms), for example, look suspiciously like phalluses (Maya 2004–8, 5:29), playing well to the *Patalliro!* reader base. For the uninitiated, the series takes time to get used to—the pages are packed with images, text, and incongruous drawings, with a profusion of black everywhere. In short, *Patalliro Genji!* is not everyone's cup of tea and not a traditional girls comics. For some, it may be too much of a spoof, with a meandering plot, not very likable central characters, and requiring too much knowledge of Maya's other *manga*. Basically, the work is a parody of Maya's *Patalliro!*, transposing central characters from that work and placing them in a new setting. It might be more accurate to call it a spin-off—in the manner of *dōjinshi* fanzine productions of mainstream *manga*, in which the characters are used in original plot lines—that services Maya's trusted fan base rather than *Genji* readers.

In effect, *Patalliro Genji!* remediates a wide range of sources, referencing Maya's own *manga* and their characters, on the one hand, and *The Tale of Genji*, on the other, but also counterpointing *shōjo manga*. Maya turns girls-comics heterosexual love relationships on their heads, humorously casting Genji as the womanizer extraordinaire with the ultimate woman-killer gaze. Maya also toys with the *shōnen-ai* male–male attraction, providing titillating possibilities but not fully delivering on them. Early on, a man tries to kiss Genji (Maya 2004–8, 1:138–9), but nothing comes of it, and neither does anything come of the transposition of the male assassin Maraich from *Patalliro!* into the female young Murasaki. Maya's remediation of girls comics is counterpointed to such an extent, in both content and look, that many question its categorization as *shōjo*—but *shōjo* it is, because it was originally published in a girls-comics magazine. Remediating *The Tale of Genji*, *Patalliro!* and the *onmyōji* yin-yang boom in girls comics, Maya weaves a captivating tale for those willing to go along for the ride—helping him stand out in the crowded field of *Genji manga* in the new millennium.

Although Maya Mineo counterpoints *The Tale of Genji* so that it is barely recognizable, the second *manga* in this grouping stays the course, albeit with a twist. As indicated by its title, *The Comics Anthology of the Tale of Genji: Ms. Shining Genji's Hottie Diary* flips the gender dynamics of the tale, transposing Genji into a wide-eyed young woman and his ladies into androgynously gorgeous men. Different artists in the anthology recount Ms. Genji's relationships—with love-interest-to-be Murasaki, stepparent Fujitsubo, fragile Yūgao, and jealous lover Rokujō, but also with others—thus subverting heteronormative gender norms at the same time that they reinscribe them. Each lady-turned-beautiful-man represents a particular male type. Genji's principal spouse Aoi, for example, is deemed reserved, with glasses and a cross look on his face—"A typical testy personality," too proud to admit that he has feelings for Ms. Genji (Ryūka 2011, 17)—which resonates well with Lady Aoi in the eleventh-century tale, albeit gender-flipped and delineated in contemporary terms. Other depictions utilize trendy descriptors in vogue at the time: Yūgao is stylized as an unassertive, unaggressive, soothing "herbivore male" (Yata 2011, 27), while Akashi becomes a sexy "carnivore" male who revels in sexually proactive wild animal traits to get his woman (Kitazawa 2011, 67)—very unlike the Akashi Lady in the tale. Each sketch also includes advice on how "to hook up" with said guy. The "lowdown" on Aoi suggests that the best way to approach him is to take everything he says as meaning the opposite, for he would never admit that he craves affection (Asuka Henshūbu 2011, 116).

Wrapping one's mind around the fact that the cute girl and not the sexy young man is Genji takes some doing. Genji's "male" traits, too, must be recast as Ms. Genji's female-appropriate characteristics. Genji's propensity to bed a multitude of women, his irresistible attractiveness to women, his "manly" assertiveness in making the first move, as well as his secret love for his stepmother—all these need to be gender-flipped and remediated to fit the profile of a young woman/girl. The same is true of the ladies-turned-men, resulting in some comical situations. Utsusemi (the provincial governor's spouse) is transformed into a sexually reticent guy running away from his wife for fear of having to consummate their marriage on their wedding night (Nanda 2011, 8). Oborozukiyo, the daring, sexually available sister of Genji's archrival in the tale, is transposed into a needy, high-maintenance male, and Genji into his solicitous lover/caretaker (Kuriyama 2011, 58–62)—the antithesis of Shikibu's daring pair, who revel in the excitement of a precarious and dangerous love affair under the nose of Oborozukiyo's sister.

Ironically, despite the gender-bending of the anthology's protagonists, the maintenance of the gender roles remains in place. Ms. Genji's encounter with Fujitsubo enacts the heteronormativity dynamics, radically altering the events of the tale to do so. Visually handsome, with long flowing locks, Fujitsubo possesses the most sexually alluring, androgynous male features in the anthology, identifying him as the ideal object of desire. As happens in the tale, Ms. Genji ardently pursues Fujitsubo, pleading her case (Takashima 2011, 110–15). And per the tale, Fujitsubo's reticence and angst are evident, warding off Ms. Genji's

Figure 3.5 As the male figure, Fujitsubo initiates the lovemaking with Genji, who is gender-flipped into a young girl. Takashima Kazusa, "Fujitsubo," in Asuka Henshūbu ed. *The Comics Anthology of the Tale of Genji: Ms. Shining Genji's Hottie Diary*, 112–13. Copyright © 2011. Courtesy of Takashima Kazusa and Kadokawa Shoten.

advances with averted face, clenched fists, and expressions of pain and anguish. But unlike in the tale, because Fujitsubo is now the male figure, it is he who must make the first move, so it is he who takes Ms. Genji's face into his hands, ardently kisses her, and initiates the lovemaking in true heteronormative romantic fashion, as seen in Figure 3.5. The conventions of a *shōjo manga* deem it so.

So, does that make *Ms. Genji's Hottie Diary* just another heterosexual remediation of *The Tale of Genji*, albeit gender-flipped? Many *shōjo*-comics readers might conclude so, but for those who read Ms. Genji and her male *bishōnen* young men in conjunction with the gender configuration of their eleventh-century non-gender-flipped counterparts, the *manga* entails gender-bending at the very least, and perhaps even transgendering. Transforming Genji into an adorable girl also stretches what *shōjo* readers accept as "normative" behavior for female protagonists. As a young woman with Genji-like appeal, Ms. Genji becomes a female protagonist liberated to enact what has largely been confined to the purview of men—having many lovers and aggressively seeking out such liaisons. Taken at face value, Ms. Genji performs within normal binary gender paradigms, but her gender positionality is radicalized if we layer the identities of Genji and his ladies from the eleventh-century tale onto those of Ms. Genji and her male lovers. Perhaps considering Ms. Genji's performance as a plethora of gender positions might be too much of a stretch, but the anthology does invite a more complex transgendered reading of the (fe)male protagonists. *The Comics Anthology of the Tale of Genji: Ms. Shining Genji's Hottie Diary* remains an intriguing remediation of both Murasaki Shikibu's *The Tale of Genji* and the category of *shōjo manga*. It might even be a spoof on Boys Love/BL *manga*, another gender-reversing remediation of *The Tale of Genji*, to be discussed in Chapter 4.

Conclusion: Shōjo *Objects of Whose Desire?*

The Tale of Genji shōjo manga in this chapter run the full gamut of girls comics, enacting the tale and the category in their own images. It all begins with Yamato Waki's *Fleeting Dreams*, as it sets the tone and establishes the narrative and visual conventions for subsequent girls comics and contemporary media iterations of the tale. The girls comics that follow embody Yamato's beautiful women being swept off their feet by their objects of desire, but they do so by giving voice to women protagonists or by turning love trysts into teenybopper hide-and-seek playdates. Others contest not just the tale but what constitutes girls comics by creating parallel *Genji* universes, modernizing settings, and introducing scenarios not found in the tale. "Fictional" spheres of the tale vie with the "historical" settings of the author Murasaki Shikibu, her empress, and the empress's father Regent Michinaga, with unexpected results. Still other titles leave readers puzzling over what happened to Genji and the tale, or why Genji is a "she" on the hunt for (male) lovers.

Indeed, *The Tale of Genji shōjo manga* have a wide reach, appearing in every decade from the 1970s through the 2010s, targeting audiences from the very young (Miō) to more traditional readers (Yamato, Toba, Miyagi), and becoming texts that counterpoint the "original" story (Maya, Shimaki, Sakurada), including gender-bending (*Ms. Genji*). Fashioning alluring objects of desire for readers, for themselves, and, of course, for their protagonists, the *shōjo* artists focalize their narrative and drawing styles in numerous ways: contiguous narratives are eschewed for vignettes on individual women (Toba, Mio, *Ms. Genji*); divergent, tangential aspects take center stage (Miyagi, Maya, Sasaki); settings are displaced into very non-Heian spaces (Shimaki); and gender identities are flipped and made more fluid (*Ms. Genji*). Pretty-boy objects of desire, *onmyōji* yin-yang masters, errant boy-rulers of island nations, and high school plays on *The Tale of Genji* take center stage. Perhaps because *Fleeting Dreams* relates the story in its entirety in standard *shōjo* fashion, subsequent artists improvise at will, creating inventive new *Tales of Genji*.

And improvise they do—yet as different as they are, they all subscribe to the tenets of girls comics. They all remediate the multifaceted eleventh-century tale, largely in terms of the romantic encounters/relationships between the heroes and heroines—the standard fare of girls comics. And central protagonists are androgynously handsome *bishōnen* men/boys and sparkling, wide-eyed *bishōjo* women/girls (with the exceptions of the red-nosed princess, the antihero Genji, secondary characters, and those who populate Maya's remediation). Mainly focusing on the women and often telling the story from their perspectives, these *manga* depict the women dreaming about finding their true love—their (Heian-inspired) Prince Charming, who will sweep them off their feet and be true to them forever. Given the dynamics of Heian society, this is, of course not to be—hence the characters' agonized waiting, and their heart-wrenching, often inevitable abandonment. Girls comics' mixed messages to their girl readers preach seeking autonomy but also maintaining traditional heterosexual feminine roles. The search for the perfect object of desire goes on, and it must be pure, innocent. This means that the lows must be tempered somewhat rather than being expressed in realistic, adult terms (as in the ladies comics discussed in Chapter 5). The highs, too—in particular, the consummation sex scenes—must be demure, with nudity kept at bay and/or depicted with elegance and refinement. Nonetheless, the point is not whether the protagonists achieve their goals but that readers are engaged in the quest, participating fully in the emotions of the moment, in tandem with the beautiful people depicted on the page, as they search together for multiple and varied objects of desire and acceptable roles for girls.

In *shōjo Genji manga* remediations, then, Genji and his ladies are stunningly gorgeous and irresistible, in keeping with Yamato's *Fleeting Dreams* and Tanabe's *shōjo* cute. But it is not just girls comics that take up that look. The Yamato-Tanabe iteration has become the contemporary face of the tale, effectively reducing *Genji* to heterosexual romantic relations—that is, to a love story with handsome heroes bedding beautiful women in over-the-top settings. Films, *anime*, light novels, and musical revues—based on girls-comics stereotypes, recycled *Genji* imagery, and lines from *Fleeting Dreams* and Tanabe's novelization—enact this new mass-produced, mass-consumed, mass-processed *Genji* culture by focusing on the characters' thoughts, feelings, and emotions, all of which are overtly expressed. Gone are the complexities and ambiguities of the story—not just in terms of love, but politically, philosophically, religiously, and even interpersonally. Gone, too, is the atmosphere of the Heian period; instead, all is like the world of the Tanabe transposition, *Fleeting Dreams*, and light novels.

So, does the Yamato/Tanabe *shōjo manga*-nization of *The Tale of Genji* push the story in unintended, misplaced directions, reducing it to a too *kawaii* cute? Purists would most likely say yes. But I contend that, if we look at the precedents set through the ages, this is not unusual. *Manga, anime*, Takarazuka all-female revue performances, and even film are just new ways through which *The Tale of Genji* has transposed itself into new forms—very much in line with the *nō* focalization on women, Motoori Norinaga's use of the tale for nation-building, and the *mitate* visual puzzle *Bumpkin Genji*. Such new forms speak to and with and of the audiences of new eras in ways that they can claim as their own. As we have seen, girls comics fashion their remediations largely as objects of desire; the chapters that follow examine how *Genji* remediations expand into male–male Boys Love comics and "grow up" with their readers into *Genji* ladies comics, so as to attend to the desires of other readerships as well.

Chapter 4

BOYS LOVE *MANGA*: APPROPRIATING, (CHILD) PORN-ING, AND QUEERING MALE–MALE ROMANCES?

"This is a parallel Heian court where only men reside, a parallel world where men love another and produce male progeny. The Shining Genji, the child whom the imperially favored consort Fujitsubo bears, is fervently and deeply loved by sundry delectable men" (Saotome 2011a, 1). So opens *Genji monogatari BL ansorojii: aiyoku no otoko ōchō koi emaki* (*The Tale of Genji BL Anthology: Love Scrolls of Courtly Male Desire*, 2011). Edited by Mori Yoshimasa, the anthology includes eight episodes by different artists. In each, Genji remains a man, but his female love interests from the eleventh-century tale are transformed into *bishōnen* beautiful young men. Providing little plot or character development, the vignettes focus more surely on the foreplay and sexual encounters between the protagonists. Sensuous looks, intimate kissing scenes, lovers locked in hot embrace, and erotically charged nude bodies fill its pages. A far cry from Heian conventions, the episodes include graphically explicit sex scenes not found either in the tale or in other kinds of *shōjo manga*—for *The Tale of Genji BL Anthology* moves the *Genji* into the new realm of Boys Love *manga*.

The Boys Love subcategory of girls comics does not simply add more sex to the mix but invites a broader range of readers beyond the targeted audience of straight women. These readers bring their own specific needs and perspectives to the table and reinscribe, challenge, subvert, and recreate as they collaborate with and coauthor the Boys Love texts. To better understand how readers participate in this creation, we must first examine what constitutes Boys Love (*bōizu rabu*). Usually referred to as BL (*bii eru*), these texts encompass visual/textual narratives of "homoerotic love between male protagonists" (Wood 2006, 394) and are created by heterosexual women ostensibly for women consumers, although, as noted above, their readership is much more varied.[1] Most often, BL texts refigure the male heterosexual relationships of mainstream *manga* characters as male–male romantic relationships.[2] Featuring homosexual relations and graphic, sometimes forceful sex, they have come under attack for trafficking in pornography (specifically child porn), for encouraging rape,[3] and for appropriating the gay community. These are serious allegations indeed. Early on, it was the portrayal of homosexuality that was the aberrant issue;[4] in recent years, it is the intimation of harm to and exploitation of marginalized communities (minors and gays) that has come under fire. But

BL and *The Tale of Genji BL Anthology* are not the only offending texts. Hard-core ladies comics, *eromanga* erotic adult (male) comics, and even girls, boys, and young men comics—as well as *anime, manga,* films, video games, fan art, and fan fiction—are viewed as "harming" minors, acquiring for Japan the moniker "Empire of Child Porn" (Adelstein and Kubo 2014). Such name-calling—Japan-bashing in its newest iteration—otherizes, orientalizes, and exoticizes Japan.[5] "Weird Japan" is the term that Patrick Galbraith uses (2017b, 109). Western audiences point to *shunga* erotic woodblock illustrations as proof of Japan's kinky sexual practices, and further eroticize and infantilize Japanese women, citing the geisha as sites where (male) sexual fantasies can be fulfilled (Yamamoto 1999, 5, 23–4; Bardsley 2021, 27–9). But do Japan, *manga/anime*, and BL warrant such charges?

To seek answers, we must examine what constitutes BL, what needs and desires they serve, and for whom. But matters are complicated by BL's relationship with two other male–male *manga* narratives: *shōnen-ai* (also translated as boys love), and *yaoi* (an acronym, explicated below, highlighting its focus on sex). Male–male romances in fact first appeared in the 1970s, as relationships between beautiful adolescent boys in suggestive, non-sexually explicit stories such as Hagio Moto's (1974) *The Heart of Thomas* and Takemiya Keiko's (1976) *A Poem of Wind and Trees* (Wood 2006, 395). These relationships turned explicit in the 1980s *dōjinshi* fanzines that posited slash-fiction-like relationships between mainstream heterosexual male protagonists. In the 1990s, male–male narratives became commercially viable and were labeled *shōnen-ai, yaoi,* and BL. Considered subcategories of girls comics, these male–male narratives remain distinct and separate in their orientation and construction, except in one respect—whether overtly aggressive and graphically eroticized or not, all relationships are enacted in the name of true love. Despite what some depictions may look like, engaging in sex exclusively for sexual gratification runs counter to the golden rule of both BL and girls comics.

From what I have been able to ascertain, most scholars, practitioners, and readers in the United States and Japan use these three different terms for male–male narratives to signal the amount of sexual content in the titles. The least graphic of the three, *shōnen-ai*, posits romances that gesture toward but do not involve sexual engagement (Wood 2006, 395), so some use it to designate narratives such as those by Hagio and Takamiya that were produced in the early 1970s (Suter 2013, 547–8; Johnson pers. comm.; Emma Hanashiro e-mail). *Yaoi*—an acronym for *yama nashi, ochi nashi, imi nashi* ("no climax, no punch line, no meaning," Schodt 1996, 37)—represents the other extreme, encompassing *manga* that are more sexually graphic and that often "forgo coherent plot development in favor of using every available opportunity to get the beautiful male characters in bed together" (Wood 2006, 395). Many use the term *yaoi* largely for *dōjinshi* fanzines (Suter 2013, 547; K. Saito 2011, 172). Others contend that it has been displaced by the term BL—which previously only designated narratives appearing in mainstream publications (Thorn e-mail; Emma Hanashiro e-mail; Johnson pers. comm.).

Generally speaking, the term *shōnen-ai* has come to be less used, while the terms BL and *yaoi* function in four iterations.[6] Publishers and *manga* websites in the

United States, however, utilize all three terms: *shōnen-ai* signals nonsexual, erotic male–male stories that focus more on relationships; *yaoi* indicates sexually explicit male–male narratives that put less effort in the storyline (Wood 2006, 395, 410; Wang e-mail); and BL has a wider purview, encompassing titles that fall in between *shōnen-ai* and *yaoi*, and serves as an umbrella term for the above, and even for fan works based on Japanese titles that are produced in other countries (Wang e-mail; Nagaike and Suganuma 2013). What is clear, then, is that several terms for largely female-targeted, male–male romance narratives are in circulation. Although their definitions and usage are fluid and overlap, scholars, readers, and BL writers usually select BL or *yaoi* as a blanket term when discussing and engaging with these narratives. For this study, I utilize the term BL for commercially published works, reserving *shōnen-ai* for early 1970s works and *yaoi* for fanzines.

Reading BL Tales of Genji

Pleasuring Whom? Challenging What? Provocative How?

To return to our pressing question: how did BL romances that are premised on true love come to be charged with trafficking in child porn/pedophilia, encouraging rape, and appropriating gay culture? The ebb and flow of Japan's economic and political fortunes, and the shifting political, cultural, and social climates of countries that consume Japanese popular culture mark the change. But the rumblings have been around a long time: when I gave presentations on *manga* to US audiences in the 1990s and 2000s, as Cool Japan was trending (McLelland 2017, 5–6), there were always questions—Why the violence? Why the sexuality? Aren't *manga* comics supposed to be for children? "I am appalled that my grandson is reading this kind of material," a K-12 educator told me. *Manga* were uncool—very uncool, destructive even. More alarm bells went off as the presence of graphic and violent sex scenes in (hard-core) ladies comics[7] and adult male *eromanga* erotic comics grabbed the attention of western media (Shigematsu 1999, 127).

Addressing Charges of Child Porn/Endangerment: Subversive Complexity That Is More Than Meets the Eye

It was in 2014 that things really heated up internationally. Under pressure from abroad, Japan banned the possession of child pornography (which expanded its 1999 criminalization of the production and dissemination of child porn), but was vilified and labeled the "Empire of Child Porn" for failing to criminalize "fantasy images" of *anime* and *manga* figures who appeared to be minors (McLelland 2017, 1; Galbraith 2017b, 109; see also Adelstein and Kubo 2014). Stricter regulation of visual (*manga* and *anime*) "representations of characters who may 'appear to be minors'" became the clarion call, and countries such as the United States, the UK, Canada, Sweden, New Zealand, and Australia passed stringent laws prohibiting the trafficking of such "child abuse publications" (McLelland 2017, 9, 11). As a result, although later overturned, in 2010 a Swedish *manga* translator was prosecuted for possessing computer cartoon images depicting minors engaged in sexual activity; less lucky, a UK man was convicted of possessing child porn based on cartoon images of sexualized minors, while a US collector was charged for a similar crime but avoided a trial through a plea bargain (McLelland 2017, 9, 12). US citizens going into Canada with print or digital copies of Japanese popular culture content have been detained, questioned, and in one case arrested on child pornography charges by Canadian Customs Officers (McLelland 2017, 13). In Australia Mark McLelland began providing explicit instructions on what kinds of images could be discussed and shown in class to comply with child pornography laws (2017, 14). One of his PhD students discovered that even materials for academic purposes could be refused entry if found to be "objectionable" and be retrieved only after a protracted legal process (Stapleton 2017, 134, 138–45). It really hit home for me when a scholar and friend based in Canada felt compelled to remove all "manga and anime–related materials" from her laptop when she traveled and placed much of her *anime* and *manga* collection into storage in the United States because it "could potentially be counted in Canada as child porn" (Orbaugh 2017, 97).

So how did Japan come to be so "uncool" and accused of enabling the exploitation of the vulnerable? In terms of BL *manga*, it is the construction and interaction of the male leads—the *seme* and the *uke*—that are at the fault lines. As designated by BL conventions, the *seme* (or "attacker," in translation) initiates the sexual relations. Often bigger in build, older, and more "masculine," he looks as if he is taking advantage of the younger, more passive *uke* (or "recipient/receiver"), who is slighter in build and more "feminine" in appearance.[8] This impression deepens as the *seme*'s overtures appear to overpower the resisting *uke*. But a show of force by the *seme* and resistance by the *uke* are all part of an orchestrated sexual dance to heighten the erotic tension and enable lovers to engage in sexual activity. No matter how much the *uke* welcomes the attention, he must initially exhibit shock and push back on the *seme*'s advances.[9] In accordance with the give-and-take of girls-comics and BL-comics romantic encounters, the *uke* comes to understand that the *seme*'s aggressive overtures stem from the *seme*'s intense love, and the *uke* responds in kind. Without an understanding of the characters and their relationship—and the conventions of girls and BL comics—the sexual encounter looks very much like the older, bigger, adult *seme* exacting his will upon the weaker, smaller, "underage" *uke*.

In *The Tale of Genji BL Anthology*, Genji and Hanachirusato perform to a T the girls-comics and BL-comics sexual tropes described above. In the episode Genji goes to visit Hanachirusato before he goes into exile for angering his rivals at court. Unlike the other gorgeous young men, Hanachirusato is older, but in the BL world of the anthology both are drawn much younger in age and the encounter is read solicitous and enjoyable. An astute reader of this manuscript queried me about how that was possible given that, on the left-hand page in Figure 4.1, Genji appears terrified and in pain.[10]

The answer is twofold: first, the presentation and interpretation of facial expressions in Japan differ from those in the west and, second, they are highly

Figure 4.1 Hanachirusato comforting and teaching Genji the ways of love. Mijuki, "Hanachirusato," in Mori Yoshimasa, ed. *The Tale of Genji BL Anthology: Love Scrolls of Courtly Male Desire*, 108–9. Copyright © Mijuki 2011.

context- and in-group specific and imbedded in the conventions of the venue—in this case the BL-comics remediations of *The Tale of Genji*. Studies[11] indicate that generally speaking in Japan revealing strong emotions and looking directly into people's faces are to be eschewed, so Japanese focus on the less overtly expressive eyes to portray feelings. This results in more subdued, controlled, and subtle expressions of emotions. In contrast, westerners use the entire face and especially the mouth to analyze facial gestures and read feelings, because the mouth is the most expressive part of the face. From a western perspective, Genji's mouth, open and in the shape of a circle, in the second panel on the left-hand page in Figure 4.1, makes him appear to be in pain and even terrified. Japanese, however, give more weight to the eyes, so, if we look more closely, we see that they have not changed much in shape or expression from the panels of the right-hand page where he is unafraid and even content. Fine lines appear under his eyes on both panels as well, revealing that he is blushing and is actually a bit embarrassed. But why is he embarrassed and not fearful? Herein lies the importance of context specificity and, more importantly, "in-group advantage in emotional recognition" (Yuki et al. 2007, 303).

Using facial expressions, dialogue, and sexual BL conventions, Mijuki expertly sets the stage to ensure that the encounter transpires between a solicitous older lover and a willing and appreciative younger partner. She begins by emphasizing Hanachirusato's role as caretaker: Hanachirusato is quick to pick up on Genji's anxiety about leaving the capital and assures him that things may be difficult now, but he is destined for great things. He adds that he, Hanachirusato, will always be there for him (Mijuki 2011, 106). A full-page close-up of Genji's face signals how deeply he is touched by Hanachirusato's care (Mijuki 2011, 107), and the gentle kiss he receives in the top panel of the page on the right in Figure 4.1 (in BL poetics parlance) alerts readers that the comfort will be sexual in nature. The second panel on the same page also reveals the exterior of a building and the single word "Aa—," denoting surprise. Appearing superfluous, the panel marks the shift to the sexual encounter with the flowers in the foreground indicating that the intimacy is premised on love. Should there be any doubt, in the panel below, Genji compliments Hanachirusato on his skill in bed, signaling that the next moves will be equally welcome. Hanachirusato accedes, replying that he has been practicing for Genji's sake, and engages him in lovemaking on the left page.

In Mijuki's vignette Genji looks ten or eleven, while Hanachirusato is in his twenties (in the tale Genji is twenty-five and Lady Hanachirusato is thirty-five)— and from a non-in-group perspective it also looks as if Hanachirusato is pushing Genji into an unwanted encounter. But Genji has given his permission to move forward and, as explained previously, no matter how forceful it may appear, BL sexual encounters are premised on love and are enacted as carefully choreographed, eroticized dances that provide agency for both parties. As the *seme* Hanachirusato must be the initiator and the *uke* Genji must initially respond to these advances with surprise, if not alarm. In other words, Genji must play, as Linda Williams explains earlier, the role of the woman who can only enjoy "bad" girl pleasures of sex outside marriage by being "forced" into them. In such a scenario the woman cannot overtly express her enjoyment, let alone her desire for sexual gratification. She must appear coerced to engage in sex: anything to the contrary would label her promiscuous. Thus, here, too, Genji must look embarrassed rather than enthusiastically engaging in sex. His hesitation, as previously mentioned, is depicted by the fine lines under his eyes in the three panels on the left-hand page of Figure 4.1. It is a display not of pain or terror but innocence, for Genji must play the role of the "good" boy who is forced into sex in order to reap the benefits of "bad" boy sexual pleasures.

For two more pages, 110–11, Genji continues this performance, blushing profusely and even asking Hanachirusato to stop, as is required of a "chaste" lover. It is only on the last page 112 of the episode that the full import of the encounter is revealed. After the two pages of sexual activity, Genji is neither traumatized by nor upset about what has happened. Rather, he rests serenely in Hanachirusato's embrace and formally asks Hanachirusato to be with him always—signaling that he accepts the sexual intimacy that transpired between them. Genji is grateful for Hanachirusato's love and validates Hanachirusato as his caretaker par excellence who knows best how to console him in his most trying moments. Mijuki's profile of a bashful but content Genji,[12] followed by close-up of a pleased Hanachirusato, further assures us that the lovemaking was not predatory or one-sided but reciprocal in nature, per BL love conventions. Knowing that in the tale

Hanachirusato functions as one of Genji's earliest sexual mentors is also crucial in fully contextualizing the encounter.

Not just in this episode but in others as well, the anthology takes care to explain that the *seme*'s forcefulness comes from love and that the *uke* Genji, although initially surprised by its intensity, responds in kind. For example, in Genji's encounter with Oborozukiyo (the sister of Genji's rival Empress Kokiden in Murasaki Shikibu's tale), Yamada Botan's adult male Oborozukiyo relentlessly pursues the "child" Genji, bending the smaller Genji to his will. But here, too, the situation is not what it seems. Oborozukiyo's rough overtures are not just to get his way but are indicative of his passionate love for Genji—a love so heartfelt that Genji comes to understand its depth and responds by professing his own love for Oborozukiyo through word and deed (Yamada, B. 2011, 72–3, 78–82).

But why portray Genji as a child? In the anthology's episode with Fujitsubo, Genji is a young boy in the early days of the relationship, but with Oborozukiyo, Akashi, and the young Murasaki, Genji is definitely older. Nonetheless, he occupies the weaker, more passive *uke* role in the male–male narratives in the anthology and is "made" to engage in sex. The explanation is twofold: first, Genji is the "hero" of the anthology, and here the hero is not the *seme* but the *uke*, who is so passionately desired and for whom the *seme* will do anything. The *uke*, then, is not a weak, less desirable, or "passive" victim; indeed, by being in the position of acquiescing to or denying the *seme*'s overtures, Genji actually "calls the shots." Thus the eleventh-century tale's alpha-male Genji becomes a "passive" *uke*, but one with power over the more experienced *seme*s, effectively complicating the Heian heteronormative notions of masculinity. The BL text also pokes fun at the alpha male: reconfigured as an adorably cute *uke*, Genji closely mirrors the function of the middle-aged *oyaji* businessman in post-2000 "New Wave" BL titles. Viewed by BL practitioners as a symbol of "phallic power" who regulates and objectifies Japanese girls and women (see Nagaike n.d.), in these recent works the formidable *oyaji* businessman is cutified and divested of status and power, just as Genji is the BL anthology.

Do *manga* fictional images, specifically those of underage-looking *uke*, constitute child endangerment/child porn? *The Tale of Genji BL Anthology* indicates otherwise, or at least asks for further consideration of the context in which such images are used, arguing first and foremost that the Genji *uke* is a fictive representation of another fictional character from a literary tale—not a human child who has been harmed in the production of the *manga*, as Orbaugh points out happens in other *manga* (2017, 94). The Genji *uke* and the various *seme*s also function in specific ways within the narrative of each episode. Although it may seem that the adult-looking *seme* is taking advantage of an unwilling *uke*, the Genji *uke* reveals that the sexual interaction is complex, and is premised on love rather than violence/violation.[13] Lastly, although the artists construct their characters to look underage, by Heian standards they are old enough to engage in sexual relations—and most of them are old enough even by contemporary standards.

Addressing Charges of "Rape": Engaging in Phantasy/Play, Seeking Equality

Targeted for depicting seemingly underaged *ukes* in sexual relationships, BL *manga* are also charged with the flagrant use of force employed by some *semes* during the sexual encounter. The most prominent example in the anthology occurs between Genji and Rokujō, Genji's older, more experienced lover, whose jealousy in the tale transforms her into a living spirit that ultimately kills Genji's wife Aoi and the love of his life, Murasaki. With such a backstory at the ready, artist Saotome Ageha portrays the two lovers in passionate embrace from the first page (Saotome 2011b, 22).[14] She, nonetheless, takes care to properly contextualize the now-male Rokujō's bedding of Genji in Figure 4.2—much as Mijuki does with Genji and Hanachirusato above.

Most importantly, Saotome shows that Genji has enjoyed Rokujō's advances in the past and has felt safe and beloved during their lovemaking. On pages 22–3, Genji revels in Rokujō's ministrations and asks for more—even professing his love and expecting the same from Rokujō. Fearful that he will be abandoned, Rokujō is reluctant to confess his love (Saotome 2011b, 23–4). And true to his fears, Rokujō hears that Genji is seeing someone else—though the next time they meet Genji dismisses it as gossip and teases Rokujō about being jealous (Saotome 2011b,

Figure 4.2 Rokujō taunts Genji that his pleas to stop belie the pleasure he is experiencing from Rokujō's ministrations. Saotome Ageha, "Haven Rokujō," in Mori Yoshimasa, ed. *The Tale of Genji BL Anthology: Love Scrolls of Courtly Male Desire*, 30–1. Copyright © Saotome Ageha 2011. Courtesy of Saotome Ageha and Kadokawa.

28-9). Angered that Genji does not understand the depth of his love, Rokujō unleashes his frustrations in Figure 4.2, announcing in the last two panels of the right-hand page that, since Genji likes it rough, he will give him what he wants. On the same page and across to the left page, Rokujō declares, "You won't just visit me, so I will stomp on you, rape you, and will sear myself onto your memory, so it is me you see no matter whom you sleep with." In the leftmost set of panels on the same page, Rokujō taunts Genji: "Your 'no' really means 'yes!' Why are you resisting now when you always so gladly spread your legs apart for me before?"

Rokujō's treatment and taunting of Genji is so violent and aggressive that Genji says it is over and does not visit Rokujō again in this episode (Saotome 2011b, 34). What is surprising, however, is that in Figure 4.2 Genji looks fearful but more surprised and a bit embarrassed: he has the same "chaste" lines of embarrassment under his eyes that appear on his face in moments when he felt safe and enjoyed Rokujō's attention (Saotome 2011b, 22-3). And, although his eyes and his mouth exhibit more surprise and reluctance than is found in his reactions in his sexual interaction with Hanachirusato in Figure 4.1, they share much in common. Genji's mouth, open and rounded in appearance, evokes fear, but, at the same time Rokujō points to Genji's looks of embarrassment (depicted as lines under his eyes) and his sexual arousal as indications that Genji's words of protest belie his enjoyment of Rokujō's advances. Rokujō's violent and aggressive bedding of the underage Genji *uke* here reads like classic rape, but scholar Setsu Shigematsu emphasizes that, as horrific as this appears, scenarios such as these do not denote rape. Rather, they are carefully choreographed to express the overpowering love that the *seme* has for his beloved, in this case Rokujō's obsessive love for Genji. And these are not "real rape" but are divorced from reality. They are read as play—erotic play, "phantasy,"[15] a fictional trope through which women readers can acknowledge and act upon their sexual desires in safe ways, without guilt or fear, for the bodies are not female and "otherized" as male, and they remain in the imaginary (Shigematsu 1999, 140).

As we can imagine, this trope, found in BL and ladies comics, has caused great consternation and has been censored both inside and outside of Japan for appearing to sanction predatory behavior (see introduction for a fuller discussion). Yet it does not encourage sexual violence in any shape or form, and operates as a fictional, narrative trope to circumnavigate the ways in which female gender roles are constituted and maintained in Japan. Since the Meiji period (1868-1912), social, cultural, and governmental norms have mandated that women be "good wives and wise mothers" (*ryōsai kenbo*) and engage only in reproductive sex within the confines of marriage, to produce (male) offspring who become military or corporate warriors. Women who do not follow these conventions are regarded as prostitutes at worst and bar-club hostesses at best. Good wives and wise mothers are discouraged from expressing their sexual desires or their enjoyment of being powerfully desired,[16] so BL and ladies-comics artists invented a phantasy trope in which such "good girls" would be "forced" to enjoy and express their sexuality (Shigematsu 1999, 142-4). Shigematsu references female protagonists in ladies comics, but the purpose and effect of this phantasy is the same for BL practitioners who identify not just as heterosexual but gay, lesbian, transgender, and in-betweens.

What is clearly understood between artists and readers is that these scenarios remain narrative tropes, existing solely in the imaginary and removed from reality.[17] Readers participate in these scenarios precisely because they occur in the imaginary and do not threaten their well-being, thereby providing a sanctuary where experimentation and pleasure transpire not just for women but other gender-identified readers. Scholars, artists, and readers alike adamantly argue that these scenes neither sanction nor invite rape in any shape or form in real life for any readers (Shigematsu 1999, 147–8), and that the queering of these encounters—the superimposing of "female" desires and bodies on male bodies—distances the phantasy even further from real life and makes the encounters safe for consumption for not only straight but also gay/lesbian/transgender and other-gendered readers.

In her study *Women Read Pornography*, Mori Naoko examines Japanese readerly responses submitted to questionnaires and write-in opportunities afforded by hard-core BL and ladies comics to determine how the trope operates. She finds that 2D sexual encounters are enjoyed as fantasy, precisely because they reside in the imaginary and creators make every effort to construct them as fictional and, most importantly, as not terrifying or too close to real life (2010, 173–4, 188). Even in violent sexual scenes, Mori writes, visual and textual stratagems are used to ensure that the sexual encounter transpires between two equals, with the *seme* acting out of overwhelming love for the *uke* and the *uke*, surprised and even resistant at first, coming to understand and reciprocate the *seme*'s passion. She argues that the visual and textual coding embedded in the facial expressions and inner dialogues of the characters further indicate that the pleasure and enjoyment is shared by both parties (2010, 160–1)—as we saw in the Genji-Hanachirusato encounter above.[18] Relying on subtle facial features and BL conventions, the Genji/Rokujō encounter, discussed above, also features a similarly situated moment: Genji's expressions of surprise, a blush of embarrassment, and then pleasure and arousal belie his words asking Rokujō to stop (see Figure 4.2), which becomes clear when parsed in tandem with the visual and textual coding and Rokujō's dialogue. Much of Genji's reluctance, too, is couched in his role as an unwilling partner forced to engage in sex against his will for the maintenance of his status as a "good" boy.[19] To further minimize the negativity of Rokujō's advances, Saotome marshals another stratagem identified by Mori Naoko—the use of the *seme*'s internal and external monologue delineating concern for how his actions have affected the *uke* (Mori N. 2010, 173–5). The *uke*'s internal monologue often expresses his pleasure as well (Mori N. 2010, 164), but in this scenario Saotome focalizes Rokujō lamenting his rough and insensitive treatment of Genji, a tear rolling down his cheek (2011b, 35–6). Taken together with Genji's look of embarrassment and his sexual arousal despite his protests, the situation is much more complex than simply one of Rokujō's taking advantage of Genji.

But can the specter of rape be banished simply by appealing to the fictionality of the Genji/Rokujō encounter, as in the case with the underage Genji *uke* in the Genji/Hanachirusato episode? In other words, can this "phantasy rape" constitute not "real" rape but "rape play" because it takes place between two fictional characters in the imaginary, separate from the lived experiences of producers, consumers, men, women, and children? Studies by Fujimoto (2015), Galbraith (2017a and 2021), and Khan and Ketterling (2019) have concluded in the affirmative and an interrogation of how it operates within the confines of male–male narratives will be equally instructive. According to one theory, the male–male *seme/uke* dynamic enables readers to transcend the reality of the hierarchical construction of gender roles and (female) desire imposed by the patriarchal Japanese society. By positing two male characters, women readers can experience romantic relationships as equal partners (Wood 2006, 401; see Mori N. 2010). Critics contend that this extreme measure is taken because heterosexual couplings in Japan automatically render the man higher and the woman lower, literally and figuratively. With both *manga* protagonists being male, readers do not identify as female, leaving them free of their prescribed gender identities—and therefore free to participate as a "male" in a more equal and mutually rewarding and satisfying relationship.

BL *manga* also go out of their way, through character construction, dialogue, and illustrations, to mitigate sexual hierarchy. As discussed above, the visuals and the text make clear that in BL *manga* the *seme*'s aggressive posture does not stem from a desire to dominate but from his overwhelming love for the *uke*, and the *uke* is not forced to comply but does so out of his own free will and desire (Wood 2006, 403). He simply looks as if he is being coerced to maintain his "good" boy paradigm status. The result is a mutually pleasurable fulfillment for both parties (Wood 2006, 401; see also Mori N. 2010). The encounter between Genji and Murasaki in the anthology portrays just such an idealized interaction (Motoi 2011, 64–5). To emphasize their lovemaking as conducted between equals, artist Motoi Tatsuno draws them as similar in age (despite Murasaki being eight years Genji's junior in the tale) with the dark-haired Murasaki taking the lead. Once again the lines under Genji's eyes indicate embarrassment and "chaste" reluctance rather than dissatisfaction with Murasaki's ministrations.

A second theory explaining why BL traffic in male–male narratives lies in their subversion of heteronormative expectations that restrict female erotic activity to marriage and reproductive sex.[20] With both protagonists being male, BL practitioners can transcend their genders and safely take up "multiple (if contradictory) subject positions" in the imaginary (Penley 1992, 480, 488–9). They can assume not just the positions of traditional "feminine" *uke* "objects of attraction" but also the roles of heretofore males-only *seme* "subjects of actions" (see Suter 2013, 550 and Mori N. 2010). BL readers, then, can become not just objects of desire but initiators of desire as well. The sexual and gender ambiguity visually encoded in the characters' appearances—the highly stylized androgynous, beautiful men, as we saw in the Rokujō/Genji encounter above (Figure 4.2)—make identifying with either protagonist easier. Nonetheless, the *seme*, as the bigger-build initiator directing the sexual encounter, raises charges of reinscribing heteronormative relations that position the male over/above the "female," as we see in the Genji/Fujitsubo encounter in the anthology drawn by Nakao Motoko. The episode opens with Genji relentlessly pursuing Fujitsubo, as he boldly lands a kiss

(Nakao 2011, 15). Initially rebuffing the overture, the older Fujitsubo dramatically changes course and takes Genji into his arms on page 16.

Declaring "Are you ready for this?," Fujitsubo assumes the "masculine" *seme* role and initiates the sexual encounter on page 16. A surprised and embarrassed Genji (depicted by the lines under his eyes) is swept up by Fujitsubo's passion on page 17, and even weakly declares "This is wrong" on the following page 18, as is required of the *uke*'s in initially responding to sexual overtures. But ultimately this is a dream come true for both parties. Fujitsubo thus enacts the "male"-on-top sexual heteronormativity, but the fact that both partners are men puts a different spin on the interaction. First, the normative heterosexual hierarchy is not as automatic because neither protagonist is gendered female. Second, the presence of the alpha-male Genji as *uke* means that the *uke* positionality is not passive, weak, or "below" that of the *seme*. And lastly, as evidenced by the engaged participation of both lovers, their mutual pleasuring transforms them into what Kumiko Saito terms "subjects of love and being loved" (2011, 185).

Addressing Charges of Appropriation: Gay Culture and the Queering of BL

Although performing as subjects of love and being loved, freed of patriarchal normativity and gender expectations, is provocative and exciting for BL practitioners, using male lovers to serve the needs of BL's targeted "straight" women/girl consumers has raised charges of appropriating the gay bodies. Should the interests of one marginalized community supersede the well-being of another? This is the question at hand. In the early days of BL production, gay men viewed BL as works largely by women and for women that did not concern them. But things changed in 1992, when gay activist and drag queen Satō Masaki accused BL comics of appropriating and discriminating against gay men. In an article in the feminist magazine *Choisir*, Satō charged that BL stereotyped gay men as androgynous, replicated mainstream homophobic comments and situations, and did not address the lived experiences and concerns of homosexual men in Japan.[21] This triggered the Yaoi debates (*Yaoi ronsō*) between the gay community and the BL proponents.

Taken aback by these charges, female BL producers and consumers contended that BL texts were not about homosexuality but performed as safe spaces where women sought "refuge from a misogynist society" (Vincent 2007, 72). In their minds making both partners male circumvented the heteronormative sexual power dynamic, leveled the playing field, and firmly placed the interaction in the imaginary. This strategy did not sit well with BL detractors, but there is more here than meets the eye as we have seen in how the male protagonists in *The BL Anthology* enact differently positioned identities—male, female, in-betweens, and even gay. Of note as well is the double standard that allows male fantasizing of female–female sexual acts in lesbian *yuri manga* but disallows females from doing the same with male–male acts.

More recently, in what some call the second debate, Ishida Hitoshi has argued that this still constitutes "representational appropriation"—the co-opting of images of gay men at their expense (2015, 229). Reminiscent of the defense mounted against charges of BL's endangering children and supporting sexual violence, female proponents appeal to BL's positionality as fiction, that is, as texts residing in the imaginary with no links to "real" life. Scholar Hori Akiko acknowledges that the *seme/uke* pairing may indeed appropriate elements of gay culture, but argues that this should not preclude BL/*yaoi* from simultaneously resisting and subverting mainstream norms (see Hori 2013, pars. 14–15 for more information). And we find that such is the case not just for "straight" women but also for other positionalities, including gay men, as we will see below.

Kazumi Nagaike and Tomoko Aoyama further caution against critiques that are based on "identity-politics stance"—that is, on the notion that gay narratives created by gay men should not be exempt from charges of "false presentations" of the gay experience on the basis that their identity automatically authenticates the experiences and gives them the "right" to describe those experiences without interrogation (2015, 125). They also warn against simplistically pitting women against gay men, as the Yaoi debates have done. Instead, they ask that we look at the processes through which stereotypical images have developed within specific historical, social, and cultural contexts, and that we examine the depiction of male–male romantic and erotic relationships in BL as well as in gay *manga*, so as to better contextualize and nuance our readings of male–male romances. Most tellingly, they also call for research tracking the changes in how BL is read and about the readers who peruse it (2015, 126).

For instance, some suggest that BL readers are largely female and that they are drawn to male–male homoerotic romances because they enjoy watching pretty boys engage in sex.[22] This may be true for some readers, but I argue that the gazing is not simply voyeuristic but transgressive, queer, and multivalenced. No doubt BL replicate normative conceptualizations of sexual identity, behavior, and desire—and privilege the needs of "straight" women in many ways—but the *seme* and the *uke* also collapse "the hetero/homo binary" and enact what Alan Williams calls "a multitude of gender performances" (2015, par. 22). These performances call into question traditional, monolithic constructions of love, desire, and of being—opening up, in Eve Sedgwick's words, a "mess of possibilities" that complicate and queer the ways in which women, girls, and others envision their sexuality (qtd. in Wood 2006, 397). BL also channel Judith Butler's formulation of queer theory, in *Undoing Gender*, as resisting regulation of identities or prioritizing some above others, and "insist[ing] that sexuality is not easily summarized or unified through categorization" (qtd. in Wood 2006, 409).[23]

Such performances are premised on the way that BL and *manga* are constructed and read. For one, their cute *kawaii*, large-eyed characters trigger an affective bonding among character, producer, and consumer known as *moe*, or "euphoric response [by readers] to fantasy characters or representations of them" (Galbraith 2009b). This bonding allows readers and creators to "dwell with and on [*anime* and *manga*] characters" and fully identify with them, no matter how differently positioned they may be from their own gender, species, or existence (Galbraith n.d.2). This is possible because these *manga* figures are fictional and

2D, and can only be engaged in the imaginary—a "pure" space unsullied by the real—where exploration of the most "perverse and polymorphous possibilities" transpires (Galbraith 2009b). In such spaces, female desire can superimpose itself onto the BL male bodies (Nagaike, qtd. in A. Williams 2015, par. 22), replicating a *nō* actor's subsuming onto/into his (male) body the desire of the female body he is performing.[24] Neither "gender" is erased. Rather, genders and sexualities are queered—moving beyond male or female, heterosexual or homosexual, enacting fluidity and noncontainment, and replicating what Alan Williams in another context calls "non-identitarian" (2015, par. 13) sexual and gender play.

We can see this dynamic play out in Genji's encounters with Hanachirusato, Oborozukiyo, Murasaki, and Fujitsubo. The lovemaking appears to be occurring between two males, but if we take into account the characters' androgyny and sexual ambiguity, and view the male lovers as stand-ins for female consumers who seek to escape from societally imposed gender regulations, we see that the erotic encounters between Genji and his ladies-turned-beautiful-boys point to an "open mess of possibilities" that is not just straight or female but lesbian, bisexual, *fujoshi* rotten girl, *fudanshi* rotten guy, gay male, and "non-identitarian." A 2012 survey tracked the consumption motivation of BL fans and reported that the readership did indeed include different sexualities: less than half (43.23 percent) self-identified as heterosexual, while 56.77 percent identified as homosexual, bisexual, asexual, or "other." In fact 20.30 percent of the nonheterosexual respondents indicated heterosexual with homosexuality, pointing to the in-between-ess of sexual identities.[25]

Other studies show that lesbian and bisexual desires have long been evident among BL practitioners, but that many readers with these interests identify as heterosexual females to avoid being "otherized" for possessing "unacceptable desires" (Welker 2011, 222).[26] Early on, readers used 1970s *shōnen-ai* love between androgynous boys in girls comics to "explore homoerotic desire, either as a beautiful boy or as herself" (Welker 2006, 865), or employed male–male eroticism depicted in *Barazoku* (Rose Tribe), a 1970s–1980s magazine for homosexual men, to validate their own same-sex/lesbian/non-normative gender identification (Welker 2011, 212). But it is the fanzine *fujoshi* "rotten girls" practitioners who perfect the queering. Primarily female, *fujoshi* use the ironic, negative designation of "rotten girls" (in the same ways that "queer" and "gay" have been reappropriated) to express pride in what others deem an "abnormal" and immature interest in romantic and erotic relations between male characters. Often transposing heterosexual male relationships portrayed in mainstream *manga* into homoerotic couplings, the *fujoshi* fans[27] interact with the pairing of boys and men and open up "alternative sites and different dimensions" of what constitutes sex, sexuality, and even gender (Shigematsu 1999, 128). *Fujoshi*, then, take mainstream heterosexual pairings (although any object, place, etc. can become objects of their fantasies), queer them, place them in stories of their own creation, and then run with them in the imaginary. Thus, in the BL *Genji* anthology, Saotome Ageha enacts a *fujoshi*-esque move, transposing the male Genji and female Rokujō from the tale into male lovers, and has Rokujō enact play rape with Genji. But, as noted above, the rape play neither advocates nor condones rape in any shape or form in the real world, and exists only as a "perverse and polymorphous possibility" in the 2D imaginary.

Fujoshi have been around since the 1970s, when girls comics developed, but they came to the attention of the media in the 1990s and became a phenomenon in the mid-2000s (see Galbraith 2011, 217–19). They now have their own proprietary gathering site known as Otome Road, in the Ikebukuro district in Tokyo, that functions very much as Akihabara does for *otaku* dedicated fans, who tend to be male but also include female aficionados. *Fujoshi* generally form networks around their shared interests and participate in an almost exclusively female fandom (see Hestor 2015 for more information). Less is known about their male counterparts, *fudanshi* "rotten boys," but they, too, queer BL. Kazumi Nagaike traces the term to the mid-2000s, where it first surfaced in a survey tracking BL male readers (2015, 190). The readers in the survey presented in different genders and sexualities, but Nagaike limits her examination to heterosexual male readers, mapping out how they use BL to challenge and seek alternatives to the socially mandated conventions of masculinity (2015, 190–1).

Reminiscent of the ways in which *fujoshi* queer BL male characters to broaden notions of feminine sexuality and desire, male *fudanshi* readers use BL to interrogate compulsory gender norms and expectations that define men as powerful and as the privileged gender and class in a modern, "masculinized nation" (Nagaike 2015, 204). The BL construction of feminized androgynous men allows *fudanshi* to "self-feminize," to identify with and embrace the "female"-ascribed traits of "weakness, fragility, and passivity" that have been banished from masculine identities in the name of the strong, silent, tough "man's man." A *fudanshi* positionality may act as a foil behind which to hide gay sexuality, but at the very least it provides heterosexual male readers with respite from the "masculine" *seme* initiator image (Nagaike 2015, 193, 196). Performing as the alpha-male-turned feminized, younger, and passive Genji *uke* allows many a *fudanshi* reader to find solace in and engagement as the "other."

But what about gay men, from whom the 1990s and more recent pushback evolved? Are they now more open to BL male–male romantic relationships, as *fudanshi* male practitioners have exhibited above? Much to my surprise, there appears to be a 180-degree shift among some gay men. In his article "Japanese Gay Men's Attitude towards 'Gay Manga' and the Problem of Genre," Thomas Baudinette determines that some gay men use BL in tandem with *geikomi* (gay comics, also known as *bara*, that are written for and by gay men) to construct and express their sexual identities and desires. Interviewing six gay men on how and what they consume, Baudinette found that BL titles play as crucial a role as *geikomi* gay comics do in the construction of gay subjecthood and the expression of gay desire (2017, 59). Rather than viewing BL and *geikomi* as oppositional, the six informants regarded them as two sides of the same coin (Baudinette 2017, 59). The two categories—or genres, as Baudinette calls them—are stylistically and thematically different. BL is *shōjo*-esque, featuring *bishōnen* beautiful androgynous men and focusing on romance and a " 'softer' masculinity," whereas *geikomi* is viewed as depicting gay men enacting "wild, rough and uncontrollable urges" in " 'hyper-masculine' visions of gay desire" (Baudinette 2017, 63–4). For the six men, then, the two genres complement each other: BL speaks to gay men's yearning for the "spiritual and emotional love" of romantic relationships, while *geikomi* recognizes their craving for "carnal lust and bodily desire" (Rang, qtd. in Baudinette 2017, 65). The two are not only not in opposition but are in dialogue as they work in tandem to construct gay subjectivity and to express gay desire.

Further research of online platforms frequented by gay men, conducted by my research assistant Jorge Rodriquez between July and August 2021, substantiates many of Baudinette's claims. A few people on the social news website and forum Reddit take issue with BL as "damaging and off-putting" to gay men, and a blog damns *yaoi* production (Rodriguez n.d.), but on the whole the tide appears to be turning on the concerns raised by the 1990s Yaoi debates. Not limited to Baudinette's informants, American and other English-speaking gay participants across the world who engage the group chat Discord servers and Tumblr blogs also consider BL to be a part of gay media, because both BL and *geikomi* center on "gay men, relationships, and sex" (Rodriguez n.d.). As with Baudinette, Rodriguez finds that the two categories are perceived as different in art style and body types, and as thus fulfilling different purposes and needs. The slim, androgynous *bishōnen* beautiful boys images and narratives are tagged as BL, while the bigger, rougher, hypermasculine male ones are labeled *geikomi*. Baudinette indicates that his informants use both sets of fantasy figures for masturbatory purposes, but, in line with Sonia Ryang's conclusions (qtd. in Baudinette 2017, 65), Rodriguez discovers that the English-based platform users seek out BL media for the development of the romantic progression of the male–male relationships depicted in stories—although their use as sexual stimulation and gratification is not precluded. In contrast, *geikomi* are mainly accessed for gay pornographic consumption. Thus for all intents and purposes, Baudinette's claims of the turning of the tide on the perception of BL media by gay men appear to be on target, and he and Rodriguez urge scholars to investigate consumer practices through the lenses of their consumers to obtain a broader sense of what constitutes BL and *geikomi*.

Conclusion: Addressing Difficult Topics

The what, the why, and the for whom of BL—and of *manga*—have changed over time, and as a result, Japanese popular culture has become an "uncool," treacherous enterprise in some circles in recent years. The religious right and native Japanese residing in the United States have taken to task those who teach and study *manga* and *anime* (Miller 2017); one scholar has been labeled the "lolicon guy"/a practitioner of child porn and has faced personal and professional consequences for working with BL (Galbraith 2017b); and legal concerns about possession of *manga* and *anime* images considered "objectionable" in the eyes of the law have dogged another scholar (Orbaugh 2017, 97). In 2017 McLelland wrote that no student in his classes has ever been "morally outraged" by *manga* content (2017, 13), but today things have changed dramatically. The COVID-19 pandemic, global conflicts, the controversies surrounding reproductive rights as well as the Black Lives Movement, the #MeToo Movement, and the deaths of George Floyd and others at the hands of police—all these have accelerated the polarization and shifting of the cultural climate in the United States. The call to end discrimination and violence and to protect marginalized communities must be heeded, for it speaks to central ills in the American landscape. At the same time, the ways these and the alarming opposing concerns (promoted by the MAGA Make America Great Again movement allied with conspiracy theorists) have been raised in blogs, the news, and social platforms have polarized the country and drawn lines in the sand as to what is morally and ethically acceptable. This has resulted in "canceling"—or at least making off limits—discussions not in agreement with some readers/viewers' ideological positions. It has also given rise to privileging western-based values in determining what is and is not appropriate to read, think, and discuss, while differently configured moral, ethical, and aesthetic frames of references are disregarded and even demonized. Black-and-white considerations of what is inappropriate, harmful to different communities, and/or morally bankrupt, without regard for the social, historical, political, and cultural circumstances in which texts arose, have co-opted discussions of every kind.

Debates and discussions that call upon participants to "choose sides," so to speak, have taken over classrooms, and my *manga* course that I taught in 2021 was no exception. The *manga* we read were put to the litmus test: Do they or do they not appropriate gay men, use underage-looking characters, objectify females, or portray unacceptable characters and behaviors? The presence of any of these resulted in the "canceling" of the *manga*—or of fixating on these elements at the expense of all else.[28] Often little attempt was made to examine how these components played out in the specific *manga* title, or to see how they developed within the specific cultural, social, and historical contexts of Japanese society. This was not true of all the students, but several vocal voices contended, for example, that the boys comics *Azumanga Daioh* is problematic because the ten-year-old female Chiyo character channels the pedophilic gaze, and because the male pervert history teacher's actions are disgusting and have no place in a *manga*. These elements took on a life of their own and overshadowed the story, which chronicles the camaraderie that develops among a group of female high schoolers who help each other through high school against all odds. No proof that Chiyo's character engages readerly pedophilia was provided, nor was there any further interrogation of the function of the history teacher within the story. As a slice-of-life *manga*, *Azumanga Daioh* depicts "real" life, which does include unsavory persons like pervert males, and a closer, more nuanced reading reveals that the male teacher is not allowed to ogle the girls—at each juncture he is ridiculed and vehemently challenged by the women teachers and girls.

The shift to assessing *manga* based on personal opinions and ideological stances marks how much times have changed, as students insert their own lived experiences and political points of view into another culture without conducting further research, questioning their own views, or examining how things/

situations/characters work within the fictional context of the *manga* in question. There is no room for parody, complexity, subversion—or a role for fiction; all is seen as black and white, and anything that does not fit into their sense of what is "correct" is simply canceled. Objections to *manga* now come from the right and in some instances from the left. But what do we do with this state of affairs? As our study of the charges of child porn, rape, and appropriation leveled against BL have shown, we must intervene. Viewers' readings are not to be dismissed out of hand—but we must insist that readers better contextualize the works, conduct nuanced examinations that allow for complex, even paradoxical readings, and come to understand the development of *manga* within specific cultural, social, and historical contexts.

We cannot shy away from studying difficult topics—they are here, and we must understand the why and the how of this. We must insist that different frames of reference be acknowledged and addressed. As Kristen Cather argues, as perverse as topics like erotic *eromanga* may be, they add to our "existing knowledge" of another culture and our "understanding of how our bodies and sexualities are shaped" (2017, 88). If we heed what is occurring in these texts, we see that there is no simple alignment of the abuser versus the abused. Children, women, and marginalized communities are not automatic victims, nor are fictionally based *manga* images of sex and violence automatically harmful and abusive.[29] Nuanced, careful readings must be conducted to rewrite the uninterrogated representations of Japan as the "Empire of Child Pornography" or "Weird" (Cather 2017, 88) that the media, global obscenity laws, the religious right, and the "extreme left" have left in their wake.

BL media have become moving targets, vilified and "canceled" for victimizing marginalized communities, but such approaches tell only half the story and circumvent the discussion of difficult topics. Literature means different things to different people and has always been read in myriad ways and by myriad individuals. BL and *manga* are no exception. Consumed and queered in multiple ways, BL have acceded to the needs and desires of readers as varied as heterosexual men and women, lesbians, bisexual men and women, and gay men whom BL has been thought to appropriate and discriminate against. Even antigay comments such as BL characters declaring that they are "not gay, but just in love with a man" have been read differently, depending on the perspective of who is consuming the work and how they are doing so. Some have parsed such content as homophobic, but others as "non-identitarian"—that is, as moving beyond the usual labels afforded them to describe their genders and sexualities (A. Williams 2015, par. 13). Thus there is no doubt that BL reinscribe mainstream heteronormativity and stereotypes of gay men, yet they also provide space for men, women, in-betweens, and even gay men to subvert, and also free themselves from, their compulsory genders and sexualities.

Many readings are in play simultaneously, so privileging one over the other is not the answer. Ultimately, once a text sees the light of day, readers will take it and run with it, making the consumers the arbiter. This may sound like eating one's cake and having it, too, but as explicated earlier, Japanese language, literature, and culture (of which *manga* may be one of the most adept practitioners) allow for interlocuters/listeners/readers to fill in the gaps in the narrative with their own stories and meanings.

I term this collaborative readership "coauthorship." As a result of this collaboration of producers, consumers, and texts, many impulses exist together and in tandem. The acceptance of one does not automatically deny another; one discourse can become normalized and take precedence for some, but fluidity, ambiguity, and oppositionals on a continuum are the preferred methods of engagement. Who, then, can represent gayness? Should identity politics hold sway and secure that privilege only for gay men, or for the straight women who traditionally produce BL *manga*? Is it permissible to consume BL in the guise of something else? Do the producers and creators of BL acknowledge their queer fans, and should they do so? The very specialized and varied contexts in which BL are produced, consumed, and read raise challenging issues involving gender, sex, sexuality, identity, and fictionality, about which much, much more research must be conducted, since BL has so provocatively opened the door to their riches.

So, does readerly queering push *The Tale of Genji* in unintended and even misplaced directions? I would argue no. Murasaki Shikibu may not have envisioned her tale transforming into an exclusive male–male world, but her narrative contains many such moments, including Genji's interaction with the brother of the provincial governor's wife and comments by male courtiers who are so struck by Genji's beauty that they find themselves musing, "If only he were a woman." *The Tale of Genji BL Anthology* seductively brings these elements to the fore, calling into question issues of gender, positionality, and desire, and ushering the *Genji* remediations into the new arena of Boys Love and *yaoi* fanzines. Readers can now queer same-sex relationships, dispense with gender and sexual identities, or explore the feminine/passive or masculine/take-charge aspects of themselves in and through the protagonists—readings that the artists may not have been aware of or necessarily targeted, and for which they may not take any responsibility. The point is not so much that the *manga* are read in particular ways, or that the protagonists secure their love interests, as that their readers are participating fully in the emotions of the moment in tandem with the protagonists, as they search together for multiple and varied subjects of love and desire and that disparate and seemingly contradictory threads can and do exist in parallel to and along a continuum with each other. Chapter 5 looks at another group of readers and showcases what they translate from the age-old tale.

Chapter 5

LADIES COMICS: SUBJECTS OF CONSUMPTION, PRODUCTION, AND DESIRE

Fragile, liquid-eyed beauties being swept off their feet by their one true love are images that charm girls-comics readers, but as consumers grow up, they yearn for more adult fare. *Rediisu komikku*, or *redikomi* (ladies comics),[1] the topic of this chapter, rise to the occasion, producing remarkable titles, including the *Genji manga* within this category. Generally catering to eighteen- through thirty-five-year-old female readers, these remediations focalize women protagonists, both narratively and visually, in exquisite close-ups at their moments of sexual ecstasy. In ladies-comics *Genji manga*, the search for Prince Charming is displaced to the seventeenth-century "love capital" Yoshiwara, jealousy and hysteria are wielded as weapons, and Genji and his cronies are pronounced rapists in a critique serialized in a Kyoto newspaper. No longer about sweet, innocent girls, ladies comics depict adult protagonists engaged in adult relationships—featuring female leads who seek agency over their lives as subjects rather than objects of their desire, consumption, and production.

This shift in focus from object to subject in ladies comics coincided with several social and political events in the 1980s and 1990s, when the bubble economy allowed less mainstreamed sectors, including women, to prosper. The passage of Japan's 1986 Equal Employment Opportunity Law leveled the labor playing field for some women, providing them with more disposable income, while a few universities instituted women studies programs (Kitamura 2008, 345–6). The 1990s feminist movement encouraged women to push back on the "good wives, wise mothers" paradigm by expressing their sexual needs and desires outside of marriage and procreation. The politically progressive 1990s featured five laws, including the Basic Law for a Gender Equal Society, creating a "state feminism" favorable to women (Kano 2011, 43–9). Feminist scholars teamed up with party leaders and bureaucrats from 1995 to 1999 to pass legislation that helped women and were also enabled by global support from the 1975 through 1985 United Nations Decade of Women and a series of World Conferences on Women in 1975, 1980, and 1985 (Kano 2011, 55, 45–6). Domestically, more women had entered the workforce and were engaged in politics since the 1980s.

In tandem with this focus on women's issues, ladies comics increased in numbers and circulation.[2] Ladies-comics *Genji manga* followed suit and were bolstered in the 2000s by the millennium celebrations of the tale despite a backlash against the liberalization of women's issues in the new millennium.³ Many of the titles centered on the women relegating Genji to a "mechanism" through which the women express, explore, and enjoy their sexuality in safe fictional spaces. The women protagonists also harness "negative" female traits, such as hysteria and jealousy, to establish their subjectivity. Mainstream (patriarchal) society in the Heian and subsequent periods deemed these dangerous and destructive, because women in these states disrupted and challenged male control. In *The Tale of Genji* Rokujō famously uses jealous rage to push back on society, but in ladies comics other women, such as Murasaki, also get into the act. Subjecthood in fictional space, if not in real life, is extended to readers as well. Taking advantage of *manga*-reading strategies, ladies-comics creators provide collaborative space for readers to use their emotional and psychic energies to fill out the experiences unfolding on the page. In this way readers come to participate in agonies, ecstasies, and rejections alongside the protagonists. Much as we found in girls comics, the collaborative, participatory readers come not simply to care and identify with the protagonists but to "become" them, "performing" in tandem with them as if they, too, are undergoing the sting of unrequited love, the rapture of fulfillment, and the torment of abandonment and rejection.

In both girls-comics and ladies-comics *Genji manga*, Genji remains important as the source of sexual bliss. But the performative space afforded to ladies-comics readers differs from that offered to their girls-comics counterparts in one marked way: unlike in girls comics, where the objects of desire are men and men occupy much of the frame times, in ladies comics it is all about the women. Of course, Prince Charming is best if he is the fabulously handsome Genji, whose sexual attractiveness and prominence rival no other, but in ladies comics it is the encounter itself—the chance for the women to give themselves up to the pleasure of the sexual encounter without guilt, fear, or worry—that is the goal for protagonists and readers alike.

Early on, ladies comics' creation of subject positions through highly sexualized depictions resulted in their being labeled erotic and pornographic (Schodt 1996, 124). But as the category grew, it introduced alternative lifestyles for women beyond that of being housewives, and entertained not just love and romance but topics such as legal, child care, and work advice and friendship, mother-in-law, medical, and sex issues (Ogi 2003, 783, 780; Ito 2009, 116). At present, ladies comics constitute three types—(1) romance/fantasy, (2) drama, and (3) the sexually erotic.⁴ Romance/fantasy *redikomi* target younger women and focus on the protagonists' finding their man. The lead figure falls in love, undergoes obstacles but ultimately overcomes them, and finds happiness. The drama subcategory features working women, wives, and mothers engaging in emotionally uplifting experiences, while others explore darker themes of mother- and daughter-in-law relationships, domestic violence, and adultery. The last subcategory—the sexually graphic, hard-core titles—constitutes only 20 percent of the market, and protagonists in these narratives are often exposed to incest, oral and anal sex, bondage, self-eroticism, and voyeurism.⁵ Although the categories are fluid and can blend together, finding all three residing in one title is rare (Ito, pers. comm.).

Establishing Subjects of Desire, Consumption, and Production

Six of the eight *Genji manga* ladies comics examined in this section reside in the romance/fantasy subcategory, with drama subcategory influence, while two gesture toward hard-core ladies. The titles constitute two groups: "Enacting *Genji* Ladies Comics" and "Pivoting *Genji* Ladies Comics." Anchoring the first group, Ide Chikae's *Genji monogatari: uruwashi no karan* (*The Tale of Genji: Elegant Dissolution*) serves as a baseline for the category. She focuses on the women characters and "grows up" their relationships with Genji into adult encounters, complete with adult highs and lows, wielding "negative" hysteria and jealousy to establish the women as subjects of consumption and production. Next, in her *Genji monogatari* (*The Tale of Genji*), Maki Miyako depicts women fighting to determine their own fates in the midst of political struggles that use them as marriage pawns and make life hard for their menfolk as well. The last two authors in this group of four—Teradate Kazuko in her *Yōhen genji monogatari* (*The Tale of Genji Mutated*), and Kira in her *Genji monogatari* (*The Tale of Genji*)—focus on the young Murasaki as she develops her subjecthood as an adult and as a young woman, respectively.

The titles in the second group, "Pivoting *Genji* Ladies Comics," stay true to the tenets of ladies comics but focalize love, desire, and subjecthood in innovative ways. Hazuki Tsuyako unabashedly eroticizes her *Manga gurimu dōwa: enbun genji monogatari* (*Erotic Talk: The Tale of Genji Grimm Fairy Tale Comics*), centering on Genji's aggressive sexual bedding of his stepmother Fujitsubo, and Fujitsubo's lady-in-waiting doing the same with her young lover. Bandoh Iruka's *Manga gurimu dōwa: kuruwa genji* (*Grimm Fairy Tales: Prostitute Quarters of Genji*) transposes the tale to the seventeenth-century courtesan world of Yoshiwara and compellingly critiques the commodified love sold to the highest bidder. Abandoning a contiguous narrative, the third creator in this group is Sakurazawa Mai, who utilizes different artists to zoom in on individual women and their fashioning of "different Genjis" based on their needs and desires in her *Genji koi monogatari* (*The Love Tale of Genji*). In yet another move, Takenaka Ranko introduces a Lady Manga to critique Genji and the Heian period in her *Heian no torendi dorama genji monogatari mangachō* (*The Heian Trendy Drama: The Tale of Genji Manga Notebook*).[6]

Enacting Genji Ladies Comics: Focalizing Subjects of Jealousy, Abandonment, and Unrequited Love

Powerfully focalizing the women, Ide Chikae's[7] (2008) *The Tale of Genji: Elegant Dissolution* provides the baseline for what constitutes a romance/fantasy work in the ladies-comics category. Not shy about nudity, Ide portrays in adult terms the sexual and erotic desires of the women characters from their own point of view. Her purpose is to provide her readers a safe, beautifully constructed space where they can indulge their sexual fantasies with the man of their dreams. Ide's *Genji* also places the women protagonists (and readers) front and center, making them less objects responding to Genji's sexual advances than subjects of their own desire. Of course, Heian sexual mores did not allow women to initiate sexual encounters, but in the moment of consummation it is the women who take ownership. Thus it is their perspective, their enjoyment and fulfillment that take center stage—all done in a gorgeous and sumptuous drawing style that brings out the beauty and elegance and subjecthood of the female protagonists.

Ide's *Genji* story, then, is about the women in it, and they love deeply and richly in the arms of their beloved Genji. In particular, the encounters between Genji and his stepmother Fujitsubo, and between Genji and his young love Murasaki, are marked by extravagant lovemaking that focalizes the women's enjoyment and pleasure over the course of several pages. What is striking about these moments is that the women submit to Genji's advances not to give in to him but to obtain erotic freedom for themselves and their readers. Much as the young woman in *Fifty Shades of Grey* becomes the submissive sexual partner of a dominant man, so Ide's protagonists engage their male partners not to be dominated but to enact their desires, with their female audiences following suit. Thus in the encounter between Fujitsubo and Genji, Genji is the initiator but not the focus. Rather, Genji functions more as a means through which Fujitsubo enacts her desire, so that it is Fujitsubo who fills the frame, reveling in her pleasure as a subject and not as an object of Genji's desires. In Figure 5.1, for instance, it is her full face that is visible to readers (in contrast to Genji's profile), beckoning readers to experience her rapture with her.

For Ide's women, then, the ultimate joy lies in being loved—or made love to even once—by the supreme heartthrob of the times, Shining Prince Genji. Ladies fall all over themselves to be with him and are willing to engage in sex anywhere, as is the case with Fujitsubo's lady-in-waiting, who offers herself as a substitute for Fujitsubo in the garden outside of Fujitsubo's rooms. Others will give up their lives in Genji's stead, as Yūgao does when Rokujō's living spirit comes to attack Genji for abandoning her. Genji is a wildly satisfying lover and a gallant hero for so many. He also causes much grief and pain, but ironically, these moments, too, enable the production of female subjectivity.

Abandonment, intense desire, and jealousy place women in untenable positions, but they also spur them to action, so "unbecoming" female traits of strong emotion are seen giving women agency. In Volume 1, for example, Genji has been drugged and brought, unconscious, to Aoi's rooms by her brother Tō no Chūjō. Aoi thinks that Genji has passed out drunk and is embarrassed that she must go to these lengths to make love to her husband, but she takes charge and initiates the lovemaking. While Aoi is on top of him, Genji awakens, crying out to her to stop, but to no avail, as Aoi climaxes. To retain Aoi's positionality as a "good girl," the scene ends with Aoi feeling humiliated at what she has done. Nevertheless, in this episode Aoi acts upon her desires and gives Genji some of his own medicine: she is on top, literally and figuratively, and has her way with him (Ide 2008, 1:338–9). When I asked Ide about this scene, she explained that it was important to portray Aoi as a woman who did not hide her jealousy and who

Figure 5.1 Fujitsubo is captured at the height of her sexual pleasure with a solicitous Genji looking on. Ide Chikae, *The Tale of Genji: Elegant Dissolution*, 298–9. Copyright © Ide Chikae 2008. Courtesy of Ide Chikae.

expressed her true feelings in ways that spoke to and for all women who had been wronged (Ide, pers. comm.).

Another woman who feels very much wronged by Genji is his lover Rokujō, and she takes her jealousy to extremes. As happens in other remediations, Rokujō leaves her body as a living spirit that attacks and kills Genji's lovers. The vengeful spirit lashes out at Genji's wife Aoi for usurping not only Rokujō's spot along the Aoi Festival procession route but also her place in Genji's affections, by bearing his son (Ide 2008, 2:124–8). The depiction of the ferociousness of the spirit's attack is matched by few other *manga*, bringing to the fore the frightening consequences of a woman scorned. And Rokujō's fury knows no bounds, for her apparition takes the unprecedented step of attacking Genji in another incident (Ide 2008, 1:190–2). Genji draws his sword but can do no more as Rokujō renders him unconscious (Ide 2008, 1:192)—and establishes her woman-scorned subject position.

A page-turner, Ide's *Genji* sits at the center of what constitutes ladies comics. Spotlighting in an adult register the life concerns and experiences of her protagonists, Ide focalizes her characters, drawing them large, with almost no background detail, so that readers can take up all points of view—fluidly becoming the women who love and are loved by Genji, but also becoming the Genji who loves and is loved by them. Fostering coauthor, in-group readers, Ide's *Genji* encourages readers to transcend the difference in time and place and live/share the experiences of the protagonists as if they were their own. For Ide, portraying the depth of her women characters' love and desire without reservation is key, entailing a sensitive yet graphically realistic and hard-hitting depiction of the high and low points, the joys and agonies of life, and the sexual desires and fulfillment, not just psychologically and emotionally but physically as well. And her portrayal of Rokujō aptly embodies what makes for a successful *manga*. In Rokujō's relationship with Genji and her transformation in and out of being a living spirit, Rokujō runs the gamut of obsessive, compulsive love, uncontrollable jealousy, unbridled competition, hurt pride, an unfathomably deep desire for revenge, utter shame and humiliation, and deep regret for what she has done. Few characters fit so well into Ide's formula—or are so well suited to undergoing Ide's transformation of girls-comics *kawaii* cute objects of desire into ladies-comics subjects of consumption and production who have agency and power.

Serialized in 1986 and published in book form in 1988, our next *manga*, Maki Miyako's[8] *The Tale of Genji*, is the earliest work in the ladies-comics category. As such, it takes to heart its mandate to provide adult fare, and centers on the trials and tribulations of women inhabiting a patriarchal, highly stratified world. It also reaches beyond the women and includes court intrigues, political power grabs, and townscapes and peoplescapes of the period. What come alive on the pages of Maki's *Genji* are not only the intimate sexual encounters between lovers and the agonies suffered by the women but also the exuberance of children at play, the buzz of courtiers plotting the demise of their enemies, and the bright, infectious energy of carpenters at work on Genji's new mansion, as we see in Figure 5.2.

Nonetheless, as the first example of how ladies comics "grew up" their young female protagonists, Maki's six-volume remediation portrays women living under the harsh realities of the patriarchal, polygyny one-man, many-wives social system, in which romantic relationships are conducted not for love but to traffic women as erotic objects for male/family political gain. All seem hopeless under these insurmountable conditions that the realistic *gekiga* style so effectively evokes. Originally more the purview of young men readers, *gekiga* often critique the sordid underbelly of industrialized landscapes (S. Suzuki 2013, 54–5, Kinsella 2000, 24–7; Nagayama 2021),[9] so *The Tale of Genji* is a far cry from the gritty, somber cityscapes Tatsumi Yoshihiro (the inventor of the term *gekiga*) utilizes to capture the lives of the disenfranchised in postwar Japan (S. Suzuki 2013, 58–60). But in Maki's hands the tale is transposed into unflinching, realistic peoplescapes of unhappy marriages, political power struggles, and vexingly difficult relationships—all the while depicting the nobility of the downtrodden and of the women who fight to become subjects in a society organized to keep them objects.

Maki masterfully portrays her women protagonists—primary and secondary[10]—engaged in a valiant struggle for subjecthood. She unerringly places them in trying gender, political, and social realities that force them to "prostitute" themselves to sire imperial heirs and forge powerful alliances for their male relatives, which often result in abandonment, jealousy, and unfulfillment. By tapping into these negative "female" emotions, Maki brings to life men's worst nightmare—a powerful Rokujō who breaks free and challenges male control. Angered that Aoi is about to bear

Figure 5.2 A vibrant peoplescape of carpenters at work on Genji's fabled Rokujō Mansion, filled with their lively discussion about Genji's plans for his new abode and two of its future inhabitants in the foreground. Maki Miyako, *The Tale of Genji*, 5: 224–5. Copyright © Miyako Maki/Leijisha 1997–8. Courtesy of Maki Miyako/Leijisha.

Genji's child, Rokujō vents her displeasure, turning a peony black with the blood she draws digging her nails into her palm (Maki 1997–8, 4:31–2). Before she is fully aware of what is happening to her, Rokujō turns into a malevolent spirit at Aoi's bedside (Maki 1997–8, 4:49–51), transforming into a deadly being whom the male constituency can no longer fully banish or control.

Maki also fashions other ways in which women produce subjecthood. For instance, she has two rivals for Genji's attention, Murasaki and the Akashi Lady, overcome their rivalry and forge an alliance in the heart of Genji's fiefdom, his Rokujō-in mansion. The two women are in love with the same man and should be at odds, but both independently realize that they are but pawns in Genji's quest for power. To best the rival Kokiden faction, Genji must install his daughter as empress, requiring both women to do the unthinkable: the Akashi Lady must relinquish her daughter, and Murasaki must raise her rival's offspring as her own. The Akashi Lady laments that this "ask" amounts to "only winter, women's winters … for Murasaki and for me" (Maki 1997–8, 5:284–5). But Maki turns these winters into spring—as the two women work together to take charge of their lives. Murasaki raises the princess, but when the princess enters court as the imperial consort, Murasaki relinquishes the honor of accompanying the princess to her biological mother, Lady Akashi.

Facing seemingly insurmountable odds, Maki's female protagonists struggle to position themselves as stewards of their own fates in a patriarchal society where men control their lives—mirroring the circumstances of Japanese women, and hence of Maki's readers. To "sell" or promote her protagonists' attainment of subjecthood under such dire circumstances, Maki imbues them with determination, agency, and strength. She also constructs them as attractive, consumable, and relatable, so that her readers can identify with them, care for them, and share in their struggles to attain subjecthood. *Manga* are very adept at creating readerly engagement, but Maki marshals slice-of-life strategies to ensure that, despite the separation of a millennium, audiences can participate in the Heian world as if it were their own. She mounts "warm and fuzzy" places and experiences that transcend time and place—children at play, people toiling at tasks of building houses, preparing meals, making love, living and dying. This establishes a home where "there is no need to explain oneself" and where readers can engage, connect, and consume without reserve (Kondo 1997, 189), so that the everydayness of life is forged into a "collective memory," a nostalgic, shared "psychological realism" (Kondo 1997, 195), creating an in-group invested in the narrative. Provided with special access, readers take the next step and become coauthors "transposing people whom they know onto the characters," individualizing and tailoring the stories for personal consumption and engagement (Wang 2013, 36, 39–40).[11]

At the end of the day, Maki's *The Tale of Genji* is a *gekiga* slice-of-life narrative that focuses on the women characters and depicts their efforts to craft themselves as subjects of production, consumption, and desire. Yet Maki's coverage is more evenly distributed than that of other ladies comics because its male and female Heian inhabitants—with their loves, hates, political intrigues, and affairs of the heart—are seen through a realistic *gekiga* lens. Maki makes the period come alive by depicting a wide range of characters going about their daily lives, thus drawing in her readers to care about her protagonists and grooming them to become in-group, coauthor readers who jointly share and participate in the protagonists' experiences as subjects of consumption and production.

Maki's *Tale of Genji* reveals a great deal about its male characters as well, Genji in particular. The *manga*'s emphasis on the political, its showcasing of the specificities of court life, and its care in presenting the thoughts of Genji and other men, as well as the women, point to its *gekiga* political, social roots. In the end Maki does not romanticize the Heian period: her tale ends with an ominous view of Genji's pinnacle of success, his Rokujō-in mansion. Genji has attained the highest of ranks, Honorary Emperor Emeritus, and acquired great wealth, but many of the women in his household have left his fabled Rokujō-in, and it lies freezing in the moonlight, the autumn wind blowing (Maki 1997–8, 6:284), presaging a less-than-kind world for the aging Genji.

Maki Miyako and Ide Chikae thus established ground zero for ladies comics, using readerly collaborative, participatory, and performative coauthorship, and "female" jealousy and hysteria, to foster readerly agency in tandem with the agency they offer their protagonists. The last two artists in the "Enacting *Genji* Ladies

Comics" group, created by Teradate Kazuko and Kira, also privilege the female perspective and the construction of subjecthood, albeit using different strategies. Both center on one figure, Murasaki, the child-woman raised by Genji to be his ideal wife. Teradate marshals jealousy to "mutate" the kind and gentle Murasaki from the tale into a conniving and jealous spouse who is a master at managing her rivals and keeping Genji all to herself. In contrast, Kira gives Murasaki agency through a coming-of-age story—depicting a sweet and innocent child-woman on the cusp of entering adult love, life, and tribulation.

Published in 2001–2, the title of Teradate Kazuko's four-volume *The Tale of Genji Mutated* signals the "wicked" nature of her remediation. Originally appearing in 2000–2 in *The World's Scariest Children Tales*, Teradate's series eschews the lush beauty of Ide's remediation and features a harsher, more photo-realistic style that is replicated in its adult narrative content and depiction of sexual encounters. Like other ladies comics, it dispenses with the contiguous narrative and mainly centers on the fortunes of one character, although each chapter is named for a different woman.[12] Graphic and dark sexual encounters[13] abound, although they lessen in Volumes 3 and 4, in which Genji is less successful in consummating his relationships, as he ages or as impediments arise.

Equally formidable is Teradate's evocation of the women's jealousy. The most startling examples are found in her portrayal of Murasaki, as she schemes against her rivals for "possession" of Genji. Depicted as Genji's thoughtful, kind, and long-suffering unofficial wife in the eleventh-century tale and in other *manga*, here Murasaki is transformed into a possessive, exceedingly jealous woman. Even as a young child she precociously asks Genji to make her his wife: her jealousy is so intense that she leaves her body as a living spirit to spy on the coupling of Genji and his principal wife Aoi (Teradate 2001–2, 1:31). This sets Murasaki upon a lifelong path of jealous rage and exacting revenge against any woman who comes between her and her beloved Genji. So intense is her desire that, contrary to the tale, Murasaki appears at Aoi's bedside as a living spirit to make her suffer, revels in her rival Fujitsubo's demise, and dies leaving Genji with the mistaken impression that she had a relationship with his son Yūgiri (Teradate 2001–2, 1:38–9; 3:33; 4:194–5).

As unladylike and vindictive as Murasaki's parting shot at Genji appears to be, she acquires agency through such moments—and through doing battle with formidable foes such as Fujitsubo and Akashi. Fujitsubo's rank, her similarity to Genji's mother, and her bearing Genji a son place Murasaki at a disadvantage, as does Akashi's position as a mother. Not to be outdone, Murasaki takes matters into her own hands, skillfully dispatching them both. Rokujō's all-consuming jealousy, which results in Yūgao and Aoi's deaths, however, poses a different kind of challenge. To indulge in jealousy and revenge as Rokujō does would be the ultimate subject-position builder, but it would also mean social suicide, so Murasaki exacts revenge in her own way, by intimating that she had a relationship with Genji's son Yūgiri (Teradate 2001–2, 4:193). Genji—and Teradate's readers—are shocked, and it is only after Murasaki's death that Genji recognizes her as "the one he was seeking," thus finally providing her with the subjecthood that so evaded her in life.

The drawing style and narrative of *The Tale of Genji Mutated* attest to the adult interests and expectations of Teradate's audience, so Genji is no longer the ideal handsome male who fulfills the romantic aspirations of young lovers. Closer to real life, he represents the unattainable beloved who causes unmitigated anguish. Yet Genji also provides the height of ecstasy and erotic fulfillment, for he unabashedly services the women sexually. This does not make Teradate's *Genji* pornographic, but it provides sexual gratification for the women characters and for its primarily adult female audiences. The transformation—the *yōhen*—of Murasaki from a sweet and innocent girl into a vengeful, jealous woman, all for the love of an unattainable object of desire, enacts the cost of loving. It also allows those who have suffered the agony of unrequited love to give full reign to their jealousy, to vent revenge and havoc in ways not permitted in polite company—and in the process constitute themselves as powerful subjects of consumption and identification, if only within the space of perusing the *manga*.

The last title in this grouping, Kira's 2005–6 *The Tale of Genji*, adopts Teradate's strategy of focalizing Murasaki but does so with a twist. Murasaki is not vicious or manipulative but a sweet and innocent child-woman who, with the help of Genji's brother-in-law and friend Tō no Chūjō, performs the unimaginable feat of turning Genji into a better man—and lover. As a coming-of-age narrative of a young woman, Kira's work is actually for a slightly younger demographic located in the interstice between girls comics and ladies comics. It was, however, serialized in the ladies-comics magazine *YOU*, which ostensibly makes it a ladies-comics *Genji*, in much the same way that *Patalliro Genji!*'s serialization in a *shōjo* magazine makes it a girls-comics *Genji*. The focus on the female protagonists and their construction as subjects of consumption and production also make it so, as does the adult treatment of the encounters between Genji and his ladies. The lack of readings for the Chinese characters for all but the Heian terms is further proof of its adult status. But the storyline, the characterization, and especially the drawing style give Kira's *Tale of Genji* a very *shōjo*-esque look. A cheerful, naïve, and fetching Murasaki, a pretty-boy Genji, and a very upbeat, cute, and friendly Tō no Chūjō (with a pug nose!) appear to belie its ladies-comics categorization. The other personas, including the "older woman" Rokujō, are also *kawaii* cute. With elements of both girls comics and ladies comics, it would be best to categorize Kira's remediation as a girls/ladies hybrid, a pre-ladies-comics *manga* that establishes female subjecthood through a coming-of-age story rather than through an expression of sexual freedom and desire.

Kira expertly maneuvers through these parameters. In accordance with ladies comics, Murasaki is at the center as subject matter and narrating voice. Thus she appears in virtually all thirteen episodes and the two additional chapters, conceived as an innocent, pretty girl who wants to grow up and be beautiful. She is refreshingly straightforward and speaks her mind, operating as a foil to expose the artifice of the adults. A child developing into a young woman, Murasaki situates herself as the perfect young-ladies-comics heroine (see Ogi 2003, 791) seeking love, but not girls-comics true love or ladies-comics sexual fulfillment. In the tradition of magazines like *Young You*, *Young Rose*, and *Feel Young*, Kira's *Genji* contains some sexuality but maintains the *shōjo* taboo against the portrayal of graphic sexuality. But per the conventions of ladies comics, it also embeds Murasaki in the social, cultural, and political realities of the day. In sum, it maintains the *shōjo* propensity to dream about love but also calls for adherence to adult social obligations (Ogi 2003, 791–6).

As a young ladies' heroine, Kira's Murasaki seeks to capture the heart of the most-sought-after man at court, but using less grown-up methods. Since this is a difficult path to tread, Kira must also ensure that Genji's philandering does not destroy the *shōjo*-esque aspect of the *manga*. Thus Kira has Genji sow his wild oats with his wife Aoi, his young middle-ranking lover Yūgao, and his lover-turned-avenging-spirit Rokujō before Murasaki makes her appearance. Thereafter, the game is to have Genji remain true to Murasaki and Murasaki alone. To enable such a tale, Genji's attraction to and interactions with other women are downplayed or even expunged, as in the case of his relationship with the Akashi Lady. As a result, Genji is stylized as a kinder, gentler, more thoughtful lover and not as a Don Juan lover who has his way with women. He is solicitous and does not force himself on Murasaki, waiting patiently to consummate their relationship until she is ready—which, unlike the tale, happens after his return from exile in Suma, making his abstinence in Akashi a powerful profession of his love for her. Throughout, he is also open with Murasaki, telling her everything, and even declaring that he will not marry the Third Princess because of the anguish it will cost Murasaki. And, as a measure of Murasaki's "adult" subject position, she encourages him to do so, citing the emperor's ill health and the price Genji would pay for disobeying him.

As Murasaki enters the murky waters of adult love, she finds that Genji's relationship to Fujitsubo is not simply that of stepmother and stepson (Kira 2005–6, 4:46–7). She struggles with the knowledge that Genji may love her only because she looks like Fujitsubo (Kira 2005–6, 4:67–70). Murasaki's distress, and the cost of her coming to terms with the adult consequences of loving Genji, are delineated through visual images with little text. An even more powerful moment depicts Murasaki witnessing the arrival of the Third Princess as Genji's new wife (Kira 2005–6, 4:120–1). A two-page spread with no text portrays Genji carrying the princess in his arms. No words are necessary to express the complex feelings in play, as the princess's slightly embarrassed but coquettish visage is juxtaposed against the darker, half-hidden figure of Murasaki viewing the scene from a distance. In both these instances we see Murasaki "grow up" and increase her stature right before our eyes, as she deals with new challenges.

Kira draws her *Genji* in simple black lines against white backgrounds, with just the hair, men's *eboshi* hats, and a few furnishings inked in. This is paired with flat, expressionless faces. But as the story progresses, Kira utilizes these sparsely drawn facial features to convey complex emotions, bringing to life her *Tale of Genji*. A bright, spunky young Murasaki who grows up but retains her signature outbursts until the end (accompanied by a caricatured, cute Tō no Chūjō) gives Kira's comics the air of a *shōjo manga*, but one that operates as a young ladies comics within the interstices of *shōjo* and adulthood by constructing subjecthood in nonsexualized ways.

Pivoting Genji Ladies Comics: Empowering Graphic Sex, Different Genjis, and Feminist Critiques

The female protagonists we have discussed thus far secure their agency by energizing their "negative" female emotionality and challenging the patriarchy, but they operate within societal conventions. The women protagonists in this section forge their subjecthood in unconventional ways, pivoting the category in the process. Hazuki Tsuyako's *Erotic Talk*, for one, uses eroticism to establish agency for her protagonists. Bandoh Iruka's *Prostitute Quarters of Genji* is marketed as "Adult women fairy tales" (2010–11, 1:254), but rather than hardcore sex scenes, it depicts women engaging on their own terms in an economy where sex and love are commodified. Some sell sex to get revenge, others refuse to abide by its rules altogether. In *The Love Tale of Genji*, Sakurazawa Mai features six vignettes, each with a different female lead drawn by a different artist, to map out how the characters of the women dictate the contours of their relationship with Genji, and even his look and feel. In *The Heian Trendy Drama: The Tale of Genji Manga Notebook*, Takenaka Ranko comes up with an innovative scheme. Male courtiers have their way with women in the *Genji* story, but in the outer narrative frame, author Murasaki Shikibu and the ladies-in-waiting critique Genji and the patriarchal Heian period from a twenty-first-century perspective supplied by a stand-in for the artist, Lady Manga.

Turning to Hazuki Tsuyako's one-volume work, appropriately entitled *Erotic Talk: The Tale of Genji*, we find that it is composed of five stories and one addendum (plus an unrelated short story). Published in the *Grimm Fairy Tales* series in 2010, it first appeared in the 2004–5 *The Experience of Love: Special Deluxe* ladies magazine, and has all the markings of the category of erotic ladies comics.[14] The scenes depict women having their robes ripped off and their backs arched, bare breasts thrust forward, engaging in sex acts. Some cry out, "Stop! Stop!"—in earnest or not entirely so, reminiscent of the BL Genji/Rokujō encounter discussed in Chapter 4 (Hazuki 2010, 30, 72, 138–9). This no doubt adds to the intense, frenzied, bordering-on-violence aspect of these portrayals. A closer look at the stories, however, reveals that these scenarios are constructed to enable "good girls" to embrace the moment without guilt and indulge in sexual pleasures usually reserved for "bad girls." Some viewers, as noted in Chapter 4, would read these encounters as abusive and humiliating to women, but they enact phantasy consumption sites that are located in safe 2D spaces where women experiment with and enjoy sex, and that have been carefully crafted by the artists to divorce readers from the harsh realities of everyday life (see the introduction for further discussion).

In Hazuki's remediation, the two female leads—Genji's stepmother Fujitsubo and her lady-in-waiting Ō no myōbu—enact their sexual desires in graphically explicit sex scenes. To enable Fujitsubo, consort to the emperor, to remain a "good girl" while giving her sexual desires free rein, Ō no myōbu initiates the meeting, and Genji "forces" himself on Fujitsubo. The encounters are powerfully and explicitly rendered, a consumable spectacle over several pages in which Fujitsubo unabashedly expresses her pleasure and fulfillment (Hazuki 2010, 40-2, 74-7, 140-2). "Made" to do it, Fujitsubo nonetheless owns her pleasure. In an even more subjecthood-creating move, she chooses motherhood and protecting her imperial son and "dumps" Genji—marking Fujitsubo's control over her destiny.

As highly charged as the Fujitsubo/Genji encounters are, the *manga* would not be R-rated ladies if it ended there. Hazuki adds another tale out of whole cloth. Not of high status, Ō no myōbu has more latitude to follow her sexual desires, providing ample opportunity to eroticize the *manga*. Ō no myōbu readily succumbs to Genji's seductions and then indulges herself with a servant boy, Seo, who is so smitten with her that he leaves the palace to live out his days "servicing" her. As Hazuki puts it, she took great liberties in fashioning Ō no myōbu, who had almost no footprint in the Murasaki's tale. In Hazuki's hands Ō no myōbu becomes a "smart," "resourceful," "beautiful" woman (2010, 252–3) who creates her own subject position by seeking sex where she may. Ō no myōbu seduces the shy, (puppy) love-struck, younger Seo, even mocking him that his "tool" is small (Hazuki 2010, 125–7)—and taking over the initiator position usually reserved for men in comics. Fujitsubo is the central figure and Ō no myōbu functions as her foil, but Ō no myōbu develops a subject positionality that rivals that of her mistress.

Ostensibly a *manga* about the eleventh-century tale, the addendum story appended at the end of the volume has no basis in the tale and portrays Seo pursuing Ō no myōbu. Playing well to readers' fantasies of being passionately courted by a young "ripped" stud, the episode opens in dramatic fashion, with Seo searching for Ō no myōbu. She is asleep in her home but hears a noise and goes out to investigate, only to have her breasts grabbed from behind. Shocked at the identity of those hands, she is overcome by Seo's passion, and he beds her in short order (Hazuki 2010, 173–6). She also seduces Seo later in the episode (Hazuki 2010, 198–202) and reacts positively when Seo steals into her room, fondles and licks her breasts, and masturbates on her stomach on yet another occasion (Hazuki 2010, 182–4).

In the end Hazuki's *Genji* remediation is a tale of two strong women who know what they want and how to get it. In the main narratives, lavish, sexually explicit scenes between Genji and Fujitsubo take center stage. It is Ō no myōbu's presence that enables Fujitsubo to make overt her desires and jealousies in ways that Heian and contemporary Japanese mores would not readily allow, but Ō no myōbu also indulges her own desires in the addendum. In contrast to the women, the men are less fully conceived. Genji is frivolous, rather shallow, and largely driven by a powerful libido; the emperor is kind and forgiving but clueless; Seo is young, powerfully built, and sexualized primarily to fulfill Ō no myōbu's erotic desires. The focus, then, is on the women—it is their needs and their pleasures that are at the center—and the men serve as means through which these desires are fulfilled. Erotic ladies comics are produced by women for women to promote erotic enjoyment and foster sexual arousal, and Hazuki remediates her *Genji* into a vehicle that positions characters and readers to pleasure themselves as subjects of highly eroticized sexual consumption and production.

The second title, Bandoh Iruka's *Prostitute Quarters of Genji*, published in 2008–11 in the same *Grimm Fairy Tale Comics* series as Hazuki's transposition, is set in the seventeenth-century licensed quarters of Yoshiwara, so we would expect sex scene after sex scene, but Bandoh has other plans. Sex is still the name of the game, but Bandoh dwells not on the moments of sexual pleasure but on the cost to the inhabitants residing within an economy where love and sex are commodified.[15] These moments also establish subjecthood. The women use their commodified positionalities to climb to the top of the sexual food chain—and gain revenge. They also find ways to escape Yoshiwara's grasp, or destroy its hold over them. By transposing the setting, the protagonists, and the situations of the eleventh-century tale to the licensed quarters, Bandoh also creates a *mitate*[16] visual puzzle and calls upon readers in the know to figure out who the players are, which events correspond to which *Genji* happenings, and what Tokugawa texts are being elicited to fill out the contours of her *Genji*.

Bandoh's transposition of the *Genji* to New Yoshiwara is bold and innovative, and from the outset she makes it very clear that it does not provide sexual freedom for the female courtesans or their guests. Following the precepts of the seventeenth-century New Yoshiwara,[17] Bandoh surrounds her Yoshiwara with walls with only one access point, so that the clientele (merchants and samurai) and the courtesans remain under tight control. She replicates Yoshiwara's ways of conducting business, so courtesans are sold to brothels and must buy out their contracts and cover their living and clothing expenses. A rigid hierarchy is in place, and rules of conduct for courtesans and clients are carefully monitored. Any breach—such as escaping for the courtesans, or "buying" one courtesan and sleeping with another for the client—results in stiff penalties, seeming to leave little room for female agency. Yoshiwara's commodified love economy also mirrors the Heian use of "love" and romance for political and economic gain, and Bandoh positions the *Genji* protagonists accordingly: Gen or Genya, the object of desire for many women, is Genji's surrogate; Fujitsubo, Aoi, Rokujō, and Yūgao remain similarly named but are now courtesans in this brave new world, commensurate with their ranks in Murasaki Shikibu's tale. Aoi and Rokujō, as daughters of imperial family members in the *Genji*, are *oiran*, the highest-ranking courtesans, while Yūgao is an apprentice geisha.

Reconfigured as courtesans serving the sexual needs of male customers, the Gen/Genya women enact erotically charged sex scenes, but an examination of one of the most provocative reveals that something else is afoot. In the opening pages of the *manga* Gen is summoned to "do his job," and he fondles and stimulates a nude Aoi—who begs him to stop (Bandoh 2010–11, 1:11–15). It looks as if Genji is forcing himself upon a defenseless Aoi, and if the mini-arc ended here, that would indeed be the case. Yet Gen is very solicitous in the aftermath. He is there when Aoi awakens, wipes away her tears, and even pours her tea, which she bats away in anger. She slaps him across the face—all of which Gen takes in stride. Undaunted, he lays out the stark reality of Yoshiwara: that Aoi has been sold to the brothel by her merchant husband and must make the best of it. Providing her with the skills to succeed, Gen challenges her to "beat the system" and become

Figure 5.3 On the right page Aoi walks in procession to the teahouse as a top-ranking courtesan in full regalia, and on the left page she catches the eye of Gen, the Genji stand-in and most sought-after man of Yoshiwara. Bandoh Iruka, *Prostitute Quarters of Genji*, 1: 40–1. Copyright © 2010. Courtesy of Bandoh Iruka and Bunkasha.

an *oiran* courtesan, the highest subject position within Yoshiwara—which Aoi attains, exacting revenge on her errant husband (Bandoh 2010–11, 1:18–19, 20–5).

Bandoh's task is to tell the stories of the women—and she depicts them at the mercy of Yoshiwara's commodification of love, but also attaining sexual fulfillment and subjecthood. We witness the trauma of Aoi's sale to Yoshiwara and her ensuing sexual initiation into the courtesan world, but also her rise to top courtesan, as we see in Figure 5.3.

Ironically, the red-nosed princess surrogate, Sue, escapes Yoshiwara's avarice because of her unattractive exterior, which Bandoh intimates hides an inner, more important, honest personality (2010–11, 2:125–7). But many are not so lucky, as they are flogged for running away or forced to commit double suicide to be with their lovers (Bandoh 2010–11, 2:80–6; 3:123). The most riveting storyline involves Rokujō. The pleasure quarters is *the* site for the pursuit of love/objects of desire, but only in play and never in earnest, for falling in love and pursuing one man would destroy the very sexual, economic foundations upon which Yoshiwara is built. Such exclusivity would result in women not doing their "jobs" as objects of desire for any man willing to pay for their services—something which the licensed quarters cannot tolerate and against which many protagonists rail to no avail. Not surprisingly, Rokujō pushes back in extravagant fashion, losing her high rank in Yoshiwara but securing her own personhood in the process.

The object of Rokujō's desire is, of course, Gen, and, although she has been banned from visiting him after he has been wounded, she goes to him anyway (Bandoh 2010–11, 3:127–30). For her disobedience, she is forced to undergo the humiliating punishment of squatting over a bowl of water into which her private parts are reflected (Bandoh 2010–11, 3:146–7). Customers pay to look into the bowl of water, and Rokujō's punishment continues for three days. When Gen arrives on scene and disavows any feelings for her, she pours hot water on her left eye and face, effectively ending her career as an *oiran* (Bandoh 2010–11, 3:199–200). An unexpected resolution to say the least, yet the story does not end there: Rokujō is demoted—rather than killed, as was the convention—and escorted by Gen to her new brothel in the backwaters of Yoshiwara.

In the last scene, Rokujō turns toward the reader in a close-up profile—her forehead and left eye bandaged. Disfigured and sans her *oiran* finery, Rokujō displays an almost frightening kind of dignity that far outshines the beauty she possessed as a top courtesan (Bandoh 2010–11, 3:210–12). By damaging her face—stripping away the outward glamour that commodified her—Rokujō takes control of her life and frees herself. Is her escape complete? It is hard to say, but she has certainly attained the dignity of agency, and the presence of Gen, the ultimate amorous man in Yoshiwara, escorting her to her new abode points in that direction. Depicting the trials and tribulations of the working women of Yoshiwara, embedded in tales of love, sex, and desire, Bandoh remediates the *Genji* into a narrative that is less about sexualized, eroticized desire as about looking beyond Yoshiwara as the site of erotic fantasy for men. In doing so, Bandoh's *manga* reveals the cost exacted from all who reside there—courtesans and, yes, even the *kōshoku ichidai otoko* (the amorous man par excellence).

Transposing the tale to Yoshiwara, Bandoh's *Prostitute Quarters of Genji* also operates like an elaborate *mitate* visual puzzle, challenging readers to decipher which characters and episodes from the tale are being evoked and how they have been retooled. It remediates Tokugawa literary texts, the most prominent of which is Ihara Saikaku's *The Life of an Amorous Man*. Stylized as the most famous lover in Yoshiwara, Gen invokes Saikaku's Genji-like lover who beds nearly four thousand (wo)men,[18] while brothel proprietor Ohama, known for her sexual prowess, calls to mind the licentious protagonist of Saikaku's *The Life of an Amorous Woman* (Bandoh 2010–11, 1:104). Most prominently, Bandoh repurposes a third Tokugawa prose genre, the *ninjōbon* (sentimental fiction), which focuses on "emotion, sentiment, romantic love" from a feminine point of view (Shirane 2002, 760). In vogue around 1818 to 1844, it targeted a female rather than male or mixed readership and focused on the trials and tribulations of the courtesans (Shirane 2002, 760–2). Thus Bandoh's *Prostitute Quarters of Genji* creates several visual puzzles—we discover aspects of *The Tale of Genji*, Yoshiwara, and Tokugawa literary texts, but also come face-to-face with the human condition of the Gen(ji) women and their success in establishing subject positions despite the "hard knocks" of two worlds, the Heian and Yoshiwara, which strive to make women objects and not subjects.

In 2001 our next author, Sakurazawa Mai, takes a different tack, composing six self-contained stories of Genji's relationships with women from the eleventh-century tale.[19] Using different artists to illustrate the stories, Sakurazawa visually and narratively highlights how the needs and circumstances of each woman construct a "different" Genji object of love. In Fujitsubo's story, subtitled "Her Stepson: Forbidden Love with Genji," Fujitsubo's subject position as Genji's stepmother and the mother of his unborn child gives her the courage to select motherhood over romantic love. The chapter on Oborozukiyo, the sister of Genji's rival at court (entitled "Fervent Love," with the addendum "An Intense Love That Burned in the Interstices of Factional Struggle"), reveals a daring woman who chooses a dangerous love despite the costs. Sakurazawa throws into sharp relief these different loves, providing space for readers to add their own emotional energy and knowledge to perform in tandem with the protagonists.

The variations in the personalities of the women (a vibrant young girl, an unassuming country girl, a proud, regal woman), their status (stepmother, supposed daughter, cousin), and their situation (the emperor's consort, an older lover, the sister of Genji's enemy at court) all fashion how their loves and their stories play out. Thus, as indicated by the subtitling of her story, Fujitsubo is mesmerized by Genji but regrets her tryst with him as her stepson and gives up everything to protect her own infant son (Sakurazawa 2001, 1:57–8, 74). In contrast, the young Murasaki finds happiness, taking solace in the fact that Genji loves her, despite his relationships with other women (Sakurazawa 2001, 2:75). And Oborozukiyo finds peace with the steadfast, kind, and loyal Crown Prince Suzaku rather than the exciting but unreliable Genji (Sakurazawa 2001, 2:182). The Tamakazura story, subtitled "Her Stepfather: Her Bewildering Love with Genji," depicts a very different Genji who eschews a relationship with her because he does not want to betray Murasaki (Sakurazawa 2001, 1:120, 115), as well as a Tamakazura who chooses marriage to a suitor to avoid hurting Murasaki.

Despite Genji's casting a spell on them, the women in Sakurazawa's anthology take control of their lives—or at least of their feelings for Genji—and come to terms with them. One memorable exception is Rokujō. Here, too, as in the tale, Rokujō is courted by Genji and succumbs to his charms only to be abandoned for other love interests. To add insult to injury, Aoi's men unceremoniously push her carriage out of the way to make room for Aoi, whom Genji formally acknowledges as he rides by in the Aoi Festival procession. Seething with anger and humiliation, Rokujō morphs into a demon and attacks Aoi just as Aoi is giving birth to Yūgiri. Fully clothed, Rokujō accosts Aoi, screaming how dare Aoi bear Genji's child (Sakurazawa 2001, 1:184–5). On the following two pages, Rokujō violently lifts Aoi by the hair and claws at her stomach (Sakurazawa 2001, 1:186–7). Only when we turn to pages 188 and 189 do we realize the extent of Rokujō's fury, as she laughs hysterically and rips something out of Aoi—a fetus. Other *manga* have featured violent scenes, but nothing as gruesome or fearsome as this! Such a scenario is not part of the eleventh-century *Genji*, nor does it fall within purview of Heian aesthetics—but Rokujō and her subject position will not be denied.

Equally startling is the portrayal of Genji's cousin Asagao, whose love for Genji is billed as licentious. A luxuriously dressed woman baring a substantial set of breasts suggests something more than romance (Sakurazawa 2001, 2:83). But what follows seems to belie our suspicions, as a very staid encounter between Genji and Asagao unfolds. Suddenly the scene darkens, revealing a bridge with figures in muted silhouette—and a pair of breasts sans a head, thrust out from a kimono (Sakurazawa 2001, 2:89). Even larger breasts appear, and we find that Asagao is using them to seduce a man, the scenario ending with several very graphic copulation scenes (Sakurazawa 2001, 2:90–1). The text explains that Asagao has a secret life in which she goes out at night to satiate her sexual desire. What she apparently fears most is falling in love with Genji and then being abandoned, so she roams the streets at night seducing random men.

Although Asagao gives her body to unknown men on the streets, she keeps a tight rein on her heart, for she is irresistibly drawn to Genji and knows that, once she gives herself to him, he will abandon her and move on to another woman. Tormented with desire for Genji and while in the throes of the graphically depicted sexual encounter with the commoner noted above, Asagao has an epiphany: the only way to ensure that Genji desires her forever is to keep him at bay and never allow physical consummation of their relationship (Sakurazawa 2001, 2:105–7). This is a startlingly brilliant and innovative reading of the sixteen-year-long, "platonic" relationship between the Genji and Asagao which in Shikibu's tale transpires through letters and nothing more. Tellingly, Asagao's answer to managing her unrequited love for Genji is juxtaposed with her appointment as the Kamo Priestess, who must eschew sexual relationships for the length of her service.

In Sakurazawa's anthology the women establish their subject positions through the different kinds of love that they create with Genji. Genji is supposedly the same person, but each love reveals a different aspect of his personality that is brought to the fore by the needs, the desires, and the character of each woman. This is especially apparent in the consummation scenes, which visually and narratively signify the differing consumable spectacles of love enacted by each woman. The ways in which Genji loves—and, in many instances, leaves—the women are striking, and strikingly different. Sakurazawa contends that the construction of the different loves is dependent on the personalities of the women, but they also result from the ways in which the women visualize and experience Genji. In each encounter readers come face-to-face with a different man of sorts. Genji is handsome and alluring across the board, but each woman protagonist crafts a different Genji by "dovetailing" with a different aspect of his persona. He can be a cute young boy who grows up to be an earnest lover (Fujitsubo) or an accomplished, polished young aristocratic lover (Murasaki), but he can also be a self-assured dandy who provides invigorating sexual gratification (Oborozukiyo) or a more earthy, licentious, eroticized object of desire (Asagao).

Published in 2001, at the beginning of the millennium celebrations for *The Tale of Genji*, Sakurazawa's stories might best be described as remediations of love, lust, and desire—but also of the tale as one unified whole, and of Genji as the "same" personality throughout. The different artists in the anthology use different drawing techniques to bring to the fore the multifaceted aspects of Genji's character and how different women bring out different Genjis—something that the eleventh-century tale, as discussed in Chapter 1, does so effectively. We have seen other collections of *Genji* stories centering on individual women, but the use here of different artists in tandem with narratives by a single author casts into sharp relief the very individual quality of the women characters' experiences of love and of Genji, and prominently highlights the construction of *The Tale of Genji* as a collection of vignettes rather than a contiguous narrative. No doubt the anthology's depiction of Rokujō's attack on Aoi and its rendering of Asagao as possessed by insatiable lust make for startling new looks at Genji's ladies. To this, Sakurazawa adds at the end of each depiction gossip-magazine-like assessments of the women and a tongue-in-cheek interview with Genji—all narrated in very contemporized terms.

Taking a humorous and lighthearted approach, our last *manga*, Takenaka Ranko's *The Heian Trendy Drama: The Tale of Genji Manga Notebook*, takes a hard look at the plight of women in their relationships with men. Focusing less on the emotional and romantic and more on the social costs to women of living in a patriarchal society, it, nonetheless, situates women in subject positions from which they critique the Heian world(s) and lampoon the men for their licentious behavior and self-absorbed quests to have their way with women. In creating her *manga*, Ranko deployed a double-frame structure and a unique distribution system: she places the "fictional" world of the tale within a "historical" world populated by Murasaki Shikibu and other ladies-in-waiting, and then serialized it as a comic strip *manga* in a newspaper, the *Kyoto Civilian News*. Appearing every Sunday over fifty weeks in 1998, each installment provided a cohesive mini-unit with a beginning and, more importantly, an end that formed some closure but that also "hooked" readers into reading the next installment. Each installment covered a great deal of ground, for space was short and the tale was long.[20]

Running two narratives concurrently, Ranko has Murasaki Shikibu compose her *Tale of Genji* against the backdrop of a discussion with other ladies-in-waiting. Ranko also creates a fictional Lady Manga (not found in the tale) who is ostensibly there to do "research" for her *manga* version of the tale, but who then participates in the discussions as a stand-in for twentieth-century readers—and for Ranko herself. Not a time traveler but a girl from the country, much like the daughter of Tō no Chūjō (Genji's brother-in-law in the tale), Lady Manga is unfamiliar with the protocols at court and requires instruction in the cultural and gender mores of the times. More importantly, she is free to poke fun at and satirize them—which she does with great aplomb, resulting in a feminist, or at least woman-centered, critique of the tale and of the outer-frame Shikibu world. Highlighting the difficulties that women endure at the hands of men in a male-dominated society, she assesses everything with great humor, tempering the feminist edge of her critique.

Nor is it only Lady Manga who criticizes the strictures placed on the women in Ranko's *manga*: the women in the *Genji* story and also in Shikibu's time object to the treatment of women at court as well. The Shikibu-world ladies refer on several occasions to the behavior of men at court as "sexual harassment," or tantamount to it (Takenaka 1998, February 8, p. 8A; February 15, p. 8B; March 8, p. 8B; March

22, p. 8A). In the tale, many are distressed by Genji's philandering. Murasaki describes Genji's consummation of their relationship as a case of her being "roughed up" (*rambōsareta*, a euphemism for sexual assault/rape) by someone whom she regarded as an older brother and not a perspective husband (Takenaka 1998, April 19, p. 8B). Ranko gets in her own "punches" as well. Drawing herself in *chibi* miniature humorous caricature in dialogue boxes positioned at the end of the weekly installments, she labels Genji "an unbelievable debauchery-ridden, shallow playboy who would be laughed at by [one of the great lovers of the period,] Ariwara no Narihira" (1998, January 25, p. 8B), and deems "sexual harassment" at the Heian court "harsh" (1998, February 8, p. 8B). The visual and textual portrayals are highly critical of men, especially Genji. In one instance he is labeled a stalker and portrayed as a dog wagging his tail, as he literally "hounds" Fujitsubo (Takenaka 1998, April 12, p. 8A), while in Figure 5.4 he gleefully looks on at his "new toy," the young Murasaki, whom he has just abducted and placed in a bird cage.

Ranko utilizes the outlandish Lady Manga, the over-the-top depiction of Genji and other men in compromising positions, and Ranko's own caricatured *chibi* self-portraits to deliver her negative appraisal of the behavior of the men and the difficult positions in which they place women. She also enlivens her story with catchy, modernized subtitles that signal the content of the installment. For example, "The Demon of the Heart #1: It's a Festival, A Fight, a Mono no ke Spiritual Possession (Aoi)" points to the clash at the Aoi Festival between Rokujō and Aoi (Takenaka 1998, March 29, p. 8A), while young Murasaki's plight is summarized as "Cinderella's Misfortune #2: The Bird May Escape but Not the Princess in the Cage (Wakamurasaki)," referring to Genji's spying on Murasaki as she laments the escaping of her pet bird, and his caging of her (Figure 5.4). Ranko adds witty, covert references to news items from 1998: for instance, "The Sexual Harasser Is Not Just the President: He Is Closer and Farther (Kashiwagi)" (February 8, p. 8A) introduces "The Broomstick" chapter in which Genji and his friends gather to discuss the merits of women, but it satirically references the sexual harassment charges levied against former President Bill Clinton by Monica Lewinsky that year. Japanese celebrities are not immune either, as Singer Go Hiromi's tell-all book, *Dirty*, and his sensational divorce from actress Nitani Yurie are derided by the ladies from Shikibu's time as a book that Genji would no doubt give his stamp of approval (Takenaka 1998, April 19, p. 8A).

Criticisms of male lust and ill-treatment of women are often playful and delivered in humorous fashion, but Ranko's *manga* ends with a scathing critique of the period, as both Lady Manga and her friend the *maihime* dancer from her hometown embark upon very un-Heian professions—the former vows to become a *manga* artist, and the latter opens her own dance studio. They pointedly note that there are no records of women artists, let alone *manga* artists, from the period—but no matter, they plan to change that by taking up careers that are not beholden to men and establishing themselves as subjects who take control of their lives. The subject positions held by Lady Manga and the dancer are anachronistic, unhistorical, and humorous, but Ranko uses both Lady Manga and the dancer and Shikibu and the ladies in the "historical" narrative frame to critique the

Figure 5.4 On the right page the ladies from Shikibu's world are talking when there is a sudden shift to Genji's world in the last frame on the lower left. The young Murasaki's grandmother worries about Murasaki after her death, and Genji in the top three frames on the left gallantly says he will take care of Murasaki, only to put her in a cage in the bottom frame. Takenaka Ranko, *Heian Trendy Drama: The Tale of Genji Manga Notebook*, February 1, p. 8AB. Copyright © 1998. Courtesy of Takenaka Ranko and *Kyoto Civilian News*.

male-dominated Heian world. Without a doubt the women in ladies comics turn female emotionality on its head and find agency in abandonment, jealousy, and unrequited love—and in humor and critique as well.

Conclusion: Adult Subjects of Consumption, Production, and Desire

Targeting adult women readers and writers, ladies comics "grow up" girls comics, and the *Genji* remediations are no different, as cute large-eyed figures are replaced by men and women with adult bodies and more realistically drawn faces. But that is not all: female objects of desire are transposed into subjects of consumption and production. This is not to say that protagonists in girls comics never occupy subject positions, but the poetics of the category naturalize any erotic stirrings as love rather than sexual desire, and, with the exceptions of BL and *Patalliro Genji!*, require its protagonists to be demure objects waiting to be swept off their feet by their Prince Charmings. In contrast, in ladies comics many bets are off because the readership is now eighteen through thirty-five and beyond. Protagonists more stridently recreate themselves into subjects and take control of their (erotic) destinies. They are still very much in search of their Prince Charmings, but want to be sexually and emotionally satisfied in adult fashion. Thus, both visually and narratively, the protagonists take charge, despite the fact that in Heian society women were dependent on men for their economic, social, and sexual fulfillment. To mark this change, with a few exceptions (such as Maki's work), the *Genji* ladies comics focalize the women, so that they are front and center. The men serve as the means through which the women's desires are enacted. Orchestrated as moments in which "good girls" can engage in and enjoy "bad girls'" sensual pleasures fully and freely, without guilt or fear of repercussions, these *manga* are conceived as safe, phantasy 2D spaces far from the reality of daily life and, more importantly, separate from real injury, humiliation, or hurt—for readers or for any real-life woman.

Even more prominently than in *shōjo manga*, then, ladies comics showcase the hard truth of romance in adult fashion. Love has its highs, its thrills, its glory, but also the agonies of waiting, of unrequited love and desire, and of abandonment. In these stories love can turn young girls/women into political pawns, whether to gain ascendency at court or for monetary gain (Maki, Bandoh); it can generate intense jealousies that steal away or poison childhoods (Teradate, Kira), cause devastating retaliation (Teradate), or even create monsters (Sakurazawa). Love can bring on the self-destructive, humiliating behavior of having sex with an unconscious husband (Ide) or of destroying one's looks and livelihood for someone who will not return one's love (Bandoh). But it can also be the ultimate flexing of sexual prowess and desire by hypersexualized women (Hazuki), and even a critique of the patriarchy (Takenaka).

In the midst of these and in other struggles, however, the women protagonists in *Genji* ladies comics take action—and in the process produce subjects worthy to be consumed and, of course, to identify with. The young Murasaki inspires Genji's friend, Tō no Chūjō, to be her champion, creating a more thoughtful Genji (Kira). Maki's Murasaki and Akashi Lady regain their humanity when they realize that they are both victims of Genji's love, rather than rivals for it. Inconceivably, Ide's Rokujō gets some "payback" by attacking Genji and driving him to illness, while Sakurazawa's Asagao takes control of her sexuality and gives Genji a taste of his own medicine—unrequited love. And no one can diminish Rokujō's inner strength and beauty as she frees herself from the political sexual economy of Yoshiwara (Bandoh), nor fail to applaud Aoi's exacting punishment of a betraying husband or Sue's choosing to leave Yoshiwara (Bandoh). Nor can we not see the wisdom in Fujitsubo's decision to reject Genji's overtures so as to protect her son and save Genji from himself (Hazuki, Sakurazawa). Even Ō no myōbu's spurning of Genji and attracting a young stud many years her junior go a long way in heralding the subjecthood that so many of the women protagonists in the ladies comics attain (Hazuki), and that their readers so desire.

Diverse and inventive on their own terms, the *Genji* ladies comics take the same *Tale of Genji* that is remediated by girls comics and give the female protagonists more agency. Depicting women whose fates are so closely linked to men's, the artists and writers of the *Genji* ladies comics nonetheless establish ways in which women protagonists become the subjects of their destinies—or at least to discover how to unabashedly express their wants, even if only in the pages of ladies comics. In the process, they also provide safe ways for readers to acquire their own subject positions—through which they can fully identify with adult women enacting adult erotic desires and jointly participate in sex as a consumable spectacle. These *manga* make plain the avenues through which women can own their own desires and use them in ways that challenge and subvert expectations of proper female sexuality, replicating the powerful queering of the *Genji* in *The Tale of Genji BL Anthology* (discussed in Chapter 4).

Chapter 6

SHŌNEN BOYS/SEINEN YOUNG MEN MANGA: MALE PERSPECTIVES REFRACTED

If we thought the ladies *Genji manga* were a motley crew, the male-oriented titles are even more so, for the *Genji* aesthete male courtiers, composing poetry and engaging in incense and painting contests, would be considered "sissy" by *shōnen* boys-comics standards and not in their wheelhouse by *seinen* young-men-comics heroes. A counterpart to girls comics, boys comics are geared toward eight- to eighteen-year-old males and feature adventure, camaraderie, loyalty, and fight scenes, while young men comics cater to eighteen- to thirty-year-old males and often showcase action, violence, and sex, although not exclusively so, but render characters, plots, and themes more complex and in less black-and-white terms.[1] As a result, the *Genji manga* artists in this chapter turn to humor, gritty realism, over-the-top hypersexuality, and parody to tell their *Tales of Genji*.

The selections comprise three groups—"*Shōnen* Boys: Focalizing the Funny," "*Seinen* Young Men #1: *Gekiga* Realism and Soft Porn," and "*Seinen* Young Men #2: Eye-Candy Panty Shots and Cherry-Picking the *Genji*." In "*Shōnen* Boys," Akatsuka Fujio makes Genji a bumbling, "unhandsome" lover who lusts after women, while Koizumi Yoshihiro "cutifies" Genji into a roly-poly chestnut, sympathetically bringing to the fore Genji's very human foibles that are costly to those around him. In "*Seinen* Young Men #1," Tomi Shinzō adopts the ultrarealistic, dark *gekiga* dramatic drawing style of Koike Kazuo and Kojima Goseki's *Lone Wolf and Cub* to dispassionately look at a society that traps all its inhabitants. In contrast, Egawa Tatsuya centers on Genji's male gaze lusting after female bodies—producing a soft porn *Genji manga*. Composed by women, the two titles in "*Seinen* Young Men #2" transpose the *Genji* to the twenty-first century, upending the tale in inventive ways. In the first Inaba Minori focalizes the Genji surrogate, but uses his ogling of female breasts and bottoms as a means through which the female protagonists manipulate him. Reminiscent of Nakamura Hikaru's *Saint Young Men*,[2] artist est em "cherry-picks" only Genji from the tale and plops him down in contemporary Japan, with hilarious results.

The Male Perspective, from Boys to Men

Despite the variety of approaches of the male-oriented *manga* discussed here, all focus on Genji. No longer just an empty-center excuse for women to be on stage, a desirable other, or the means through which female erotic desire is enacted, in these remediations Genji and his story retake center stage—even if he receives a gentle dressing-down at the hands of humorist Akatsuka or is portrayed as a young man at the mercy of Inaba's modernized women. Nonetheless, for full engagement all the works still require readerly collaboration—knowledge not just of the tale but of works by the artists in question, of the adult *manga* arena, and of other *manga* in the category.

Shōnen Boys Manga: *Focalizing the Funny*

Focalizing the funny—transforming the tale into a slapstick comedy or a *kawaii* cute gag piece—seems like a dubious way to entice boys-comics readers,[3] who expect action-packed narratives featuring high-stakes sport matches, dangerous quests, or pitched battles against insurmountable enemies. But Akatsuka Fujio's *Akatsuka Fujio no manga koten nyūmon genji monogatari* (*Akatsuka Fujio's Manga Introduction to Classical Literature: The Tale of Genji*) and Koizumi Yoshihiro's *Ōzukami genji monogatari maro n?* (*Grasping the Gist of The Tale of Genji, I/Chestnut*) bank on tempting their fan base with their brand of humor. So, much like Akamatsu Ken's *Love Hina* lead, their Genji surrogates marshal their personal "charm" and "sexual prowess" to woo the ladies at the court. But, unlike in the eleventh-century tale or *Love Hina*, Genji is not the handsome ideal love interest whom women seek. Rather, Akatsuka deploys a physically unattractive "un-hero" from his gag *manga*, backstory and all, while Koizumi transforms Genji into a very cute roly-poly courtier whom no one can fault or stay angry at for very long.

Publishing his 1983 *Genji* remediation as part of his *Introduction to Classical Literature* series, which includes *The Pillow Book*, *Heike monogatari* (*The Tale of Heike*), and *Oku no hosomichi* (*The Narrow Road to the North*), Akatsuka[4] includes instructional information, chapter summaries, and the like, but also employs visual and textual intertextuality to engage his fan base. He populates his *Genji* with characters from his gag comics and "mashes" the material culture and language discourses of the eleventh and the twentieth centuries together in incongruously funny ways. Iyami (Nasty), the "bad boy" from *Osomatsukun* (*Mr. Nothing Special*, 1962),[5] "crosses over" to the *Genji* world, becoming Iyami Genji. Visually and textually, "Me," as the character calls himself, blends his Iyami "backstory" appearance and personality with that of the eleventh-century Genji—resulting in the antithesis of a handsome heartthrob. Iyami Genji now sports buckteeth and bulging eyes, is uncouth and self-centered.[6] He is also always at the ready to con someone—usually a woman. But, unlike truly evil villains, such as Sherlock Holmes's nemesis, Professor Moriarty, he is not very smart or successful in his escapades, and thus has an endearing quality about him.

Akatsuka creates his funny by mishmashing contemporary concepts and situations with those of the Heian. Throwing together twentieth-century slang with a pinch of the comedic, pseudo-classical language, topped off with silly word-and-image play, Akatsuka adds layer upon layer of the incongruous. And true to his vision, Akatsuka plumbs every event and relationship for its fullest comic potential—the red-nosed princess Suetsumuhana episode (1983, 69–71), for instance, providing a perfect opportunity. The scene opens with the would-be lovers meeting for the first time as a snowstorm rages outside. The lights suddenly go out, and Iyami Genji's long-awaited first look at the princess is thwarted (Akatsuka 1983, 70). The lights go back on, and lo and behold, in the topmost panel in Figure 6.1, the red-nosed princess's face comes to light—literally illuminated by lightning bolts and popping red particles.

Certainly not the beauty he expected, in second panel on the right Iyami's visage shatters—his upper face separating at the jaw, his hair radiating out in black spikes, his eyes becoming red stars, and his huge buckteeth splaying outward. Suetsumuhana is humorously caricatured, but the butt of the joke is Iyami Genji—as he chides himself for letting his womanizing get the best of him.

Figure 6.1 Iyami Genji gets his first glimpse of the red-nosed princess and reacts in exaggerated fashion, his face shattering in surprise. Akatsuka Fujio, *The Tale of Genji*, 71. Copyright © Fujio Akatsuka 1983. Courtesy Akatsuka Fujio.

In Akatsuka's hands, the "high art" courtier world of Genji is transposed into the "low art" popular culture of Iyami Genji, full of puns, jokes, and even scatological humor. Exceedingly lowbrow and slapstick in conception, Akatsuka's *Genji* is intended not to ridicule or denigrate the eleventh-century classic or the red-nosed princess but to render the *Genji* more accessible and engaging to his readers—at Iyami Genji's expense, of course! In the end Akatsuka creates a funny, accessible, over-the-top *Genji* that is a far cry from—or way below—Murasaki Shikibu's creation, but exceedingly enjoyable and entertaining. The idea is not to make the plot irrelevant or to be irreverent, but to bring Genji down a notch or two and make him fodder for a laugh or two—or three.

The inventive reworking of the boys-comics category that requires visual and textual literacy from other venues continues with Koizumi Yoshihiro[7] in *Grasping the Gist of The Tale of Genji, I/Chestnut?* Genji's male perspective on the happenings in the tale is still very much in play, but visually and narratively, Koizumi brings a very unexpected look to his 2002 remediation—no doubt resulting in his being awarded the Sixth Excellence Prize in Manga from Japan Media Arts Plaza (Japan Media Arts Plaza n.d.). Koizumi begins the fun with the title *Ōzukami Genji monogatari maro n?* The first three words mean "grabbing hold of *The Tale of Genji*"—in other words, providing the gist of the tale. The last three syllables "maro, n," are a clever play on word—and image—that requires knowledge of classical Japanese and a bit of French. The central character modestly calls himself "Maro," a post-Heian reference for the first person. But when "maro" is joined to the "n," it forms "maron," a French foreign loan word for "chestnut." What do chestnuts have to do with the *Genji*? Everything—as we are soon to find out!

Witness the two pages allotted to chapter 1, "Kiritsubo" (Figure 6.2), which are in color in the original. Reading page 12, on the right, from top to bottom in Figure 6.2, we see the emperor and the Kiritsubo Consort in love in the first frame, and in the second, their baby—but, lo and behold, it is not a human child but a *maron*, a chestnut named *Maro* (Koizumi 2002, 12–13)! Needless to say, Empress Kokiden, the mother of the first prince and heir to the throne, is not amused by the union and hounds the Kiritsubo Consort to death in frames 3 and 4. In the first frame on the left (page 13), the emperor is despondent over the passing of the Consort, but in the discursive economy of the eight-frame *manga* he finds an enchanting replacement in his new empress, Fujitsubo, in the following frame. With equal speed Genji grows up, comes of age, marries Lady Aoi in frame 3, and declares in the following frame his love for Fujitsubo with the caveat, "But Fujitsubo is Papa's wife, huh?" A disarmingly cute statement, conveyed in Koizumi's gentle ironic fashion, this masks Maro's later cuckolding of his father.

Using eight frames on interfacing pages, rather than the story *manga* format of other *Genji manga*, Koizumi depicts all fifty-four chapters of the tale in one volume. As evident in the "Kiritsubo" chapter, this calls for extreme distillation of the story at great discursive speed, but Koizumi is a master at capturing the "essence" of the story in a few deft strokes and pithy prose. He carefully pairs just the right image with the right narrative description and dialogue, so it is pitched

Figure 6.2 Koizumi succinctly depicts the first chapter of the tale "Kiritsubo" in eight frames: the romance between Maro's parents, which results in his birth and his mother's death on page 12; his father's subsequent marriage to Fujitsubo; and Maro's falling in love with her on page 13. Koizumi Yoshihiro, *Grasping the Gist of The Tale of Genji: I/Chestnut?*, 12–13. Copyright © 2002. Courtesy of Koizumi Yoshihiro and Gentōsha.

perfectly—but it also requires high literacy in *The Tale of Genji*. Short and sweet, the frames fluidly relate the main events of the tale. In the "Kiritsubo" chapter, discussed above, they speak of the unusual love affair between the emperor and Maro's mother, the cost of that love, Maro's birth, and the beginning of Maro's lifelong pursuit of his stepmother.

Koizumi does not shy away from the trials and tribulations of court life— the violence of harassment, the tragedy of death, and the debilitating sorrow of Maro's illicit feelings for his stepmother—but these moments are tempered and minimized by the brevity of the piece and Koizumi's gentle, cute drawings. The vibrant, happy colors—which are not replicated here and are absent not just in other *Genji* remediations but in most *manga*—also help. Referencing the polychromatic twelfth-century Genji scrolls and the fifteenth-century Tosa paintings, they are a feast for the eyes, inviting us to linger longer on each frame. Life, riddled with thwarted desires and even death, is harsh, but a bubbly *maron* surrounded by brightly colorful hues takes a bit of the sting away.

Koizumi also does not leave the entire burden of narration to the eight frames. In between the chapters he includes information on the characters and the period.

To support Chapter 1, for example, he adds a genealogy of the characters, explains the hierarchy among the imperial consorts and the marriage customs, and details the Korean soothsayer's prophecy of Maro's future (2002, 14–19). For other chapters he adds maps and explanations on clothing and other accouterments, and also inserts poetry—some solo and some *zōtōka* exchanges between lovers—done in brush-like calligraphy with modern translations alongside.

Comprising 255 pages, Koizumi's *Genji* follows the basic storyline and chapters of the eleventh-century tale and covers all fifty-four chapters—a tour de force, to say the least.[8] The *manga* is divided into three segments, covering Genji in the first two and his presumed son, his grandson, and the three Uji princesses in the third. Yet ultimately it is about Genji—or Maro, to be exact. Cute and cuddly as a baby, Maro remains a roly-poly chestnut with an *eboshi* hat throughout, even as he grows up to be a powerful figure at court. He ages little and is drawn with sweat drops of embarrassment, distress, and concern. Although he does force his attentions on his stepmother Fujitsubo, the love of his life Murasaki, and Yūgao's daughter Tamakazura, he is bumbling, and much less suave and debonair than a girls-comics Lothario, so that in the end he also appears less "blamable" for his actions. Perhaps this is because the women tend to forgive him. Or perhaps it is because Maro is not a human but a chestnut, and a cute one at that, so he more sympathetically and gently embodies our human foibles of love, desire, vulnerability, and weakness. Hiding behind a foil of *kawaii* cuteness, Koizumi tempers Maro's—and, by extension, our own—shortcomings, providing space for thoughtful self-reflection that does not wallow in self-pity or defensiveness.

But why a *maron*? Koizumi writes that, in 1987, a confectionary company asked him to create a logo character to advertise a new product. The project never got off the ground, and he stuffed his design, Ma, n?, into a drawer. On a lark, Koizumi began his *Genji*, and Ma, n? became his male lead Genji. Nine years later—six years to detail the story, and three to illustrate it—*Ōzukami* was born. But why a gentle, fumbling *maron*? Koizumi's cryptic comment, tucked away in the afterword of his *manga*, claims that Heian courtiers look a lot like Maro. But examining his series *Butta to shattaka butta* (Pig/Buddha and the Phony)[9] provides some clues. Reprinted beginning in 2003, *Pig/Buddha and the Phony* has captivated *manga* audiences with its poignantly funny and on-target scrutiny of the foibles of humankind in love, agony, and self-doubt. Those asked to carry the burden of human vanity and vulnerability, however, are not people but delightfully cute and chubby pigs in pink, cream, and purple, in wigs like Miss Piggy, in neckties or sunglasses, dressed up like Buddha or in Elvis costumes—in other words, reminiscent of Maro. Populating the four-frame *manga*, the pigs act out the anxieties of first dates, the fear of relationships, life, love, hates, likes, happiness—the list goes on. Koizumi provides pithy one-liners and succinct dialogue, replete with puns and "truths" about the human condition. The series is aptly named *Butta to shattaka butta*—which playfully includes puns for "pig" (*buta*), the "Japanglish" pronunciation of Buddha (*butta*), and *shattaka butta* (someone who pretends to know what is going on but really doesn't). These pigs tell us how the contemporary world goes round, while a cute and cuddly *maron* Shining Prince Genji provides a glimpse into the Heian court of old.

Seinen *Young Men #1:* Gekiga *Realism and Soft Porn*

From the slapstick and cute funny boys *Genji manga*, we move to *seinen* comics, which target eighteen- to thirty-year-old young men. Texts in this demographic often employ themes and scenarios found in boys comics, but in a more mature register. They also cast a wider net, encompassing, for instance, an examination of what constitutes humanity vis-à-vis cyborgs (*Pluto*), the story of a doctor haunted by saving the life of a murdering psychopath (*Monster*), and even a sensitive portrayal of a young boy's sexual coming-of-age story (*Wandering Son*). Nonetheless, what distinguishes young men comics is a more realistic approach emphasizing the grayscale of existence—heroes are not entirely good, nor villains purely evil, so the stories are more complex, often exploring philosophical questions without giving any one protagonist the moral high ground. Not restricted to adventure and camaraderie, Tomi Shinzō's *Genji monogatari* (*The Tale of Genji*) replaces the gentility of the Heian period with the stark realism of Koike and Kojima's *Lone Wolf and Cub* and Inoue Takehiko's *Vagabond* samurai narratives but without the blood and gore, while Egawa Tatsuya's *Genji monogatari* (*The Tale of Genji*) hypes the sexual and erotic and ventures into soft porn.

Tomi Shinzō's (1991) *gekiga Genji* places the tale in a Tokugawa-esque setting reminiscent of the 1960s, when *gekiga* participated in a worldwide countercultural rebellion against the Establishment (see S. Suzuki 2013, 55). Utilizing the hallmark bleak realism of the style, Tomi remediates the glory and glamour of the Heian court into depictions of men and women struggling against societal mores and obligations. The prose introductions to the three volumes make that eminently clear, as Tomi rails against political expediencies that force men and women to use marital relationships to better their positions, that tax and terrorize farmers, and that cause even the rich to live stressful, anxiety-ridden existences (Tomi 1991, 1:8–9; 2:8–9; 3:8). In Tomi's estimation, no one has the good life in the *Genji* world.

Tomi's *manga* thus reads like a cold critique of the socioeconomic conditions of the Heian-displaced Tokugawa-esque society. He evokes the lonely fugitive existence of *Lone Wolf and Cub* and the hopeless cog-in-the-wheel lives of urban factory workers fighting their way through the industrial grime and dirt of early-twentieth-century Japan in Tatsumi Yoshihiro's *A Drifting Life*. Strict, rectangular panels with little layering, anatomically correct bodies that feature nudity in a no-nonsense, non-gratuitous manner, and facial expressions that are dour and unattractive—all these speak to the *manga*'s theme that everyone, even Genji, suffers. Genji's existence is depicted as an unrelenting, heart-wrenching string of losses. His mother dies in front of his eyes; his wife Aoi passes away, while Rokujō and Utsusemi abandon him (Tomi 1991, 1:40–1; 2:142–9; 3:189–95; 1:131–7). He is all but destroyed by his stepmother Fujitsubo's rejection of his advances and her taking the tonsure (Tomi 1991, 1:236–7; 2:250–2). But it is the depictions of Genji's exile to Suma that speak most poignantly to the hardness of his life: the political animosity that drives him from the capital, his leaving everyone he loves, and the desolate living conditions in Suma, crowned by the fury of the storm, take up a good one-third of Volume 3 (Tomi 1991, 3:15–16, 17–46, 80–95). And although Tomi's remediation focalizes Genji, it also vividly portrays the harsh realities for women in the intense rivalries at court to secure the emperor's favor, thus adding elements not found in other *Genji manga*. Tomi's *manga*, for example, opens with Genji's mother Kiritsubo no kōi making her way to the emperor's quarters. A needle-like object, placed by supporters of her rival Empress Kokiden, catches on her robes and sends her sprawling, coughing up blood (Tomi 1991, 1:17–20). In another instance Genji's stepmother Fujitsubo passes Kokiden in the palace, and the air between the two crackles with animosity (Tomi 1991, 2:228–30).

The stark graphic *gekiga* drawings of sweaty bodies, and of faces contorted in pain, grief, and humiliation, underscore the difficulty of living in the *Genji* world. Everyday occurrences such as childbirth speak less to the joy of a new life than to the pain experienced by the mother. In love scenes, the erotic excitement and pleasure are often overshadowed by forced compliance or feelings of guilt and remorse. The emphasis of the *manga*, then, is on the harsh, the tragic, and the serious: very little levity is present, even in the usual comic-relief depictions of the red-nosed princess and episodes that include the older, licentious lady-in-waiting Gen no naishi. Moments of hardship and tragedy are depicted in slow-motion cinematic shots with no dialogue—heightening the emotional cost. In one scene, depicted on page 36 (the right-hand page) in Figure 6.3, Genji's mother leaves the palace to recuperate from her ill-treatment at court. En route to her home, she vomits blood and tumbles out of her oxen cart to her death on page 37 (the left-hand page). Not conceivable by Heian standards, such embellishments drive home Tomi's point that court life is harsh and unrelenting: love trysts are foils for political gain; jockeying for positions of power is fierce; hardships, physical and emotional, are simply a way of life.

The series covers only sixteen chapters of the tale, and Tomi's graphic depiction of death and suffering prevails, although somewhat mitigated by moments like the ending, where the provincial governor's wife Utsusemi's humanity, as she visits the grave of her deceased husband, shines through. More beautifully drawn than others, Genji's radiance also dispels the gloom. He is beautiful not just outwardly but inwardly as well: he is kinder, gentler, more solicitous than his eleventh-century counterpart. His keenly felt grief over the deaths of Yūgao and Aoi, his sorrow over parting with Rokujō and even Utsusemi testify to that (Tomi 1991, 1:179; 2:143–51; 3:226–9; 1:131–8). He also forgives the ghost of the caretaker's daughter for killing Yūgao (which in the tale is attributed to Rokujō); he stops seeing Akashi in deference to Murasaki; and he even puts covers over his sleeping men in their home while in exile (Tomi 1991, 1:182–4; 3:148–50). Glimpses of such a Genji, although few and far between, work to soften Tomi's social critique a bit.

Egawa Tatsuya writes our second *seinen* title in this section, also entitled *The Tale of Genji*, which he began in 2001 with the intent of creating one volume for each chapter of the tale, although only seven volumes have been published to date.

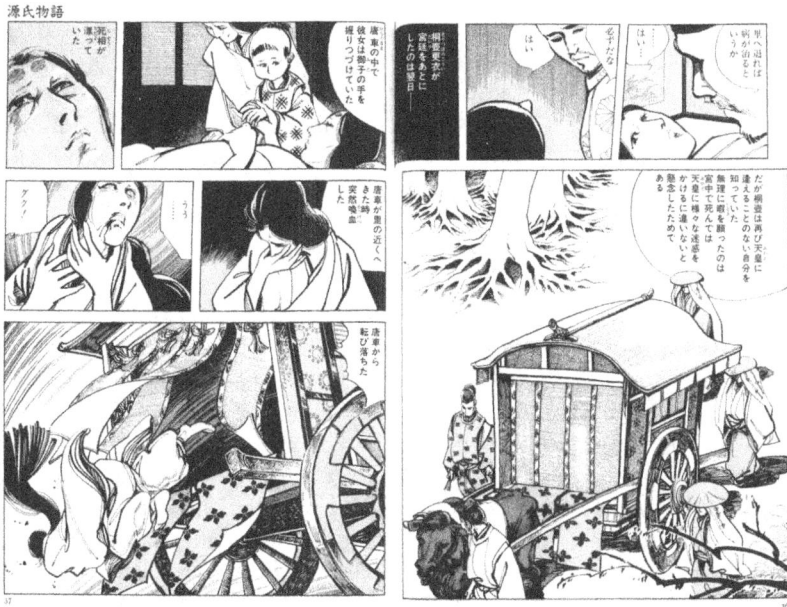

Figure 6.3 Tomi embellishes in graphic fashion Genji's mother tumbling to her death, as an illness, perpetrated by the harassment she suffers at court, gets the better of her. Tomi Shinzō, *The Tale of Genji*, 1: 36–7. Copyright © 1991. Courtesy of Tomi Shinzō and Geibunsha.

An established artist, Egawa is well known for his works such as *BE FREE!* (1984) and *The Tokyo University Story* (1992–2001), and for challenging the limits of what constitute young men comics (MANGASeek and Nichigai Associates 2003, 68; Nagatani 1994, 70). Not surprisingly, his *Tale of Genji* features nude, sweaty bodies in amorous embrace, a male gaze, and explicit sex scenes that many would consider highly eroticized and more appropriate for adult male audiences.[10] It also focalizes the sex scenes above all else, especially in the early volumes, and in ways that make his *Genji* a counterpart of erotic ladies comics. But the series is published by Shūeisha, a mainstream publisher, and following the usual conventions for categorizing *manga*, it falls within the rubric of young men rather than adult men.[11] Nonetheless, it remains an outlier, for Egawa pushes the envelope of mainstream *manga*. The eleventh-century tale describes instances where Genji's advances are unwanted, or are at least met with complicated feelings (e.g., by Fujitsubo or the provincial governor's wife who thereafter remains faithful to her husband), but Egawa makes these encounters seductive, consensual, and universally welcomed. Genji thus sweeps the women off their feet and gives his willing partners a night to remember, making them objects of his desire—unlike the innocent romances of girls comics or the construction of female agency in ladies comics.

As such, it is the female nude body that is almost exclusively on display. The overriding gaze is male, and the sexual moments cater to men readers. This raises several questions: Is Egawa's graphic sexually gratuitous? Is his portrayal historically accurate, or is it just trafficking in hyperbole? And if the latter, is it done to shock, and to cater to his fan base of male viewers, or is something else also in play? When all is said and done, Egawa relishes the controversy—but he also contends that he is simply making plain the sexual and political dynamics that the eleventh-century tale shrouds in secrecy and misplaced elegance. Placed at court to further the agendas of their respective families, the consorts and attendants serve at the (sexual) pleasure of the emperor, reduced to vying for imperial favor and the opportunity to bear a royal male offspring. The women thus constitute a harem with no sexual outlet other than to await their "turn" at servicing the emperor (Egawa 2001–5, 1:20). Egawa literally describes them as dogs in heat, and depicts several masturbating to satisfy their sexual needs (2001–5, 1:20–5). The stakes are high and the competition dirty, as evidenced by the treatment that Genji's mother, the emperor's favorite, receives at the hands of the other women. Ever extreme in making his point, in one telling scene Egawa depicts a lady defecating in a box and then ordering her attendants to smear the feces on the halls through which Genji's mother must pass on her way to the emperor's rooms (Egawa 2001–5, 1:47–8). Egawa makes plain the central purpose of the emperor's bevy of ladies, his graphic and base depictions reducing them to sex-driven animals.

A similar kind of overdrive is evident in Egawa's depiction of the sexual encounters between Genji and his women. With the exceptions of two volumes, the series contains numerous sex scenes. In one sequence, Genji spends a record sixty-eight pages (twenty-six of them while she is asleep) deflowering Utsusemi's stepdaughter (Egawa 2001–5, 3:119–86). He fondles her breasts and genitalia and applies his final ministrations before he enters her. But far from over, the last forty-one pages detail the stepdaughter's eager sexual awakening and her transformation into a sex-crazed young woman (Egawa 2001–5, 3:145–85).

Further questions remain: What is Egawa doing? Is this pornography, erotic art, or just a *manga* trafficking in shock value? Or is he trying to demean women? No doubt many people, especially women, are greatly put off by the graphically explicit sex scenes that portray men engaged in steamy, sweaty sex with women. Egawa's depiction of Heian female sexual and body politics, and Genji's encounter with Utsusemi's stepdaughter in the episode discussed above raise charges of violation, for what is more invasive than being viewed in the nude without permission, or being sexually stimulated while sound asleep? All have the markings of a horrific experience for women of any era. Yet what of the stepdaughter's reaction? In the tale she offers no resistance and wants Genji to visit her again—circumstances that Egawa embellishes at will. In his remediation, the stepdaughter is delighted and excited about what is happening to her and comes back for more and more (2001–5, 3:164–72). In effect, Egawa portrays the young woman as an insatiable sex machine, but he is very careful to draw her in a cute, comic, hyperbolic *manga* style, placing her and the encounter well away from the real world. Pulling all the stops in the initial consummation scene, Egawa depicts the woman freefalling through phantastic space, while Genji's penis (with his head at its tip) makes its way through the young woman's body and out her mouth in an over-the-top, phantasmal manner, so very far removed from the real world. Unreal, outrageous, hyperbolic—what was Egawa thinking?

The charge of sexual violence against women can indeed be levied against Egawa's hypersexualization of *The Tale of Genji*—and second-wave feminism would be in the vanguard, attacking Egawa's objectification of women's bodies and trafficking of women "as sexual spectacle" under an intrusive male gaze (Jackie Stacey, qtd. in Grossman 2020, 287). Feminist scholarship in the 1980s and 1990s, however, would challenge this assessment, arguing that women are not "homogeneous," that the male gaze is not "monolithic," and that popular culture is not "univocal," nor the "spectator … fixed by the text to a predetermined gender identification" (Grossman 2020, 288). Women, gazes, audiences, and even genders are disparate, multifaceted, fragmented, and fluid. All are further embedded in race, class, sexuality, and in what Setsu Shigematsu calls "historical, cultural, ideological, and economic expediencies," as well as power dynamics (199, 128).

How much more is this the case when cultural, global, and genre border crossings occur, as in Egawa's case. *Manga* studies have shown that *manga* are particularly adept at encouraging readers to identify with their protagonists and to take up multiple positionalities regardless of the genders and sexualities inhabited by the readers. The reading strategies employed (which scholars have called Japanese *manga* or media literacy, an economy of desire for images) allow practitioners to commit fully to their fantasy/phantasy 2D *manga* (and *anime*) worlds—and engage them only in the imaginary and in specified in-group venues. *Fujoshi* rotten girls consumers of BL/*yaoi* have perfected this engagement into an art form. Moreover, as we saw in the introduction, Japanese speakers continually craft themselves to fit the parameters of differing social contexts—formal/informal, at work/at play, with whom, where, and when (see Kondo 1990)—so they are well situated to explore the in-betweenness of different identifications, and to occupy a host of queer readings, as we have seen among BL consumers. Egawa's *Genji* draws in (wo)men readers (straight and queer) who lust after Genji's role in the stepdaughter's sexual awakening—and for the opportunity to experience the stepdaughter's "first time." Perhaps other (fe)male readers, too, would respond to Genji's advances as enthusiastically as the stepdaughter does—or desire the *seme*-like initiator role occupied by Genji. Still others—male and female, straight and otherwise—dream of giving in to their desires fully and becoming like the "sex machine" stepdaughter. All do so within the safe spaces of their imaginary and regulated in-group events, which allow unfettered freedom—separate from the mainstream real world and its rigid rules of social decorum and behavior.

As is the case with other audiences, *manga* audiences, including readers of Egawa's *Genji*, are not monolithic but "fragmented, polymorphous, contradictory, and nomadic" (Doty, qtd. in Grossman 2020, 288). They produce readings that complicate and challenge the very texts themselves, as the examples above suggest.

Alongside male gazes that objectify women's bodies in the service of voyeuristic pleasure, queer readings run rampant—subversive, but also complicit at the same time. Thus, utilizing sex that smacks of sex for sex's sake, gratuitous to plot, image, and story, Egawa creates spaces where readers can express and engage their (fe)male sexual fantasies, hyper-eroticizing and fetishizing body parts.

In his eroticized *manga*, Egawa constructs an array of bodies in hyperbolic and extravagant fashion that disengage from real life and 3D female bodies. The enormous, oversized bosoms bursting out of robes, the wildly ecstatic reactions after a night of frivolity with Genji, the profuse sweat rolling off nude bodies during the sexual encounters, phalluses decked out with Genji's head—all these spotlight Genji's unfettered lust through what Klar calls "comic specific bodies." These bodies can do and be things that are far beyond the physical laws of real life: they are resistant to injury, resurrect themselves continually, and can parody gender, age, and other species (Klar 2013, 128–31), thus stabilizing and destabilizing the reading process. The Akatsuka and Koizumi remediations already discussed poke fun at Genji's *suki* lust, but Egawa's sensationally exaggerated bodies, body parts, and sex acts are so over-the-top that one cannot help but wonder whether Egawa is slyly laughing at Genji and the male gaze, lampooning them for their excesses—at the same time that he enables both the enjoyment of male desire and multiple queer readings.

Notably, this ridicule of male lust and desire can be construed as being directed not simply at the fictional Genji but at the imperial family at large, for maintaining a harem of imperial consorts at the beck and call of the emperor. By one account Egawa's *Genji* was the first time that the imperial family had been so scandalously treated—its sexual mores, although from more than a millennium before and no longer in practice—aired in such appalling fashion.[12] By bringing grotesque humor and exasperating hyperbole to the fore in transposing the sexual and power politics of Murasaki Shikibu's tale, Egawa invites us to take up different positionalities to see which ones fit, to explore a bit, to be grossed out a lot, and to take his portrayals of the imperial family, male lust, (wo)men's comic-specific bodies, and women's lives with many grains of salt. Or perhaps not. One never knows for sure because Egawa keeps pushing the envelope, delighting some, shocking many, and definitely challenging all—yet somehow remaining within the decorum required of mainstream journals. Quite the agitator, Egawa provokes reaction in and engagement by his readers, as he takes his works to the edge of what is appropriate and then pushes them one step over the line—or maybe two or three.

Seinen *Young Men #2: Eye-Candy Panty Shots and Cherry-Picking the* Genji

The last two titles discussed here take young men comics in different directions, transposing the *Genji* to contemporary Japan and enacting a more powerful female presence. In her *Minamoto-kun monogatari* (*The Tale of Minamoto-kun*), Inaba Minori recasts Genji as a college student and plays to her young men audience but also places her young, naïve Genji stand-in at the mercy of her women protagonists.

Artist est em's *Ii ne! Hikaru genji-kun* (*Twitter "Likes"! Shining Genji-kun*) is even more off the beaten path. Not only does the artist dispense with Genji's perspective, but she removes all the women in the eleventh-century tale, plopping Genji into contemporary Japan as the "roommate" of a young woman named Fujiwara Saori. Genji sheds his Heian robes for sweats and tennies and acquires an iPhone as he tries to acclimate to the twenty-first century—with some engagingly funny results.

Reminiscent of Takahashi Rumiko's 1982–97 young men comics *Maison Ikkoku* (*Maison Ikkoku*), in which a young man falls for his older, more experienced landlady, Inaba's 2012–19 sixteen-volume *Tale of Minamoto-kun* features adult eroticized romantic interactions between the protagonists, but with one marked difference: the central protagonist is not the suave, debonair Genji of old, or even the adult Genji in Egawa or Tomi's remediation, but an earnest, sexually naïve young college student. Renamed Minamoto-kun—the vernacular Japanese reading of the surname Genji, plus the diminutive *kun* (rather than *san*, the adult equivalent of Mr.) appended to his name—Minamoto Terumi is designated as junior to—or a peer of—the women in the *manga*. The ramifications are clear: Terumi is not "manly" in the usual sense of the word, and is even stylized a loser, because he has never had a girlfriend and knows very little about women. To add insult to injury, all through junior high and high school, Terumi was mercilessly harassed by a girl who was angered that Terumi and not she was deemed the cutest "girl" in school (Inaba 2012–19, 1:3, 5–6). Even in college, Terumi (whose name could refer to a female) is often mistaken for a girl, and he makes a stunningly beautiful one when he dons female garb.

For most of the series, Minamoto-kun is very much at the beck and call of his aunt, Fujiwara Kaoruko, who takes him in after he is driven from home by his father. A *Tale of Genji* scholar, Kaoruko tasks Terumi for help with her research. This would not ordinarily be cause for alarm, but Kaoruko instructs Terumi to enact *The Tale of Genji* by romancing—in effect, bedding—fourteen women. Terumi reacts in disbelief, mirroring our reactions as readers. But he grudgingly acquiesces because he sees it as a chance to shed his past and remake himself into a skillful lover if all goes well. The operative phrase is "if all goes well," for Terumi is not the irresistible, man-in-control eleventh-century Genji—and his "targets" are not Heian woman under patriarchal control. Rather, they are powerfully reconfigured contemporary spin-offs of Genji's ladies[13] with Aunt Kaoruko at the helm, acting as a kind of Murasaki Shikibu to Terumi's tale. As a result, the women make Terumi their boy toy, harnessing his lustful male gaze to get him to do their bidding.

In one such instance Terumi is instructed to court Tokonatsu Yū. Unlike her delicate counterpart Yūgao in the tale, who dies at the hands of Genji's jealous lover, Yū is an energetic fitness instructor who becomes engaged to Terumi, only to terminate the relationship and strike out on her own. Similar interactions in which the women call the shots continue throughout the sixteen volumes, as Inaba transposes the Heian women into vibrant modern figures who control their desires—and their destinies. Even the timid red-nosed princess Suetsumuhana, who acts as comic relief in the original tale, is transformed from an unattractive,

Figure 6.4 Unbeknownst to Yū, Terumi spies on her lifting her top to cool off. Fan-service close-up of her breasts is very much on display, but on the left page we also see Terumi's sense of shame at being a "peeping Tom." Inaba Minori, *The Tale of Minamoto-kun*, 7: 42–3. Copyright © 2012–19. Courtesy of Inaba Minori and Shūeisha.

old-fashioned princess into a pixie-porn-video-game voice actor! At first she is so painfully shy that she can barely be in the same room with Terumi, but in the end her desire to succeed as a voice actor pushes her to proposition Terumi to sleep with her as a "study strategy," so that she can audition for her part with real-life experience and conviction (Inaba 2012–19, 9:103–7).

As a young men's title, *The Tale of Minamoto-kun* must also perform for the target demographic, so panel after panel shows Terumi ogling female bodies. But Terumi's gaze operates differently from the lust and swagger of Egawa's Genji. Rather, Terumi is depicted with a blush under his eyes shamefacedly sneaking a peek at women's bodies, as in his guilty appreciation of Yū's chest when she lifts her top to cool off in front of a fan in Figure 6.4.

In other instances, the display of women's bodies suggests something different. Eroticized eye candy for certain, they also tease and manipulate Terumi—and, by extension, readers. In fact the women control the staging of their sexualized bodies, regulating how much, how little, for whom, when, and why they display them. Thus Terumi ogles and objectifies the women's bodies, but the women use this looking to reel him in by his lustful nose and get him to do their bidding.

The women are in charge, but the person orchestrating it all is Terumi's aunt Fujiwara Kaoruko. Her surname alludes to the *Genji* author Murasaki Shikibu and the powerful Northern Fujiwara Branch Regent Michinaga who was the power broker behind the family's dominance at court. Kaoruko does not have a court over which she holds sway, but she is very much in charge: she sets the narrative in motion by tasking Terumi to bed the women; she acts as his sexual instructor, teasing and taunting him with her body; and she "stage-manages" how and where Terumi "seduces" his targets. "Look, touch, but no sex"—that seems to be her mantra to Terumi about her body, and one to which he fastidiously adheres because she is his aunt. Known throughout the university for her beauty—sexual prowess and allure—Kaoruko is the heartthrob of Terumi's best friend Murakami and other males, and is not ashamed to flaunt her physical assets. Her actions vis-à-vis Terumi borders on incest, alluding to the eleventh-century *Genji*'s relationship with his stepmother, the import of which becomes clear at the end of the series.

Throughout the series Kaoruko is very much in control and maintains her role as the master puppeteer: she appears several times in every volume and keeps tabs on Terumi's activities, strategizing with him beforehand and debriefing him after, guiding and directing him as she sees fit. Cold, dispassionate, and interested only in the success of her research, Kaoruko appears in Volume 11 to be pining for Terumi, who is away at a driving-school boot camp trying to protect Tamakazura Ruri (Inaba 2012–19, 11:191–6). Up to this point she has been aloof, displaying no interest in Terumi in over two thousand pages, but now something seems to be afoot. The series' denouement produces some startling revelations—for Terumi and for readers as well.

The *manga* continually subverts the male gaze and depicts the women having a field day leading Terumi around by the nose. Terumi very willingly goes along with the agenda, earnestly trying to win over the women not by overpowering them but being kind, solicitous, and by reining in his own needs and attending to theirs. Why such a thoughtful, kind, and malleable Genji lover? Parody is very much in play, but its full impact is not revealed until nearly three-fourths into the concluding volume. After disappearing for a length of time and returning home, Kaoruko dares Terumi to stand up to her sexual ministrations and then gives him two hours to do the same to her (Inaba 2012–19, 16:114–53). It takes only one lick of Kaoruko's tongue on Terumi's penis for him to fall, whereas when it is Terumi's turn he must work for two hours to finally achieve his goal—and Kaoruko's approval and admiration. They engage in mutual pleasuring, and readers expect this to be the "climax" (no pun intended!) of the series, but there is much more. After their lovemaking, Kaoruko reveals that she is Woman #14—in other words, Terumi's Fujitsubo, parodying Genji's lifelong pursuit of his stepmother Fujitsubo and thereby transforming the eleventh-century *Genji*'s mother complex into an aunt complex. But there is still more: we find out that Kaoruko promised Terumi's mother that she would raise him to be an ideal man with whom fourteen women would fall in love (Inaba 2012–19, 16:164, 168–9)—this time enacting a parodic reversal of the eleventh-century *Genji*'s raising the young Murasaki to be the perfect woman. The series ultimately closes with the two engaged in three months of nightly bliss, Terumi proving that he has indeed grown up to be a lover of principle and great skill. Kaoruko also announces that she is leaving Shiun University and tasks Terumi to commence his own *The Tale of Minamoto-kun*!

Navigating uncharted waters indeed, Inaba has one more thing up her sleeve—focalizing Terumi's cross-dressing performances. She hints at this early on, through his gender-neutral name, and also through positioning him as the prettiest girl in junior high. But rather than only maintaining his male persona, Terumi embraces his "feminine" self and increases his cross-dressing activities in college. In most cases he does so at the behest of his aunt: to "man" the information booth at Shiun University's Open Campus Day as a girl, and to greet visitors as a female *maiko* attendant at a shrine run by his cousin Asahi's relatives (Inaba 2012–19, 7:3–9; 9:62–3). In one of the most striking scenes, Terumi goes against Kaoruko's wishes and enters the Miss Shiun University bathing-suit contest, bringing down the house by beating six female contestants, including his archrival Chūjō, although he pulls out before he is awarded the crown (Inaba 2012–19, 8:152–80). As the series progresses, however, Terumi uses his female impersonation to help young women whom he is tasked to win over: in Volume 11 he goes undercover as a female high school student to protect his tenth target, Tamakazura Ruri, from an unwanted suitor, and in Volume 14 he dresses as a girl to accompany Oboro Tsukiko (Woman #11) to a love hotel so that she can conduct research for her novel and get over her fear of men (Inaba 2012–19, 11:136–60; 14:13–29).

The cross-dressing in Inaba's *manga* no doubt speaks to the eleventh-century Genji's ability to turn the heads of men as well as women, and gender flips Genji's taking to bed a young male attendant in lieu of the attendant's sister, but Inaba hints at something more. Most *Genji manga* retain Genji as a male, his ladies as female, and the romantic performance as heteronormative. But like *The Comics Anthology of the Tale of Genji: Ms. Shining Genji's Hottie Diary* and *The Tale of Genji BL Anthology: Love Scrolls of Courtly Male Desire* (discussed respectively in Chapters 3 and 4), Inaba's remediation messes with gender identities and dynamics. Angered at being mistaken for a girl in junior high, Terumi does not operate as a transgender person in the usual sense of the positionality, yet there is his curious entrance into the Ms. Shuin University contest as a girl donning a bathing suit. In Volume 12 a shamefaced Terumi in female guise gives a bath to an unsuspecting Tamakazura Ruri, heightening the (heterosexual) sexual tension between them if we take Terumi's gender as male, but also opening up same-sex lesbian sexual attraction if positioning Terumi as a girl (Inaba 2012–19, 12:69–90). The blurring of the lines occurs in other instances as well: Terumi dresses as a girl to show Oboro Tsukiko the sexual ropes at the love hotel; his cousin Asahi moons over the female-attired Terumi at her family shrine (Inaba 2012–19, 14:12–28, 45–96; 11:59, 62–7). Readers "know" that Terumi is male and that the attraction is heterosexual, but his image as a girl provides ample room to queer the interaction as a female-female encounter and to ruminate on what constitutes "normative" sexual, gender, and erotic performance.

Inaba's *Tale of Minamoto-kun* and its categorization as young men *manga* signal early on that this fascinating series will remediate the Heian tale in ways different from girls, ladies, or even boys comics. It centers on the male lead but transposes the accomplished and successful lover Genji into a naïve, inept young protagonist of eighteen who attempts to come of age sexually by romancing modernized, highly capable versions of Genji's ladies. Sophomore-ish in his fixation on the breasts, buttocks, and cleavage of (un)suspecting women, Terumi blunders his way through many a relationship with the women. Largely told from Terumi's perspective, the *manga* is filled with blow-by-blow accounts of his attempts to win over the women, replete with nude bodies, bosoms, and appropriate "sound" effects, no doubt to capture the attention of its primary young men demographic. And like Egawa's soft porn remediation, the *manga* does its job effectively, the early volumes going into numerous reprintings.[14]

For most of the series as well, Terumi's voyeuristic male gaze remains in play, even though Kaoruko and the women turn it back onto him and use it to manipulate and control him. The *manga* parodies his lovemaking efforts and his fetishizing male gaze, yet three-fourths of the way through the final volume, as we have seen, Inaba reveals a much different narrative by turning *The Tale of Genji* on its head—upending not just Genji's performance as a lover but his love for Fujitsubo, his mother complex, and especially his grooming of a young Murasaki to become his ideal wife and lover. Terumi is not a Don Juan but an earnest and solicitous lover; he does not have a mother complex but an aunt complex; and he is raised by a woman to become an ideal lover for women. Thus Terumi's cross-dressings, covert and overt, are designed to teach him how to better service the women in his life. "Becoming" a girl gives Terumi "insider" knowledge of what a woman wants in a lover. A male version of a (female) Takarazuka *otokoyaku* male lead and a *seme/uke* rolled-into-one, Terumi is schooled in what turns women on. He is thereby transposed into the perfect lover for heterosexual "conquests," while his dual male/female, male-gaze/cross-dressing positionalities also open queering opportunities for readers who seek same-sex female as well as heterosexual attraction and desire. For readers of *The Tale of Minamoto-kun*, the cross-dressing, *seme/uke*-rolled-into-one, Takarazuka-male/female performer Terumi may indeed be their dashing, heartthrob Shining Prince.

From a young, naïve Genji surrogate coming of age as a woman's ideal lover, we move to est em's *Twitter "Likes"! Shining Genji-kun* (2016), which places the Genji in contemporary Japan "rooming" with a young woman, Fujiwara Saori. Displaced from Heian Japan to contemporary Tokyo, Genji still turns heads and receives approving looks from women—this time signaled by the numerous "likes" he receives for his posts on the social media platform Twitter (now known as X). Here, as in Inaba's work, the diminutive "-*kun*" appended to Genji's name indicates that this new Genji is not the unapproachable emperor's son, but one whom Saori can consider her social equal, friend, and even love interest.

Twitter "Likes"! Shining Genji-kun was first serialized in *Feel Young*, a ladies-comics magazine that often stars women in their early twenties juggling careers and romantic relationships, as well as those in their thirties and forties attempting to maintain work-life balance. *Feel Young* has been home to the likes of Unita Yumi's *Bunny Drop*, about a single man raising his grandfather's love child, and Sakurazawa Erica's *Between the Sheets*, featuring a young woman protagonist who falls in love with her female best friend, so est em's *Genji-kun* fits in well with such company, although its similarity to Nakamura Hikaru's young men comics *Saint Young Men* is striking. Much like Buddha and Jesus—the two protagonists in *Saint Young Men* who come down to Tokyo for a vacation from their holy duties—the Genji figure in *Twitter "Likes"* comes to contemporary Tokyo from the eleventh century and must adapt to his new surroundings. A gently humorous and different look, est em's remediation successfully enacts a crossover ladies comics and young men comics *Saint Young Men* lookalike that signals the artist's work across the BL, *yaoi*, boys, and young men *manga*, and also her border crossing of gender- and age-targeting categories (Berndt n.d.).

A one-volume work of 198 pages, the story ventures far afield from Murasaki Shikibu's tale: the only Heian references document Genji's brief return to his ladies after his first appearance in Saori's apartment and a short contemporary reenactment of the tale on TV. What transcends the temporal divide, however, is Genji's effect on women—they go as "goo-goo-eyed" over him in the twenty-first century as they did in the eleventh. But primarily a gag *manga*, *Twitter "Likes"!* focuses more on Genji's funny encounters with twenty-first-century mores. Its creator, est em, cleverly sets up the humorous clash between the Heian and the contemporary from the get-go (est em 2016, 7–33): the female protagonist Saori comes home exhausted from her unfulfilling job hoping to spend a relaxing weekend, but curiously, she puts up Heian-style *sudare* bamboo blinds to give her apartment an "Asian" flare and burns incense that she bought in Paris. A puzzling set of events, but it all makes good sense if we have been paying attention to the beginning of the *manga*. It opens with the iconic words *izure no oontoki nika* (In which era was it?), the opening lines to *The Tale of Genji* (which evoke memories of high school literature class for Japanese readers), and then continues in classical Japanese, contrasting the unremarkable cog-in-the-wheel office lady Saori with the laudable Kiritsubo Consort, Genji's mother, who is of low rank but extraordinary nonetheless.

Why est em makes the contrast is not clear, but one thing is certain: Saori's world is about to be turned upside down as the incense reaches out into the past and beckons Genji, who emerges through the *sudare* arrayed in his Heian attire and *eboshi* hat. A shocking encounter for both characters, each interprets the situation through his/her respective historical and class-appropriate lens. In a kind of reverse anachronism, Genji grabs Saori, as he might a lady on one of his nocturnal trysts, but he quickly determines that she must be a *mono no ke* living spirit who has come to possess him, because she appears to have on a facial mask. Saori in turn sees Genji as an intruder, so she grabs a bat, knocks him out cold, and calls the police. Totally out of his element, Genji is about to be hauled off to the station when Saori inexplicably blurts out that she knows him—albeit only from her high school classical literature class. From his speech and dress Saori determines that her intruder is the Shining Prince Genji (est em 2016, 36–8).

Inexplicable and incongruous as this may be, Saori "saves" Genji from the gallows, so to speak. Thus begins his adventure, as he sheds robe, *eboshi* hat, and the Heian period for sweats and, later, khaki pants, a jacket, a wool cap, and contemporary Japan. Even in modern times, he receives admiring looks from women as he experiences Tokyo with great enthusiasm and aplomb. His innocent delight is infectious, and is expressed in a novel mixture of Heian and modern ways: when he tastes a *matcha* tea frappé for the first time, for example, he bursts into poetic song, creating a thirty-one-syllable *waka* poem to express his delight (est em 2016, 66–7). He does likewise when he has a marshmallow-and-strawberry-dipped-in-chocolate dessert, and falls in love with soufflés and Mont Blanc pureed chestnut confectionary (est em 2016, 142–3, 148). He also goes off to compose more poems with a poetry circle of senior citizens and runs a marathon with Saori, only to literally chase after a cute runner, leaving Saori in the dust (est em 2016, 132, 164–6). But Saori's reaction to Genji's Heian lifestyle is also telling. He explains that he was on his way to exile in Suma for bedding his brother's imperial consort when he stumbled into the twenty-first century. Operating from the contemporary reader's perspective, Saori is scandalized that Genji committed adultery with his brother's wife and that he has numerous other women lovers as well. Her consternation over Genji's loose morals is, however, displaced by her fear that Genji might turn his womanizing attention to her—but this, too, she dismisses when she realizes, with some regret, that Genji has not made any moves on her (est em 2016, 70–2)!

Such concerns notwithstanding, Saori worries about Genji's well-being, especially his getting lost while she is at work, so she gives him an iPhone and sets up a Twitter account for him, so he can take pictures and she can contact him (est em 2016, 126–9). When she teaches him how to use the phone and the account, Genji processes these things in terms of what he knows: his selfie, for example, is first likened to a mirror and then to a painting; his sending of his selfie, along with the *waka* poem he composes to express his pleasure in it, is understood as "couriering" a hard-copy Heian *fumi* letter (est em 2016, 74–83). Within an hour of the posting, he receives thirty *Ii ne* "likes" on his Twitter account (est em 2016, 84)—astounding Saori but also cleverly translating Genji's allure into modern terms. Soon Saori finds she is falling for him and is relieved that Genji is unable to return to the Heian period. But, as she is about to confess her feelings, they are hit by a truck. Saori regains consciousness in the hospital, only to find that Genji is gone (est em 2016, 189–94). Devasted, she searches for him but finds no trace of him: she is back to her old drudgery and decides that she needs to get over him. She goes to terminate his Twitter account but finds that he has three thousand followers—and is not only alive but has several selfies with different women! The *manga* ends with Saori tweeting her "like" to his last post, concluding that the Heian heartthrob Genji has transformed himself into a twentieth-century one (est em 2016, 198).

Far afield from the tale, the Heian period, and the other young men *Genji manga*, est em's *Twitter "Likes"! Shining Genji-kun* and Inaba's *The Tale of Minamoto-kun* focus on Genji but deflect him in different ways. Neither makes Genji a strong male. Inaba fashions a young, naïve college student at the beck and call of women, whereas est em depicts a Genji very much out of his element, but whose appeal is funneled through a wonderfully expressive appreciation of things modern, from ice cream to exquisite chocolates to selfies and Twitter. Both Minamoto-kun and Genji-kun are outliers and present very different sides of the Heian Genji—the former is the butt of jokes, surrounded by eye-candy panty shots with highly sexualized overtones, yet nevertheless succeeds in "conquering" fourteen women by being sensitive to their needs, while the latter is alluring and attractive to women but without overt sexuality. Women are attracted to and attractive to the Genji stand-ins in both remediations. With Inaba, the women use Terumi to fulfill their needs in ways reminiscent of ladies comics, and in the process transform Terumi into their ideal man. With est em, Saori takes up an advisory, caretaker role to a charming Genji who is so artless, clueless, and extremely candid in his encounters with the twenty-first century that Saori can scarcely be blamed for falling for him even without the usual sex, seduction, or even romance. Saori's dull and boring life comes alive as she spends time with Genji-kun, thus helping us see a different side of Murasaki Shikibu's Genji. Genji-kun is a lady killer still, but more truly an *ikemen* hottie guy who is attractive in looks and in personality, possessing beauty and allure that can cross a millennium. All he needed to do so was the right guide, est em's female protagonist Fujiwara Saori, who just might be a descendant of Shikibu of the Northern Branch of the Fujiwaras.

Conclusion: Lusting after the Genjis

The male-oriented *Genji manga* discussed in this chapter constitute six titles, fewer than any other category discussed here because *The Tale of Genji* remediates less easily into boys comics and young men comics than it does into girls comics and ladies comics. But what male-oriented *Genji manga* lack in numbers they make up for in breadth and reach. Unable to deploy the usual boys-comics adventure, battle, and comradery, Akatsuka and Koizumi create gag comics with two unlikely Genjis—a bucktoothed, slapstick nasty, and a roly-poly chestnut. The *seinen* young men offerings, too, are wide-ranging—Tomi showcases people, including Genji, trapped by the obligations that rule their lives in a Heian-turned-Tokugawa-esque society, in stark, ultrarealistic *gekiga* style. Egawa employs a cherubic-looking Genji who engages in graphically explicit sex scenes, depicted in an extravagant style, that shock but also parody and lay bare the cruel sexual mores of the Heian court. Utilizing parodic comic-style bodies, Egawa also provides space not only for the exploration of male desire but for queer reading strategies as well. In the newer young men remediations by female artists, Inaba features buxom women, panty shots, and a very naïve and unsure Genji surrogate who parodies Genji, his lifelong pursuit of his stepmother, and his raising of an ideal wife. In contrast, est em eschews the tale altogether and produces a Genji exploring the delights of contemporary Tokyo under the guidance of a young woman who might be construed as a Murasaki Shikibu "descendant."

As different as these remediations are, all focalize Genji's *suki* lusting after women. Akatsuka lampoons it by creating an unhandsome Iyami Genji bumbling his romantic way through the *manga*. Koizumi gently pokes fun at it by transforming Genji into a cute chestnut who fulfills his desires even at the expense of those around him. Brazen in style and sexually graphic in content and image, Egawa's *manga* puts Genji's unfettered sexual appetite on full display—depicting him deflowering a virgin for sixty-eight pages. Not to be outdone, Inaba presents her own brand of interrogating male lust. Catering largely to young men readers, she populates *The Tale of Minamoto-kun* with eye candy but uses these images to transform the Genji surrogate into a sensitive lover who serves her modern spin-offs of the eleventh-century Genji women. The remaining two artists discussed in this chapter utilize Genji's *suki* tendencies in a different manner: est em takes Genji out of his Heian element and remediates his attractiveness into socially acceptable twenty-first-century terms—namely, Twitter "likes"; Genji still has his stuff and can strut it, albeit through a new venue. Tomi, in contrast, subsumes Genji's *suki* under the grim reality of Tokugawa-esque life, in which societal, familial, and sexual obligations and concerns take precedence over the pursuit of women.

Hence four of the six *manga* examined here objectify, parody, and even lampoon the male gaze, but all six also share other things in common. Five, for example, traffic in humor—gag, hyperbolic, over-the-top, or bemused. Five tell their story from a male perspective. All six center on the Genji figure more fully than in girls-comics and ladies-comics adaptations, and tell his story. In addition, to a greater extent than for other remediations in this study, these six titles require literacy beyond both the eleventh-century tale and their own respective demographic categories. This is because the *Genji* does not lend itself to the usual parameters of boys comics, and because the young men's comics category allows for wide exploration and an "anything-goes" policy. With no adventure or little comradery to be had in Murasaki Shikibu's tale, Akatsuka's *Genji* weaves a complex intertextual tapestry, requiring knowledge of the eleventh-century tale but even more familiarity with Akatsuka's gag comics. Readers must transpose from his oeuvre the characters and their backstories that he uses to represent the *Genji* figures. Knowledge of Japanese comedian routines, contemporary cultural analogies, pseudo-historical language, and contemporary slang is imperative. Koizumi follows suit, harkening back to his *Pig/Buddha and the Phony* comics featuring adorably accessorized pigs performing very human, revealing quirks, while literacy in eight-frame gag comics, the *Genji* scrolls, and the Tosa paintings is needed as well.

The young men works also require knowing the tale and the comics categories. For Tomi's remediation, understanding the philosophical and political underpinnings of the *gekiga* style and Tatsumi Yoshihiro's *A Drifting Life* better situates the transformation of the Heian court into the dark, ultrarealistic, entrapping Tokugawa-esque world. Familiarity with *Lone Wolf and Cub* and other young men comics brings better contextualization as well. Egawa's remediation, in turn, requires readerly facility in the eleventh-century tale's storyline, personages, and events, but also familiarity with the cultural and orthographic practices of the Heian period on the one hand, and with erotic portrayals and adult male erotic *manga* on the other. Inaba's *Minamoto-kun* calls for knowledge of the tale but also detailed knowledge of the personalities of Genji's women: only then will readers be able to fully capture the clever ways in which Inaba has contemporized each woman. Understanding the function of panty shots and buxom women in young men offerings, how the male gaze works, and how it operates in the earlier young men comics *Chobits* (2001–2) by CLAMP and *Maison Ikkoku* (1982–97) by Takahashi Rumiko is critical as well. Finally, est em delicately balances knowledge of twenty-first-century Japan—the social media platforms and devices, the food, the accoutrements—with Heian customs to create her brand of humor produced in their disjuncture. The merging of the young men comics *Saint Young Men* with the ladies comics' search for an ideal man generates even more humorous moments.

But as different and similar as these male-oriented remediations of Genji are—*ikemen* handsome and not so handsome, inexperienced youth and super-lecher, roly-poly chestnut and Edo-esque courtiers—the Genjis in these remediations provide singular and novel looks at the tale, highlighting certain aspects and bringing out others that we would have never dreamed of. Who indeed is the real Genji—or does it matter?

Chapter 7

EDUCATION FOR SOFT POWER, NATIONAL
PRIDE, AND FEMINIST CRITIQUE: *GENJI* IN *JŌHŌ*
INFORMATIONAL *MANGA*

When I taught Tsuboi Koh's *The Illustrated Tale of Genji: A Classic Japanese Romance* in class, students often asked, "What are '*jōhō* informational *manga*'?" Not a household word even in Japan, informational comics are generally used to make school curricula, corporate manuals, project plans, and government white papers more accessible, and are ubiquitous in Japan for that reason. They teach people how to bank, how to support an aging parent, how to face death—and even instruct a young mother how to network in a new neighborhood.[1] Hence the existence of *Genji jōhō manga* stands to reason; yet what was as surprising to my students as it was to me is that these informational comics teach readers to view the tale in very specific ways—including as a database of the best of Japanese culture and as a literary masterpiece, on a par with classic western works, that garners the respect and support of both domestic and global audiences. Ostensibly educational in nature, this reading of *The Tale of Genji* carries a great deal of clout, and like all *manga*, these informational comics are very successful in reaching and working with different audiences through their gender- and age-marked content, narrative conventions, and drawing styles. And, as teaching tomes, they also preclude presenting Genji or the tale as deviant or highly erotic.

The authority afforded the *Genji* and other informational comics comes from their genesis in the 1950s as tools to teach history, geography, and the sciences to children and, later, to instruct adults in business, politics, education, and literature (Kure 1997, 207–8; Kinsella 2000, 71–7). These comics are marketed as factual and objective, but in fact they "inform" from particularized political, cultural, and social points of view—some, for instance, proselytize religious cults, while others endorse ultranationalistic claims that Japan fought the Second World War to stop "white people from colonizing Asia" (Gravett 2004, 119). Even pioneer Ishinomori Shōtarō's (1986) *Japan Inc: An Introduction to Japanese Economics in Manga*, which jump-started the informational comics industry (Kure 1997, 207), purports to simply explain Japanese economics, but it does so in ways sympathetic and laudatory to Japan. Scholar Sharon Kinsella contends that, in the hands of the Japanese government, *manga* such as *Japan Inc* disseminate Japanese culture abroad in "a more official and managed" manner (2000, 13)—to garner goodwill[2] and enhance Japan's image as vibrant, hip, and contemporary. "A form of implicit political revisionism," they provide a positive view of the Japanese military-industrial complex—its large corporations, legislative branch, and military forces.[3] Hirokane Kenshi's 1983–92 nonerotic adult men comics story *Section Chief Kōsaku Shima* (about an ethical, "good guy" salaryman rising through the ranks of corporate Japan), for example, puts a more positive face on Japanese industry, while Kawaguchi Kaiji's 1988–96 *Silent Service* does the same for the military in its narrative of a renegade Japanese submarine captain and crew taking on global superpowers to save the world.

It is difficult to ascertain the exact influence that *manga* have globally. However, riding the *anime*, music, fashion, and food Cool Japan wave that was prominent in the 1990s through 2010s—and to some extent even today—*manga* do gather cultural status and goodwill for Japan. *Genji manga* do similar work for the tale, building upon the 1910s and 1920s efforts that used the tale to anchor Japan's bid to modernize. Cashing in on its positionality as the world's first novel, on equal footing with Marcel Proust's *Remembrance of Things Past*, *The Tale of Genji* helped situate Japan as a modern, global nation-state. To this day the tale maintains international prominence as one of the few Asian literary works included in world literature collections such as the Penguin Classics series.

Marketed to the Japanese people as a source of national pride and a globally acclaimed masterpiece, the tale has bolstered Japan's national identity domestically as well (see Caddeau 2006, 8, 3 for more information). It was nativist scholar Motoori Norinaga who argued in the eighteenth century that the "essence" of Japanese culture lay in *The Tale of Genji*; in the 1910–1920s the tale was first deployed in statecraft; by the 1930s it appeared in primary through high school textbooks to foster national pride (T. Suzuki 2008, 244, 271); and after the Second World War it bolstered Japan's peace-loving status and signaled its reentry into the new world order. The well-regarded Heian scholar Ikeda Kikan has heralded the tale as Japan's "grandest and greatest novel," and as one "praised by people all over the world as one of the world's classics" (Ikeda, qtd. in T. Suzuki 2008, 277).

The Tale of Genji's positionality as a national treasure that legitimizes the authority of the state and its superiority in the twentieth century (Caddeau 2006, 3) remains to this day. At the November 2008 Millennial Anniversary Memorial Ceremony of the tale's inception, in the presence of 2,400 attendees, an actress stand-in for its author Murasaki Shikibu proclaimed that the *Genji* is not just a "Japanese classic" but a "world classic" influencing the arts, performance, and craftwork, and deeply touching the hearts of readers the world over. Not just a literary work but a life guide, she noted that the tale is "the crystallization of the wisdom of humanity" and that it answers existential questions such as "What is a human being? What is life?" (qtd. in Emmerich 2013, 16).[4]

As would be expected, the *manga* remediations of the tale are also not innocent in rewriting history or perceptions of Genji and the tale. *Bunkashi manga* ("literary manga"), an informational comics subcategory that includes the *Genji manga*, originated as a public relations stratagem to attract Japanese audiences who normally do not read literary works (Kinsella 2000, 73). But the *Genji jōhō manga* do much more than entice new readers—they highlight certain aspects of the tale, focalize the point of view of Genji or the women, utilize specific drawing styles and the like to map particularized versions of the tale. They also call upon learned scholars, educators, and famous *manga* artists and novelists to write treatises to direct the reading of the tale. Some promote the women, others temper Genji's image and laud the tale as a globally acclaimed masterpiece of which readers should be proud—while concomitantly taking pride in the nation and culture that produced it. Moreover, as educational tomes, they are regarded as providing the "true" interpretation of the tale. To this we can add the *Genji manga*'s appeal to a new stratum of niched audiences. Throughout the ages, the *Genji* transpositions have provided differently situated bodies with the political and cultural right to rule (landed warlords in the fourteenth and fifteenth centuries) or to serve as the cultural brokers of their times (the twelfth-century court or the Edo townspeople). The *Genji manga* in their mainstream and especially their informational iterations do the same today, this time in the name of eliciting goodwill and positive appraisal for Japan, creating pride in nation and state, and serving as a coping mechanism in times of adversity. The timely millennium celebration of the tale from 2000 to 2008 epitomized the confluence of all three impulses, as we saw in the introduction.

Informational Genji Manga *Speak*

The first *Genji manga* was a girls comics published in 1974, with other categories following in the 1980s and 1990s, and informational *manga* were in the mix early on, highlighting the tale's educational importance, with the three most recent *jōhō manga* appearing between 2010 and 2014. Well-regarded *manga* artists (Tsuboi Koh and Hasegawa Hōsei) were recruited to illustrate the tale; many titles (by Kuwata Jirō, Maruyama Kei, Hasegawa, Hanamura Eiko, Variety Art Works, and Sanazaki Harumo) have become part of classical and general literature *manga* collections; and one *Genji jōhō manga* (by Saeki Nao) was ensured of wide distribution under the auspices of the Kumon reading program network. Two (the Tsuboi and Mihashi Mari versions) enlisted a Heian literary scholar as a consultant to enhance the accuracy and prestige of their interpretations, and even the government got into the act, "commissioning" Toba Shōko (whose work is categorized as a girls comics in our study) to fashion a *Genji manga* based on their *anime* series on classical literature. All in all, the reach is deep and wide.

But as broad as the informational offerings may be, all ten (not including the Toba and Akatsuka remediations discussed in Chapters 3 and 5, respectively) fall into three major groupings, categorized by the age and gender of their audiences: *manga* for children, for adult males, and for adult women. The *manga* discussed below under "Informational Children *Manga*: Less-Gendered, Cute, Straightforward Narratives" target young children and employ a more gender-neutral *manga* style than those in the next two groups. Maruyama and Kuwata write for the very youngest readers, while Saeki and Kishida write for older elementary school students. The *manga* discussed under "Adult Informational

Manga #1: 'Unmarked' Male Views" includes offerings by Tsuboi, Hasegawa, and Variety Art Works. Tsuboi adapts his realistic children's educational *manga* drawings to be more age appropriate for adult readers, Hasegawa employs a classical scroll painting technique, and Variety Art Works utilizes an adult-oriented realistic style of drawing, but all relate the story from Genji's point of view, their orientation very male, with the experiences of the women remaining in the background. In contrast, the titles under "Adult Informational Manga #2: 'Marked' Women's Concerns" are by three female artists, Mihashi, Hanamura, and Sanazaki, and operate very much within the mainstream of *josei* (women comics) if not *redikomi* (ladies-comics) remediations (see Chapter 5). The drawing styles and narration depict the concerns and issues of the women in the tale. Thus, although the informational comics do not portray Genji as an ideal object of desire, as girls comics do, or focus on safe spaces where readers can give full rein to their sexual desires, as is found in ladies comics, or even create slapstick gag lovers or roly-poly chestnut to elicit laughs among young boy readers (see Chapter 6), the age- and the gender-targeting stratagems remain very much in play.

Informational Children Manga: Less-Gendered, Cute, Straightforward Narratives

In keeping with comics for younger readers, the plots and characters of texts in this grouping are clear and straightforward. Moreover, all but one appear in collections that operate like a literary canon by standardizing for schools and parents the titles that constitute the pillars of Japan's national literature. The Maruyama and Kuwata texts, both entitled *Genji monogatari* (*The Tale of Genji*), appear in ten-by-seven-inch *ehon* picture books[5] favored by younger readers. Maruyama's remediation was in its eighth printing in 2003, and an expanded fifteen-volume edition appeared in 2009. Saeki Nao's *Kumon no manga koten bungakukan genji monogatari* (*The Kumon Manga Literature Classics Tale of Genji*), for older children, is published by and used in the Kumon Educational learning centers throughout Japan. For older elementary schoolchildren, Kishida Ren's *Manga genji monogatari* (*Manga Tale of Genji*) is the only title not part of a collection of classical literature, but its commentaries and the *manga* itself construct Genji as an honorable hero whom readers should admire.

Our first children's work, Maruyama Kei's[6] (1998; reprinted in 2003 edition) *The Tale of Genji*, appears as Volumes 4 and 5 in the ten-book *Komikkusutorii watashitachi no koten* (*Comic Stories of Our Classics*), which features literary works from the Nara (710–784) through the Tokugawa (1600–1868) periods. The series introduces Japanese literary classics to elementary students but also to junior and senior high students and adults, and an emeritus professor prominently authorizes it as a "fun" and accessible way to read the *Genji* story. To help the process along, the *manga* includes readings for the Chinese *kanji* characters, footnotes, and cultural notes. It also directs the reading and interpretation of the tale through chapter synopses, character profiles, and essays detailing the role and importance of the tale in classical literary history.[7]

The *manga* opens with a two-page spread situating Genji against a backdrop of simulated gold-leaf-decorated paper and signaling his centrality in the series. It utilizes titles that are based on but do not replicate those in the eleventh-century tale. Volume 1 focuses on Genji and his liaisons with his stepmother Fujitsubo, his first wife Aoi, the ill-fated Yūgao, the young Murasaki, his older lover Rokujō, and Akashi, the mother of his daughter. Volume 2 still revolves around Genji, although the second and third generations make their appearance. Only 259 pages long in its two volumes, the work focuses on Genji and the main female characters, with little on the subsidiary characters. The last ten Uji chapters, featuring the third generation, are reduced to nineteen pages.

Utilizing a cheery, *shōjo*-eseque style (reminiscent of her work in girls comics), Maruyama puts an age-appropriate "happy face" on her *Genji*. She makes her story straightforward—accessible, clear, concise, and easy to follow. She uses simplified language, and the dialogues and narration are short and to the point. No nudity or hot and heavy scenes—the love trysts are configured as couples lying in bed side by side or are confined to a chaste kiss or two (2003, 4:62–3). Death scenes are eschewed—the deceased look as if they are simply asleep (Maruyama 2003, 4:47–8, 134; 5:109), while the harsh realities of polygynous marital relations are omitted. Mindful of contemporary attitudes, Maruyama also downplays Genji's "playboy" persona and minimizes the unsavory elements of his personality: both his abduction of the young Murasaki and the consummation of their bond as husband and wife are greatly muted (2003, 4:64–5, 86). Rather, Genji is depicted as good, bright, handsome, cheerful, and an exceedingly kind and responsible person. His womanizing *suki* lust and self-centered ways expunged, Genji is thoughtful of others and their feelings. He faces up to his misdeeds—apologizing to Murasaki for marrying the Third Princess, looking appropriately remorseful when Murasaki is saddened by his going to visit Akashi, and, even more surprisingly, expressing his regret to his father for cuckolding him (Maruyama 2003, 5:69; 4:132, 64).

Genji's apologies whenever he does something wrong, taken in tandem with instances where he is told not to cry, such as when his mother leaves the palace and upon her death (Maruyama 2003, 4:21–3), reflect not just a kinder, more sensitive Genji but "teachable moments" that aim to instill honorable and praiseworthy behavior in young readers. Yet the women readily accept Genji's transgressions, even enabling him whenever they can. Murasaki, for example, lets Genji visit other women and offers to raise Akashi's daughter without being asked, while Akashi is sad but not hurt when Genji returns to the capital without her (Maruyama 2003, 4:131–3; 4:115). Little jealousy or anger on the part of the women is depicted— they "let him off the hook" in ways that few other portrayals do. This whitewashed Genji does surface in mainstream girls *manga*, but Maruyama's remediation, touted as educational and used in classroom and at other official sites, gives much more authority to the positive reading of Genji and the tale.[8]

All in all, Maruyama's *The Tale of Genji* is a teaching tome attempting to provide a contemporary rendering of the tale. Augmented by historical and cultural explanations, it elects to follow the dominant narrative, thus focalizing on Genji and his liaisons with the principal women. To reach its young audiences and make

Genji a more honorable hero, it rewrites Genji as kinder and more thoughtful than he is in Murasaki Shikibu's tale—and depicts the women as acquiescing to his other lovers and even enabling his philandering ways. It also does not dwell on the "sketchier" sides of Genji's personality—his womanizing, his having many lovers, and his abducting the young Murasaki, among other things. The *shōjo*-esque drawings stylize the characters as cute and adorable and the tale as cheerful, happy, and accessible, erasing the dark and problematic aspects of Genji and the world he inhabits. Perhaps these choices are necessary for works targeting the youngest of readers, but it makes for a revisionist reading of Genji and the Heian period.

The second picture book, also entitled *The Tale of Genji*, comprises Volumes 5 through 7 in the *Komi gurafikku nihon no koten* (*Graphic Comics Japanese Classics*) series on Nara- through Tokugawa-period works. These *Genji* volumes, published from 1993 to 1995, cover much the same ground as Maruyama's do, but with two differences: they use *manga* texts and images with photographs of sites and objects, as well as reproductions of paintings and scrolls, to tell the tale. Presumably this better contextualizes the tale, but the conflation of present-day locales with the imaginary spaces depicted in the tale attempts to historize the tale in ways that cause some concern.

Kuwata Jirō is the artist; Tsuji Masaki, a well-respected novelist and scriptwriter for *anime* and dramatic pieces, writes the storyline; and a cadre of photographers provide the photos.[9] Using a media-rich format, the *manga* does a good job relating not only Genji's youth and glory days but also his darker side, which is brought to the fore by including a twelfth-century *Genji* scroll reproduction portraying him looking pensively at his reputed son Kaoru, who is not his biological offspring (1993–5, 7:53). Kuwata also does a good job with the women, portraying their interiority as well as that of other male characters. Hence Genji is not the golden boy, all sweetness and light, as seen in Maruyama's depiction, but is presented in a more balanced fashion, and one that is closer to his portrayal in the eleventh-century tale. The *manga* also does not shy away from grief or sorrow: both Genji's heart-wrenching distress when Murasaki dies and his own demise, depicted as a black silhouette etched against a grainy background signaling the end of his life, are beautifully done (1993–5, 7:117, 127).

As informative as this work is, combining *manga* drawings and text with photographs and art reproductions impedes the flow of the narration in some instances and causes confusion in others. And as noted above, the conflation of present-day locales with the imaginary spaces depicted in the tale is disconcerting. Casting a currently existing building as the location where Genji takes Yūgao for the tryst that ends in her death makes it seem as though Yūgao is a living person rather than a fictional one (Kuwata 1993–5, 5:41). Presenting Ninnaji Temple as the site to which Suzaku, Genji's half-brother, retires once he abdicates the throne (Kuwata 1993–5, 7:2) implies that Suzaku actually resided at the temple and transposes him into a living personage from the historical past. The commentaries take up a similar refrain: the second essay, for example, contends that the tale portrays specific Heian emperors—that Genji's father, the Kiritsubo Emperor, represents Emperor Daigo who reigned from 897 to 930 and that Genji and Fujitsubo's son Reizei is (based on) Emperor Murakami (Kuwata 1993–5, 6:i). Outlining several theories assessing the tale, the third commentary also argues for the historicity of the tale—that it is a record of the social and cultural aspects of the period, that the Buddhist impermanence of human life in the tale is a primer of moral instruction for the Heian courtiers, and that the tale personifies the "essence" of what constitutes Japan (Kuwata 1993–5, 7:i). Presenting the tale as fact/history imbues it with an authenticity and authority of lived lives that are not the case.

Less cute and sweet than Maruyama's informational *manga*, Kuwata's *Tale of Genji* uses text multimedia, and commentaries to direct the reading of the text, but in the end it proves difficult to traverse, requiring readers to digest a great deal without an established rhythm or flow. It also asks readers to see the tale as more than a fictional repository of the life of one handsome and talented Genji and argues for viewing Genji as Michinaga, transforming fictional characters into historical figures, and understanding the tale as a primer of the Buddhist concept of human life—in effect situating the tale as fact and not just fiction, and asking the tale to do much more than it was ever conceived to do.

The next two titles, which target older elementary school readers, do not historicize the tale but do stay on mission in terms of directing specific interpretations of the tale. This is especially true of the first, Saeki Nao's 2004 (first published in 1990) remediation, which is only forty-nine pages long and radically condenses the tale—so much so that it can be hard to follow. For example, Genji meets young Murasaki and brings her home to his mansion in six-and-a-half pages (Saeki 2004, 51–7). This includes Murasaki's grandmother refusing Genji's offer to become Murasaki's guardian and then passing away on the same page! Murasaki also reaches maturity in the course of a single page, although the montage of her growing up is skillfully executed (Saeki 2004, 58). Other events occur at such speed that the reader has no time to participate in the grieving, the suffering, or the joy. In most cases readers can follow the plot and the passage of time because they are referenced by Genji's age or indicated as "three years later," but the lack of character interiority makes for little readerly emotional investment in the characters and impedes full appreciation of the tale.

Readers must also fill in the gaps with information from the commentaries. Elementary schoolteacher Torii Hiroko writes several of them, giving general information on the tale, the author, and the literary, historical, economic, political, and social landscape of the times (2004, 151–9). But she also goes one step further, touting the *Genji* as "the greatest classical Japanese work." In her estimation the author evokes a wide spectrum of human emotions, and the construction of the women trapped in lives they cannot control poignantly embodies *mono no aware* evanescence of all things (2004, 154–5)—the essence of Japanese-ness. In his introduction Professor Hirata Yoshinobu does his part, echoing the injunction presented at the millennial celebration of the tale, which proclaimed Genji's trials and tribulations to be life lessons on how to be human (2004, 4–5). In its seventeenth printing in 2004, Saeki's remediation continues to preach that the *Genji* provides life lessons and is the greatest work in classical Japanese literature and even of Japanese-ness—reaching many through its Kumon Educational Japan centers located all over Japan (Kumon n.d.).

The last *manga* for children, Kishida Ren's 2002[10] (first published in 1996) *Manga Tale of Genji*, covers forty-one chapters in four volumes and also follows the lead of an academic, former Keio University Professor Nishimura Tōru, who cautions against viewing Genji as a playboy. Nishimura argues that Genji's philandering is an enactment of a practice of old in which emperors and imperial princes took wives from different lands to exercise their rule and authority over these regions (2002, 1:4–5). He also introduces a narrative frame that is important in the tale but not found in other remediations—the presence of a lady-in-waiting narrator relating the tale to an intimate few (2002, 1:5). Two young women eager to hear about Genji ask about him on the day of his funeral, and the in-text narrator obliges (Kishida 2002, 1:10–11). Nishimura adds that tales like the *Genji* were written by women and read aloud by ladies-in-waiting—but that was not always the case.[11]

Following Nishimura's lead, the Kishida *Genji* remakes Genji into a kind, thoughtful ideal man. Not only does he do right by the women characters, but he is solicitous of others as well. He feels badly for the anguish he causes Murasaki by marrying the Third Princess, and he openly blames himself for his exile and its cost to his men, both in loss of rank and in having to leave their loved ones (Kishida 2002, 3:266, 270; 2:69, 79, 93). This care and remorsefulness are suggested in other *manga*, but Kishida takes extra care in presenting Genji as kind and likable.

As the *manga* progresses, Genji becomes less shining and laudable, but he still retains his status as a remarkable, if not totally ideal, person. Kishida achieves this by constructing the women as loving him deeply and forgiving him, no matter the cost. Murasaki, for one, acknowledges the agony that Genji has put her through, but expires happy to have been loved by him (Kishida 2002, 4:210). On her deathbed Fujitsubo laments that she could not openly express her love for Genji (Kishida 2002, 2:248). The mutual respect and care that two rivals for Genji's affection, Murasaki and Akashi, afford each other also let Genji "off the hook" for putting them in untenable situations (Kishida 2002, 3:240). This is not to say that the eleventh-century tale contradicts these conclusions, but Kishida makes every effort to make plain Genji's goodness no matter what he does.

All in all, the Kishida remediation is praiseworthy for its attention to detail and for its attempt to be faithful to the *Genji*,[12] but in keeping with other remediations in this section, it presents Genji as a laudable hero—kind, sensitive, and with little to tarnish that reputation. The Kishida *manga* also does not depict the women characters pushing back against Genji or Heian court culture, thus allowing Genji and the practices of the period to look good, with the educational bent of the *manga* giving credence to this reading.

Adult Informational Manga #1: "Unmarked" Male Views

In keeping with the revisionist educational mission of informational comics, the children *manga* make Genji nicer than the eleventh-century tale does, and the Heian period brighter and shinier. The adult-oriented informational *manga* in

7. Education for Soft Power, National Pride, and Feminist Critique   147

this section follow suit—recouping Genji's image and viewing the Heian court as populated by beautiful people and filled with gloriously extravagant material culture. Addressing general audiences, these titles are actually "unmarked" male views, basically telling the story through Genji's eyes. The viewpoints of the women, their interiority, and their side of the story are often not fully explored, or mainly serve to tell the male-oriented Genji story. But each is remarkable in its own way. Tsuboi Koh's *The Illustrated Tale of Genji: A Classic Japanese Romance*, for one, primarily relates the tale through the eyes of the three generations of the male members of the Genji family, providing little of the women's perspectives, but doing so with a quiet elegance and beauty. Variety Art Works' *Genji monogatari manga de dokuha* (*Reading The Tale of Genji through Manga*), too, focuses on Genji and his male offspring with only a few moments highlighting women's concerns, but it takes a dramatically delightful turn toward the end. Hasegawa Hōsei's *Genji monogatari* (*The Tale of Genji*) also adopts Genji's perspective to relate his narrative, but Hasegawa's lush portrayal of the material culture of the period takes precedence.

We begin with Tsuboi Koh's[13] single-volume *Genji*—remarkable for its quiet beauty and also for being one of only two remediations available in English. Published in Japanese in 1989, it was followed seven months later by an English edition, translated by Alan Tansman. The *manga* covers thirty-six of the *Genji*'s fifty-four chapters and is notable for its condensation, allotting two hundred pages to Genji, fifty to his son Yūgiri and his son's friend Kashiwagi, and fifty to Genji's grandson Niou and his reputed son Kaoru. Tsuboi did the adaptation and illustrations, while renowned Heian scholar Shimizu Yoshiko served in a supervisory capacity. It is not clear how much direction Shimizu provided, but the focalization is mainly on the male characters and their relationships, with little presentation of the women's interiority.

Working within the short length of his remediation, Tsuboi devises some highly effective ways to condense the tale. He first highlights the characters above all else, distinguishing the "good," important personages from the secondary and not-so-good figures through his drawings. Genji, his stepmother Fujitsubo, and the love of his life Murasaki, as well as his son Yūgiri, grandson Niou, and presumed son Kaoru are drawn as *bishōnen/bishōjo* (beautiful men/women), while secondary characters are less attractive and more comical. The "villainous" Kokiden, for example, contorts her face in anger over Genji's mother's success at court and Genji's steady rise to power (Tsuboi 1989b, 108–9). Great care and more frame time are allotted to moments of importance as well. Genji's first glimpse of Fujitsubo covers the end of one page into the next, as his wonderment and delight are reflected on his face (Tsuboi 1989a and 1989b, 26–7). Figure 7.1 (which is read from left to right in the English version) shows a Genji in the lower right frame of the left-hand page, looking surprised at an image of himself walking down a corridor. It is only in Figure 7.2 (the Japanese version, which reads from right to left) that we see that Genji is actually looking at the figure of a woman on the next page walking down the hall, her full-portrait figure revealing that it is his love interest, his stepmother Fujitsubo.[14]

Figure 7.1 In the transposed English version, the left-hand page (page 26) depicts Genji looking at himself walking down the corridor. Tsuboi Koh, *The Illustrated Tale of Genji: A Classic Japanese Romance, English Edition*, 26–7. Copyright © 1989. Courtesy of Tsuboi Koh and Kadokawa.

Genji's fateful departure to Suma comes to life as well in one of the most beautiful frames in the *manga* (Tsuboi 1989b, 112). Startlingly crisp, the sharply etched thick black lines of the silhouetted oxen cart speak eloquently to the sadness and loneliness accompanying the departing entourage. But its sharpness is also muted by the gentle elegance and aestheticization of the moment.

Due to the brevity of his piece, Tsuboi omits eighteen chapters that delineate secondary threads of the story, but also condenses others in ingenious ways. In the "Hotaru" ("Fireflies") chapter, for instance, he distills the action into two interfacing pages: Tamakazura, Yūgao's long-lost daughter, is seated to the right on page 174,[15] with her shoulders hunched and a look of great embarrassment on her face as she realizes that one of her suitors, seated just beyond the raised curtain of state on the succeeding page, has seen her face illuminated by the fireflies that Genji has purposely let loose. Genji sits to the lower left of page 175, still holding the cloth in which he had hidden the fireflies, clearly reveling in his voyeuristic enjoyment of Tamakazura's chagrin and his suitor brother's delight.

Tsuboi's *Genji* is elegant, stately, and refined, enacted in slow-moving, exquisite tableaus, as seen in the "Fireflies" chapter and the Suma processional silhouette cutout. Dynamic departures indicate moments of special notice: the winds whipping about in the "Nowaki" ("Autumn Winds") episode, for example, speak to

Figure 7.2 In the Japanese version, page 26 is on the right and is situated so that Genji is looking across to page 27 (on the left) at Fujitsubo. Tsuboi Koh, *The Illustrated Tale of Genji: A Classic Japanese Romance, Japanese Edition*, 26–7. Copyright © 1989. Courtesy of Tsuboi Koh and Kadokawa.

the sexual arousal that Genji's son Yūgiri experiences when he is afforded a look at his beautiful stepmother Murasaki (Tsuboi 1989b, 182–3). But most dynamic and captivating is the Suma storm when it threatens to sweep Genji out to sea (Tsuboi 1989b, 124). Plumes of water churn around a frame that shows three figures with Genji's frantic countenance superimposed above them, thus juxtaposing the violence of the sea with the paralyzing fear of the static figures.

In sum, Tsuboi enacts a twentieth-century *manga* recreation of the Heian world through his clear, clean illustrations of the events and personages. He provides a balanced presentation of the four generations of the Genji family, but he also signals which aspects of the tale are important and how to read them, through his narration, drawing style, and allotment of frame time. His selection of chapters and events centers on Genji and his male progeny and their point of view, so Murasaki's shocked reaction to being so roughly initiated into marital relations by Genji is well done but lacks the muted delicacy of its eleventh-century counterpart. Rokujō also appears, more malevolent than in the eleventh-century tale but without a fuller exploration of the horror she feels at her living spirit killing Genji's lovers. Beautiful men/women portrayals separate the central from the secondary characters, but also the "good" from the "bad" personages. No doubt the brevity of Tsuboi's remediation and the need to contemporize the story for a modern audience, for whom clarity and a love story would be more salable, have much to do with the ways in which Tsuboi's remediation is directed. But it retains a quiet, muted elegance that tells us much about Genji's world.

The second work in this group, Variety Art Works' 2010 *Reading The Tale of Genji*, *manga*-nizes world literary works and nonfiction writings and sums up the *Genji* in a single volume. And like Tsuboi's remediation, it condenses and compresses the tale from a male point of view. The result is mixed: births, deaths, and the passage of time occur in quick succession, so that Genji's reputed son Kaoru's courtship of the oldest of the Uji princesses is dispatched in one-and-a-half pages, with her death announced in one line on a third page (Variety Art Works 2010, 153–4, 155)! But in other instances the pacing is seamless and effective. The Suma storm, Genji's visit from the ghost of his deceased father, and his escape to Akashi are very dramatically presented in the course of one-and-a-half pages (Variety Art Works 2010, 108–9).

As with Tsuboi's remediation, the *manga* directs us in how to "read" the protagonists. Genji is made to look good—handsome, kind, and self-reflectively thoughtful. Even Genji's physical consummation of his relationship with the young Murasaki is reworked: his actions are depicted as a matter of course, and Murasaki sheds tears of joy at what happens and at his words of encouragement (Variety Art Works 2010, 95–6). This enabling of Genji is not just a one-off: when Genji agonizes over telling Murasaki about Akashi and his daughter with her, Murasaki forgives him, saying that his actions are warranted because she herself cannot bear children (Variety Art Works 2010, 118–19). On her deathbed, Murasaki acknowledges the anguish Genji has caused her but admits that she loves Genji, and concludes that her life was a happy one (Variety Art Works 2010, 145).

Yet what this remediation excels at is the use of humor and the presentation of cultural information in a concise and engaging manner. For example, the Rainy Day discussion, in which Genji and three courtiers rank the merits of women, is dispatched in one frame but skillfully segues into an explanation of Heian marriage and traits that make men and women attractive marriage partners (Variety Art Works 2010, 50–3). Cute comic figures gleefully enact how marriages begin and end—"divorce" simply entailing the husband telling his wife that he will not be back!—but the women get their payback, for the last frame shows an ominous figure, billed as a "creature of unknowable origins," into which spurned women morph (Variety Art Works 2010, 53).

Another hilariously entertaining bit of good fun occurs in the Uji segment of the *manga* at the expense of Genji's reputed son Kaoru and grandson Niou. Niou is rendered a conniving, unlikable playboy and Kaoru as highly emotional and lustful—a complete turnaround from Murasaki Shikibu's tale's staid, serious courtier seeking the religious life. In the Variety Art Works remediation, Kaoru is gleeful in "scoring" Ukifune (2010, 160). He locates her at a priest's house and entreats her to return with him, but Ukifune rebuffs his overtures on page 185, saying, "All men are alike. They only bring sorrow to women." Kaoru erupts in such anger on the next page that the old nun, the priest's sister, knocks him out cold with one punch. Certainly not something that would happen in Heian times, this scores points with contemporary readers. Although the episode does have

Ukifune ruefully lamenting at the bottom of page 186, "Men are creatures who only think of themselves and I have suffered so," it is wonderfully comic as well, accompanied by funny asides with the priest asking the still out cold Kaoru face down on the floor if he wants to go into training with the nun (2010, 188).

The old nun goes on to lecture Ukifune not to take the tonsure but to go out and live life. She counsels her to find love, have children, and become a nun when she is old. Things did not work out with Kaoru or Niou, she explains, because they are not good people, and Ukifune is too young (Variety Art Works 2010, 188). Fight off whatever life throws at you and live, the nun tells her. The *manga* ends with a full-page image of Ukifune in traveling clothes, a wide smile on her face, with the text noting that there is an adult woman living in Uji who shows no hint of past sorrows (2010, 190). Unusual to say the least, Variety Art Works is much more upbeat than the tale itself is, and its innovative end centering on Ukifune is replicated in only one other remediation, Yamato Waki's *Fleeting Dreams* (discussed in Chapter 3)—but, of course, sans the "punching out of Kaoru's lights"!

Without a doubt the Variety Art Works remediation directs audiences to read Genji as better than he is in the tale, and Kaoru and Niou as worse. Genji's stature is greatly enhanced, forgiven and enabled by the women at every turn. At the same time, however, this *manga* exhorts women, even if only through Ukifune, to fight for their dreams and themselves—to find love and family and happiness. Are these but ways to make the tale accessible to contemporary audiences? Are they just spice added to an age-old tale to get people to pick it up and read it? Or is this done to poke fun at the tale itself, at Variety Art Works' instructional presentation of it, and/or even at the *manga*'s readers? The *manga* never says, but in the end it delivers a great deal of cultural information quickly, efficiently, and effectively; it is highly accessible and fun; it relates the high points of the narrative, albeit in a way that is a bit "fast and dirty"; and finally, it challenges us all to decipher within it what is and is not historically and narratively accurate.

Last in the "unmarked" adult male offerings is Hasegawa Hōsei's[16] *The Tale of Genji*, which was published as Volumes 3 through 5 in the 1996–7 *Manga Nihon no koten* (*Japanese Classics in Manga*) series under the editorship of veteran *manga* artist Ishinomori Shōtarō, known for *Japan, Inc.* and for his epic forty-eight-volume *Manga nihon no rekishi* (*The History of Japan in Manga*). Hasegawa is one of several mainstream artists whom Ishinomori recruited to produce a stellar collection of *manga* transpositions of classical Japanese literature. Hasegawa covers the first forty-one chapters of the tale, ending with Genji's demise. Unlike in many remediations, Hasegawa uses the titles from the eleventh-century *Genji* and, like Murasaki Shikibu, adds the extra chapter "Kumogakure" ("Hiding Behind the Clouds") in title only, thus announcing Genji's departure from the story. Hasegawa intended to complete the tale, but to date no additional volumes have been published.

Like the other *jōhō* remediations in this section, Hasegawa highlights Genji and the unmarked male point of view, but his forte is the presentation of material culture. Gone are Tsuboi's quiet elegance and Variety Art Works' *manga* cute, replaced by a bold density of detail. Intricate designs cover every square inch of *byōbu* standing screens, decorative boxes, and kimonos—complete with layout and execution reminiscent of a Tokugawa-era scroll.[17] Witness the famous practice concert session that Genji organizes in preparation for his brother Suzaku's fiftieth birthday celebration (Hasegawa 1996–7, 5:102–3). On a two-page spread, Genji's ladies, rehearsing for the performance, are positioned diagonally from right to left in the upper half of both pages. Beyond the drapes in the foreground sit the courtiers who have come to hear the rehearsal. Arranged in tableau fashion, the women are identified by name. And identified they must be, for without knowing which instrument each lady plays, we would be hard-pressed to recognize each musician. All the figures in Hasegawa's illustrations, male or female, are graced with plump faces, high foreheads, narrow eyes, thick eyebrows, and tiny mouths, in scroll-painting style. Drawn in the minimalist *hikime kagihana* (line eyes and tiny fishhook noses) mode, their faces convey little emotion and allow for almost no individual or gender differentiation.

Perhaps it would be more accurate to say that it is not Hasegawa's lack of interest in people but his use of traditional *emaki*-scroll-and-painting conventions that result in his drawing of people in this fashion. Even the highly charged encounter between Genji and his stepmother Fujitsubo is sketched with little facial emotion. Rather, following the conventions of scroll painting, the intensity of the moment is highly stylized, portrayed through the disorderly lines of the robes and Fujitsubo's hair in disarray (Hasegawa 1996–7, 3:99). Hasegawa's depiction of Genji's subsequent attempt to visit Fujitsubo (1996–7, 3:202) is equally stark—the figures are stilted stick-like figures placed at awkward angles, while two straight white lines on Genji's cheeks convey his tears. In Hasegawa's pictorial economy these unnatural poses best reflect the emotional agony of the moment, although in Volume 5 he does skillfully manipulate light, darkness, subtle shadings, and images to enable readers to shadow Genji's son Yūgiri's friend Kashiwagi as he picks his way through the darkness to reach the rooms of Genji's wife, the Third Princess (1996–7, 5:118–21).

If clandestine seduction scenes are not his strong suit, Hasegawa excels at tableau-like scenes depicting groups in motion, such as in the clash between the entourages of Genji rivals Aoi and Rokujō during the Kamo festival, which emanate power and energy (1996–7, 3:169). The scene is fluid and convincing: there is nothing stilted or awkward about it, and we can almost hear the pushing and shoving of the two tussling groups. Even more impressive is his attention to the details of the material culture—to the pattern and design of rooms, oxen carts, furniture, *byōbu* standing screens, and kimonos—the stuff of everyday living. Doing extensive research on the layout of dwellings, the placement of furniture, and the movement of the figures in scrolls and paintings,[18] Hasegawa lovingly lays out his scenes employing another artistic style, *fukinuki yatai* (open roof architectural bird's-eye view), to great effect, as seen in Figure 7.3, where he conveys in a single page Genji's courting of Utsusemi, the provincial governor's wife.

So sumptuous are the details of the interior of the governor's mansion—from its gently swaying drapes and curtains of state to its beautifully appointed sliding doors and gorgeously patterned furniture and kimono designs—that the people

Figure 7.3 As he sets the scene for Genji's seduction of the provincial governor's wife, Hasegawa details the material culture of a Heian mansion. Hasegawa Hōsei, *The Tale of Genji*, 3: 39. Copyright © 1996–7 Hasegawa Hōsei and Chūō Kōron. Courtesy of Hasegawa Hōsei and Chūō Kōronsha.

almost disappear into the surroundings. Only when we look closely do we see the governor's wife tucked away in a room at the top left corner of the page, with Genji sitting in the room next door, privy to the gossip wafting alluringly from the next room: "Oh, to be able to see Prince Genji up so close!" "He's so young, but he already has a wife!" "But rumor has it that he still makes secret visits elsewhere." The stage is beautifully set for boy to seek out girl, though exquisitely fashioned screens, doors, and drapes stand in the way in all their detailed multiplicity.

Hasegawa retells the *Genji* in a fast-paced, energetic, straightforward way that is in keeping with the ambience of his hometown Hakata on the island of Kyushu.[19] Without complex facial expressions to slow the reader down, the traditional scroll-painting drawing style complements the rapid pacing, and it also enables the production of sumptuous, detailed renderings of things and settings—the material culture of everyday Heian life that Hasegawa marshals to tell his *Genji* story. Hasegawa uses the layouts of rooms and buildings, the paintings on the doors and standing screens (which he meticulously draws), and the detailed designs of chests and trays to bring the tale to life, thus helping readers understand the full splendor of *The Tale of Genji* and of the Heian period that produced it. Hasegawa is not minimizing the dialogic interactions or the personages or the events—he is simply choosing a different and wonderfully expressive way to instill pride in the tale.

Adult Informational Genji *Manga #2: "Marked" Women's Concerns*

The unmarked male informational comics are marketed for general consumption, but as our discussion thus far has made clear, *manga* artists do gender- and age-target their remediations. The titles in this last grouping target their audiences through their drawing styles and content, and also marshal support for their readings of the tale from additional sources. Thus Mihashi Mari's *Manga genji monogatari* (*The Manga Tale of Genji*) called upon Heian literary specialist Shimizu Yoshiko (who also consulted on Tsuboi's remediation, discussed earlier) to explain the structure and storyline of the tale, and to examine the role of marriage and the positionality of women during the Heian period. Shimizu ends her introductory essay with a call to readers to think more deeply about the difficulty of women's lives through the lens of Ukifune's trying circumstances (1988, 1:3–5). Mihashi follows Shimizu's lead and focalizes the women in an over-the-top manner. The second *manga* in this group, Hanamura Eiko's *Genji monogatari* (*The Tale of Genji*), even more prominently centers on the women, highlighting the costs rather than the joys of being loved by men like Genji. Novelist Setouchi Jakuchō adds her voice in a concluding essay, contending that being loved by the ideal man did not bring the women happiness. Lastly, Sanazaki Harumo's *Meisho o manga de: genji monogatari* (*The Masterpieces through Manga: The Tale of Genji*) much more straightforwardly depicts the agonies of the women characters. Loving their man brings dire consequences for the women, but each woman uses her experience to provide life lessons and opportunities for readers to try out.

7. Education for Soft Power, National Pride, and Feminist Critique   155

The focus on women in these titles may come as no surprise, but their emphasis on the difficulty of women's lives also spoke to a shift in Japan's national policies from a period of progressive legislation in the 1990s to a right-wing backlash in the 2000s (see Chapter 5). Technically speaking, Mihashi Mari's[20] two-volume remediation first appeared in 1988, as the women's movement was gaining momentum, but its republication in 2002 resonated with its readers, as the dream of a gender-equal society faded. It follows the progression of *The Tale of Genji* rather faithfully, completing all fifty-four chapters, although with several two-page distillations. It not only focalizes Genji and his relationships with his women but also powerfully presents the plight of the women in an extravagant emotional register that delineates the intense pressures placed on women vying for the love of the same man in the polygynous marital conditions of the Heian period. The emotional costs of jealousy, worry, and despair are prohibitively high: Mihashi depicts Genji's archenemy Kokiden sprouting horns both when she is bested by Genji's mother (1988, 1:24) and, later, when Fujitsubo is promoted to empress, as seen on the left in Figure 7.4. Kokiden rants: "What! He made her empress. Unforgivable! I hate that woman! "The Emperor—how could he make someone like Fujitsubo empress! Prepare rites to place a curse on her!" Kokiden's rage comes into even sharper relief, juxtaposed against the preceding right-hand page

Figure 7.4 Empress Kokiden sprouts horns, revealing the ferocity of her jealousy over Fujitsubo's promotion to empress and giving birth to a son who becomes crown prince, despite the biological father being Genji and not the emperor. Mihashi Mari, *The Tale of Genji*, 1: 110–11. Copyright © 1988. Courtesy of Mihashi Mari and Heibonsha.

where the emperor makes Fujitsubo's son crown prince. Unbeknownst to Kokiden, however, Genji, a sweat droplet running down his face, is put on the spot as well, as the emperor comments on how much the crown prince resembles Genji.

Even Fujitsubo bares her teeth in rage at having to bear Genji's illegitimate child, while Akashi wails bitterly at having to give up her daughter to Murasaki to raise in her stead (Mihashi 1988, 1:232–3). But it is in Volume 2 that Mihashi most powerfully explores the precarious lives of the women trapped in a male-oriented sexual economy in which not having a husband leaves a woman and her family without a livelihood, yet finding a husband results in heartache, anguish, and endless sorrow. To mark these words, Volume 2 portrays Murasaki suffering from unrelenting insomnia as she endures Genji's marriage to the Third Princess (1988, 2:115–16). The princess fares no better, becoming pregnant by Kashiwagi, Genji's son's friend. Yūgao's long-lost daughter Tamakazura, Kashiwagi's wife Ochiba, and the Uji princesses also all suffer. As Murasaki declares, "No matter which world it be, the relationship between a man and a woman is like an ephemeral lovers' tryst in a dream. A woman's tortured and sorrowful heart is not something that can be understood by a man" (Mihashi 1988, 2:297).

Focalizing the concerns of the women but intertwining them with the stories of Genji and his male progeny, Mihashi creates a dark rendition of the tale and the Heian period. Jealousy causes women to grow horns, relationships with men bring great sorrow, women must bear babies they do not want or give up ones whom they treasure. Life is hard and cruel. But what about the men? They weep and wail, and suffer political setbacks and the loss of loved ones, and, in Genji's case, experience exile, but the *manga* concludes that their lot as men provides them with a modicum of a better life. As excessive as Mihashi's portrayal of Heian life and the tale is, her rendition has been very popular, for by 2002 Volume 1 had been reprinted fifteen times, while Volume 2 had undergone twelve reprints. In all likelihood, only Yamato's *Fleeting Dreams*, a favorite *Genji* remediation among college entrance-exam takers, exceeds this number. Perhaps the compactness of Mihashi's rendition, its less *shōjo*-esque orientation, and Shimizu's academic authority account for its popularity. Successful in highlighting the cost of the Heian male-oriented sexual economy on women, Mihashi's *Genji* describes the women characters' trauma in an emotional register and with an intensity that greatly exceeds those of the eleventh-century tale and that resonates with modern audiences.

The next woman-authored text is Hanamura Eiko's[21] (2013) three-volume *The Comics Classical Literature Tale of Genji*, which is part of a series of five titles published by Shōgakukan. It documents Genji's life from his birth though his elder years. Hanamura's delicate drawing style and focalization of the female characters, and their experiences and interiority, remediate ladies/women's comics. However, her Genji is not just the ideal object of desire through whom the women's sexual and erotic desires are realized; rather, he is often the cause of the women's angst and unrelenting sorrow. On the one hand, then, Genji operates in Hanamura's *manga* as the handsome, eternally desirable darling of court society. His less laudable actions are downplayed: his abduction of the young Murasaki, for example, is muted and turned into a plus that features a solicitous and tender Genji (Hanamura 2013, 1:118). His moments of remorse are also brought very much to the fore: he feels badly about not letting the Akashi Lady see her daughter until she enters court, and even admits that he was thoughtlessly cruel to Murasaki by marrying the Third Princess (Hanamura 2013, 2:268; 3:12–13). On the other hand, the costs to the women who form liaisons with this Shining Prince are immense. Genji's stepmother Fujitsubo lives in paralyzing fear and remorse after her illicit encounter with him; Yūgao pays with her life; Genji's older lover Rokujō becomes a living spirit killing off his lovers; and his archenemy's sister Oborozukiyo forfeits her chance of becoming empress. Hanamura skillfully speaks to the precarity of the lives of her contemporary readers, as she highlights the social and financial challenges they face in the new millennium (see Allison 2013).

The root cause of these sufferings, as Hanamura sees it, is the positionality of women in Heian society. Murasaki laments the fate that has befallen Ochiba after the death of her husband Kashiwagi, Yūgiri's friend. Having the misfortune of being born female, Ochiba has no control over her own destiny. Like other women, she can never fully breathe the air outside but must live a cloistered life, suppressing all emotions. She can say little and must simply look pleasant—a life that Murasaki deems not worth living (Hanamura 2013, 3:200). Forty-seven pages later, on her deathbed, Murasaki also expresses similar sentiments, this time cautioning the Akashi Empress not to become like her. A woman, Murasaki maintains, is a sorrowful creature—a creature who says nothing, who must kill her desires and her being, and who must do the bidding of others (Hanamura 2013, 3:247). What is most remarkable about these injunctions is the depth of their anguish and despair and the fact that they are uttered by Murasaki, who in the eleventh-century tale appears to have won the prize, so to speak, by capturing the heart of the much-sought-after object of desire, Genji.

In giving voice in Hanamura's *manga* to her deep sorrow, which is not as overtly expressed in the Heian tale, the fictional Murasaki (and perhaps, Hanamura may be suggesting, as other *manga* artists have, the historical Murasaki Shikibu, author of the tale) cautions her twenty-first-century readers about the costs of loving someone like Genji. Receiving body blow after body blow, Murasaki encounters two she cannot survive—Genji's marriage to the higher-ranking Third Princess, and the ironic realization that both she and the princess are nothing more than stand-ins for Genji's true love, Fujitsubo (Hanamura 2013, 3:6–7, 10). Much earlier in the chain of events, in the double-page tableau shown in Figure 7.5, Hanamura expertly captures Murasaki's visceral shock, in medias res, when the Third Princess enters Rokujō-in attended by forty ladies-in-waiting—the sheer power and grandeur of her newest competitor completely overwhelming Murasaki.

To make matters worse, Genji selfishly believes that he has suffered more than Murasaki, and hastens her death by staunchly refusing her request to take the tonsure (Hanamura 2013, 3:92–4). Unlike in other *manga* versions, Murasaki cannot overcome the sorrow and anguish of loving Genji, and only in death does she find the peace and security that she sought in life (2013, 3:248–51).[22]

Figure 7.5 Murasaki is overwhelmed by the power and prestige of her new rival for Genji's love, the Third Princess, as she "invades" Rokujō-in with her army of ladies-in-waiting. The depths of Murasaki's anguish is reflected in her silent address to Genji: "I have no home to return to, should the Princess steal your heart." Hanamura Eiko, *The Tale of Genji*, 2: 284–5. Copyright © Hanamura Eiko/Atelier Eiko Co. 2013. Courtesy of Hanamura Eiko/Atelier Eiko Co.

In sum, although the handsome Genji is the de facto hero, Hanamura's *Genji* is about women struggling to find their way in the Heian period's polygynous, patriarchal society. Novelist-turned-nun Setouchi Jakuchō champions this reading in her 1998 modern Japanese rendition of the tale, and argues for it here as well. She contends that the true heroes are not the men but the women—Rokujō's presence adding immeasurable depth and complexity to the tale (2013, 3:282). She also maintains that the women are not downtrodden but possess a much-feared "secret weapon"—the ability to take the tonsure and put themselves beyond the reach of men, parents, and even ladies-in-waiting who dictate who has access to them and who can marry them. As nuns, the women subvert the gender dynamics of the times, becoming off limits to suitors and to families using them as marriage pawns. Religious vows afforded women control over their lives, and even a position from which they could more dispassionately assess the behavior of the men (Setouchi 2013, 3:284–5), as we see in the case of Fujitsubo, Utsusemi, the Third Princess, and especially Ukifune.

In an even more surprising move, Setouchi Jakuchō contends that the male fear of women's taking the tonsure is still alive and well. She writes that when she took her vows in 1973, her friends' husbands were afraid that their wives would "shame" them by doing the same (2013, 3:285). (One astute reader saw the taking of tonsure as related to the increasing resistance against marriage and the bearing of children by contemporary women.) It is difficult to know how pervasive Jakuchō's claim is, but it brings into focus the fictional Murasaki's injunctions to readers—and perhaps what Hanamura considers to be the educational mission of her *Tale of Genji*: the relating of the sorrowful story of embattled women who nonetheless retain their dignity through death, taking religious vows, and even through morphing into an avenging living spirit—and who through these struggles provide spaces for readers to do the same.

Our final *manga* of the chapter—and the study—is a one-volume remediation by Sanazaki Harumo,[23] in a series that includes her work and *manga*-nization of author Dazai Osamu's novels. Published in 2010, it purports to relate the tale in full and opens with Genji, but its "educational" mission is for each female protagonist to tell her own love story, so that contemporary readers can vicariously engage with and learn from them. Depicted largely from a female perspective, the *manga* portrays in an adult and realistic fashion (but with little nudity and eroticism) women being swept off their feet by a dashing hero, the love of their life. Like Sakurazawa's ladies comics, the man Genji remains the same, but each woman constructs a different kind of love: Genji's stepmother Fujitsubo views her love as forbidden, a sin she must bear the rest of her life; his neglected wife Aoi sees her "love" as humiliating and demeaning, as Genji forces himself upon her; his archenemy Kokiden's sister Oborozukiyo engages in a gloriously romantic and dangerous love under the light of the shining moon, but away from the watchful eye of her sister; and Genji's older lover Rokujō's jealous and all-consuming love morphs her into a possessing, killing spirit, but one that is depicted with kindness and compassion (Sanazaki 2010, 96–7, 104–6, 107–8, 76–82).

Most complex of all is Sanazaki's depiction of Murasaki's love. Early on, Murasaki is an eager, young woman, happy in Genji's embrace, but the years and the "other women" take a toll on her. Even more than in Hanamura's portrayal, a surprisingly unromanticized rendering of Murasaki's relationship with Genji unfolds, in which a motif of coldness signifies Murasaki's sense of betrayal as she discovers that Genji has "warmed" himself with the Akashi Lady while in exile, leaving Murasaki herself chilled and alone in the capital (Sanazaki 2010, 140–1). This motif returns with a vengeance in the wake of Genji's marriage to the Third Princess: in a two-page spread, Murasaki feels her white body etched against a black background growing colder and colder as her love for Genji ebbs away (Sanazaki 2010, 166–7). Murasaki falls ill on the next page and passes away without forgiving Genji, much in the fashion seen in Hanamura's remediation.

Hanamura focuses on the women but tells their stories in conjunction with Genji, whereas Sanazaki centers on the women and uses Genji more as a catalyst to enable the narrative—an aspect that may make Sanazaki's *Genji* appear to be more in keeping with the ladies comics discussed in Chapter 5 than with informational *manga*. Yet her remediation appears in a series that not only *manga*-nizes other literary works but also lacks the ladies-comics eroticization and overt sexuality, thereby making it more suitable for this chapter—and, as an educational tome, perhaps gain it more credence and cultural capital authority.

Conclusion: Cultural Repository, National Treasure, Global Masterpiece

Constituting one-fourth of the titles discussed in this study, informational *jōhō manga* are a mainstay of the *Genji manga*. Their mission is to teach and educate readers about the tale, and they do so in particularized ways. Like *Japan Inc: An Introduction to Japanese Economics in Manga*, informational *Genji manga* (and their mainstream counterparts) traffic in global and domestic cultural capital and soft power, garnering cultural prestige and goodwill for Japan abroad and fostering national pride at home. A part of the *manga*, anime, music, and fashion facets of Cool Japan, the informational *Genji manga* tout the tale as a masterpiece on a par with great western novels—and engage in what Sharon Kinsella terms the "implicit political revisionism" that puts a more positive spin on things Japanese and takes care not to give rise to charges of sexual violence or appropriation of underaged/gay bodies.

As such, informational *Genji manga* are age appropriate to the youngest through adult readers. Some focalize Genji and the male point of view, others examine what it means to be born female in a society where men can have multiple wives, and still others downplay Genji's unfavorable traits. As disparate as these readings are, their status as educational tomes means that *jōhō manga* are often taken at face value and considered the authoritative, vetted reading of the tale. Learned scholars, famous *manga* artists, and renowned novelists lend a hand, writing commentaries and introductions that endorse appraisals of the tale as a source of national pride, a database of Japanese culture, and a globally acclaimed masterpiece—in keeping with the initiative set in motion by Motoori Norinaga in the eighteenth century.

As we have seen, informational *Genji manga* present in three groupings—less gender-marked versions of the tale for children, adult unmarked male iterations, and adult marked female remediations. In addition to being audience appropriate, these groupings are nuanced in other ways as well. The section on "Informational Children *Manga*" features four comics for elementary schoolchildren, and makes Genji and the tale praiseworthy in the eyes of young readers. Genji is, then, rewritten as a likable, nice guy, a thoughtful, much admired and respected lover, while the Heian period is presented as laudable and worthy of great pride. Purporting to be faithful to the tale, the four remediations in this group in fact minimize some elements, enhance others, and omit still others to make the tale appropriate for young audiences and deserving of its billing as a national treasure. The three male remediations in the section on "Adult Informational *Manga* #1" also "inform" readers in particular ways. They underscore the important characters and events (Tsuboi), make Genji "look good" (Tsuboi, Variety Art Works), and give an unexpected call-out to women (Variety Art Works). One even touts the richness and splendor of the material culture of the Heian period, and by implication of the society and country that produced it (Hasegawa). All three are marketed for general audiences but relate Genji's story largely from Genji's own point of view—often at the expense of the women protagonists—thus making these *manga* male in orientation.

In contrast, the titles considered in "Adult Informational Manga #2" are composed by girls-turned-ladies-comics artists. Ranging from the over-the-top (Mihashi) to the sympathetic (Hanamura) to the teachable (Sanazaki), their drawing styles and focalization on the women characters in the tale make their works unmistakably adult and female—with the "ideal" Genji and the male-dominated, polygynous Heian society becoming culprits responsible for the deplorable circumstances in which the women live. The educational mission of viewing *The Tale of Genji* as a national treasure and the essence of Japanese-ness remains intact, but in different ways than in the *manga* in the other two groupings. Genji and the Heian court are not honorable and praiseworthy but epitomize the challenges of the human condition. Living with and sharing their pain and sorrow in love, life, and death, the women protagonists in these *Genji jōhō manga* help readers find comfort, solace, and guidance in ways that *manga* are so adept at providing.

The hope in all these informational *manga* is that readers will come to find in the *Genji* the best of Japanese culture—with which to ease their souls and to face brave new worlds.[24] Hugely accessible and pitched to particularized audiences, *Genji* informational *manga* invite readers to connect with the tale's emotional, cultural, and aesthetic sensitivities that can overcome much and even answer such existential questions as "What is a human being? What is life?"—as was promised in the 2008 Millennial Anniversary Memorial Ceremony commemorating the inception of the tale. After all, *The Tale of Genji* is a Japanese classic, a world classic, a "crystallization of the wisdom of humanity"—which the *Genji manga* simultaneously support, parody, and challenge.

Chapter 8

CONCLUSION: THE CULTURAL DNA OF THE (MANGA) TALES OF GENJI

Since its inception in the eleventh century, *The Tale of Genji* has had an exceedingly good run, being transposed from era to era, from medium to medium, and assembling a rich array of remediations fashioned to serve differing political and cultural brokers. In premodern times readers were treated to hooknosed, slits-for-eyes Genjis, stately male *nō* actors performing Genji women, and sword-wielding samurai Genjis enacting *mitate* visual puzzles; in the modern era, we see female *otokoyaku* male-specialist Genjis, Genji's ladies transformed into gorgeous BL studs in *manga* offerings, and much more. In this final chapter, we look back on the tale and its remediations—what they meant to different interpretative communities, what the *Genji manga* in particular added to our *Genji* adventure, and what the future holds for the venerable old tale.

In its earliest iterations, *The Tale of Genji* remained within the borders of Japan and was used as a tool though which movers and shakers sought to establish sovereignty and identity. The Heian court, warrior landed lords, townspeople, and especially the eighteenth-century nativist scholar Motoori Norinaga realized that the tale personified something special about Japan. After the 1868 Meiji Restoration, the Japanese government, too, recognized the tale's potential in forging identity and cultural currency, and wielded it in statecraft: it was first deployed in the 1910s and 1920s to secure membership in the community of nations; next, to prove after the Second World War that Japan had shed its bellicose, aggressive ways; and finally, in the new millennium, to garner global goodwill and accolades for producing the world's first novel. Male writers and kabuki performers marketed their male-perspective *Genji* remediations for general consumption. Female/feminine-oriented repurposings also took shape, through novels authored by women and the romanticized, mass-produced and mass-consumed Yamato/Tanabe *Genji* transpositions.

The *Genji manga* were very much a part of this new landscape, digging deep into their respective categories to bring to the fore funny, serious, highly romantic, erotic and otherwise renderings of the tale. The *manga* explored nooks and crannies of the tale, pulling and stretching and expanding it in ways that author Murasaki Shikibu might never have dreamed of, but in the process opening up new vistas for the tale. Wildly inventive, the remediations targeted women and girls but also men and boys, and had their pulse on the interest and desires of contemporary Japanese society. Creating age- and gender-centered, niched in-groups, the *Genji manga* enabled fantasies, savory and otherwise, to flourish but only in the imaginary and prescribed mainstream venues. Media literacy, reading strategies, and the deployment of reading selves assured that would be so.

Regulated by venue (formal/informal, public/private) and by the age, rank, and gender of the participants involved, and tailored to fit the parameters of the context, the Japanese selves who participate in fantasies keep all within the imaginary and basically out of real life. The Japanese "I" is not a single unit but is instead fluid, shifting, and numerous—each self within it being tailored to the specificities of any given context, and deployed accordingly. Thus, in Japan, for a salaryman in a suit and tie to close a formal business deal at a neighborhood rugby game would be seen and felt to be as "inappropriate" as a drunk soccer fan showing up in a company board room. Appropriateness is key, and publicly sanctioned *soto* outside-directed selves must conform to the strictures of the collective, while *uchi* personal insider-focused selves can be safely utilized within the private domain of fantasy. As a result, these selves that spy on female bodies, engage in sexual experimentation, or are entranced by underaged females exist in Japan in the private domain of the imaginary virtual space of reading *manga* and other prescribed venues—and only engage characters and scenarios that are fictional, separate, and distinct from reality.

This compartmentalization of selves is the modus operandi for Japanese selves, so that any emergence of the wrong one in the wrong venue is canceled and censured by a social peer pressure system that is highly effective and more far reaching than any experienced in the United States. As in many societies, acceptable behavior is normalized through educational, religious, law, and media institutions in Japan, but appropriateness is also overseen and enforced more rigorously by one's peers. Hence the check on a person's interactions is constant and comes from all quarters—teachers, parents, bosses, and friends but also shop clerks, passengers on trains, and even strangers on the street. Society at large keeps everyone in line through gentle nudging, hostile stares, and even loud, public reprimands from the taxi drivers, middle-aged women, and the like (although such strictures are less prominent post-pandemic).

The constant monitoring of behavior in Japan keeps the imaginary in the imaginary but also allows it to prosper and flourish as we saw in the rich expanse of *manga* and *Genji manga*. Bound by a cultural literacy that is ingrained in those who have grown up with what Fujimoto Yukari calls "a culture of drawing and fantasy ... where the desire is for ... the [fictional] image" (qtd. in Galbraith 2017a, 115), readers can let their fantasies run wild, for fantasies will remain fantasies within authorized, prescribed spaces. Variously labeled as an economy of desire for the image, *anime* orientation, or *moe* imagery literacy, this media literacy teaches its practitioners to seek the fictional and eschew the real. Consequently, *manga* and *anime*'s representations of underaged bodies and the utilization of gay bodies remain fictional and do not reference nor harm real-life sentient beings. Despite finding some adult comics "nasty," Fujimoto is against censoring them and would agree with video game creator Kagami Hiroyuki that the production of "even the most objectionable of sexual expression and imagination" must be permitted in order to safeguard the "freedom of expression and imagination" (Galbraith 2017a, 115, 118).

The so-called "deviant" and "unsavory" are deployed in the fantasy worlds of *manga, anime,* and computer gaming. They are fictional, confined to the private domain of the selves that take part in that imaginary. Research has not shown that these depictions contribute to sexual violence against women or girls, and some have even led to reparative effects such as helping to overcome the fear of rape in a safe environment, allowing for safe mediated spaces within which to erotically explore and experiment, and even providing venues where men can be more self-reflective regarding the sexual choices they make. (See Khan and Ketterling 2019; Galbraith 2017c.)

Locating/Situating the Genji *Manga*

To some, the presence of selves who engage in "inappropriate" fantasies only in the imaginary sounds like subterfuge aimed at countering the recent pushback against *manga/anime*/computer games. But for the Japanese, these context-specific selves and the existence of the imaginary are not an indulgence but a necessity: the fantasy-based self and its imaginary space, in particular, act as escape valves in a society where behavior is still regulated and controlled. Deployed only in the imaginary and regulated in-group venues, these selves and their fantasies are often viewed as alarming by non-in-group viewers. But when we look carefully at how they are established and employed within the specificities of the *Genji manga* titles, we find that they provide workarounds vis-à-vis social conventions, and space for identity formation and experimentation; they challenge and interrogate male lust and use the tale to garner goodwill and prestige. They do not advocate rape, violence, or appropriation, and regularly subvert and parody what is being portrayed. They queer male bodies and embody gender/nongendered/in-between positionalities.

In other words, fantasies operate within the social, cultural, and aesthetic imaginaries that govern the lives of the men, women, and children of Japan. Our study has looked at male- and female-targeted *Genji* remediations and has found that each category works within its own self-imposed imaginary-based parameters. For women and girls, the *manga* provide exquisitely fabulous dress-ups—shy, sexy, provocative ways through which to establish alluring identities in a society that privileges men. Through the pages of the *shōjo Genji manga*, girl readers can stylize themselves as stunningly beautiful objects of desire who are longing to catch and be caught by their Prince Charming objects of desire. The cost of true love is high, and the agonies of loving and being loved are played for keeps. It can end in death, in (unknowingly) killing rivals, in forfeiture of personal happiness for the good of the family, in displacement into another time period, or even in self-exile to ensure that one's love is not put in peril. Girls are provided with an array of love interests: dashing, dreamboat heroes, a scoundrel-turned-good-guy, an earnest high schooler, an unapologetic womanizer, a sweet, let's-all-be-friends play pal, and even a fetching "she." In dialogue with these love interests, girl readers can choose differing acceptable roles as modern girls: they can fall madly in love, be strong and independent, engender a love that transforms a bad boy, or embody transgender personas. Far beyond their daily lives, readers can occupy a different time and place where handsome men vie for their hand, where yin-yang masters are called upon to combat loves deep and fierce, where a girl can be on the hunt for romantic action. Unlike ladies comics and BL *manga*, girls comics fantasies are set up with love at center and great care is taken to keep them innocent and true and, most importantly, like all *manga* yearnings, they are constructed to unfold only in the imaginary. Fantasies can thereby be unabashedly experienced in fictional settings that do not demean or endanger young girls.

Girls comics hint at Genji's womanizing and at his abducting of the young Murasaki—elements that are an inherent part of *The Tale of Genji*'s erotic, moral, and aesthetic DNA but that are frowned upon by contemporary standards. Ladies comics more straightforwardly present unsavory behavior by Genji and other men as they press their attentions on women, and especially by Genji as he initiates the young Murasaki into married life. Such encounters might even be called rape in the modern vernacular, but the ladies-comics artists are clear and very careful in devising these scenarios as narrative tropes designed to allow "good girls" to express and enjoy sex and erotic desires while still remaining "good girls" in mainstream society. Known as "play rape," they are workarounds of social conventions that prevent women from expressing and enjoying their sexual desires outside of marriage and procreation. Ostensibly, created by straight women for the pleasure and enjoyment of women, these titles are actively sought out by women readers. Their fictional tropes are also created for enactment within the safe space of the imaginary, and are set up so as not to make readers feel threatened or to encourage injury to real-life women. Complex and roundabout as such tropes may be, they allow women to acquire agency over their bodies and desires, to become mistresses of their sexual fantasies and desires safely and freely. Even the negative traits of jealousy, abandonment, and unrequited love are marshaled to acquire agency. As such, a devious Murasaki, for example, defends her turf and secures Genji's attention at all costs (Teradate), while strong emotions are also used to craft different Genjis—an earnest lover, an accomplished aristocratic suitor, a self-assured dandy (Sakurazawa). Other *Genji manga* present a Murasaki residing in the interstices between girls and ladies comics (Kira), or use newspaper serializations to call Genji and his cohorts on the carpet for their deplorable treatment of women (Takenaka). Still others elicit concern about their ostensible commodification of female bodies for the pleasure of men (Hazuki, Bandoh), though when we examine them with more care, we find that the sexualization and objectification of women are used by the women characters and their readers to gain agency over their sexual fantasies and desires. And all is for the pleasure and the gratification of their producers and consumers and experienced only within imaginary and other sanctioned spaces.

Even in *The Tale of Genji BL Anthology* edited by Mori Yoshimasa, in which male–male romances appear to appropriate gay men and reduce them to uniformly androgynous, feminized bodies, we find that these tropes operate as a workaround of the social convention that automatically places the male on top of the female in heterosexual coupling scenarios. By positing two males, female artists and readers can distance themselves, embody both the "passive" loved one and the "aggressor" lover positionalities, and engage both these roles in an equal relationship as fantasies in the imaginary. This ability of women readers to "un-gender" themselves via the two same-sex protagonists depicted in BL *manga* has enabled not only *fujoshi* "rotten" girls but also *fudanshi* "rotten" straight male readers, lesbians, bisexual men and women, and even gay men to secure gender in-betweenness via which to live out their unfettered desires within the space of reading a *manga*. Because they reach beyond socially sanctioned gender and age restrictions, these explorations have encountered pushback for their destabilization of the male/female gender binary and other positionalities. When read within the context of straight, gay, lesbian, in-between positionalities, however, these *manga* provide complex readings that are fluid and in flux, at times seeming to impinge on one group for the pleasure of another but also safeguarded from doing so by their deployment within the compartmentalized, context-appropriate virtual spaces of the reading of a fictionalized *manga*.

The *Genji* boys comics and young men comics cast into further relief *The Tale of Genji*'s moral, ethical, and artistic DNA—revealing that the elegance and gentility of the tale hide some hard truths. Tomi Shinzō, for one, unflinchingly exposes the dirty, ugly political truth about the Heian court: men, women, even children were but pawns in the acquisition of power, making anything approaching a self-determined life untenable for all. Other titles interrogate male lust, Genji's insatiable desire to have his way with women. The boys *manga* lampoon and gently poke fun at an inept, unhandsome Genji (Akatsuka) and a roly-poly chestnut stand-in (Koizumi), but the depth of that desire cannot be denied. Egawa Tatsuya's remediation lays it all out there, trafficking in soft porn with nude, sweating bodies, fan-servicing his readerly demographic. But once again, when we look more closely, we find that the spectacle is multifaceted. On the one hand, it puts Genji's unfettered lust and desire on full display for male enjoyment; on the other, it parodies that lust in a hyperbolic, over-the-top manner that interrogates its viability and maligns its very existence. And, as we found in the BL readings, these nuances open up queer readings for differently situated readers—even the targeted male ones. Inaba Minori's young men's title also allows the male gaze to have its day, and more. Fan service, eye-candy cleavage, and panty shots abound, but these are used to manipulate and subvert the male gaze. Transposing the tale to contemporary Japan, and the suave, debonair Genji into a naïve, inept college student, Inaba sets up her Genji stand-in to attend to the needs of fourteen formidable, vibrant women and become their ideal lover. Looks can be deceiving indeed, for the sexualized women in the Inaba title are complexly rendered, and it is they who come out on top, both literally and figuratively. Here, too, what appears to demean and objectify women is actually turned on its head to serve the women—an apt metaphor for what is happening in many of the *Genji manga* in this study.

The Tale of Genji's cultural, moral, and ethical concerns appear most prominently in the last set of *manga* examined here, the informational comics whose mission is to celebrate the *Genji* as a literary masterpiece that is on a par with western works and a repository of the best of Japanese culture. Anxious to instruct domestic readers to view the tale as a national treasure and a globally lauded masterpiece, the practitioners in this category go out of their way not to run afoul of any ethical or moral concerns of western and Japanese readers alike. To accomplish this, they make Genji a gracious and generous lover, and downplay his having many wives and love interests and his using romantic trysts to gain political ascendency at court. Age- and gender-appropriate informational texts for children feature *manga*-cute figures and construct Genji as a role model whom children can look up to. Adult-male-oriented texts bill the Heian period as a wondrous place populated by beautiful people (Tsuboi), the Heian court as an exquisitely rich and elegant material landscape (Hasegawa), and Genji as a kind, thoughtful, elegant hero worthy of adoration (Variety Art Works). In contrast, the female artists Hanamura, Mihashi, and Sanazaki focus on the trials and tribulations suffered by the women as a result of loving Genji and living in the Heian patriarchal society. They do not laud the period, but they credit the tale for operating as a template of life lessons and a coping mechanism to help readers face the sorrows that life brings. Touting their version as the "real" Genji, all these informational *manga* posit that *The Tale of Genji* not only constitutes the best of Japanese culture but offers readers solace and can give meaning to their lives. Eschewing graphic sexuality and anything else that could elicit censure from some readers, these *manga* thus strive to put the *Genji*'s best foot forward.

As we have seen above, *The Tale of Genji* has been lauded as a masterpiece and a national treasure at home, and as a means of garnering goodwill and admiration abroad. It has withstood the test of time as few works have, adapting throughout the ages to numerous and various media and venues, old and new, to the delight of audiences both domestic and global. Pictorial, textual, dramatic, musical, operatic, and material arts transpositions—you name it, and there may very well be a *Genji* remediation. The expanse of *Genji* events and activities during the millennial celebrations of the tale spanning 2000 through 2008 attest to this and more. *Manga* joined the parade and utilized word and image to provide space for their in-group constituencies to explore, experiment, and dream—creating specially coded worlds that readers decipher by collaborating, participating, and performing in tandem with the protagonists, thus enriching these in-group interpretative communities of producers, consumers, and texts.

Nevertheless, as we have also seen, the liberatory and exploratory space afforded to one marginalized group may simultaneously appropriate and objectify other marginalized groups, hence uncooling Cool Japan. Boys, young men, and adult men comics, BL comics, and even girls *manga* have come under fire for their portrayals of young-looking/underage protagonists with mature bodies engaging in sexual activity. Ladies and young and adult male comics are cited for objectifying and demeaning female bodies. BL male–male sexual scenes and body types are docked points for appropriating the gay community. The pushback has been severe at times, and the moral and ethical differences real. But, as this study has shown, there is more to the matter than meets the eye and the issue complex. Cute young protagonists have long been accepted as part of the *anime* and *manga* universes, with the firm understanding that these portrayals are fictional and do not endanger real children. The seemingly forced sexual domination and humiliation of women are actually marshaled by female artists for female readers precisely to enable, in safe spaces, the exploration and expression of sexual desires deemed inappropriate for "good girls." Fujimoto Yukari goes so far as to say that tropes of rape, sadomasochism, and brutal sexual encounters are used in the imaginary as a catalyst to awaken women's sexual desire. The gazes on (fe)male bodies are also not monolithic and are interpreted in different ways by different people/readers for different purposes. And they are embedded in historical, cultural, ideological, and moral expediencies that, depending on the perspective, deem such visual and textual narratives inappropriate or appropriate, perverse or exhilarating, obscene or liberating. *Fujoshi* rotten girls, *fundashi* rotten boys, bi/transsexual (wo)men, and lesbian women have used these fictional fantasies to escape their gendered bodies and inhabit "others," and to embody gender- and reality-free non-identitarian aspects of their beings. All explore, interpret, and fantasize to their hearts content, queering the *manga* in ways that may well venture beyond the wildest dreams of their producers.

As unruly and over-the-top as they may be, these musings are confined to the imaginary and are constructed to be all play—remaining well beyond the reach of the everyday. *Fujoshi* girls fans and more conventional Japanese alike are masters at keeping their fantasies in check, enacting them only in fictional spaces. Even when cosplaying, these selves appear only at sanctioned conventions and expos and in the pop culture meccas like Akihabara and Otome Rōdo (Maiden Road) in Ikebukuro, never at work or in other public venues. Fantasies stay in the imaginary and are kept separate from reality. These performances are also not just for fun but prove to be integral as coping mechanisms. Operating as much needed escape valves from the rigor of their enactors' societal roles, the imaginary "I"s in the virtual spaces of the reading of *manga* carefully keep illicit desires from bleeding into daily life.

Has the *manga*-nization of *The Tale of Genji* therefore led the tale in unintended and even misplaced directions that have exposed it to censure? I would argue no. Although Murasaki Shikibu could not have envisioned her tale morphing into a cornucopia of pop culture graphic novels that would encounter pushback a millennium after she wrote it, it is irrefutable that her eleventh-century narrative contains many moments that raise concerns for today's audiences. The tale and its *manga* remediations provocatively bring these to the fore, causing consternation among some but also calling into question significant issues of gender, positionality, and desire. Readers can now queer same-sex/heterosexual relationships, dispense with gender and sexual identities, or explore the stereotypical feminine/passive versus masculine/take-charge dichotomy and all the other aspects on that continuum, participating fully in the emotions of the moment in tandem with the *Genji*'s protagonists, as they search together for multiple and varied subjects of love and desire.

Back to the Future: The Tale of Genji's *Cultural DNA*

The Tale of Genji has prospered and remained relevant through the premodern and modern ages: the twentieth century alone witnessed the Japanese government marshaling the tale for nation-building several times. It has also recompositioned itself in three *Genji* booms. In the most recent of these, it joined forces with *manga*, *anime*, and popular culture, emerging as the Tanabe/Yamato mass-produced, mass-consumed *Genji* culture—Cool Japan *Genji*. The 1980s decade of women, feminism, and the millennial celebration of the inception of the tale all nurtured its longevity, revealing time and again the tale's centrality as the holder of the cultural, moral, and erotic DNA of Japan. But will the *Genji* continue to be relevant in the twenty-first century, as print texts lose more and more ground to digital and electronic media? Will anyone care about a musty old story from the eleventh century in classical Japanese that is too difficult for contemporary Japanese audiences to parse? Taught in high school classical Japanese courses, it may survive in those circles, but will it ever be able to hitch its wagon to another medium as ubiquitous and wide-ranging as *manga*? Can it jump to new delivery systems? Will we see a YouTube enactment, a podcast dedicated to the tale, a sixty-second TikTok video, or some buzz on the social news website Reddit? What will it take to put the *Genji* back into the Japanese, let alone the global, economy?

As bleak as the future of literary works may appear to be, some intriguing possibilities reside in interactive electronic platforms. As students read less and less and move away from print text, new ways to teach literature to a new generation must be forged. Digital storytelling platforms such as storify.com, which touts itself as a "mobile friendly, media-rich, and highly interactive" medium that is "fun yet informative," could be employed to keep Murasaki's work alive and well and bring readers back to the tale. Virtual interactive sites could also entice users to role-play different *Genji* characters and move about in a virtual Heian world. One of the most intriguing possibilities is the visual novel (VN), which encompasses features of a novel and a video game.[1] Digital in format, a VN uses text, voice-overs, music/sound, and pictures to provide an interactive story-reading, participatory experience. Usually employing multiple storylines or narrative branches, these nonlinear stories present multiple endings depending on the choices made by the player at clearly demarcated decision points. The stories are complex, with the digital medium allowing for exploration of finely calibrated nuances, moral stances, and perspectives. Interactions with characters and multiple dialogue choices form the basis, and provide "readings" that extend into different storylines. Kinetic novel VNs offer only one route and a single storyline, however, relying on their visuals, sound effects, and emotion to capture and draw in the reader/player. They can generally be completed within ten hours, whereas a dating sim (or romance simulation) VN such as *Amagami SS*, in which the player has the chance to date six girls, can take up to fifty hours to conclude. Decisions are made at intermittent junctures to determine how the relationship with a particular character will evolve. Once the relationship reaches its completion, the process must be followed with each of the other characters to reach the final end of the game. Finally, *eroge* or erotized VNs traffic in erotic action, although the best ones develop meaningful characters and deep relationships and use eroticism primarily to develop the plot.

Two students in my *manga* course created a VN that parodied the dating sims and the different *manga* categories (see "Doki Doki Manga Genres"). They devised cat-character sprites that embodied the girls-, boys-, young men, and ladies-comics *manga* categories, and set them up so that the player must choose which persona the player wants to hang out with. Hosting only a few narrative branches, their VN is a simple piece by industry standards. Nonetheless, it showcases VN's applicability to telling stories, its ability to entice and engage consumers with fun visuals and catchy dialogue, and its strengths in greatly enhancing the interactive and immersive experience of novel "reading"/video gaming. In effect, my students' VN enriches and makes fully virtual the *manga* experience in every way. It allows reader-players not only to be collaborative but especially to be participatory and performative.

Enabling the first-person perspective, such VNs create the player as a full-fledged participant residing in the VN world and interacting with other characters. They allow virtual spaces where the imaginary self can live out his/her fantasy fully confined within the virtual "pages" of the VN. Virtual novels are *manga* on steroids, bringing new dimensions to the table that allow fantasy selves to thrive and be free in ways that are slated to outstrip the feats that niche-targeted *manga* have performed in the late twentieth and early twenty-first centuries. VNs may well offer the ultimate remediations of the age-old *Tale of Genji* in its ongoing journey through time and space, across cultures and oceans. But will VNs enable the *Genji* to be fully translated and finally understood in ways that have evaded its printed novel versions and its modern text/image *manga* transpositions? Only time will tell. My hope is that our journey here, through all the splendidly configured Genjis and *Genji manga*, will entice others to take *The Tale of Genji* to the next step—to another generation, to a virtual novel,[2] and beyond.

NOTES

Introduction

1 Of note, within its pages *The Tale of Genji* has scenarios that raise concerns, but these elements were less evident in its text-based and film-based remediations. *Manga*, however, made visual/visible the tale's sexual and erotic conventions; the male/female social, political, and sexual hierarchies that govern their bodies; and the amorous activity among young protagonists.
2 I thank Jan Bardsley and Jack Abecassis for their invaluable reading of and insightful help in shaping this chapter.
3 The first type illustrates scenes taken from textual narratives but also includes the uploading of pictures and texts to computers for easier access. In type two, the electronic version improves on the older printed version, providing better resolution of images and adding sound or video. In type three, the new medium attempts to refashion the older. Thus source material like television or movie clips can be taken out of context and rearranged in a "collage" or "photomontage" that might appear on a website or in a news clip. In the last time type, the new medium tries to "absorb the old medium entirely," although total erasure is not possible. Examples of computer games like *Myst* and *Doom* that remediate film fall into this category (see Bolter and Grusin 1999, 44–7).
4 Remediation also operates within a single medium such as when film "borrows" from other films or when a painting "incorporates" other paintings (see Bolter and Grusin, 49). As we will see in the ensuing chapters, the *Genji manga* actively remediate other *manga*.
5 Emmerich contends that what he terms the *Genji* "replacements" displace the tale (2013, 10–11), but I concur with Atkins that translations of the tale and other reworkings do not efface the eleventh-century tale (2015, 182). Rather, as I argue, the adaptations serve as transpositions that different cultural and historical constituencies used to establish their identities.
6 The *manga* craze hit its high in 1995 and has been on a decline since even with the shift to digital platforms. But despite the waxing and waning of *manga*, they have remained ubiquitous in Japan and are used to teach accessing bank accounts and loans, proselytize new religions, and even recruit for the Self-Defense military force. In conjunction with other facets of pop culture such as fashion, music, and *anime*, *manga* often function as part of Cool Japan's global soft-power diplomacy.
7 I use the lower case "western" rather than the upper case "Western" to highlight that there is no monolithic "West" in opposition to a monolithic "East." By "west" I primarily mean the United States, Canada, Australia, New Zealand, the UK, France, Germany, and other western European countries (the demarcation of which the conflict between the Ukraine and Russia has put into high relief).
8 *Manga* sales have steadily dropped since 1995, but in 2019 paper *manga* sales clocked in at 166.5 billion yen (about $1.57 billion), while digital *manga* rang up 258.3 billion

yen ($2.43 billion) (National Publishing Association/Publishing Science Institute 2020). The COVID-19 pandemic accelerated the move to digital. The future of *manga* in Japan is unclear, and hopes for growth reside in markets outside of Japan (Horn 2018).

In the United States, the year 2007 marked the highest figures ($210 million), tanking at $65 million in 2012, but it has been making a comeback: $110 million in 2016 (Alverson 2017). In 2020 COVID-19 shuttered things, sending publishers scrambling to adapt. Demand for *manga* went online and publishers created new digital distribution channels, and digital sales tided them over (Aoki 2020). ICv2 reports that the 2021 sales clocked in at 24.4 million volumes, an increase of 160 percent from the previous year (Griepp 2022).

9 See Kern (2006) on *kibyōshi* (yellow books) as a precursor but not progenitor of *manga*, and Köhn (2007) for an opposing view. See also Schodt (1983, 28–67) and Ito (2008) for further information on the genesis of *manga*.

10 In the early 1970s *gekiga* developed into "third-rate *gekiga*" or erotic *manga*, which is a precursor of contemporary erotic *eromanga* (Nagayama 2021, 59–65). See Nagayama (2021) for an instructive study on how *eromanga* developed and incorporated erotic memes from Tezuka, boys, and girls comics along the way.

11 Some *manga* are four to eight frames in length, but most are story *manga* first appearing in *manga* magazines. See Schodt (1983, 18–20, 12–14) and Gravett (2004, 13–14). Some *manga* are serialized for years—one of the longest, *Golgo 13*, a James Bond–like spy *manga*, has been in publication since 1969 (Kinsella 2000, 44; McCarthy 2014, 36). The creator of *Golgo 13*, Saitō Takeo, passed away in 2021, but the staff at Saito Publication will continue to produce it (Hodgkins 2022).

12 "Genres" indicate the topic/theme of romance, fantasy, sports, and the like, while "categories" reference gender/age demarcations, but categories operate very much like genres. I follow the lead of Schodt (1996) and scholars Yonezawa (1987), Natsume (1999), Gravett (2004), and Lehmann (2005) in determining the mainstream categories to be boys, young men, girls, ladies, and adult men comics, although Nagatani (1994) sets up a system mixing and matching age/gender, topic, mode of production, and drawing and narrative styles. Needless to say, crossovers and the blurring of the boundaries are a matter of course.

13 Also known as *eromanga* or erotic *manga*, they are wide ranging and encompass countless art styles with 30 percent of their artists being women in 2014 (Galbraith and Bauwens-Sugimoto 2021, 39). See Nagayama (2021) for an informative study of the category.

14 Thorn (n.d.2, 5). See Yoshihiro (1993, 41–8) on the development of girls comics as well as Kusaka (2010) for more general information. In English, see Shamoon (2012), Schodt (1983), and Gravett (2004). See also Yamada T. (2006) and Yonezawa (1987), although M. Takahashi is critical of Yonezawa's assessment of the *shōjo* style (M. Takahashi 2008, 122). Prough (2010) provides an instructive look at how the industry fosters its readers and artists.

15 I am indebted to Haruo Shirane for the translation of this title.

16 The good wife/wise mother paradigm, operating since the late nineteenth century, dictated that women's sexuality and sexual activity be confined to marriage and the production of children. Sex for exploration and pleasure was frowned upon.

17 At the outset, in 1980, only two ladies-comics magazines were in circulation, but they had increased to forty-eight by 1991 (Shuppan qtd. in Ogi 2003, 780). Others say that by the end of the 1980s more than one hundred were being published, with fifty-seven

of them boasting a total circulation of 120 million by 1993 (Schodt 1996, 124). In 2005, 64.5 million copies of ladies-comics magazines were sold (Ito 2010, 89).
18 Schodt (1996, 56) and Kinsella (2000, 146–8). See also Nagayama (2021) on the regulations on erotic manga and McLelland (2015) for an informative study of the strictures placed on BL in the new millennium.
19 See Shigematsu (1999, 127 and 151n1). See also Kristof's November 5, 1995, comment in the *New York Times* and Shigematsu's assessment (1999, 152n5).
20 Jones (2005, 97). Allison conflates ladies comics with male-oriented erotic comics and deems the depiction of the women in both to be "misogynistic" (1996, 78). Some feminists would agree, characterizing pornography as demeaning to women, although many take a more nuanced, positive view, contending that women are reclaiming pornography for their own purposes. See Dworkin (1979) and Dines (2010) for the former view, and L. Williams (1999) and Taormino et al.'s (2013) edited anthology for the latter. Smith and Attwood note that a resurgence of the anti-porn movement has been on the rise since the early 2000s (2013, 42).
21 See Galbraith (2021, 71), McLelland (2017, 1–3), Galbraith and Bauwens-Sugimoto (2021, 13–14), and Library of Congress (2014) for more information. Khan and Ketterling would call the labeling a case of Orientalism and Yellow Peril, which situates the Orient as perverted and sexually deviant (2019, 357, 363–6).
22 See Allison (1996, 170–2) for further explanation. As with the case with Kristof above, Allison appears to be predominantly talking about the erotic ladies comics, which comprise only 20 percent of the category but does not make that distinction. In his chapter on regulation Schodt describes how *manga* artists managed the highly sexual and violent while skirting censorship (1983).
23 A sense of duty and obligation still plays a central role in contemporary Japan. Stories abound of Japanese dying from overwork (*karōshi*), the expectation of wives to work, take care of the home, and raise the children, and for children to do well in school, despite the lack of employment opportunities. Japanese society has changed from a "middle-class" corporate-family model of lifetime company employees and stay-at-home housewives of the 1960s and 1970s to the present "gap society" where social inequalities reign, but maintaining middle-class status remains in force for 90 percent of the population. See Hommerich, Kikkawa, and Sudo (2021a and 2021b) and Higuchi (2021) for further information.
24 See Miyake (1993) for the deployment of these readers in *The Tale of Genji*. Galbraith describes a similar kind of symmetry occurring between player and character in adult computer games, identifying it as a special feature of Japanese video games. (Male) players take up the first-person perspective of a female character and make choices for the character but in the process undergo the consequences of their choices with the character. As a result, one *manga/anime* critic reported that he became more thoughtful and responsible in making his decisions (Galbraith 2017c, 77–81).
25 Lunning defines cosplay as a "fictional mode of existence" rather than a single performance, arguing that cosplayers blend the fictional aspects of the characters they embody with their real-life identity as a student, part-time employee, and the like. She writes that *anime/manga/otaku* interests have become mainstreamed, influencing high fashion, winning Oscar awards, and populating internet content, but that cosplay is still enacted in specialized, safe spaces like conventions and photo shoots and must be defended "from mainstream culture, peers and even family" (2022, 64–8, 74, 70–1, 109).

26 A contemporary analogy would be the selves created for different social platforms. On a *Daily* podcast both the host and the reporter expressed concerns about accessing the Threads app, a competitor to X (previously Twitter), through their Instagram account. They feared exposing their more private Instagram personas on Threads which, like X, traffics in quick, short messages directed at a large audience. Tellingly, both participants called these personas, selves, differently configured "faces" constructed for specific social media sites that mimic the deployment of context-specific Japanese selves.

27 Unisex and regionally based "I"s also exist. A transvestite man may opt for "atai," while rural older women often favor "ore." My gratitude to an astute reader who pointed this out.

28 The possibility of violent video games (and also *manga* and *anime*) harming women and girls and of encouraging participants to enact sexual violence is a hotly debated topic (see Galbraith 2021, 10–24). After reviewing studies on the topic and examining the societal impact of "RapeLay," an erotic Japanese video game, Khan and Ketterling found that "no empirical evidence … clearly shows that sexually violent media, whether film or video games, cause people to be violent" (2019, 393). Two studies by Zendle, Cairns, and Kudenko (both in 2018) and another by Coulson and Ferguson (2016) also argue against "simplistic cause and effect connection between the media we consume and real-life aggression or violence" (Khan and Ketterling 2019, 379). Fujimoto and Shigematsu concur (qtd. in Galbraith 2017a, 122). Frühstück views the "sex and sexuality in visual culture from erotic woodblock prints to video games" as "resistance against … governmental suppression" (2022, 167), while Khan and Ketterling make a case for "reparative readings" of such media (2019, 379–93).

29 I am indebted to Backnik (1982, 6–7) for the translations of these terms. Doi T. provides some of the earliest discussion of the *uchi*/soto trope.

30 Many studies have been conducted on *otaku*, most recently Galbraith (2019) and Galbraith, Kam, and Kamn (2015).

31 As a counterpoint, Khan and Ketterling argue that rape fantasies help manage the fear of rape in the "safe mediated distance" of the computer games in much the same way that happens with terror in horror movies (2019, 382–5).

32 Similar labeling and targeting operate in computer gaming as well. The packaging for the adult game RapeLay advised that it was for those eighteen and older and was not to be sold to anyone younger or placed where it would be accessible to them (Galbraith 2017a, 121).

33 Nagayama provides a different reading of eroticism and sexuality, arguing that pornography "complements" the male-dominated heterosexual family and marriage system of modern Japan by serving as a safety valve to "cool" things off (2021, 203).

34 Galbraith argues that the gamers of *bishōjo* cute girls computer games establish relationships with fictional female characters in ways that replicate real-life interactions. They consider the characters to be their "wives" or "girlfriends" and interact with them as if they are real. The gamers are fully aware that these characters do not inhabit the 3D, physical world and eschew it, actively creating an alternative existence in a 2D, *anime/manga*/gaming environment populated by fictional characters and the company of like-minded aficionados. See Galbraith (2021, Chapters 4 and 5).

35 I am indebted to Brendan Elliot (2004) for alerting me to Tateishi Kazuhiro's website and twenty of the forty published versions of *Genji manga* (see Tateishi 2004). My study examines thirty-four of these, mentions the two earliest, and refers to four

less intensively because they are similar to the other titles I discuss. These last four are Saotome's *Iro otoko hikaru genji* (*The Sexy Shining Prince*, 2013), Okano et al.'s *Genji monogatari: koi to shiraseba* (*The Tale of Genji Comics Anthology: If We Let Them Know It's Love*, 2006), Hanazono's *Haya gen: hayayomi genji monogatari* (*Quick Gen: Reading the Tale of Genji in a Flash*, 2012), and Nanateru et al.'s *Manga de yomu genji monogatari* (*Reading the Tale of Genji in Manga*, 2014, 2016).

Chapter 1

1 The women were not entirely at the mercy of men. Cavanaugh (1996) shows that they controlled the dyeing and sewing (but not the distribution) of robes, which were used as currency. Yoda notes that they were adept at rebuffing poetic sexual overtures by men, as witnessed by Fujitsubo successfully thwarting Genji's advances (2004, 134–6).
2 Some say four hundred people; others, such as McCullough, indicate about a thousand (1968, 15).
3 Ukifune's name speaks to her existence as a tiny boat buffeted by the winds and tides of love, loss, and desire for redemption.
4 See Bowring (1988) for a succinct and informative summary of the tale and an astute rendering of the fluidity of its narrative points of view; see Field (1987) for a provocative delineation of the challenges to the throne, the role of several central women characters, and their substitution and displacement as Genji seeks his mother figure; and see Shirane (1987) for an illuminating explication of the influence of the poetic *waka* tradition and the utilization of antecedent *monogatari* tale plot and thematic conventions on the narrative construction of the *Genji*.
5 See Kikuta (1967) for more information.
6 I will be using Royall Tyler's translation of *The Tale of Genji* and, following the convention in the field, the English and modern Japanese translations will be cited by their translators and not the author Murasaki Shikibu.
7 See Rodd (1984) for full translation.
8 Kondo (1990, 33). See Lebra (1984, 294–5). I am indebted to Kondo for alerting me to Lebra's study. Fujii also astutely argues that western realist novels center the narrative on "an individuated self ... whose psychology and actions constitute the object or content of narration" (1993, 19).
9 Kikuta, pers. comm. This dovetailing of characters is mirrored in the fluidity between poetry and prose, among genre categories and disciplinary fields (literature, politics, etc.), and even between buildings and their environs, as already mentioned, but it is essential in interpersonal interactions. See Tanaka (1995) and Doi T. (1973) for how *amae no kōzō* (the functionality of indulgent dependency) factors into the ways in which personhood in Japan is constructed.
10 Invoking Bakhtin's dialogic notion of textual subjects as narrated and not "discrete subjects" or "unitary, closed individual[s]," Fujii posits that characters in the late-nineteenth- through early-twentieth-century Japanese novel function as non-individuated subjectivities formulated in similar fashion (1993, 34). Bakhtin contends that a narrated subjectivity results from the novel's focus on the utterances of the protagonists in a specific time and place (1984, 336, 276). Booker expands the notion further: "Dostoevsky does not create and describe fully formed and finalized

characters; instead he lets those characters evolve in dialogue with their author and with the other characters" (1996, 112).
11   They are also called base poems or allusive variations (Shirane 2007b, 606).
12   The Rokujō lineage is particularly resonant in portraying "surface depth" characterization, specifically jealousy and revenge. Pursued by Genji, Rokujō succumbs to his charms, only to be displaced by other women. Overcome by jealousy, Rokujō unleashes her living spirit and attacks Yūgao. Rokujō is horrified by what she has done but is unable to contain herself. But at the same time that her jealousy is ravaging Genji's women, Rokujō enables his ascendency at court through her daughter who becomes Genji's ward. Even Genji's fabled Rokujō-in mansion housing his women is built in part on land where Rokujō's mansion formerly stood and was conceived to appease her spirit. Thus, although she is spurned by Genji romantically, in the end Rokujō gets her revenge by possessing Genji's women and affecting his life well after her demise.
13   Tyler (2001b) makes the difference even clearer by naming Yūgao "The Twilight Beauty"—delicate and exceedingly short-lived, residing in the interstices of sunset and nightfall.
14   This reading stance was adopted for prose/tales as well, and in fact it comes full circle in the targeting of *manga* audiences in contemporary times—which runs counter to the broadening of audiences in the west through the novel. More on this later when discussing specific *manga* audiences in Part II.
15   Fish's interpretive communities have been critiqued as lacking historical specificity (Shepherd 1989, 96–7), but the Heian courtiers were in no danger of that.
16   I am indebted to Paul Cahill for delineating the importance of the reader's complicity in the collaboration of the reading of the tale.
17   It is not clear that a definitive "you" can be ascribed to indicate the reader, but, much like the "public narrator" whom Lanser delineates, the *Genji* narrator "brings into existence a fictional world ... [and] is capable of addressing a reader-construct who represents the public" (1981, 138). But the *Genji* narrator is much less well-defined than Lanser's "public narrator."
18   The ubiquitous narrator is not like Marlowe in *The Heart of Darkness*, who is a character in the narrative, nor does she function as a stand-in for the author, as we see in eighteenth-century novels by Daniel Defoe, Henry Fielding, or S. Richardson, in which the author interacts directly with the audience by posing rhetorical questions or addressing concerns that the author presumes the audience may have.
19   See Horton's article, "They Also Serve: Ladies-in-Waiting in *The Tale of Genji*" (1993) for a fuller explanation of the ladies-in-waiting as ubiquitous but unobtrusive presences, outlining their historical functions in service to their "male and female principals" as well as their narrative function in *monogatari* tales.
20   Kikuchi Yasuhiko, pers. comm. See Kondo (1990); Fowler (1988, 5–7, 28–9); Harada (1975, 510–11); and Backnik (1982) for further information on the ways that the modern Japanese *watashi* "I" or the classical first-person *waga* and *ware* lack the exclusivity of personal pronouns in English.
21   See Miyake (1993, 84–5). A similar process is evident in the ways in which a *nō* actor takes up his role. The ritualistic donning of the mask enables him not just to "simulate" the other (who can be of a different gender because all actors are male) but to "embody" or "become" the other by "releasing himself into the otherness of the role, allowing his body to be used as a 'vessel' or 'receptacle' [*ki, kimatsu*] for the body of the other" (Brown 2001, 25).

Chapter 2

1. Shirane writes that the adaptations of the tale have created a *"Genji* culture" that has a global as well as domestic reach (2008a, 1). I am indebted to his edited volume *Envisioning the Tale of Genji* for discussion of several adaptations.
2. I am indebted to Meech-Pakarik (1982) for the history of *Genji-e*. I thank Bruce Coats for outlining the parameters of the *Genji-e* tradition and for pointing out the significance of Kunisada in this narrative. For a concise listing of *Genji* paintings in Japanese, see Komachiya (2008). See Taguchi (2009) for information on the iconography used in works on the *Genji* theme.
3. Hasegawa adapted the layout and design of spaces and accoutrements from *emaki* scrolls and *ekotoba* (painting manuals for painters and calligraphers) to draw his *manga* (1996-7, 5:250-2; 3:269-70; 4:268). Both Egawa Tatsuya and Ide Chikae studied Heian-period materials to ensure the accuracy of their *Genji manga* (Lehmann 2005, 63; Ide, pers. comm.).
4. The Kamakura (1185-1333) and Muromachi (1333-1600) eras constitute the medieval period, although some scholars have recently pointed to the fourteenth century (when the Heian courtier-based framework began to erode) as the true start of the period (Colcutt 2008, 1). The *Encyclopedia Britannica* and the Weatherhead East Asian Institute at Columbia University educational site identify the medieval period as beginning in the late twelfth century, however, so I have followed suit.
5. Gotoh Museum Presenter on the *Genji Scrolls* pers, comm. Lippit agrees that vast resources and planning were required, though the circumstances of the scrolls' production remain unknown (2008, 49-50).
6. Taguchi (2009, 6-7) and Murase (2001, 18-19). The central *Genji* illustrations were by the Tosa School, but the Kanō, Kaihō, and Rimpa schools also produced their own paintings. For more information, see Murase (1983, 15), Tamamushi (2004), and Carpenter and McCormick (2019).
7. See Yamanaka (2008), Brown (2001, Chapters 2 and 3), and Goff (1991) for more information on the impact of the *Genji* on the *nō* theatre. Digests summarizing plotline, key scenes, and the meanings of the poems were also available providing painters, poets, and other practitioners access to the tale (Shirane 2008a, 22), but left much latitude for "translation" of the tale.
8. Harper (1993, 30). See Harper (1993 and 1994) for an informative introduction to the genre. See Marra (1984a, 1984b, 1984c) for *A Nameless Notebook*. The *Genji* was also an indispensable source for female poets like Nun Abutsu (1222?-1283) (Ii 2008, 165, 167). See Rowley (2010) for the role the *Genji* played in the lives of aristocratic women from its inception until the eighteenth century, and Allen (2004) for the significance of the pictorial *Genji-e* in elite women's lives in the seventeenth century. See Kornicki (2005) for a discussion of its suitability for women readers.
9. See Kern (2006) for a translation of Santo Kyōden's *Edo umare uwaki no kabayaki*.
10. Kern argues that technical differences, the historical hiatus between *kibyōshi* and *manga*, and the prominent influence of western comics on *manga* make the two separate entities (2006, 130), while Köhn questions Kern's contention that modern *manga* have no linkage with *kibyōshi* (2007, 237). My sense is that the modern *manga* gained inspiration from premodern Japanese works, merged these with western formats and techniques, and established their own new genre.

11. An English translation by Richardson and Tanonaka (1985) gives it the title *The Rustic Genji of a Bogus Murasaki*.
12. Marcus (1992, 139); see 124–8 for a plot summary. Emmerich contends that the eleventh-century *Genji* was virtually unknown to ordinary townspeople, so the *Bumpkin Genji* was less a parody than a reintroduction or a replacement of the tale (2013, 10–11). My sense is that some (elite) readers were aware of the *Genji*, its digests and pictorial renditions, so that considering *Bumpkin Genji* a parody of the tale is plausible. See Emmerich (2013) Part 1 for a discussion of the *gōkan* (combined booklets) *Bumpkin Genji* that merge text with Kunisada's images.
13. Emmerich argues that *Bumpkin Genji* was the sole means by which readers of these periods came to know the tale, or at least that the eleventh-century tale existed more as "a reflection on *Inaka* [i.e., *Bumpkin*] *Genji*, and not the other way around" (2008, 212–13 and 2013, 51), but the Tosa prints and other visual renditions of the tale were also very much in vogue at that time. The popularity of *Bumpkin Genji* was real: writer Kōda Rohan credits it for inspiring the sudden outburst of everything from "[*Genji*] garden decorations to trinkets and fashion accessories, ... *Genji* oil, *Genji* rice crackers, *Genji* sushi, and *Genji* soba noodles" (Caddeau 2006, 4)—yet considering *Bumpkin Genji* the only source of this branding craze oversimplifies the situation.
14. See Rowley (2000) for information on Akiko. See Midorikawa (2003 and 2010) for a fuller account of several of the translations of the tale. The second half of Emmerich (2013) also deals with translations, and he credits Suematsu for establishing the *Genji*'s position in world literature.
15. Largely self-taught in classical Chinese and Japanese, Waley never visited Japan but came to know the tale through *nō*, and produced what Hirakawa credits as an exceptionally fine translation (2008, 49). De Gruchy writes that readers were "moved" by Murasaki's tale but more so by Waley's prose, believing that Waley had "upgraded" the original—so much so that they credited him with producing a stellar work of English literature rather than just a translation of Murasaki's tale (2003, 130–2).
16. Tanizaki completed three novelizations of the tale, and authors Enchi Fumiko, Tanabe Seiko, and Setouchi Jakuchō followed with their versions in the 1970s and 1990s. Seidensticker, Tyler, and Washburn completed their English versions in 1976, 2001, 2015, respectively.
17. I am indebted to Tateishi for signaling the presence of the 1950s and 1980s booms, although he does so only in passing (2008, 303, 315).
18. See Caddeau (2006, 12) on the use of the *Genji* in this period.
19. Nathan wrote a biography of Mishima in 1974 addressing Mishima's homosexuality, but Mishima's widow blocked its publication in Japan, threatening to deny permission to publish Mishima's works should any publisher do so. For a fuller explanation of the construction of Japan as infantile and female to the west's male, see chapter 1 of Yamamoto's 1999 study.
20. Kitamura (2008 and 2000, 160, 149n2). The latter provides sales numbers for modern prose translations of the tale by Yosano Akiko (1,720,000) and Tanizaki Jun'ichiro (830,000), revealing that Yamato Waki's closest competitors were Tanabe Seiko at 2,500,000 copies sold and Setouchi Jakuchō at 2,100,000 in 2000.
21. Tanabe's novel was first serialized in the *Asahi Weekly* from late 1974 through 1978, and later published in five volumes in 1978–9. It streamlined and simplified the grammar, language, and content of the Murasaki's tale, translating the tale into an idealized romance that spoke to female readers of all ages (see Kitamura 2008, 332–4).

22 In keeping with this new *Genji* culture, the Takarazuka revue staged two grand shows in 1981 and 1989 based on Tanabe's novelization (Kitamura 2008, 341; Tateishi 2005b, 186–7), while three *Genji manga* targeting female audiences were produced in the 1990s. An outlier to the female emphasis, Hashimoto Osamu's 1991–3 *Yōhen genji monogatari* (*The Transformed Tale of Genji*) focalized Genji, his male interiority, and the "darkness of the heart" in psychological detail (Kitamura 2008, 346–7).

23 The term "Japan's National Cool" was popularized by McGray in 2002. Others call the phenomenon J-Cult (Iwabuchi 2002) or Japanimation (Uyeno Toshiya, qtd. in MacWilliams 2008, 13).

24 I thank Bruce Coats for the introduction to the Miyata (2001) and Ishidori (1999) illustrations.

25 An underwater love scene between Genji and his older lover Rokujō in her bathing room is added. Genji's stepmother Fujitsubo goes out nightly to a shrine to pray for Genji when he falls ill and then meets him by chance there. On another occasion Genji is attacked by ruffians and, in the words of one of my students, he "takes out his sword and goes all action hero and takes out the ruffians without suffering a scratch"—no doubt very entertaining and riveting for the audience but anachronistic at best.

26 Shin'nosuke debuted in a 1983 production of *The Tale of Genji*, but he took the name Shin'nosuke VII in 1985 and the name Ichikawa Ebizo XI in 2004, according to the online website Naritaya. In a special magazine edition, produced by Heibonsha on the Kabuki *Genji* productions that covers both performances, the actor was still called Shin'nosuke then (Takahashi Y. 2001). Today he goes by the name Ebizo; his son is Shin'nosuke VIII. My gratitude to an astute reader for alerting me to the change.

27 The website is no longer active, and, on a personal note, my mentor at Tohoku University Kikuta Shigeo and several of his students gave lectures in Sendai, one of the selected sites.

28 See Tomita (1999). The symphony was subsequently recorded by the London Philharmonic Orchestra in conjunction with a synthesizer, koto zither, and other traditional Japanese instruments, under the title *Genji monogatari gensō kōkyō emaki* (*Genji Fantasy Symphonic Scroll*). It is also called *Genji Monogatari Illusion Symphony Picture Scroll*.

Chapter 3

1 Many treatises discuss the meaning and origin of the *kawaii* cute phenomenon, which is one of the few female-driven aesthetics and is primarily associated with the large-eyed, innocent look of girls comics, Hello Kitty, and the frilly look of Victorian-infused Lolita fashion. See Kinsella (1995) and Treat (1996) for further information. *Otaku* designates a "fanboy [or fangirl] a hardcore or cult fan," who immerses him/herself in *anime, manga*, and video games (Galbraith 2009a, 171). See T. Saito (2007) for more information. *Moe*, "to bud or sprout," is a homophone for "to burn" and is used to indicate "a euphoric [highly positive] response to fantasy characters" by fans (Galbraith 2009b). See Galbraith (n.d.2, and 2017a) for further information. Galbraith also argues that computer gamers engage so fully with the fictional 2D world of *anime/manga* that they eschew the 3D natural world reality and create an alternative

mode of existence for themselves in the fictional 2D through what Galbraith terms the ethics of media literacy or alternately the ethics of *moe* (2021, 183–8).

2. The remaining three girls comics in the *Genji manga* category include two early remediations. The first, by Kimura Jin, later known as Mitsuhi, is entitled *Shinhan Genji monogatari* (*The New Edition Tale of Genji*) and was published in January 1970 in volume 9 of the *Josei komikku elle* (*The Women's Comics Elle*) magazine. Little is known about the *manga* itself, but it is mentioned by Tateishi (2005c, 191–2). Mori Yukiko followed with her *Genji monogatari* (*The Tale of Genji*) in 1974, which consists of three chapters centered on Genji but treats him more like a real-life figure than a fictional one. There is little nudity, and emotions are subdued. With no screen tones or shading, the visuals are reminiscent of black-ink *sumie* drawings (1974, 72, 46–7, 133). The third title, *Genji monogatari komikku ansorojii: koi to shiraseba* (*The Tale of Genji Comics Anthology: If We Let Them Know It's Love*), by Okano et al., is very similar to other girls *Genji manga* and is not discussed in the study.

3. Kitamura (2008, 334–5); MANGASeek and Nichigai Associates (2003, 404). M. Takahashi (2008, 130–5) discusses the ways in which *shōjo* comics' innovations were misunderstood by critics. Gravett (2004, 79) provides a succinct description of their drawing innovations.

4. I am grateful to Kiriko Komura for alerting me to the "Iroha" poem, and to Emmerich for pointing out the usage of "asaki yume miji" in the poem. Of note, the phrase "asaki yume mishi" does not appear in *The Tale of Genji*, but the poem is recorded in its entirely on the last page of Volume 10 of Yamato's *manga*, marking Genji's passing.

5. *Shōjo manga* often feature handsome male leads, while the female characters are "ordinary girl" personages like Bunny with whom readers can readily relate, although as part of the magical girl subcategory, Bunny and her friends are also tasked with saving the world.

6. Kitamura (2008, 336–8). See also Kitamura (2000, 153–2 [the page numbers proceed in reverse order in this work]). Numerous articles have been written on *Fleeting Dreams*. Tateishi suggests that the success of the *manga* lies in Yamato's ability to translate into girls comics the age-old story of young women overcoming adversity and succeeding, while Hirota contends that it lies in the *manga*'s making overt the feelings of the women (Tateishi 2005c, 198; Hirota 1997, 47, 49).

7. Kitamura comes to a similar conclusion, persuasively arguing that Ukifune has become her own person, finding her rightful place by taking the tonsure. Kitamura points to a series of pages in the *manga* (Yamato 1980–93, 13:184–6) in which a voice assures Ukifune that she can live her life alone, free of others, and that only those who have wept and suffered in love can free themselves of all entanglements and live out bigger, richer dreams that transcend gender, sexuality, and time (Kitamura 2000, 152–151 [the page numbers proceed in reverse order in this work]).

8. Hijikata (2005, 26–7). Tateishi identifies lines from Tanabe's novelization of the tale that have been used without attribution in the film *A Love of a Thousand Years*, and even in *Fleeting Dreams* (2005a, 150 and 2005c, 199).

9. A fourth title, *The Tale of Genji Comics Anthology: If We Let Them Know It's Love* (2006), by Okano et al., belongs to this grouping and portrays women who know that their love for Genji is doomed, but it does not add a great deal to the *Genji manga* corpus, so it is not included here.

10. Very little can be found on Toba's background, so her humorous, tongue-in-cheek home page (available in 2005 but no longer so, due to her death in 2008) becomes our only source. Covers of her *manga*, images from her other works, and a link to

a cat named Mania were available. She was born on January 4, was blood type A, and a Capricorn who liked action movies and video games. She also drew herself in caricature, toothbrush in hand, towel draped around her neck, hair awry, her eyes tightly closed, with the description *mōningu bakuhastsu musume* ("The morning imploding girl").

11 From 1989 to 1991, the Japan Broadcasting Corporation (NHK) aired on television *anime* versions of six classical works, *Makura no sōshi* (*The Pillow Book*), *Tsurezuregusa* (*Essays in Idleness*), *Sarashina nikki* (*The Sarashina Diary*), *Kagerō nikki* (*The Kagerō Diary*), *Ise monogatari* (*The Tales of Ise*), and *The Tale of Genji*. These were then commissioned as *manga* and published from 1991 to 1995 by Kadokawa Shoten. All but *Essays in Idleness* were reprinted by Homesha in 2006: Volume One comprises *The Pillow Book*; Volume Two, *The Kagerō Diary* and *The Sarashina Diary*; and Volume Three, *The Tale of Genji* and *The Tales of Ise*.

12 See p. 350 of the 2006 Homesha edition.

13 Suter characterizes Toba as a "soft-core Boys Love" artist (2013, 557n7), but Toba's *Yasashii himitsu no mori* (*The Gentle Forest of Secrets*, 2001) and other titles indicate a girls-comics art style reminiscent of 1980s and 1990s CLAMP, a celebrated team of female *manga* artists. Consisting of Ōkawa Ageha (also known as Nanase), Igarashi Satsuki, Nekoi Tsubaki, and Mokona, CLAMP is well known for their diverse styles, from sci-fi to romance, from *seinen* young men to children's *manga*. See https://clamp-net.com/about for information on the artists and their works. In English see Lehmann (2005, 32–47, 116–17).

14 Disputes over Japan's participation in the Gulf War escalated, while the 1995 release of poisonous sarin gas in a Tokyo subway by the religious cult Aum Shinrikyō and a devastating earthquake shook the nation to its core. The new millennium brought its own troubles: a US submarine collided with a Japanese high school fishing trawler; Prime Minister Koizumi Jun'ichirō angered China and Korea by visiting the Yasukuni Shrine where the ashes of war criminals are housed, and deployed Japanese ships to the war in Afghanistan.

15 Hayasaka Akira, a novelist, screenwriter, dramatist, and stage director who has won numerous prizes, wrote the script for the film and is listed on the cover of Sasaki'a *manga*, but in light of the differences between the film and the *manga*, it appears that Sasaki created her own adaptation.

16 Tateishi is highly critical of the film for its "preposterous 'creativity'" (2008, 316)—an assessment with which I concur. Shikibu's husband dies at the hands of pirates, Genji and the Akashi Lady engage in an underwater love scene, and Shikibu and her daughter pull in fishnets in the hinterlands of Echizen while former idol Matsuda Seiko sings from rooftops. But most alarming are the imperialist and nationalistic gestures—evidenced by the tributes brought by China, Korea, and the Ryūkyū Islands for the coronation ceremony for Genji's son, and in the assertion that *The Tale of Genji* is "the world's greatest novel written exactly one thousand years ago."

Tateishi notes that some read the film as a parody of the *Genji*, for Shikibu is critical of her husband Nobutaka and Regent Michinaga for treating women like marriage pawns, yet Shikibu herself grooms Shōshi to be an imperial consort and bearer of the emperor's children, muddying the waters of the film's view on patriarchy. See Tateishi (2008, 316–21 and 2005a, 138–9, 149, 49–51) for more information.

17 Very little can be found on the artist—on the inside jacket of Volume 1, Miō writes that she was born in Kyoto on September first and is a Virgo. She loves gourmet food and going to the gym. Her debut work, *Todoite MY VOICE* (*Please Reach, My*

Voice), was published in June 2004 in *Shōjo Komikku* (*Girls Comics*), and she adapted *Towazugatari* (*The Confessions of Lady Nijō*) into *manga*. On the last page Miō explains that she has loved classical Japanese literature since middle school, so she jumped at the chance to *manga*-nize the *Genji*.

18 First serialized in *Girls Comics* for young readers from 2006 to 2009, the stories appear concurrently as Shōgakukan Flower Comics. Each of the four volumes contains four vignette-like episodes, much like Toba's, that focus on the central women (Genji's mother, his stepmother Fujitsubo, his principal wife Aoi, his jealous lover Rokujō, his lovers Akashi and Murasaki, his second principal wife the Third Princess, and the three Uji princesses), as well as on some secondary figures like the red-nosed princess and Rokujō's daughter.

19 Some online blog entries find Miō's rewriting of *Genji* a travesty and exhort her to do her research on the Heian period. Perhaps the best advice comes from a blogger who recommends Miō's remediation to *shōjo manga* and not *The Tale of Genji* readers. See Amazon Customer Review.

20 Blackface performances have been around in Japan since the 1870s and the most recent occurred in 2017 when a comedian appeared in blackface in a Beverly Hills cop skit. In 2015 McNeil successfully lobbied against two Japanese bands who planned to perform in blackface on national TV. See BBC News (2018) and McNeil (2018). In light of these occurrences, the call for Japan to be more sensitive and less "tone deaf" to racial diversity is wholeheartedly endorsed.

21 Abe no Seimei (921–1005) was active from 967 to 1005 (Shigeta 2013, 82–3, 96). Both Shigeta and Inoue postulate that Seimei held several posts at court and that he is credited with "legendary and mystical episodes" and described as possessing "extraordinary paranormal powers," including channeling spirits, ridding imperial residences of evil spirits, producing rain, and curing an emperor of illness (Inoue n.d.; Shigeta 2013, 78–81, 84, 93–4). Despite no historical records to support these claims (Shigeta 2013, 93), Seimei's legendary prowess, coupled with his apocryphal status as the offspring of a fox, gave rise to his wizard status in popular culture (Miller 2008, 32).

Miller writes that the Bureau of Onmyōryō Divination performed "rituals and magic that constituted a syncretic form of esoteric cosmology and divination" (2008, 33). See Ooms (2009) for information on *onmyōji* in the Nara period, and Bialock (2007, chapter 2) for its Heian through its Kamakura manifestations in literary texts.

22 Theories explaining the boom are as follows: (1) "a new nationalism" revived interest in history and "Japanese cultural innovation," (2) Seimei captured the imagination of youth who wanted to escape from reality and find refuge in fantasies, (3) it brought to the fore fears that resulted from the 9/11 attacks in the United States and the Japanese recession, and (4) it was associated with the popularity of the Harry Potter books (Miller 2008, 40).

23 I am grateful to Nicole Ogawa-Yukitomo for identifying these tropes.

Chapter 4

1 The readership of BL works includes lesbians, bisexuals, and heterosexual and gay men, especially in their "New Wave" iteration that challenges and subverts early BL versions. Because BL are produced as *manga*, light novels, artwork, *anime*, and video

games, they are often referred to as BL media, but we will limit our discussion to their comics versions in this chapter.

2 This turning of the gender table mirrors western slash fiction in which Mr. Spock and Captain James Kirk of *Star Trek* fame, or Harry Potter and his nemesis Draco, are transposed into lovers, but BL has some differences, as will become apparent below. See Woledge (2005) for further information on slash fiction, and McLelland (2006/2007) for the relationship between slash and BL. K. Saito also includes in this category *bishōnen* (beautiful boy), *tanbi* (aestheticism), *bara* (rose), *June* (name of a magazine), and *fujoshi* (2011, 172), while McLelland and Welker list *shōnen-ai*, *JUNE*, *yaoi*, and boys love (2015, 5). See Welker (2015) for an instructive history of male–male narratives. Here I limit my discussion to the central players in male–male narratives, BL, *shōnen-ai*, and *yaoi*.

3 After examining 110 series titles and 53,000 pages in paperbacks, comic books, and *manga* magazines available in the United States from 1999 to 2001, Perper and Cornog found that most sexualzed encounters in *manga* did not victimize or humiliate women. Rather, 92 percent of the 87 stories which depicted sexual assault exacted revenge on sexual attackers, refuting the claim that *manga* glorified sexual violence (2002, 45, 3).

4 In one such example, when I mounted a *manga* symposium in 2006 and had speakers present on *manga*, what earned ire was not the sexualized ladies comics but the mention of a budding attraction between two high school boys in girls comics. Their love consisted of longing looks and deep sighs—no physical touching or nudity—but the intimation of homoerotic, homosexual yearnings resulted in angry denunciation by a participant.

5 Khan and Ketterling contend that the controversy over the Japanese adult video game *RapeLay*—and by extension "the erotic cartoon and game culture" in Japan—mounted by western activists and politicians is "an example of orientalism and yellow peril, wherein the Japanese 'Other' was targeted as immoral, dangerous and sexually deviant" (2019, 357, 363–6). In contrast a western violent video game *Grand Theft Auto* which has a much wider and deeper distribution in the United States (holding the record for most sales) has not been "unequivocally censored" by western media nor has had legal and political actions mobilized against it (Khan and Ketterling 2019, 394).

6 These four iterations are: (1) BL and *yaoi* are considered one and the same and are used interchangeably (Mizoguchi 2003, 62; K. Saito 2011, 172); (2) BL is subsumed under *yaoi* (Nagaike 2003, 74, but she shifts to using BL as a blanket term in later publications); (3) *yaoi* (and *shōnen-ai*) are separate categories under BL (Wood 2006, 394–5); and (4) the most persuasive, BL has become the blanket term for male–male romances (Thorn pers. comm.; Pagliasotti 2008; Johnson pers. comm.; Emma Hanashiro e-mail; Suter 2013, 547; McLelland and Welker 2015, 3; Welker 2015).

See Welker (2015) for a fuller account of the integrated history of *shōnen-ai*, *yaoi*, and BL. Of note, the products of the *fujoshi* (literally, "rotten girls," the most prominent aficionados of male–male romances) are considered BL by some. However, Galbraith, who has studied the *fujoshi*, contends that these works are *yaoi*—"fan-produced fiction and art, usually manga" (2011, 212)—and not BL, which are commercially published manga.

7 The violent sexual encounters in ladies comics, however, do not operate as misogynistic violence perpetuated by a male on a female. Rather, they function as "play rape," narrative devices or tropes through which women act upon their sexual desires in safe ways and without guilt or fear (Shigematsu 1999, 147–8). Put another way, feminist scholar L. Williams notes that only "by pretending to be good and only

coerced into sex—does the woman who is coerced and punished get the 'bad' girl's pleasure. She gets this pleasure as *if* against her will and thus *as if* were still a good girl" (L. Williams, qtd. in Shamoon 2004, 97). But to be clear these spaces accede to readers' desires precisely because they are not real. They function as fictional, outside and beyond reality, and as safe places for exploration and pleasure.

8 The characteristics of the *seme* and the *uke* vary, and this traditional relationship is challenged, subverted, and rearranged at will, especially in post-2000 "New Wave" BL. This is discussed in detail below.

9 This is not just found in BL but has operated as an established convention in sexual (heterosexual) dynamics between the sexes ever since such trysts have been recorded. In *The Tale of Genji* as well, even when the attention is welcome, women must initially rebuff any overtures. The man/initiator knows that refusal is part of the dance and will push forward—and the woman/receiver is expected to accept. Galbraith notes that Kagami Hiroyuki, a writer for adult video games, describes these sexual encounters in games as "performed—or, to borrow a theatre term, played—by performers … [embodying a] constructed media fiction" (Galbraith 2017a, 16).

10 I made every effort to acquire permission for Figure 4.1 as well as two others but to no avail. Ronald Stewart, sociologist and former director of the Japanese Manga Association, noted that, when the Association mounted a BL symposium in 2021, several artists did not want to appear on Zoom or to have their photos included in the proceedings, indicating a reluctance on the part of some artists to be publicly acknowledged (e-mail). I have thus used Figure 4.1 invoking the Japanese copyright law, which is similar to "free use" copyright exceptions outside of Japan. Article 32, Section 1 stipulates that images can be used in academic publications like a quote and hence without permission from the copyright holder, as long as it is relevant to what is being analyzed and discussed (Stewart e-mail).

11 See Yuki et al. (2007) and Jack et al. (2009) for studies on the cultural differences in expressing and interpreting facial emotions in Japan and the United States.

12 Some readers might read Genji's averted visage, his not looking at Hanachirusato and expressing his contentment more straightforwardly, as indicating ambivalence, but, as noted by Yuki et al. (2007), Japanese eschew expressing emotions overtly and looking directly into people's faces, so readers must pay careful attention to what Genji says and how he acts after the encounter to interpret Genji's enjoyment and satisfaction with the encounter.

13 Orbaugh writes that there is no clear sense of "an empowered abuser group and a disempowered abused group" in pornography, and that the power dynamics in *manga* as well are "complex and shifting." She also argues that the "wide range" of *manga* narratives allows young readers "to make *informed and independent choices about their own sexualities* in a safe space." She deems this "sexual literacy" "a *child's right*" (2017, 104). The italics are hers. See Khan and Ketterling on the reparative affects of erotic games (2019, 375–93); Galbraith 2017a, 120).

14 Saotome continues her Rokujō story in *Iro otoko hikaru genji* (*The Sexy Shining Genji*), but it is not as provocative as her entry in the *Tale of Genji BL Anthology*. Of note, the artist was commissioned by the publisher to create these episodes and they do not represent her views or beliefs.

15 Fujimoto calls it "'playing sexuality' … which leads to exploration and understanding of sex(uality);" Kagami sees it as "sexual fantasy," which has positive outcomes for individuals and society (qtd. in Galbraith 2017a, 114, 121).

16 See Bullock (2010, Chapter 1) for further information on how governmental decrees regulated abortion, birth control, and sex education to enforce the "good wives and wise mothers" ideology. In vogue since the late nineteenth century, the government pressured women into roles centered in marriage and motherhood and dictated that marriage was the only outlet for female sexuality. All other sexual desires were deemed "unhealthy" (Bullock 2010, 20, 22). This ideology still remains in effect today (McLelland and Welker 2015, 10).
17 See Galbraith (n.d.1 and 2015) on how *fujoshi* consumers and other *manga* readers maintain a strict separation of the imaginary and the real/reality, invoking what Galbraith and others call media literacy. The fantasy world operates as an alternate space, as a means to escape the rigidity of Japanese society for all takers. Acting out fantasies in the real world brings swift condemnation, although incidents of young people behaving inappropriately have risen since the 1990s. See the introduction to the present volume for a fuller explanation.
18 Mori N. finds that the *uke* may verbally tell the *seme* to stop, but his thoughts reveal that the *seme*'s ministrations are thrilling and enjoyable, and the *uke* does not want the *seme* to stop (2010, 173–5). In other cases, the aftermath of the encounter is depicted as positive, as the *uke* agrees to go out on a date or blushes happily when reference is made to the encounter.

 Fujimoto further argues that the prevalence of the rape and sadomasochistic tropes in BL does not demean or endanger women but in fact gives girls agency (qtd. Shamoon 2004, 78–9, 85). McLelland and Walker write that the "re-appropriation" of male characters in BL/*yaoi* romances enabled women artists and readers to consume "sexual scenarios including sadomasochism and rape" that have been "the preserve of male sexual fantasy" (2015, 10).

 There is no doubt that those who have been assaulted would find these scenarios unsettlingly and difficult to keep separate from real-life world experiences, but, as discussed in the introduction, such viewers would be forewarned not to engage these categories. There is no guarantee, but most would not venture into these *manga* knowing their content, any more than they would engage pornography targeting men.
19 Genji's not returning to visit Rokujō again is not explained, but it could be due as much to his embarrassment in enjoying Rokujō's rough sex as to the ferocity of the encounter.
20 This theory is promoted by Midori Matsui and Ueno Chizuko (Suter 2013, 548–4). Wood identifies other scholars of a similar mindset (2006, 396).
21 See Nagaike and Aoyama for a succinct summary of the scholarly appraisals of the issues and how they played out in the debate (2015, 123–6). Also see Vincent (2007, 69–77), and Lunsing (2006, pars. 14–18, 26–34). Baudinette points out that the depictions of gay men in *geikomi* gay comics, produced for and by gay men, are "equally fantastic" and are not more "authentic or real" than BL constructions (2017, 65).
22 Ishida Minori and Mark McLelland suggest that this is what drives BLers (Suter 2013, 549).
23 I thank José Cartagena-Calderon for alerting me to Sedgwick and Butler's articulation of queer theory, and for his insightful assessment of them.
24 In *nō* theater, a male actor assumes a female body and not vice versa, but this has much in common with what *manga* fans enact.
25 These figures are from Zsila et al.'s (2018) survey entitled "Loving the Love of Boys: Motives for Consuming Yaoi Media," which primarily centered on US and

Hungarian respondents. The full data are as follows: 43.23 percent identify as heterosexual; 20.30 percent as heterosexual with homosexuality to some extent; 13.54 percent as bisexual, 4.01 percent as homosexual with heterosexuality to some extent; 14.09 percent as homosexual, 0.28 percent as asexual; 2.76 percent as unsure about their sexual orientation; and 1.80 percent as "other" (Zsila et al. 2018). There were 724 participants—420 men and 212 women.

26 Imahashi notes that the Japanese public has become more accepting of LGBTQ people. The attitude is still tolerance (qtd. in Johnson 2020, 135)—a kind of "as long it is not my child" attitude at best, but the Japanese Diet just passed the Japan Equality Act in June 2023. A first of its kind, it directs the Japanese government to "promote understanding" of LGBT people and "to avoid 'unfair discrimination' of sexual orientation and gender identity." The consensus is that it is not far-reaching enough (K. Doi and Worden 2023). Johnson speaks to the ways in which a primarily music-based set of performances known as visual *kei* (translated as "visual type") serves as another arena in which fans and performers can "dabble in queer ideas and practices" and enact queer identities in a relatively safe and "noncommittal" manner (2020, 134).

27 Matsui Midori views *fujoshi* as "girls with penises" who seek male personas as the only way through which they can express their sexuality (qtd. in A. Williams 2015, n55), but *fujoshi* do not seek to be male or see their female positionalities as undesirable; instead, they use the imagined male–male pairings to seek out alternatives that are beyond male or female, gay or straight, so Freud's penis-envy is less applicable here.

Galbraith also notes that *fujoshi* do not shun "real" or even heterosexual relationships. Rather, their *moe* world often operates in tandem with their lived experiences: some fans are married or have boyfriends and live "normative" lives, but concurrently participate in a community of shared BL/*yaoi* practices (2015). See Hestor (2015) for information on how the *fujoshi* fandom operates.

28 No doubt the isolation brought on by the pandemic, and having class via Zoom, impeded the more even-keeled in-person discussions that usually transpire in my classroom.

29 Orbaugh argues that "the harm … in *eradicating* sexual images and narratives (that have not harmed any actual person in their production) is … far greater than the potential harm caused to society by manga." She writes that she knows "about child abuse first-hand" and that "what saved [her]" was not "silence about sex" but "reading and writing and using [her] imagination to try to understand … unequal power and domination and betrayal." Psychologists and therapists have shown that narrative is "the *only* thing that provides effective healing from trauma" (Orbaugh 2017, 106, 105).

Chapter 5

1 Some call this category *josei* women comics, but Thorn considers *redikomi* and *josei* to be two separate categories (e-mail). Ito pegs ladies-comics readers at fifteen through forty-four years old (2002, 69) and Ogi, at twenty-five to thirty (2003, 780), although women in their forties and fifties read them as well.

2 The 1980s saw just two ladies-comics magazines (Ogi 2003, 780), but by 1993 fifty-seven magazines, boasting a circulation of 120 million in print (Schodt 1996, 124). Ito puts the figures at more than one hundred in the late 1980s (2010, 75). Sales dropped in the 1990s, but 42.5 million, plus 22 million special issues, were sold in

2005, not including comics through internet providers (Ito 2010, 89). The Japan Magazine Publishers Association lists magazine circulation at 718,031 from October 2018 to September 2019, not including digital sales (Japan Magazine Publishers Association n.d.).

3. The liberalization of women's issues resulted from the confluence of unusual forces that aligned in the 1990s but were not sustained in the new millennium. Factors such as a resurgence of nationalism that put gender under the microscope, a decade of economic stagnation, Japan's decline on the international stage, and little interaction of the women's movement with the international feminism unraveled much of the progress. "State feminism" and the movement also came to be blamed for the ills of contemporary society (Kano 2011, 55).

4. See Ito (2010), which provides a short history of ladies comics in Chapter 1 and examples of the subcategories in Chapters 2 and 3. A growing trend features stories based on readers' experiences that the magazines turn into *manga* (Ito 2010, 91–2).

5. Fujimoto Yukari explains these tropes as catalysts for awakening a woman's sexual desire (Shamoon 2004, 97). In one story the female protagonist is sexually aroused through masturbation, long considered the purview of male sexual activity (Shamoon 2004, 91). Her female body then does not function as a visual "turn on" for male viewers. Rather, enacting a female gaze, she spectacle-izes her body to showcase her pleasure, which in turn serves as visual trope through which readers can in tandem participate and perform.

6. Technically speaking, Takenaka's *manga* is not a ladies comics because it was serialized in a newspaper, but its themes and its critique of male privilege make it best fit in this chapter.

7. Ide generously allowed me to visit her studio on two occasions. Debuting in 1966 as a girls-comics artist, she is one of the less than 10 percent of *manga* artists who makes a living solely by creating comics. In producing her *manga* she plans how to narrate the story and then sketches out the layout and images. Once she receives editorial approval, she finalizes the layout, leaving the background and clothing to her assistants, but draws the facial expressions herself. For her *Genji manga* she studied art and reference books to learn about the tale and the period. Utilizing Yosano Akiko's translation, she determined which episodes she would depict and then sketched out her story. Ide notes that a *mangaka* must be smart and in tune with the times and with their readers. Her success at doing just that is clear in her remediation of the irascible Genji and his fabulous women. See Ito (2011) for more on Ide's life and art.

8. Maki is a classic 1950s–1960s girls-comics artist who moved to women magazines and then to ladies comics in the 1970s, producing *Akujo baiburu* (*Femme Fatale Bible*, 1980–91) and *manga* versions of several novels. Maki serialized her *Genji* remediation in *Biggu komikku foa rediisu* (*Big Comic for Ladies*), a counterpart of young men's *Big Comic*, and published her ten-volume book version in 1988–91 (see Kitamura 2008, 342–9, 355n46). It was reprinted in the *Weekly Visual Genji monogatari* in 2002–3, and won the Thirty-Fourth Shōgakukan Manga Award in 1989.

9. See Shamoon (2011) for a general description of the *gekiga* style, and Brophy (2010) to see how Tezuka Osamu utilized it in his *manga*.

10. A prominent example of Maki's portrayal of a secondary protagonist is Genji's wet nurse. Summoned by Empress Kokiden, the rival of Genji's mother, the wet nurse is ordered to poison the baby Genji but, against great odds, she disobeys (1997–8, 1:4–9).

11 *Manga* enable this process in some surprising ways: comics theorist Scott McCloud argues that the simplified, caricature drawings in comics and *manga* "universalize" the figures, allowing viewers to see a wide range of people in them, including themselves, which in turn fosters identification, whereas more detailed drawings provide too much specificity and result in making the figures "other," causing separation rather than identification (1994, 30–1, 44).
12 The *manga* covers the central women and others, such as Rokujō's daughter and the wife of Genji's son, who are not included in other remediations.
13 Genji spies on his father and Fujitsubo engaging in sex (Teradate 2001–2, 1:88–93), and, thoroughly frustrated, he imposes himself on Aoi, who seems surprised but not displeased until he utters Fujitsubo's name (Teradate 2001–2, 1:97–9). In another unusual move, the emperor and Genji discuss in explicit sexual terms—with accompanying images—the pleasures of having a young wife whom you can mold to your specific wants and needs (Teradate 2001–2, 1:115–18).
14 Sex scenes comprise a high 23 percent of the main stories in Hazuki's *Erotic Talk*, and 25 percent of the addendum (if the male "beefcake" images are included).
15 Of note is the 2006 live action film, *Sakuran* (*Blossoms Wild*), that explores similar themes of female confinement. Adapted from Mayō Anno's popular *manga* (2001–3) by the same name, it portrays the rise of the central protagonist Kiyoha to the rank of a top courtesan in Yoshiwara. It is beautifully directed by celebrated art photographer Ninagawa Mika. I thank an astute reader for alerting me to this work.
16 Shirane translates *mitate* as "visual transposition" (2008a, 10, 36).
17 New Yoshiwara was built in 1657 near an area called Asakusa (after the original Yoshiwara built in 1617 burned down), and at its height Yoshiwara housed about one thousand courtesans/prostitutes (Bandoh 2010–11, I:245). See Shirane (2002, 8–10) for further information on the licensed quarters.
18 A young courtesan notes that in Yoshiwara there roam one thousand looky-loos, one hundred dons (patrons), but only one amorous man, Gen (Bandoh 2010–11, 1:105). See the section on Tokugawa transpositions of the tale in Chapter 2 for further information on *The Life of an Amorous Man*. See also Shirane (2002, Chapter 3) for more information on Ihara Saikaku.
19 Sakurazawa composed all the stories but utilized different artists for each vignette. Volume 1 features Fujitsubo by artist Hirose Mihoko, Tamakazura by the aforementioned Ide Chikae, and Rokujō by Honjo Ru, while Volume 2 includes Murasaki drawn by Asano Maiko, Asagao by Enomoto Yumi, and Oborozukiyo by Kawanakajima Miyuki. For the sake of expediency and the fact that Sakurazawa wrote all the stories, I use Sakurazawa's name to discuss and cite the anthology.
20 *Manga* are not usually serialized in newspapers in Japan. Takenaka Ranko's remediation enacts a four-page book *manga* layout with straight-edged rectangular panels that contain dialogue and explanatory text. Clothing, accouterments, and furnishings done in Ranko's rendition of the Heian period are included, but the figures are most dominant. The weekly *manga* entries consist of two pages of panels, which I have identified as "A" and "B," moving from right to left. See Figure 5.4 for an example. I use the artist's first name rather than her surname, because that is what she calls herself in the asides at the end of the installments.

Strictly speaking, then Ranko's *manga* might have been better placed in Chapter 7 as an educational comics, but I discuss her remediation here because of her focus on women's issues and her feminist-leaning critique of the Heian male-dominated society.

Chapter 6

1. There is a third category, also pronounced *seinen* but with different Chinese characters, that targets mid-twenties through fifties adult men. Nagayama (2021) argues that it is actually very wide ranging in topic, theme, and style with 30 percent of their artists being women. (See introduction for further discussion.) Erotic *manga* are published in low circulation, semi-pornographic magazines, while young men *manga* are produced by large mainstream publishers like Kōdansha and Shōgakukan (Kinsella 2000, 44–6). See Schodt (1983) and Gravett (2004) for more information on all three categories in English. In Japanese, see Kure (1997, Part II).
2. In *Saint Young Men*, Buddha and Jesus come down from Nirvana and heaven, respectively, for a "vacation" from their duties and share an apartment in modern Tokyo. They take the subway, go to Tokyo Disneyland and the supermarket, and even create blogs—all with very funny and unexpected results.
3. See Drummond-Mathews (2010) for an introduction to boys comics and the five stages of the heroic journey that the protagonists in a typical boys comics undertake.
4. Akatsuka was born in Manchuria in 1935 and grew up in Nara and Niigata. Debuting in 1956, he has won numerous prizes, is the subject of many books, and has a dedicated museum in his hometown. See Nagatani (1994, 21–3) and MANGASeek and Nichigai Associates (2003, 8–9) for further information.
5. *Tensai Bakabon* (*The Genius Dummy*) and *Mr. Nothing Special* were published in the 1960s. See *Zen'in shūgō de ōrusutā nanoda!!* (*A Jamboree of Everyone, So It's an All-Star Billing*) for examples of these comics as well as his other hits. A bilingual volume, *The Genius Bakabon*, is also available.
6. Akatsuka selects the perfect surrogates for his *Genji* characters: Nasty Iyami notwithstanding, the sweet and lovable papa from *The Genius Dummy* becomes Emperor Kiritsubo. Innocent and upbeat through and through, papa gets duped time and again but remains undaunted and never takes things badly—an apt commentary on Emperor Kiritsubo, whose doting parental love (*oya baka*) forgives Genji all, including Genji's fathering a son with his own empress.
7. Koizumi was born in 1953 and worked for an advertisement agency and as a freelance commercial writer before debuting in 1993. His *Butta to shattaka butta* (*Pig/Buddha and the Phony*) series is discussed later in this section.
8. Koizumi adds one chapter, "Kagayaku hi no miya" ("The Radiant Sun Princess"), on Fujitsubo, to explain her relationship to Genji. He also uses what I term "lateral or surface depth" to tell his *Genji*. Just as a thirty-one-syllable *waka* poem references and then incorporates puns and images from other poems in the classical corpus to create its meaning, so Koizumi's *Genji* reaches out to the tale, other *Genji manga*, his gag comics, and to the *Genji* scrolls and Tosa paintings to augment its brief form. A case in point is the *kaimami* "peeping Tom" scene in which Maro spies on the young Murasaki as she watches her pet sparrow wing away. The positioning of Murasaki, her grandmother, and lady-in-waiting replicates the Tosa remediation to a T.
9. Koizumi published the first volume in 1993 and the third in 1999, but my citation is for the 2003–4 version. The series includes five more volumes with different titles, all of which appear to be well received by readers.
10. Klar utilizes Mariana Ortega-Brena's definition of erotic media—"anime or manga that contains 'the depiction of explicit forms of sexual activity, including different types of intercourse'" (Ortega-Brena, qtd. in Klar 2013, 122)—and notes that these

elements are found in adult male, ladies, *yaoi*, and what she terms erotic *hentai manga* (Klar 2013, 121). See Kelts (2006, Chapter 6) for more information. Nagayama and other scholars utilize the term *eromanga* (erotic *manga*) for eroticized comics.

11 As already mentioned, in Japanese both young men and adult male *manga* are pronounced *seinen* but use different Chinese characters. Schodt reads it as *seijin* (1996, 95), but in keeping with the usual convention, I use the romanization *seinen* for adult male and young men comics. Adult male comics often feature erotic content, although some, such as *Silent Service* and *Division Chief Shima Kōsaku*, deal with political and economic issues and contain little eroticism. See Schodt (1996, 101–5, 165–8) for more information.

Allison contends that the erotic adult *manga* highlight men abusing, humiliating, and even brutalizing women (1996, 63–5). In contrast, Klar argues that erotic *manga* readers more often identify with both the "victim" than the "attacker" (2013, 123–4), creating queer readings that subvert and challenge the graphic sex and violence as well as taking it at face value. See Nagayama (2021) for further information.

12 Heian scholar Mitani Kuniaki made this observation at "The Ways and Means of Women Writers—Ferris University International Conference on Japanese Literature" in Yokohama, Japan, where I was invited to present my paper on *Genji manga* on November 17, 2006.

13 The fourteen women are Momozono Asahi (Genji's cousin Asagao), Kiriyama Aoi (Genji's principal wife Aoi), Hanada Chisato (Genji's caretaker Hanachirusato), Rokujō Miya (Lady Rokujō), Kowaka Shian (Young Murasaki whom Terumi only engages in conversation), Semi Iyo (Utsusemi), Tokonatsu Yū (Yūgao), Suetsumu Hana (Suetsumuhana), Gennai Noriko (the elderly lady-in-waiting Gen no naishi), Tamakazura Ruri (Yūgao's daughter), Oboro Tsukiko (Oborozukiyo), Mitsumiya Otome (Onna San no miya), and Akashi Mutsuge (Lady Akashi), with the Fujitsubo surrogate not revealed until Volume 16.

14 Volume 1 of Inaba's *The Tale of Minamoto-kun* was reprinted nine times in fifteen months, Volume 2, five times in eight-and-a-half months, and Volume 3, three times in less than three months.

Chapter 7

1 Schodt (1996, 295–7). Gravett points out that comics have been used to convey information in the United States as well—for example, noted comics artist Will Eisner created instructional manuals on how to maintain equipment for the US army (2004, 119).

2 In 2005 former Japanese ambassador to the United States Kato Ryōzō lauded contemporary art forms like *manga* and *anime* as productive means to establish a good US-Japan relationship because they foster "people-to-people communication and mutual respect" ("Japan's Manga Comics" 2005).

3 Kinsella (2000, 71). Gravett and Schodt do not subscribe to Kinsella's views, although Schodt submits that *Silent Service*'s popularity could be attributed to its ability to "articulat[e] many of the rarely vocalized national aspirations of the general public" (1996, 167). See Shirane and T. Suzuki (2000) for an insightful examination of how premodern Japanese works were used in a similar fashion to construct a nation-building canon.

4 In times of change, distress, and great challenge, Caddeau argues, the tale provides comfort and solace to the Japanese people. The first all-female musical revue Takarazuka performance of the *Genji* in July 1919 occurred after the signing of the Treaty of Versailles and the end of the First World War, while the 2000 *Fleeting Dreams* adaptation helped its audience lament the passing of the prosperous 1960s–1980s in tandem with Genji's mourning of Murasaki's death (Caddeau 2006, 9, 13).

5 The Maruyama and Kuwata's picture books are larger in size than mainstream *manga*, but placement of the panels, the progression of the story, and deployment of characters follow *manga* conventions, hence I have considered them *manga*.

6 Debuting in 1968, artist Maruyama works in *shōjo* circles. Here, she teams up with Yanagawa Sōzō, who does scriptwriting for movies and television and has held jobs as a magazine editor and movie reporter (*Maruyama Kei Archives*). The ehon is a joint effort by Maruyama and Yanagawa, but, for the sake of simplicity, I will just cite Maruyama. A similar situation occurs with Kuwata and his collaboration with Tsuji discussed below.

7 The essays mark, for example, the shift from classical Chinese to vernacular Japanese literature, and laud the subsequent flowering of Japanese literary traditions—court women literature under the Fujiwara regency, the short prose *setsuwa bungaku*, the *monogatari* tales, and the *nikki bungaku* diary literary traditions (Maruyama 2003, 4:138–40).

8 Fujiwara no Michinaga, the father of the empress whom the author Murasaki Shikibu served, also gets a positive makeover. History generally portrays Michinaga as a shrewd, often ruthless courtier who brought Shikibu to court to enhance his political fortunes, but Maruyama depicts Shikibu as so bedazzled by Michinaga that she models Genji on him (2003, 4:4–6). Heian scholars speculate that Michinaga was only one of the figures to serve as a model for Genji, and there is no historical record of extended encounters between the author and Michinaga, so it is curious that Michinaga is given such prominence in Maruyama's *Genji manga*.

9 Kuwata, born in 1935, debuted at thirteen and has been drawing *manga* ever since. Born in 1932, Tsuji worked as an NHK producer and is credited with producing the TV scripts for *Sazae-san*, a long-running *anime* series on a family living in Tokyo, and Ishinomori's *Cyborg 009*. To simplify matters, I cite Kuwata alone, although the *manga* is the combined effort of Kuwata, Tsuji, and the photographers.

10 Kishida was born in 1962 and has published *manga*-nized versions of literary works and works on Mozart, Bach, and Chopin. Here he works with Nishimura, whose scholarship includes studies on Heian court aesthetics, love poetry, and *The Tale of Genji*.

11 Adding the lady-in-waiting narrator who is integral to the eleventh-century *Genji* is a nice touch, and this is the only *manga* that does so. Nishimura's comments on the authorship and consumption of tales in Heian times, however, raise some issues. Several prose works of the period were written by women, but the tales that were generally for female consumption were largely composed by men, and the ladies did not necessarily have them read aloud to them—although such a theory exists.

12 Kishida weaves into the narrative Heian customs and practices not found in other remediations. He details, for example, the directional taboos that prohibited courtiers from traveling to their destinations, and shows how women's hair was tied into long ponytails, pulled back behind their heads, and placed in boxes when they retired for the night (2002, 1:49, 63).

13 Born in Tokyo, Tsuboi worked for Matsuda Motors for eight years after graduating from high school before turning to drawing *manga* full time. He debuted in 1977 and serialized *Tsuboi no nihon jinbutsushi* (*Tsuboi's Japanese Historical Figures*, 1994–2000) in *The Asahi Elementary School Newspaper*. He is best known for his *manga* on great historical figures, *Nihon jinbutsushi shirīzu* (*History of Japanese Personages Series*), and his illustrated world geography, *Zusetsu manga sekai no kuniguni* (*A Manga Dictionary of the Countries of the World*) (MANGAseek and Nichigai Associates 2003, 250; Tsuboi book jacket).
14 In their earliest attempts, publishers transposed *manga* into English word order, and did so by flipping the pages. Unfortunately, this resulted in situations like the one here, or in making right-handed protagonists left-handed, so today *manga* are printed in Japanese word order, reading from right to left. A directive printed at the back of a translated *manga* cautions readers that this is the end of the text and to begin from the end of the volume.
15 For the sake of consistency, I refer here to the right-to-left Japanese pagination order.
16 Born in 1945 in the district of Hakata in Fukuoka city, Kyushu, Hasegawa is a *manga* artist, novelist, and essayist. He debuted in 1968 with a work entitled *Shōgo ni kyōkai e* (*To the Church at Noon*), for which he won COM's monthly prize for new artists. From 1976 to 1984 he serialized *Hakatakko junjō* (*A Hakata Native Through and Through*) in *Manga Action*. He wrote the *manga* entirely in the Hakata dialect, chronicling the highly energetic nature of the area, its festivals, and the like. So wildly successful was he that a Hakata boom ensued. Hasegawa has been awarded the Manga Sandē Award (1972), the Hakata Chōnin Bunka Order Award (1980), and the 26th Shōgakukan Manga Prize (1981). He has done television commercials, worked as an Asahi television newscaster, and written newspaper essays. He has also been the director of the Hakata City Hometown Museum and a visiting professor in the Department of Manga Studies, Art Division, at the Kyushu Art Junior College (see Nagatani 1994, 264; MANGAseek and Nichigai Associates 2003, 295–6).
17 I am indebted to Midorikawa Machiko for pointing out the reference to Tokugawa scrolls.
18 According to Hirota, Hasegawa wrote in a *Yomiuri Newspaper* article that he "had to read the original a hundred times to reach a decision concerning the layout of the rooms for scenes in the Hahakigi [Broom Tree] and the Utsusemi [Empty Cicada] chapters" (1997, 39).
19 I am indebted to Kiriko Komura, who is from Kyushu, for this insight.
20 The back page of the *manga* notes that Mihashi was born in Tokyo in 1960, attended Sophia University, and worked for a time for an automobile company. Her Facebook page says she is a woodblock artist and lists her exhibitions, presentations, publications, and awards. A specialist in Heian literature, Shimizu Yoshiko (1921–2004) graduated from Kyoto University with a degree in literature and was a professor at Kansei University when her foreword appeared in Mihashi's *Genji manga*. A list of her publications, largely on *The Tale of Genji*, appears on the back page of the *manga*.
21 Hanamura debuted in 1959 and in 1963 began publishing in iconic girls magazines such as *Nakayoshi* (*Pals*), *Shōjo furendo* (*Girls' Friend*), and *Māgaretto* (*Margaret*) as a pioneer of girls comics. She later moved to ladies comics and *manga*-nizing mystery novels. She received prestigious awards in 1989 and 1997, the latter for the *manga* version of *Ochikubo monogagari* (*The Tale of Ochikubo*) in The Japanese Comics Classical *Literature* series in which Hasegawa published his *Tale of Genji* (HYPERLINK \l "Hanamura 2013, 1:287").

22 Genji's callous behavior is starkly replicated in the usually dependable Yūgiri's courting of Kashiwagi's widow Ochiba, causing anguish for all: his wife Kumoinokari leaves him; Ochiba suffers the shame of being toyed with and of betraying Kashiwagi; Ochiba's mother dies crushed by the destruction of her daughter's reputation; and Kashiwagi's parents suffer Ochiba's seeming disregard of their son Kashiwagi and the breaking up of their daughter Kumoinokari's family (Hanamura 2013, 3:166–222).
23 Sanazaki was born in Tokyo in 1957 and in 2010 was a visiting lecturer at the University of Creation's Art, Music, and Social Work division. She debuted in 1981 with *I Seek Love* and has worked in mystery, romance, and the production of original works. She gives *manga* master classes in China, Taipei, France, Los Angeles, and Belgium ("Guest: Harumo Sanazaki"). The website Baka-Updates Manga lists her as a ladies comics artist.
24 This reliance on the *Genji* to provide solace is not an isolated moment, but resonates with the *iyashi* healing boom that appeared in 2004. After the bursting of the bubble and ensuing decades of recession and economic stability, many Japanese sought solace and respite from stress and anxiety in new support spaces, namely in animal cafés, which encouraged patrons to relax through engagement with cats, rabbits, and other animals and in maid cafés where customers bond with waitress, young women dressed in maid uniforms and reminiscent of favorite *manga* characters. Others turned to electronic pet and therapeutic robots in search of intimacy, social support, and interaction (Allison 2013, 96–103).

Chapter 8

1 See "A Beginner's Guide to Visual Novel Video Games" for a good introduction to and examples of VN, and "What Is Visual Novel (VN)? [Gaming Definition, Meaning]" for a description of the three basic types discussed below.
2 It appears that several VNs on *Genji* are available, although some are no longer supported and others are available only in Japanese. My appreciation to Jorge Rodriguez for locating them. (1) *Reverse Genji Romance*: https://vndb.org/v20438# by Genius Inc. (discontinued); (2) *Reverse Genji Ren'ai*: https://vndb.org/v24746# by Ciagram (available in Japanese); (3) *Genji Koi Emaki*: https://vndb.org/v16509 by Quinrose (available only in Japanese); (4) *The Tale of Genji Reverse Love Song*: https://vndb.org/v31581 by eterire (discontinued); and (5) *Genji Yumegatari*: https://vndb.org/v23576 by Genji Monogatari Ge-muka Keikaku (available only in Japanese).

BIBLIOGRAPHY

Adelstein, Jake and Angela Erika Kubo (2014), "Japan's Kiddie Porn Empire: Bye-Bye?" *The Daily Beast*, June 3, www.thedailybeast.com/articles/2014/06/03/japan-s-kid die-porn-empire-bye-bye.html (accessed November 10, 2020).

Akatsuka, Fujio (1983), *Genji monogatari* [*The Tale of Genji*], Vol. 4 of *Akatsuka Fujio manga koten nyūmon, Akatsuka Fujio's Manga Introduction to Classical Literature*, Tokyo: Gakushū Kenkyūsha.

Akatsuka, Fujio (2000), *Tensai bakabon bairingaru han* [*The Genius Bakabon, Bilingual Version*], vol. 1, trans. Zufelt, Tokyo: Kōdansha International.

Akatsuka, Fujio (2003), *Zen'in shūgō de ōrusutā nanoda!!* [*A Jamboree of Everyone, So It's an All-Star Billiing*], Tokyo: Kōbunsha Bunko.

Allen, Laura W. (2004), "Japanese Exemplars for a New Age: *Genji* Paintings from the Seventeenth Century Tosa School," in E. Lillehoj (ed.), *Critical Perspectives in Classicism in Japanese Painting 1600–1700*, Honolulu: University of Hawai'i Press, pp. 99–132.

Allison, Anne (1996), *Permitted and Prohibited Desires: Mothers, Comics, and Censorship in Japan*, Boulder, CO: Westview Press.

Allison, Anne (2013), *Precarious Japan*, Durham, NC: Duke University Press.

Alverson, Brigid (2017), "NYCC 2017: Manga Sales Continue to Rise." *Publishers Weekly*, October 13, https://www.publishersweekly.com/pw/by-topic/industry-news/com ics/article/75066-nycc-2017-manga-sales-continue-to-rise.html (accessed October 10, 2020).

Amano, Yoshitaka ([1997] 2006), *The Tale of Genji*, Text by Anri Itō and Junichi Imura and additional translation by Rachel Nacht. Milwaukie: DH Press.

Amazon's Customer Reviews (n.d.), www.amazon.co.jp/product-reviews/4091308473/ (accessed July 20, 2015).

Anderson, Benedict ([1983] 1991), *Imagined Communities: Reflections on the Origin and Spread of Nationalism*, rev. ed., London: Verso.

Aoki, Deb (2020), "Manga Publishers Are Holding Steady—For Now," May 29, https:// www.publishersweekly.com/pw/by-topic/industry-news/publisher-news/arti cle/83450-manga-publishers-are-holding-steady-for-now.html (accessed October 10, 2020).

Asuka Henshūbu (2011), "Genji monogatari kara manabu koi no tekunikku" [Love Strategies Learned from *The Tale of Genji*], in Asuka Henshūbu (ed.), *Genji monogatari komikku ansorojii: onna hikaru genji no ikemen nikki* [*The Comics Anthology of The Tale of Genji: Ms. Shining Genji's Hottie Diary*], Tokyo: Kadokawa Shoten, pp. 116–19.

Asuka Henshūbu, ed. (2011), *Genji monogatari komikku ansorojii: onna hikaru genji no ikemen nikki* [*The Comics Anthology of The Tale of Genji: Ms. Shining Genji's Hottie Diary*, Tokyo: Kadokawa Shoten.

Atkins, Paul S. (2015), "*The Tale of Genji: Translation, Canonization, and World Literature* by Michael Emmerich (review)," *Harvard Journal of Asiatic Studies*, 75 (1), pp. 179–85.

Backnik, Jane M. (1982), "Deixis and Self/Other References in Japanese Discourse," *Working Papers in Sociolinguistics 99*, Austin Southwest Educational Development Laboratory.

Backnik, Jane M. (1994), "Introduction: *uchi/soto*: Challenging Our Conceptualizations of Self, Social Order, and Language," in J. M. Bachnik and C. J. Quinn, Jr. (eds.), *Situated Meaning: Inside and Outside in Japanese Self, Society and Language*, Princeton, NJ: Princeton University Press, pp. 3–37.

Bakhtin, Mikhail (1984), *The Dialogic Imagination: Four Essays by M. M. Bahktin*, ed. M. Holquist, trans. C. Emerson and M. Holquist, Austin: University of Texas Press.

Bandoh, Iruka (2010–11), *Kuruwa genji* [*Prostitute Quarters of Genji*]. *Manga gurimu dōwa* [*Grimm Fairy Tale Comics*], 3 vols., Tokyo: Bunkasha, 2010–11. (Vols. 1 and 2 were originally published in *Grimm Fairy Tale Comics LoveSexy Special Edition* vols. from February 2008–November 2009. Vol. 3 was originally published in *Grimm Fairy Tale Comics* from March 2010–March 2011.)

Bardsley, Jan (2021), *Maiko Masquerade: Crafting Geisha Girlhood in Japan*, Berkeley: University of California Press.

Baudinette, Thomas (2017), "Japanese Gay Men's Attitude towards 'Gay Manga' and the Problem of Genre," *East Asian Journal of Popular Culture*, 3 (1), pp. 59–72.

BBC News (2018), "Japanese TV Show Featuring Blackface Actor Sparks Anger," June 4, https://www.bbc.com/news/world-asia-42561815 (accessed June 19, 2023).

"A Beginner's Guide to Visual Novel Video Games" (2020), *Hacker Noon*, November 22, www.hackernoon.com/a-beginners-guide-to-visual-novel-video-games-2f463w27 (accessed December 29, 2021).

Berndt, Jacqueline (n.d.), "Centaur, Torera & Genji-kun: The Hybrid Worlds of Manga Artist est em." *manga I*. Flyer. Stockholm: Stockholm University, February 22–23.

Bialock, David T. (2007), *Eccentric Spaces, Hidden Histories: Narrative, Ritual, and Royal Authority from The Chronicles of Japan to The Tale of the Heike*, Stanford: Stanford University Press.

Bolter, Jay David and Richard Grusin (1999), *Remediation: Understanding New Media*, Cambridge: MIT Press.

Booker, M. Keith (1996), *A Practical Introduction to Literary Theory and Criticism*, White Plains: Longman.

Bourdieu, Pierre (1984), *Distinction: A Social Critique of the Judgement of Taste*, trans. R. Nice, Cambridge, MA: Harvard University Press.

Bowring, Richard John (1988), *Murasaki Shikibu, the Tale of Genji: Landmarks of World Literature*, ed. J. P. Stern, Cambridge: Cambridge University Press.

Brophy, Philip (2010), "Osamu Tezuka's *Gekiga*: Behind the Mask of Manga," in T. Johnson-Woods (ed.), *Manga: An Anthology of Global and Cultural Perspectives*, New York: Continuum International Publishing Group Inc, pp. 128–36.

Brown, Steven T. (2001), *Theatricalities of Power: The Cultural Politics of Noh*, Stanford: Stanford University Press.

Bryce, Mio, Jason Davis, and Christine Barber (2008), "The Cultural Biographies and Social Lives of *Manga*: Lessons from the *Mangaverse*," *Scan: Journal of Media Arts Culture*, 5 (2), pp. 1–13. http://scan.net.au/scan/journal/display.php?journal_id=114 (accessed July 8, 2013).

Buckley, Sandra (1991), "'Penguin in Bondage': A Graphic Tale of Japanese Comic Books," in C. Penley and A. Ross (eds.), *Technoculture*, Minneapolis: University of Minnesota Press, pp. 163–95.

Bullock, Julia C. (2010), *The Other Women's Lib: Gender and Body in Japanese Women's Fiction*, Honolulu: University of Hawai'i Press.

Caddeau, Patrick W. (2006), *Appraising Genji: Literary Criticism and Cultural Anxiety in the Age of the Last Samurai*, Albany: State University of New York Press.

Carpenter, John T. and Melissa McCormick, with Monika Bincsik and Kyoko Kinoshita (2019), *The Tale of Genji: A Japanese Classic Illuminated*, New York: The Metropolitan Museum of Art, New York. (Catalogue that accompanied exhibit by same name from March 5 to June 16, 2019.)

Cather, Kirsten (2017), "Must We Burn Eromanga? Trying Obscenity in the Courtroom and in the Classroom," in M. McLelland (ed.), *The End of Cool Japan: Ethical, Legal, and Cultural Challenges to Japanese Popular Culture*, London: Routledge, pp. 70–93.

Cavanaugh, Carole (1996), "Text and Textile: Unweaving the Female Subject in Heian Writing," *Positions: East Asian Cultures Critiques*, 4 (3), pp. 595–636.

CLAMP, https://clamp-net.com/about (accessed June 1, 2021).

Colcutt, Martin (2008), "Japan's Medieval Age: The Kamakura and Muromachi Periods," March 27, https://aboutjapan.japansociety.org/japans_medieval_age_the_kamakura __muromachi_periods (accessed February 6, 2022). (Originally written in 2003 for the Japan Society's previous website for educators, "Journey through Japan.").

Cook, Lewis (2008), "Genre Trouble: Medieval Commentaries and Canonization of *The Tale of Genji*," in H. Shirane (ed.), *Envisioning the Tale of Genji: Media, Gender, and Cultural Production*, New York: Columbia University Press, pp. 129–53.

Coulson, Mark and Christopher J. Ferguson (2015), "The Influence of Digital Games on Aggression and Violent Crimes," in R. Kowert and T. Quandt (eds.), *The Video Game Debate: Unraveling the Physical, Social, and Psychological Effects of Digital Games*, London: Routledge, pp. 54–73.

De Gruchy, John Walter (2003), *Orienting Arthur Waley: Japanism, Orientalism, and the Creation of Japanese Literature in English*, Honolulu: University of Hawai'i Press.

Dines, Gail (2010), *Pornland: How Porn Has Hijacked Our Sexuality*, Boston, MA: Beacon Press.

Doi, Kanae and Minky Worden (2023), "Japan Passes Law to 'Promote Understanding' of LGBT People: Fight Continues for Comprehensive Nondiscrimination Legislation," *Human Rights Watch*, July 12, https://www.hrw.org/news/2023/07/12/japan-pas ses-law-promote-understanding-lgbt-people (accessed July 30, 2023).

Doi, Takeo (1973), *The Anatomy of Dependence*, Tokyo: Kodansha International.

Doki Doki Manga Genres (2021) (Instructions).

Drummond-Mathews, Angela (2010), "What Boys Will Be: A Study of Shōnen Manga," in T. Johnson-Woods (ed.), *Manga: An Anthology of Global and Cultural Perspectives*, New York: Continuum International Publishing Group Inc, pp. 62–76.

Duranti, Alessandro (1986), "The Audience as Co-Author: An Introduction," *Text: Interdisciplinary Journal for the Study of Discourse*, 6 (3), pp. 239–47.

Dworkin, Andrea (1979), *Pornography: Men Possessing Women*, London: Penguin.

Egawa Tatsuya (2001–5), *Genji monogatari* [*The Tale of Genji*], 7 vols., Tokyo: Shūeisha.

Elliot, Brendan (2004), PMJS: Listserv, March 28, https://groups.google.com/h/pmjs (accessed January 2006). (PMJS = Premodern Japanese Studies.)

Emmerich, Michael (2008), "The Splendor of Hybridity: Image and Text in Ryūtei Tanehiko's *Inaka Genji*," in H. Shirane (ed.), *Envisioning the Tale of Genji: Media, Gender, and Cultural Production*, New York: Columbia University Press, pp. 211–39.

Emmerich, Michael (2013), *The Tale of Genji: Translation, Canonization, and World Literature*, New York: Columbia University Press.

Encyclopedia Britannica Online (n.d.), "Medieval Japan," https://www.britannica.com/place/Japan/Medieval-Japan (accessed June 15, 2014).

est em (2016), *Iine! Hikaru genji-kun [Twitter "Likes"! Shining Genji-kun]*, Tokyo: Shōden. (Originally serialized in *Feel Young*, May 2015–October 2016.)

Field, Norma (1987), *The Splendor of Longing in The Tale of Genji*, Princeton, NJ: Princeton University Press.

Fish, Stanley (1980), *Is There a Text in This Class? The Authority of Interpretive Communities*, Cambridge, MA: Harvard University Press.

Fowler, Edward (1988), *The Rhetoric of Confession: Shishōsetsu in Early Twentieth-Century Japanese Fiction*, Berkeley: University of California Press.

Fowler, Edward (1991), "Rendering Words, Traversing Cultures: On the Art and Politics of Translating Modern Fiction," *The Journal of Japanese Studies*, 18 (1), pp. 1–44.

Frühstück, Sabine (2022), *Gender and Sexuality in Modern Japan*, Cambridge: Cambridge University Press.

Fuji Xerox (2001), "Fuji Xerox and Kodansha Start genji-daigaku.com," October 27, http://www.fujixerox.co.jp/eng/headline/2000/1027_genji.html (accessed July 14, 2004).

Fujii, James A. (1993), *Complicit Fictions: The Subject in the Modern Japanese Prose Narrative*, Berkeley: University of California Press.

Fujimoto, Yukari (2015), "The Evolution of BL as 'Playing with Gender': Viewing the Genesis and Development of BL from a Contemporary Perspective," in M. McLelland, K. Nagaike, K. Suganuma, and J. Welker (eds.), *Boys Love Manga and Beyond: History, Culture, and Community in Japan*, Jackson: University of Mississippi Press, pp. 76–92.

Galbraith, Patrick W. (2009a), *The Otaku Encyclopedia: An Insider's Guide to the Subculture of Cool Japan*, Tokyo: Kōdansha International.

Galbraith, Patrick W. (2009b), "Moe: Exploring Virtual Potential in Post-Millennial Japan," *ejcjs* (*Electronic Journal of Contemporary Japanese* Studies), http://www.japanesestudies.org.uk/articles/2009/Galbraith.html (accessed March 10, 2015).

Galbraith. Patrick W. (2011), "*Fujoshi*: Fantasy Play and Transgressive Intimacy among 'Rotten Girls' in Contemporary Japan," *Signs*, 37 (1), pp. 211–32.

Galbraith, Patrick W. (2015), "Moe Talk: Affective Communication among Female Fans of *Yaoi* in Japan," in M. McLelland, K. Nagaike, K. Suganuma, and J. Welker (eds.), *Boys Love Manga and Beyond: History, Culture, and Community in Japan*, Jackson: University of Mississippi Press, pp. 153–68.

Galbraith, Patrick W. (2017a), "RapeLay and the Return of the Sex Wars in Japan," *Porn Studies*, 4 (1), pp. 105–26.

Galbraith. Patrick W. (2017b), "'The Lolicon Guy': Some Observations on Researching Unpopular Topics in Japan," in M. McLelland (ed.), *The End of Cool Japan: Ethical, Legal, and Cultural Challenges to Japanese Popular Culture*, London: Routledge, pp. 109–33.

Galbraith, Patrick W. (2017c), "Adult Computer Games and the Ethics of Imaginary Violence: Responding to Gamergate from Japan," *U.S. Japan Women's Journal* 52, pp. 67–88.

Galbraith, Patrick W. (2019), *Otaku and the Struggle for Imagination in Japan*, Durham, NC: Duke University Press.

Galbraith, Patrick W. (2021), *The Ethics of Affect: Lines and Life in a Tokyo Neighborhood*, Stockholm: Stockholm University Press.

Galbraith, Patrick W. (n.d.1), 'Fujoshi,' *Japanese Media and Popular Culture: An Open-Access Digital Initiative of the University of Tokyo*, https://jmpc-utokyo.com/ (accessed May 25, 2020).

Galbraith, Patrick W. (n.d.2), "Moe," *Japanese Media and Popular Culture: An Open-Access Digital Initiative of the University of Tokyo*, https://jmpc-utokyo.com/ (accessed May 25, 2020).

Galbraith, Patrick W., and Jessica Bauwens-Sugimoto (2021), "Translator's Introduction: *Eromanga* in the Global Now," in *Erotic Comics in Japan: An Introduction to Eromanga*, trans. P. W. Galbraith and J. Bauwens-Sugimoto, Amsterdam: Amsterdam University Press, pp. 13–38.

Galbraith, Patrick W., Thiam Huat Kam, and Björn-Ole Kamn (eds.) (2015), *Debating Otaku in Contemporary Japan*, London: Bloomsbury.

Goff, Janet (1991), *Noh Drama and The Tale of Genji: The Art of Allusion in Fifteen Classical Plays. Princeton Library of Asian Translations*, Princeton, NJ: Princeton University Press.

Gravett, Paul (2004), *Manga: Sixty Years of Japanese Comics*, London: Laurence King Publishing.

Griepp, Milton (2022), "ICV$_2$ Report: U.S. Manga Sales More than Doubled in 2021: NPD Reports Sales up 160% in Units," February 28, https://icv2.com/print/article/50543 (accessed January 4, 2022).

Grossman, Diane (2020), "Sexuality and Popular Culture," in N. A. Naples (ed.), *Companion to Sexuality Studies*, New Jersey: John Wiley & Sons Ltd., pp. 281–98.

"Guest: Harumi Sanazaki," (2016), Japan Expo, April 13, https://www.japan-expo-paris.com/en/invites/harumo-sanazaki_635.htm (accessed October 2019).

Hall, Kevin (2008), "Murasaki-bot Recounts the World's (Much Debated) Oldest Novel." https://web.archive.org/web/20101112081837/http://dvice.com/archives/2008/07/murasakibot_rec.php (accessed July 5, 2020).

Hanamura, Eiko (2013), *Genji monogatari [The Tale of Genji]*, *Manga koten bungaku [Classical Japanese Literature Comics]*, 3 vols., Tokyo: Shōgakukan.

Hanazono, Azuki (2012), *Haya gen: hayayomi genji monogatari [Quick Gen: Reading The Tale of Genji in a Flash]*, Tokyo: Shinshokan.

Harada, Shin-Ichi. (1976), "Honorifics," in M. Shibatani (ed.), *Syntax and Semantics 5: Japanese Generative Grammar*, New York: Academic, pp. 499–561.

Harper, Thomas J. (1993), "*Genji* Gossip," in A. Gatten and A. H. Chambers (eds.), *New Leaves: Studies and Translations of Japanese Literature in Honor of Edward Seidensticker*, Ann Arbor: University of Michigan Press, pp. 29–44.

Harper, Thomas J. (1994), "More *Genji* Gossip," *The Journal of the Association of Teachers of Japanese*, 28 (2), pp. 175–82.

Hasegawa, Hōsei (1996–7), *Genji monogatari [The Tale of Genji]*, Vols. 3–5 of *Manga nihon no koten [Manga Japanese Classics]*, Ishinomori Shōtarō, general editor, Tokyo: Chūō Kōronsha.

Hashimoto, Osamu (1991–3), *Yōhen genji monogatari [The Transformed Tale of Genji]*, 14 vols., Tokyo: Chūō Kōronsha.

Hazuki, Tsuyako (2010), *Enbun genji monogatari [Erotic Talk: The Tale of Genji]. Manga gurimu dōwa [Grimm Fairy Tale Comics]*, Bunkasha. (Originally published in *Ai no taiken: special derakusu [The Experience of Love: Special Deluxe]*, Tokyo: Takeshobōkan, July 2004–October 2009.)

Hestor, Jeffry T. (2015), "*Fujoshi* Emergent: Shifting Popular Representations of *Yaoi*/BL Fandom in Japan," in M. McLelland, K. Nagaike, K. Suganuma, and J. Welker (eds.), *Boys Love Manga and Beyond: History, Culture, and Community in Japan*, Jackson: University of Mississippi Press, pp. 169–88.

Higuchi, Mari (2021), "Why Do Married Women in Japan Support the Unequal Gender Norm of 'Working and Caring'?" in C. Hommerich, N. Sudo, and T. Kikkawa (eds.), *Social Change in Japan, 1989-2019: Social Status, Social Consciousness, Attitudes and Values*, London: Routledge, pp. 149–68.

Hijikata, Yōichi (2005), "Monogatari • shōsetsu no naka no genji monogatari" [*The Tale of Genji* in Tales and Novels] in K. Tateishi and T. Ando (eds.), *Genji bunka no jikū* [*Times and Spaces of the Genji Culture*], Tokyo: Moriwasha, pp. 12–29.

Hirakawa, Sukehiro (2008), "*Genji monogatari* no tensaitekina eiyakusha towa ikanaru hito ka" [What Kind of Person Is the Genius English Translator of *The Tale of Genji*?], *Sekai no genji monogatari* [*The Global Tale of Genji*], Tokyo: Random House Kōdansha, pp. 45–50.

Hirata, Yoshinobu ([1990] 2004), "Hikaru genji no monogatari" [The Tale of the Shining Genji], *Kumon no manga koten bungakukan genji monogatari* [*The Kumon Manga Literature Classics Tale of Genji*], by Saeki Nao, Tokyo: Kumon Shuppan, pp. 4–5.

Hirota, Akiko (1997), "*The Tale of Genji*: From Heian Classic to Heisei Comic," *Journal of Popular Culture*, 31 (2), pp. 29–68.

Hodgkins, C. (2022), "Golgo 13 Manga Creator Takao Saito Passes Away at 84," *AnimeNewsNetwork*, September 29, https://www.animenewsnetwork.com/news/2021-09-29/golgo-13-manga-creator-takao-saito-passes-away-at-84/.177952 (accessed August 18, 2022).

Hommerich, Carola., Naoki Sudo, and Toru Kikkawa (2021a), "Understanding Heisei Japan: Anchoring Amidst Transformation," in C. Hommerich, N. Sudo, and T. Kikkawa (eds.), *Social Change in Japan, 1989-2019: Social Status, Social Consciousness, Attitudes and Values*, London: Routledge, pp. 3–15.

Hommerich, Carola, Naoki Sudo, and Toru Kikkawa (2021b), "Japan After the Heisei Period: Where Are We Headed?" in C. Hommerich, N. Sudo, and T. Kikkawa (eds.), *Social Change in Japan, 1989-2019: Social Status, Social Consciousness, Attitudes and Values*, London: Routledge, pp. 169–73.

Hori, Akiko (2013), "On the Response (or Lack Thereof) of Japanese Fans to Criticism that *Yaoi* is Antigay Discrimination," *Transformative Works and Cultures*, 12, https://journal.transformativeworks.org/index.php/twc/article/view/463 (accessed February 15, 2022).

Horn, Carl (2018), "What's New in Manga?," *Pomona College Magazine*.

Horton, H. Mack (1983), "Introduction," in K. Nishi and K. Hozumi, *What Is Japanese Architecture? with a List of Sites and a Map*, trans. and adapted by H. M. Horton, Tokyo: Kōdansha International, pp. 7–11.

Horton, H. Mack (1993), "They Also Serve: Ladies-in-Waiting in *The Tale of Genji*," in E. Kamens (ed.), *Approaches to Teaching Murasaki Shikibu's The Tale of Genji*, New York: The Modern Language Association of America, pp. 95–107.

Ide, Chikae (2008), *Genji monogatari: uruwashi no karan* [*The Tale of Genji: Elegant Dissolution*], 2 vols., Tokyo: Shūeisha. (Originally published by Sōmasha, 2002, 2 vols.)

Ii, Haruki (2008), "Didactic Readings of *The Tale of Genji*: Politics and Women's Education," trans. Saeko Shibayama in H. Shirane (ed.), *Envisioning the Tale of Genji: Media, Gender, and Cultural Production*, New York: Columbia University Press, 2008, pp. 157–70.

Inaba, Minori (2012-19), *Minamoto-kun monogatari* [*The Tale of Minamoto-kun*], 16 vols., Tokyo: Shūeisha. (Originally published in *Shūkan yongu jyonpu* [*Weekly Young Jump*], 2011–17.)

Inoue, Nobutaka (n.d.), "Abe no Seimei." *Encyclopedia of Shinto*, https://d-museum.kokugakuin.ac.jp/eos/detail/?id=9603 (accessed February 8, 2022).
Ishida, Hitoshi (2015), "Representational Appropriation and the Anatomy of Desire in *Yaoi*/BL," trans. K. Suganuma, in M. McLelland, K. Nagaike, K. Suganuma, and J. Welker (eds.), *Boys Love Manga and Beyond: History, Culture, and Community in Japan*, Jackson: University of Mississippi Press, pp. 210–32.
Ishidori, Tatsuya, illustrator (1999), *The Tale of Genji Picture Book* by Murasaki Shikibu. Retold by Setouchi Jakuchō. Introduction and trans. H. M. Horton. Tokyo: Kōdansha.
Ito, Kinko (2002), "The World of Japanese Ladies' Comics: From the Romantic Fantasy to Lustful Perversion," *Journal of Popular Culture*, 36 (1), pp. 68–85.
Ito, Kinko (2008), "Manga in Japanese History," in M. W. MacWilliams (ed.), *Japanese Visual Culture: Explorations in the World of Manga and Anime*, Armonk: M. E. Sharpe, Inc., pp. 26–47.
Ito, Kinko (2009), "New Trends in the Production of Japanese 'Ladies' Comics': Diversification and Catharsis," *Japan Studies Review*, 13, pp. 111–30.
Ito, Kinko (2010), *A Sociology of Japanese Ladies' Comics: Images of the Life, Loves, and Sexual Fantasies of Adult Japanese Women*, Lewiston: Edwin Mellen Press.
Ito, Kinko (2011), "Chikae Ide, the Queen of Japanese Ladies' Comics: Her Life and Manga," in T. Perper and M. Cornog (eds.), *Mangatopia: Essays on Manga and Anime in the Modern World*, Santa Barbara: Libraries Unlimited, pp. 3–19.
Itoh, Moriyuki (2001), "The Role of Gender and Education in the Works of Heian Women Writers," in J. Brown and S. Arntzen (eds.), *Across Time and Genre: Reading and Writing Japanese Women's Texts*, Edmonton: University of Alberta Press, pp. 244–6.
Iwabuchi, Koichi (2002), "'Soft' Nationalism and Narcissism: Japanese Popular Culture Goes Global," *Asian Studies Review*, 26, pp. 447–69.
Jack, Rachael E., Caroline Blais, Christoph Scheepers, Phillippe G. Schyns, and Roberto Caldara (2009), "Cultural Confusions Show that Facial Expressions are not Universal," *Current Biology*, 19 (18), pp. 1543–8.
Japan Magazine Publishers Association (n.d.), "JMPA magajin dēta" [JMPA Magazine Data], https://web.archive.org/web/20201114201115/https://www.j-magazine.or.jp/user/data/magdata (accessed July 5, 2020).
Japan Media Arts Plaza (n.d.), "Excellence Prize Oosukami Genji Monogatari Maro, n?" http://plaza.bunka.go.jp/english/festival/sakuin_backnumber/14/maron.html (accessed June 16, 2004).
The Japan Times (1999), "2,000 Bill to Commemorate 2000," October 6, https://www.japantimes.co.jp/news/1999/10/06/national/2000-yen-bill-to-commemorate-2000/#.XtxnMS2ZOM4 (accessed July 5, 2020).
The Japan Times (2008), "'Tale of Genji' to Grace Kyoto Coin," June 25, https://www.japantimes.co.jp/news/2008/06/25/business/tale-of-genji-to-grace-kyoto-coin/#.Xtxjri2ZOM4 (accessed July 5, 2020).
"Japan's Manga Comics Take on the US Superheroes" (2005), AFP, January 31.
Johnson, Adrienne R. (2020), "Josō or 'Gender Free'?: Playfully Queer 'Lives' in Visual *Kei*," *Asian Anthropology*, 19 (2), pp. 119–42.
Jones, Gretchan I. (2005), "Bad Girls Like to Watch: Writing and Reading Ladies' Comics," in J. Bardsley and L. Miller (eds.), *Bad Girls of Japan*, New York: Palgrave Macmillian, pp. 97–109.
Kano, Ayako (2011), "Backlash, Fight Back, and Back-pedaling: Responses to State Feminism Contemporary Japan," *International Journal of Asian Studies*, 8 (1), pp. 41–62.

Kawabata, Yasunari (1948), *Yukiguni* [*Snow Country*], trans. E. Seidensticker, New York: Alfred A Knopf, 1948. (Originally serialized in Japanese, 1935–7; publisher unknown.)

Kelts, Roland (2006), *Japanamerica: How Japanese Pop Culture Has Invaded the U.S.*, New York: Pelgrave Macmillan.

Kern, Adam (2006), *Manga from the Floating World: Comicbook Culture and the Kibyōshi of Edo Japan*, Cambridge: Harvard University Asia Center.

Khan, Ummni and Jean Ketterling (2019), "Rape as Play: Yellow Peril Panic and a Defense of Fantasy," *The Asian Yearbook of Human Rights and Humanitarian Law* 3, pp. 367–95.

Kikuta, Shigeo (1967), "Waka to monogatari" [Waka Poetry and Tales] in *Waka no sekai* [*The World of Waka Poetry*], Tokyo: Ōfūsha, pp. 7–25.

Kimura, Jin or Mitsuhi (1970), *Shinhan genji monogatari* [*The New Edition Tale of Genji*], *Josei komikku elle* [*The Women's Comics Elle*], vol. 9.

Kinsella, Sharon (1995), "Cuties in Japan," in B. Moeran and L. Skov (eds.), *Women, Media, and Consumption in Japan*, Honolulu: University of Hawai'i Press, pp. 220–54.

Kinsella, Sharon (2000), *Adult Manga: Culture and Power in Contemporary Japanese Society*, Honolulu: University of Hawai'i Press.

Kira (2005–6), *Genji monogatari* [*The Tale of Genji*], 4 vols., Tokyo: Shūeisha. (Originally published in *YOU*, 2004–6.)

Kishida, Ren, illustrator ([1996] 2002) with consultation by Nishimura Tōru, *Manga genji monogatari* [*Manga Tale of Genji*], 4 vols., Tokyo: Kawade Shobō Shinsha.

Kitamura, Yuika (2000), "Shōjo no yume no ōkan: asaki yume mishi ron" [The Young Girls' Dream Circuit: A Study of *Fleeting Dreams*] in *Kokusai bunkagaku* [*International Literature*], 3, pp. 160–47 (the pages proceed in reverse order in this work).

Kitamura, Yuika (2008), "Sexuality, Gender, and *The Tale of Genji* in Modern Translations and *Manga*," in H. Shirane (ed.), *Envisioning the Tale of Genji: Media, Gender, and Cultural Production*, New York: Columbia University Press, pp. 329–57.

Kitazawa Kyō (2011), "Akashi no kimi" [Lady Akashi], *Genji monogatari komikku ansorojii: onna hikaru genji no ikemen nikki* [*The Comics Anthology of The Tale of Genji: Ms. Shining Genji's Hottie Diary*], ed. Asuka Henshūbu, Tokyo: Kadokawa Shoten, pp. 67–76.

Klar, Elizabeth (2013), "Tentacles, Lolitas, and Pencil Strokes: The Parodist Body in European and Japanese Erotic Comics," in J. Berndt and B. Kummerling-Meibauer (eds.), *Manga's Cultural Crossroads*, London: Routledge, pp. 121–42.

Köhn, Stephan (2007), "Review of Adam Kern, *Manga from the Floating World: Comicbook Culture and the Kibyōshi of Edo Japan*," *Monumenta Nipponica*, 62 (2), pp. 235–37.

Koizumi Yoshihiro ([1993–7] 2003–4), *Butta to shattaka butta* [*Pig/Buddha and the Phony*], 3 vols., Tokyo: Media Factory.

Koizumi, Yoshihiro (2002), *Ōzukami genji monogatari maro, n?* [*Grasping the Gist of The Tale of Genji, I/Chestnut?*], Tokyo: Gentōsha.

Komachiya, Teruhiko (2008), "E de yomu *Genji monogatari*: monogatari-e to genji-e" [Reading *the Tale of Genji* through Painting: Tale- and Genji-e Paintings], in Genji monogatari Sen'nenki l'Inkai (ed.), *Sekai no Genji monogatari* [*The World's Tale of Genji*], Tokyo: Randamu Hausu Kōdansha, pp. 64–5.

Komesu, Kikuyo (2001), "'Tale of Genji' Goes to the Opera," *The Japan Times*, September 14, https://www.japantimes.co.jp/news/2001/09/14/national/tale-of-genji-goes-to-the-opera/. (accessed November 11, 2011).

Kondo, Dorinne K. (1990), *Crafting Selves: Power, Gender, and Discourses of Identity in a Japanese Workplace*, Chicago: University of Chicago Press.

Kondo, Dorinne K. (1997), *About Face: Performing Race in Fashion and Theater*, London: Routledge.

Kornicki, Peter F. (2005), "Unsuitable Books for Women? *Genji monogatari* and *Ise monogatari* in Late Seventeenth-Century Japan," *Monumenta Nipponica*, 60 (2), pp. 147–93.

Kumon (n.d.), https://www.kumon.com/ (accessed February 2016).

Kure, Tomofusa (1997), *Gendai manga no zentaizō* [*The General Fundamentals of Modern Manga*], Tokyo: Futabasha.

Kuriyama, Renji (2011), "Oborozukiyo," in Asuka Henshūbu (ed.), *Genji monogatari komikku ansorojii: onna hikaru genji no ikemen nikki* [*The Comics Anthology of The Tale of Genji: Ms. Shining Genji's Hottie Diary*], Tokyo: Kadokawa Shoten, pp. 57–66.

Kusaka, Midori (2000), *Manga gaku no susume* [*Promoting Manga Studies*], Tokyo: Hakuteisha.

Kuwata, Jirō ([1982] 1993–5), *Genji monogatari* [*The Tale of Genji*]. Vols. 5–7 of *Komi gurafikku nihon no koten* [*Graphic Comics Japanese Classics*], Tsuji Masaki, general editor, Akatsuki Kyōiku Tosho, Tokyo: Akatsuki Kyōiku Shuppan.

Lanser, Susan. Sniader (1981), *The Narrative Act: Point of View in Prose Fiction*, Princeton, NJ: Princeton Univeristy Press.

Lebra, Takie Sugiyama (1984), *Japanese Women: Constraint and Fulfillment*, Honolulu: University of Hawai'i Press.

Lehmann, Timothy R. (2005), *Manga: Masters of Art*, New York: HarperCollins.

Lewis, C. S. (1967), *Christian Reflections*, ed. W. Hooper, Grand Rapids: William B. Erdmans Publishing Co.

Library of Congress (2014), "Japan: Possession of Child Pornography Finally Punishable," https://www.loc.gov/item/global-legal-monitor/2014-08-04/japan-politics (accessed May 10, 2023).

Lippit, Yukio (2008), "Figure and Fracture in the *Genji* Scrolls: Text, Calligraphy, Paper, and Painting," in H. Shirane (ed.), *Envisioning the Tale of Genji: Media, Gender, and Cultural Production*, New York: Columbia University Press, pp. 49–80.

A Love of a Thousand Years: The Tale of the Shining Genji (*Sen'nen no koi: hikaru genji monogatari*) (2001), [Film]. Dir, Horikawa Tonkō, screenplay by Hayasaka Akira, Japan: Tōei Animation et al. (This is live action, despite the fact that the first film company is called Tōei Animation.)

Lunning, Frenchy (2022), *Cosplay: The Fictional Mode of Existence*, Minneapolis: University of Minnesota Press.

Lunsing, Wim (2006), "Yaoi Ronsō: Discussing Depictions of Male Homosexuality in Japanese Girls' Comics, Gay Comics and Gay Pornography," *Intersections: Gender, History and Culture in the Asian Context*, 12, pp. 1–16 https://web-s-ebscohost-com.ccl.idm.oclc.org/ehost/results?vid=1&sid=29c8328e-a66e-4850-b975-f4df497a8 c94%40redis&bquery=JN+%22Intersections%3a+Gender+%26+Sexuality+in+Asia+ %26+the+Pacific%22+AND+DT+20060101+NOT+PM+AOP&bdata= JkF1dGhUeXBlPXNzbyZkYj1vZm0mdHlwZT0xJnNlYXJjaE1vZGU9U3 RhbmRhcmQmc2l0ZT1l aG9zdC1saXZlJnNjb3BlPXNpdGU%3d (accessed February 15, 2022).

MacWilliams, Mark W. (2008), "Introduction," in M. W. MacWilliams (ed.), *Japanese Visual Culture: Explorations in the World of Manga and Anime*, Armonk: M. E. Sharpe, Inc., pp. 3–25.

Mainichi Shinbun (n.d.), "A Crisp Murasaki Shikibu Profile in a Kyoto Rice Field," http://video.mainichi.co.jp/viewvideo.jspx?Movie=48227968/482 (accessed October 1, 2010). (no longer available).

Maki Miyako (1997-8 [2002]), *Genji monogatari* [*The Tale of Genji*], 6 vols., Tokyo: Shōgakukan. (First serialized in *Biggu komikku foa rediisu* [*Big Comic for Ladies*] in 1986, originally published by Shōgakukan in 1988-91, and reprinted in the *Weekly Visual Genji monogatari* in 2002-3.)

MANGASeek and Nichigai Associates (2003), *Mangaka jinmei jiten* [*A Biographical Dictionary of Manga Artists*], Nichigai Associates, Tokyo: Hatsubaimoto Kinokuniya Shoten.

Marcus, Andrew Lawrence (1992), *The Willow in Autumn: Ryūtei Tanehiko, 1783-1842*, Council on East Asian Studies, Cambridge, MA: Harvard University Press.

Marra, Michele (1984a), "Mumyōzōshi: Introduction and Translation," *Monumenta Nipponica*, 39 (2), pp. 115-45.

Marra, Michele (1984b), "Mumyōzōshi, Part 2," *Monumenta Nipponica*, 39 (3), pp. 281-305.

Marra, Michele (1984c), "Mumyōzōshi Part 3," *Monumenta Nipponica*, 39 (4), pp. 409-34.

Maruyama, Kei, illustrator, and written by Yanagawa Sōzo ([1998, 2003] 2009), *Genji monogatari* [*The Tale of Genji*], Vols. 4-5 of *Komikkusutorii watashitachi no koten* [*Comics Stories: Our Classics*], Hasegawa Takashi, general editor. Tokyo Gakkō Tosho, 1998, 2003. 10 vols. Expanded 15 vols. (2009).

Maruyama Kei (n.d.), *Maruyama Kei Archives*. Maruyama-kei.net (accessed June 15, 2008)

Maya Mineo (1978-present), *Patalliro!*, 101 vols., Tokyo: Hakusensha.

Maya Mineo (2004-8), *Patalliro genji monogatari!* [*Patalliro Tale of Genji!*], 5 vols., Tokyo: Hakusensha.

McCarthy, Helen (2014), *A Brief History of Manga*, East Sussex: ILEX.

McCloud, Scott (1993), *Understanding Comics: The Invisible Art*, New York: HarperCollins Perennial (Originally published by Kitchen Sink Press, 1993.)

McCormick, Melissa (2008), "Monochromatic *Genji*: The Hakubyō Tradition and Female Commentarial Culture," in H. Shirane (ed.), *Envisioning The Tale of Genji: Media, Gender, and Cultural Production*, New York: Columbia University Press, pp. 101-28.

McCullough, Helen Craig (1968), "Introduction," in *Tales of Ise: Lyrical Episodes from Tenth-Century Japan*, trans. H. C. McCullough, Stanford: Stanford University Press, pp. 3-65.

McGray, Douglas (2002), "Japan's Gross National Cool," *Foreign Policy*, 130, pp. 44-54.

McLelland, Mark (2006/2007), "Why are Japanese Girls' Comics Full of Boys Bonking?," *Refractory*, 10, https://web.archive.org/web/20071016060453if_/http://www.refractory.unimelb.edu.au/journalissues/vol10/maclelland.html (accessed February 2, 2014).

McLelland, Mark (2015), "Regulation of Manga Content in Japan: What Is the Future for BL?," in M. McLelland, K. Nagaike, K. Suganuma, and J. Welker (eds.), *Boys Love Manga and Beyond: History, Culture, and Community in Japan*, Jackson: University of Mississippi Press, pp. 253-73.

McLelland, Mark (2017), "Introduction: Negotiating 'Cool Japan' in Research and Teaching," in M. McLelland (ed.), *The End of Cool Japan: Ethical, Legal, and Cultural Challenges to Japanese Popular Culture*, London: Routledge, pp. 1-30.

McLelland, Mark and James Welker (2015), "An Introduction to 'Boys Love' in Japan," in M. McLelland, K. Nagaike, K. Suganuma, and J. Welker (eds.), *Boys Love Manga and Beyond: History, Culture, and Community in Japan*, Jackson: University of Mississippi Press, pp. 3-20.

McNeil, Baye (2018), "Why Japan Should Consider Banning Blackface," *Japan Today*, January 25, https://japantoday.com/category/features/opinions/why-japan-should-consider-banning-blackface (accessed June 19, 2023).

Meech-Pakarik, Julia (1982), "The Artist's View of Ukifune," in A. Pekarik (ed.), *Ukifune: Love in the Tale of Genji*, New York: Columbia University Press, pp. 173–215.

Midorikawa, Machiko (2003), "Coming to Terms with the Alien: Translations of *Genji Monogatari*," *Monumenta Nipponica*, 58 (2), pp. 193–222.

Midorikawa, Machiko (2010), *Genji monogatari eiyaku ni tsuite no kenkyū* [*Transformations of The Tale of Genji: A Study of the Translations*], Tokyo: Musashino Shoin.

Mihashi, Mari, illustrator (1988 [2002]), with consultation by Shimizu Yoshiko, *Manga Genji monogatari* [*The Manga Tale of Genji*], 2 vols., Tokyo: Heibonsha. Reprinted Kōdansha, 2002.

Mijuki (2011), "Hanachirusato," in Mori Yoshimasa (ed.), *Genji monogatari BL ansorojii: aiyoku no otoko ochō koi emaki* [*The Tale of Genji BL Anthology: Love Scrolls of Courtly Male Desire*], Tokyo: Entāburein, pp. 97–112.

Miki, Minoru, composer, and libretto in English by Colin Graham (2000), *The Tale of Genji*. (Premier in June 2000 at the Opera Theatre of St. Louis, with Graham directing.)

Miller, Laura (2008), "Extreme Makeover for a Heian-Era Wizard," *Mechademia*, 3 (1): *Limits of the Human*, pp. 30–45.

Miller, Laura (2017), "Scholar Girl Meets Manga Maniac, Media Specialist, and Cultural Gate Keeper," in M. McLelland (ed.), *The End of Cool Japan: Ethical, Legal, and Cultural Challenges to Japanese Popular Culture*, London: Routledge, pp. 51–69.

Miō, Serina (2007–9), *Genji monogatari* [*The Tale of Genji*], 4 vols., Tokyo: Shōgakukan. (Originally serialized in *Shōjo komikku* [*Girls Comics*] and *Sho-Comi zōkan* [Sho-Comi Special Edition from 2006–9.])

Miyagi, Tōko, illustrator, written by Takayama Yukiko, and inked by Kawasaki Izumi (2011), *Genji monogatari: sen'nen no nazo* [*The Tale of Genji: The One-Thousand-Year-Old Riddle*], 2 vols., Tokyo: Kadokawa Shoten. (Originally serialized in *Asuka*, January–October 2011.)

Miyake, Lynne K. (1993), "The Narrative Triad in *The Tale of Genji*: Narrator, Reader, and Text," in E. Kamens (ed.), *Approaches to Teaching Murasaki Shikibu's The Tale of Genji*, New York: The Modern Language Association of America, pp. 77–87.

Miyake, Lynne K. (2000), "'Siting Translation': Translation and Classical Japanese Literary Canon Formation in the United States," *AJLS Proceedings of the Association for Japanese Literary Studies: Issues of Canonicity and Canon Formation in Japanese Literary Studies*, pp. 487–501.

Miyake, Lynne K. (2001), "Interactive Narrators and Performative Readers: Gendered Interfacing in Heian Japanese Narratives," *Women & Performance: A Journal of Feminist Theory, Performing Japanese Women*, 12:1 (23), pp. 23–42.

Miyake, Lynne K. (2008), "Graphically Speaking: *Manga* Versions of *The Tale of Genji*," *Monumenta Nipponica*, 63 (2), pp. 359–92.

Miyata, Masayuki (2001), *The Tale of Genji: Scenes from the World's First Novel*, trans. H. M. Horton, Tokyo: Kodansha International.

Mizoguchi, Akiko (2003), "Male–Male Romance by and for Women in Japan: A History and the Subgenres of *Yaoi* Fictions," *U.S.–Japan Women's Journal*, 25, pp. 49–75.

Modern Language Association (n.d.), *Approaches to Teaching World Literature*. http://www.mla.org/publications/publication-program/pub-prog-bookseries (accessed July 13, 2012).

Mori, Naoko (2010), *Onna wa poruno o yomu: josei no seiyoku to feminizumu* [Women Read Pornography: Women's Sexual Desire and Feminism], Tokyo: Seikyūsha.

Mori, Yoshimasa, ed. (2011), *Genji monogatari BL ansorojii: aiyoku no otoko ochō koi emaki* [The Tale of Genji BL Anthology: Love Scrolls of Courtly Male Desire, Tokyo: Entāburein.

Mori, Yukiko (1974), *Genji monogatari* [The Tale of Genji], Tokyo: Akebono Shuppan.

Motoi Tatsuno (2011), "Murasaki no ue" [Lady Murasaki] in Mori Yoshimasa (ed.), *Genji monogatari BL ansorojii: aiyoku no otoko ōchō koi emaki* [The Tale of Genji BL Anthology: Love Scrolls of Courtly Male Desire], Tokyo: Entāburein, pp. 55–68.

Motomi, Kyōsuke (2010–15), *Dengeki Daisy*, 16 vols., San Francisco: Viz Media. (Serialized in *Betsukomi Shōgakukan* [Shōgakukan Addendum Comics], May 2007–October 2013.)

Murasaki Shikibu: The Tale of Genji (Murasaki shikibu genji monogatari) (1987), [Animated film] Dir Sugi'i Gizabirō, screenplay by Tsutsumi Tomomi, animation director Maeda Yasuo, Japan: Asahi/TV Asahi/Japan Herold Films.

Murase, Miyeko (1983), *Iconography of The Tale of Genji: Genji monogatari ekotoba*, ed. and written M. Murase and illustrated by Tosa Mitsuoki, New York: John Weatherhill.

Murase, Miyeko (2001), "Introduction," in *The Tale of Genji: Legends and Paintings*, ed. M. Murase and illustrated by Tosa Mitsuoki. New York: George Braziller, pp. 1–21.

Nagaike, Kazumi (2003), "Perverse Sexualities, Perverse Desires: Representations of Female Fantasies and *Yaoi Manga* as Pornography Directed at Women," *U.S.–Japan Women's Journal*, 25, pp. 76–103.

Nagaike, Kazumi (2015), "Do Heterosexual Men Dream of Homosexual Men? BL *Fudanshi* and Discourse on Male Feminization," in M. McLelland, K. Nagaike, K. Suganuma, and J. Welker (eds.), *Boys Love Manga and Beyond: History, Culture, and Community in Japan*, Jackson: University of Mississippi Press, pp. 189–209.

Nagaike, Kazumi (n.d.), "Boys' Love," *Japanese Media and Popular Culture: An Open-Access Digital Initiative of the University of Tokyo*, https://jmpc–utokyo.com/ (accessed May 25, 2020).

Nagaike, Kazumi and Katsuhito Suganuma (2013), "Transnational Boys' Love Fan Studies," *Transformative Works and Cultures*, 12, https://journal.transformativeworks.org/index.php/twc/issue/view/14 (accessed March 8, 2015).

Nagaike, Kazumi and Tomoko Aoyama (2015), "What Is Japanese 'BL Studies?': A Historical and Analytical Overview," in M. McLelland, K. Nagaike, K. Suganuma, and J. Welker (eds.), *Boys Love Manga and Beyond: History, Culture, and Community in Japan*, Jackson: University of Mississippi Press, pp. 119–40.

Nagatani, Kunio (1994), *Nippon mangaka meikan* [A Dictionary of Japanese Manga Artists], Tokyo: Dētahausu.

Nagayama, Kaoru (2021), *Erotic Comics in Japan: An Introduction to Eromanga*, trans. P. W. Galbraith and J. Bauwens-Sugimoto, Amsterdam: Amsterdam University Press.

Nakamachi Keiko (2008), "*Genji* Pictures from Momoyama Painting to Edo *Ukiyo-e*: Cultural Authority and New Horizons," in H. Shirane (ed.), *Envisioning the Tale of Genji: Media, Gender, and Cultural Production*, New York: Columbia University Press, pp. 171–210.

Nakao, Motoko (2011), "Fujitsubo," in Mori Yoshimasa (ed.), *Genji monogatari BL ansorojii: aiyoku no otoko ōchō koi emaki* [The Tale of Genji BL Anthology: Love Scrolls of Courtly Male Desire], Tokyo: Entāburein, pp. 7–20.

Nanateru, Tsubasa, Kuro Nyako, and Fujimori Kanna ([2014] 2017), *Manga de yomu genji monogatari* [Reading the Tale of Genji in Manga], Tokyo: Gakken Plus.

Nanda, Chyun (2011), "Utsusemi," in Asuka Henshūbu (ed.), *Genji monogatari komikku ansorojii: onna hikaru genji no ikemen nikki* [*The Comics Anthology of The Tale of Genji: Ms. Shining Genji's Hottie Diary*], Tokyo: Kadokawa Shoten, pp. 7–16.

Naritaya (2013), https://web.archive.org/web/20130509073752/http://www.naritaya.jp:80/english/profile/ebizo.html (accessed June 19, 2014).

Nathan, John (1974), *Mishima: A Biography*, New York: Little, Brown & Company.

National Publishing Association/Publishing Science Institute (2020), "News Release," 27 July, https://hon.jp/news/1.0/0/28155 (accessed October 10, 2020).

Natsume, Fusanosuke (1999), *Manga no chikara* [*The Power of Manga*], Tokyo: Shōbunsha.

Nishi, Kazuo and Kazuo Hozumi (1985), *What Is Japanese Architecture?: A Survey of Traditional Japanese Architecture with a List of Sites and a Map*, trans. and adapted by H. M. Horton, Tokyo: Kodansha International, 1985.

Nishimura, Tōru ([1996] 2002), "Manga genji no hajime ni" [At the Beginning of the *Manga Tale of Genji*] in *Manga Genji monogatari* [*Manga Tale of Genji*], illustrated by Kishida Ren with consultation by Nishimura Tōru, Tokyo: Kawade Shobō Shinsha, 1: 3–6.

Ogi, Fusami (2003), "Female Subjectivity and *Shoujo* (Girls) *Manga* (Japanese Comics): *Shoujo* in Ladies' Comics and Young Ladies' Comics," *Journal of Popular Culture*, 36 (4), pp. 780–803.

Okano, Fumika, Sekine Kiyo, Fujikura Mao, Yagi Katsumi, Haruno Saku, and Kikuchi Kumiko (2006), *Genji monogatari komikku ansorojii: koi to shiraseba* [*The Tale of Genji Comics Anthology: If We Let Them Know It's Love*], Tokyo: Kōbunsha.

Okochi Ayaka (n.d.), "Takigi Noh," http://thekyotoproject.org/english/takigi-noh/ (accessed September 29, 2020).

Ooms, Herman (2009), *Imperial Politics and Symbolics in Ancient Japan: The Tenmu Dynasty, 650–800*, Honolulu: University of Hawai'i Press.

Orbaugh, Sharlyn (2017), "Manga, Anime, and Child Pornography Law in Canada," in M. McLelland (ed.), *The End of Cool Japan: Ethical, Legal, and Cultural Challenges to Japanese Popular Culture*, London: Routledge, pp. 94–108.

Pagliasotti, Dru (2008), "Reading Boys' Love in the West," *Particip@tions*, 5 (2), https://www.participations.org/Volume%205/Issue%202/5_02_contents.htm (accessed April 5, 2015).

Penguin Classics (n.d.), http://us.penguingroup.com/static/pages/classics/deluxe.html (accessed July 9, 2012).

Penley, Constance (1992), "Feminism, Psychoanalysis, and the Study of Popular Culture," in L. Grossberg, C. Nelson and P. Trechler (eds.), *Cultural Studies*, London: Routledge, pp. 479–500.

Perper, Timothy and Martha Cornog (2002), "Eroticism for the Masses: Japanese Manga Comics and Their Assimilation into the U.S.," *Sexuality and Culture*, 6, pp. 3–126.

Prough, Jennifer S. (2010), *Straight from the Heart: Gender, Intimacy, and the Production of Shōjo Manga*, Honolulu: University of Hawai'i Press.

Robo-Garage (n.d.), http://www.robo-garage.com/en/prd/p_04/index.html (accessed July 16, 2012).

Rodd, Laurel Rasplica, with Mary Catherine Henkenius, trans. (1984), *Kokinshū: A Collection of Poems Ancient and Modern*, Princeton, NJ: Princeton University Press.

Rodriguez, Jorge (n.d.), "BL Gei Komi in the Gay Mediascape," https://jrod04747.wixsite.com/website/post/bl-and-gei-komi-in-the-gay-mediascape (accessed October 6, 2021).

Rowley, G. G. (2000), *Yosano Akiko and The Tale of Genji*. Michigan Monograph Series in Japanese Studies, no. 28. Center for Japanese Studies, Ann Arbor: University of Michigan Press.

Rowley, G. G. (2010), "*The Tale of Genji*: Required Reading for Aristocratic Women," in P. F. Kornicki, M. Patessio, and G. G. Rowley (eds.), *The Female as Subject: Reading and Writing in Early Modern Japan*, Michigan Monograph Series in Japanese Studies, no. 70, Center for Japanese Studies, Ann Arbor: University of Michigan Press, pp. 39–57.

Ryūka, Satoru (2011), "Aoi no ue" [Lady Aoi], in Asuka Henshūbu (ed.), *Genji monogatari komikku ansorojii: onna hikaru genji no ikemen nikki* [*The Comics Anthology of The Tale of Genji: Ms. Shining Genji's Hottie Diary*], Tokyo: Kadokawa Shoten, pp. 17–26.

Ryūtei, Tanehiko (1985), *Nise murasaki inaka genji* [*The Rustic Genji of a Bogus Murasaki*], trans. D. M. Richardson and T. Tanonaka, 3 vols., Winchester, Virginia: privately published.

Saeki, Nao ([1990] 2004), *Kumon no manga koten bungakukan genji monogatari* [*The Kumon Manga Literature Classics Tale of Genji*], Tokyo: Kumon Shuppan.

Saito, Kumiko (2011), "Desire in Subtext: Gender, Fandom, and Women's Male–Male Homoerotic Parodies in Contemporary Japan," *Machademia*, 6, pp. 171–91.

Saito, Tamaki (2007), "Otaku Sexuality," in C. Bolton, I. Csicsery-Ronay, Jr., and T. Tatsumi (eds.), *Robot Ghosts and Wired Dreams: Japanese Science Fiction from Origins to Anime*, Minneapolis: University of Minnesota Press, pp. 222–49.

Sakurada, Hina (2015–16), *Kuro genji monogatari: hana to miruramu* [*The Black Tale of Genji: So Like a Flower*], 3 vols., Tokyo: Shōgakukan. (Simultaneously published in *Cheese!*, 2015–16.)

Sakurazawa, Mai (2001), writer, and illustrated by Hirose Mihoko, Ide Chikae, Honjo Ru, Asano Maiko, Enomoto Yumi, and Kawanakajima Miyuki, *Genji koi monogatari* [*The Love Tale of Genji*], 2 vols., Tokyo: Wantsū Magajinsha.

Sanazaki, Harumo (2010), *Genji monogatari* [*The Tale of Genji*], in Miki Katsuya (ed.), *Meisho o manga de* [*The Masterpieces through Manga*], Tokyo: Gakken.

Saotome, Ageha (2011a), "Joshō" [Prologue] in Mori Yoshimasa (ed.), *Genji monogatari BL ansorojii: aiyoku no otoko ōchō koi emaki* [*The Tale of Genji BL Anthology: Love Scrolls of Courtly Male Desire*], Tokyo: Entāburein, p. 1.

Saotome, Ageha (2011b), *Rokujō no miyasudokoro* [*Haven Rokujō*] in Mori Yoshimasa (ed.), *Genji monogatari BL ansorojii: aiyoku no otoko ōchō koi emaki* [*The Tale of Genji BL Anthology: Love Scrolls of Courtly Male Desire*], Tokyo: Entāburein, pp. 21–36.

Saotome, Ageha (2013), *Iro otoko hikaru genji: shitto ni modaeru toshi ue otoko rokujō no miyasudokoro* [*The Sexy Shining Genji: The Haven Rokujō, the Older Man Tormented by Jealousy*], Tokyo: Entāburein.

Sasaki, Misuzu (2001), *Sen'nen no koi: hikaru genji monogatari* [*A Love of a Thousand Years: The Tale of the Shining Genji*], Tokyo: Kadowa Shoten. (Loosely based on the 2001 film *A Love of a Thousand Years: The Tale of the Shining Genji*, screenplay by Hayasaka Akira.)

Schodt, Fredrick L. (1983 [1986]), *Manga! Manga!: The World of Japanese Comics*, Tokyo: Kodansha International.

Schodt, Fredrick L. (1996), *Dreamland Japan: Writings on Modern Manga*, Berkeley: Stone Bridge Press.

Searle, John (1969), *Speech Acts: An Essay in the Philosophy of Language*, Cambridge: Cambridge University Press.

Seidensticker, Edward, trans. (1976), *The Tale of Genji* by Murasaki Shikibu, 2 vols., New York: Alfred A. Knopf.
Setouchi Jakuchō (1996-8), *Genji monogatari* [*The Tale of Genji*], 10 vols., Tokyo: Kadokawa.
Setouchi Jakuchō (2012-13), "Genji monogatari no onna tachi" [The Women of *The Tale of Genji*] in *Genji monogatari* [*The Tale of Genji*], by Hanamura Eiko, Tokyo: Shōgakukan, 3: 282-5.
Shamoon, Deborah (2004), "Office Sluts and Rebel Flowers: The Pleasures of Japanese Pornographic Comics for Women," in L. Williams (ed.), *Porn Studies*, Durham, NC: Duke University Press, pp. 77-103.
Shamoon, Deborah (2011), "Films on Paper: Cinematic Narrative in Gekiga," in T. Perper and M. Cornog (eds.), *Mangatopia: Essays on Manga and Anime in the Modern World*, Santa Barbara: Libraries Unlimited, pp. 21-36.
Shamoon, Deborah (2012), *Passionate Friendship: The Aesthetic of Girls' Culture in Japan*, Honolulu: University of Hawai'i Press.
Shepherd, David (1989), "Bakhtin and the Reader," in K. Hirschkop and D. Shepherd (eds.), *Bakhtin and Cultural Theory: Books Are Nothing but People Speaking Publicly*, Manchester: Manchester University Press, pp. 91-108.
Shigematsu, Setsu (1999), "Dimensions of Desire: Sex, Fantasy, and Fetish in Japanese Comics," in J. A. Lent (ed.), *Themes and Issues in Asian Cartooning: Cute, Cheap, Mad, and Sexy*, Bowling Green: Bowling Green State University Popular Press, pp. 127-63.
Shigeta, Shin'ichi (2013), "A Portrait of Abe no Seimei," *Japanese Journal of Religious Studies*, 40 (1), pp. 77-97.
Shimaki, Ako (2002-4), *Gekka no kimi* [*The Prince in the Moonlight*], 7 vols., Tokyo: Shōgakukan. (Simultaneously published in *Gekkan shōjo komikku Cheese!* [*Monthly Girls Comics Cheese!*], 2002-4.
Shimizu, Yoshiko (1988 [2002]), "Maegaki" [Foreword] in *Manga genji monogatari* [*The Manga Tale of Genji*], by Mihashi Mari with consultation with Shimizu Yoshiko, Tokyo: Heibonsha, 1:3-5. Reprinted Kōdansha, 2002.
Shinohara, Shōji, Suzuki Hideo, and Hinata Kazumasa (1988), *Ehon genji monogatari* [*The Picture Book Tale of Genji*], Tokyo: Yūgen Gaisha Kichōbon Kankōkai.
Shirane, Haruo (1987), *The Bridge of Dreams: A Poetics of The Tale of Genji*, Stanford: Stanford University Press.
Shirane, Haruo, ed. (2002), *Early Modern Japanese Literature: An Anthology 1600-1900*, New York: Columbia University Press.
Shirane, Haruo (2007a), "Introduction," in H. Shirane (ed.), *Traditional Japanese Literature: An Anthology, Beginnings to 1600*, New York: Columbia University Press, pp. 1-14.
Shirane, Haruo, ed. (2007b), *Traditional Japanese Literature: An Anthology, Beginnings to 1600*, New York: Columbia University Press.
Shirane, Haruo (2008a), "*The Tale of Genji* and the Dynamics of Cultural Production: Canonization and Popularization," in H. Shirane (ed.), *Envisioning the Tale of Genji: Media, Gender, and Cultural Production*, New York: Columbia University Press, pp. 1-46.
Shirane, Haruo, ed. (2008b), *Envisioning the Tale of Genji: Media, Gender, and Cultural Production*, New York: Columbia University Press.
Shirane, Haruo and Tomi Suzuki, eds. (2000), *Inventing the Classics: Modernity, National Identity, and Japanese Literature*, Stanford: Stanford University Press.

Smith, Clarissa and Feona Attwood (2013), "Emotional Truths and Thrilling Slide Shows: The Resurgence of Antiporn Feminism," in T. Taormino, C. P. Shimizu, C. Penley, and M. Miller-Young (eds.), *The Feminist Porn Book: The Politics of Producing Pleasure*, New York: The Feminist Press at the City University of New York, pp. 41–57.

Stapleton, Adam (2017), "All Seizures Great and Small: Reading Contentious Images of Minors in Japan and Australia," in M. McLelland (ed.), *The End of Cool Japan: Ethical, Legal, and Cultural Challenges to Japanese Popular Culture*, London: Routledge, pp. 134–62.

Suter, Rebecca (2013), "Gender Bending and Exoticism in Japanese Girls' Comics," *Asian Studies Review*, 37 (4), pp. 546–58.

Suzuki, Shige (CJ) (2013), "Tatsumi Yoshihiro's *Gekiga* and the Global Sixties: Aspiring for an Alternative," in J. Berndt and B. Kummerling-Meibauer (eds.), *Manga's Cultural Crossroads*, London: Routledge, pp. 50–64.

Suzuki, Tomi (2000), "Gender and Genre: Modern Literary Histories and Women's Diary Literature," in H. Shirane and T. Suzuki (eds.), *Inventing the Classics: Modernity, National Identity, and Japanese Literature*, Stanford: Stanford University Press, pp. 71–95.

Suzuki, Tomi (2008), "*The Tale of Genji*, National Literature, Language, and Modernism," in H. Shirane (ed.), *Envisioning the Tale of Genji: Media, Gender, and Cultural Production*, New York: Columbia University Press, pp. 243–87.

Taguchi, Eiichi, ed and written in conjunction with Inamoto Mariko, Kimura Saeko, and Ryūsawa Aya (2009), *Suguwakaru genji monogatari no kaiga* [*The Easy-to-Understand Tale of Genji Paintings*], Tokyo: Tokyo Bijutsu.

Tahara, Mildred, trans. (1980), *Tales of Yamato: A Tenth-Century Poem-Tale*, Honolulu: University of Hawai'i Press.

Takahashi, Mizuki (2008), "Opening the Closed World of *Shōjo Manga*," in M. W. MacWilliams (ed.), *Japanese Visual Culture: Explorations in the World of Manga and Anime*, Armonk: M. E. Sharpe, Inc., pp. 114–36.

Takahashi, Yōji, ed. (2001), *Kabuki Genji monogatari: jūichidaime ichikawa danjūrō, jūnidaime danjūrō, shin'nosuke—san dai no hikaru genji* [*The Kabuki Tale of Genji: Ichikawa Danjūrō XI, Danjūrō XII, Shin'nosuke—The Three Generations of the Shining Genji*], Tokyo: Heibonsha.

Takashima, Kazusa (2011), "Fujitsubo," in Asuka Henshūbu (ed.), *Genji monogatari komikku ansorojii: onna hikaru genji no ikemen nikki* [*The Comics Anthology of The Tale of Genji: Ms. Shining Genji's Hottie Diary*], Tokyo: Kadokawa Shoten, pp. 107–15.

Takenaka Ranko (1998), *Heian no torendii dorama genji monogatari mangachō* [*Heian Trendy Drama: The Tale of Genji Manga Notebook*], Kyōto Minpōsha [*Kyoto Civilian News*], January 4–December 20, 1998. (Comic strip in newspaper for 38 weeks, with two pages per week.)

Takeuchi, Naoko (2011–13), *Pretty Guardian Sailor Moon*, 12 vols., Tokyo: Kōdansha Comics. (Originally published 1991–7. 18 vols.)

The Tale of Genji: A Millennium-Old Journal [*Genji monogatari: sen'nenki*] (2009), [Animated Film] Dir Dezaki Osamu, screenplay Dezaki Osamu, Morita Mayumi, and Konparu Tomoko, Tezuka Productions/TMS Entertainment.

Tamamushi, Satoko (2004), "Tawaraya Sōtetsu and the 'Yamato-e Revival,' " in E. Lillehoj (ed.), *Critical Perspectives in Classicism in Japanese Painting 1600–1700*, Honolulu: University of Hawai'i Press, pp. 53–78.

Tanabe, Seiko (1978–9), *Shin Genji monogatari* [*The New* Tale of Genji], 5 vols., Tokyo: Shinchōsha. (Originally serialized in *Shūkan Asahi* [*Weekly Asahi*], November 8, 1974–December 27, 1978.)

Tanaka, Shigeyoshi (1995), "Nihon shaki ni okeru shakaiteki kyōkai ni kansuru shiron" [An Essay on Societal Boundaries in Japanese Society], *Environment and Communication: Designated Research Report* 192–4, pp. 13–30.

Tanizaki, Jun'ichirō, trans. (1939–41), *Jun'ichirō-yaku genji monogatari* [*Tale of Genji: The Jun'ichirō Translation*], by Murasaki Shikibu, publisher unknown.

Tanizaki, Jun'ichirō, trans. (1951–4), *Jun'ichirō shin'yaku genji monogatari* [*Tale of Genji: The New Jun'ichirō Translation*], by Murasaki Shikibu, publisher unknown.

Tanizaki, Jun'ichirō, trans. (1964–5), *Jun'ichirō shinshin'yaku genji monogatari* [*Tale of Genji: The New New Jun'ichirō Translation*], by Murasaki Shikibu, 11 vols., Tokyo: Chūō Kōronsha.

Taormino, Tristen, Celine Parreenas Shimizu, Constance Penley, and Michelle Miller-Young, eds. (2013), *Feminist Porn Book: The Politics of Producing Pleasure*, New York: The Feminist Press at the City University of New York.

Teradate Kazuko (2001–2), *The Tale of Genji: Mutated* [*Yōhen Genji monogatari*], 4 vols., Tokyo: Bunkasha. (Originally published in *The World's Scariest Children Tales*, 2000–2.)

Tateishi, Kazuhiro (2004), Homepage, http://web.archive.org/web/20040702143127/ http://homepage3.nifty.com/genji-db/manga.htm (accessed June 3, 2004) (no longer available).

Tateishi, Kazuhiro (2005a), "Eigaka sarerata *genji monogatari*" [The Film-ization of *The Tale of Genji*], in K. Tateishi and T. Ando (eds.), *Genji bunka no jikū* [*The Times and Spaces of the Genji Culture*], Tokyo: Moriwasha, pp. 126–57.

Tateishi, Kazuhiro (2005b), "Kabuki to Takarazuka no *genji monogatari*" [The Kabuki and Takarazuka *Tale of Genji*], in K. Tateishi and T. Ando (eds.), *Genji bunka no jikū* [*The Times and Spaces of the Genji Culture*], Tokyo: Moriwasha, pp. 158–87.

Tateishi, Kazuhiro (2005c), "Genji monogatari no komikku to kyarakutaraizu" [The Comics and Characterizing of *The Tale of Genji*], in K. Tateishi and T. Ando (eds.), *Genji bunka no jikū* [*The Times and Spaces of the Genji Culture*], Tokyo: Moriwasha, pp. 188–225.

Tateishi, Kazuhiro (2008), "*The Tale of Genji* in Postwar Film," in H. Shirane (ed.), *Envisioning the Tale of Genji: Media, Gender, and Cultural Production*, New York: Columbia University Press, pp. 303–28.

Thorn, Rachel (2001), "Shōjo Manga—Something for Girls," *Japan Quarterly*, 48 (3), pp. 43–50.

Thorn, Rachel (n.d.1), "A History of Manga." http://www.matt-thorn.com/mangagaku/history.html. (accessed July 1, 2010) (no longer available).

Thorn, Rachel (n d.2), "The Multi-Faceted Universe of Shōjo Manga." www.matt-thorn.com/shoujo_manga/colloque/index.php (accessed July 1, 2010) (no longer available).

Toba, Shōko (n,d.), Homepage: http://www5a.biglobe.ne.jp/~ruridou/frame1.htm (accessed July 15, 2005) (no longer available).

Toba, Shōko (2006), *NHK manga de yomu koten 1: murasaki shikibu gensaku genji monogatari* [*NHK Reading the Classics through Manga: The Tale of Genji, Original by Murasaki Shikibu*]. Kadokawa Shoten, 1991, 1997. Reprinted in *NHK manga de yomu koten 3: genji monogatari • ise monogatari* [*Reading the Classics through Manga 3: The Tale of Genji and The Tale of Ise*], Tokyo: Homesha.

Tokugawa Art Museum (2005), *Kaiga de tsuzuru genji monogatari: kaki tsugareta genji-e no keitō* [*The Tale of Genji through Painting: The Illustrated Lineage of the Genji-e Paintings*], Nagoya: Tokugawa Art Museum.

Tomi, Shinzō (1991), *Genji monogatari* [*The Tale of Genji*], 3 vols., Tokyo: Geibunsha.

Tomita Isao, composer and conductor of Pasadena Symphony (1999), *The Tale of Genji*, Pasadena Civic Auditorium, Pasadena, May 11, 1999. (Accompanying electronic show directed by Mitsuru Shimizu, in which the *Genji* was Part 2.)

Torii, Hiroko ([1990] 2004), "Kaisetsu genji monogatari" [Commentary on *The Tale of Genji*] in *Kumon no manga koten bungakukan genji monogatari* [*The Kumon Manga Literature Classics Tale of Genji*], by Saeki Nao, Tokyo: Kumon Shuppan, pp. 150–9.

Treat, John Whittier (1996), "Yoshimoto Banana Writes Home: The *Shōjo* in Japanese Popular Culture," in J. W. Treat (ed.), *Contemporary Japan and Popular Culture*, London: Curzon Press, pp. 275–308.

Tsuboi, Koh (1989a), illustratrator, ed. Shimizu Yoshiko and Konaka Yōtarō, *The Illustrated Tale of Genji: A Classic Japanese Romance, English Edition*, trans. A. Tansman, Tokyo: Shinjinbutsu Ōraisha.

Tsuboi, Koh (1989b), illustrator with consultation by Shimizu Yoshiko, *The Illustrated Tale of Genji: A Classic Japanese Romance, Japanese Edition*. Tokyo: Shinjinbutsu Ōraisha.

Tyler, Royall (2001a), "Chronology," in *The Tale of Genji*, trans. R. Tyler, New York: Viking Penguin, 2: 1125–33.

Tyler, Royall, trans. (2001b), *The Tale of Genji*, by Murasaki Shikibu, 2 vols., New York: Viking Penguin.

Variety Art Works (2010), *Genji monogatari manga de dokuha* [*Reading the Tale of Genji through Manga*], Tokyo: Iisuto Puresu.

Vernon, Victoria V. (1988), *Daughters of the Moon: Wish, Will, and Social Constraint in Fiction by Modern Japanese Women*, Institute of East Asian Studies, Berkeley: University of California Press.

Vincent, Keith (2007), "A Japanese Electra and Her Queer Progeny," *Mechademia*, 2, pp. 64–79.

Waley, Arthur, trans. (1960), *The Tale of Genji in Six Parts*, by Murasaki Shikibu, New York: The Modern Library. (Originally published by G. Allen and Unwin, 1925–33.)

Wang, Xin (2013), "Slice of Life Narratives in Japanese Manga and Prose: School Life, Biting Cats, and Curry Rice," Senior Thesis, vol. 2, Pomona College, Claremont.

Washburn, Dennis, trans. (2015), *The Tale of Genji*, by Murasaki Shikibu, New York: W. W. Norton.

Weatherhead East Asia Institute Columbia University (n.d.), "Japan: Medieval Japan (1185–1600)," *Key Points Across East Asia by Era 1000–1450 CE. Asia For Educators*, http://afe.easia.columbia.edu/main_pop/kpct/kp_medievaljp.htm (accessed June 2014).

Welker, James (2006), "Beautiful, Borrowed, and Bent: Boys' Love as Girls' Love in *Shōjo Manga*," *Signs*, 31 (3), pp. 841–70.

Welker, James (2011), "Flower Tribes and Female Desire Complicating Early Female Consumption of Male Homosexuality in Shōjo Manga," *Mechadamia*, 6, pp. 211–28.

Welker, James (2015), "A Brief History of *Shōnen-ai, Yaoi*, and Boys Love," in M. McLelland, K. Nagaike, K. Suganuma, and J. Welker (eds.), *Boys Love Manga and Beyond: History, Culture, and Community in Japan*, Jackson: University of Mississippi Press, pp. 42–75.

"What is Visual Novel (VN)? [Gaming Definition, Meaning]" (2017), March 18, https://honeysanime.com/what-is-visual-novel-vn/ (accessed December 29, 2021).
Williams, Alan (2015), "Rethinking *Yaoi* on the Regional and Global Scale," *Interactions: Gender and Sexuality in Asia and the Pacific*, 37, http://intersections.anu.edu.au/issue37/williams.pdf (acessed June 15, 2020).
Williams, Linda (1999), *Hard Core: Power, Pleasure and the "Frenzy of the Visible*," Berkeley: University of California Press.
Woledge, Elizabeth (2005), "From Slash to Mainstream: Female Writers and Gender Blending Men," *Extrapolation*, 46 (1), pp. 50–65.
Wood, Andrea (2006), "'Straight' Women, Queer Texts: Boy-Love Manga and the Rise of a Global Counterpublic," *Women's Studies Quarterly*, 34 (1 and 2), pp. 394–412.
Woolf, Virginia (1929), *A Room of One's Own*, New York: Harcourt Brace Jovanovich.
Yamada, Botan (2011), "Oborozukiyo," in Mori Yoshimasa (ed.), *Genji monogatari BL ansorojii: aiyoku no otoko ōchō koi emaki* [*The Tale of Genji BL Anthology: Love Scrolls of Courtly Male Desire*], Tokyo: Entāburein, pp. 69–82.
Yamada, Tomoko (2006), "Shōjo josei manga shi gairon" [Introduction to the History of Girls and Ladies Comics], in Takeuchi Osamu (ed.), *Gendai manga hakubutsukan 1945-2005* [*The Encyclopedia of Contemporary Manga 1945–2005*], Tokyo: Shōgakukan, pp. 406–12.
Yamamoto, Traise (1999), *Masking Selves, Making Subjects: Japanese American Women, Identity, and the Body*, Berkeley: University of California Press.
Yamanaka, Reiko (2008), "*The Tale of Genji* and the Development of Female-Spirit *Nō*," in H. Shirane (ed.), *Envisioning the Tale of Genji: Media, Gender, and Cultural Production*, New York: Columbia University Press, pp. 81–100.
Yamashita, Samuel H. (n.d.), "Medieval Japan: Overview," *Two Minute Japan, UCLA Teaching About Japan Website*, http//www.international.ucla.edu/eas/japan/medieval/overview.htm (accessed August 1, 2011) (no longer available).
Yamato, Waki (1980–93), *Asaki yume mishi* [*Fleeting Dreams*], 13 vols., Tokyo: Kodansha. (Originally serialized in *mimi* from 1979–85, in *Fortnightly mimi* from 1985–6, and in *Excellentmimi* from 1985–93.)
Yamato, Waki (2000–1), *Bairingaruban Asaki yume mishi: hoshi no shō jō to ge to hana no shō jō to ge* [*Bilingual Version The Tale of Genji Fleeting Dreams: The Star Chapter, Vols.1 and 2, and The Flower Chapter, Vols. 1 and 2*], trans. Stuart Atkins and Yoko Toyozaki, Tokyo: Kōdansha International.
Yamato, Waki (2019–20), *The Tale of Genji*, [English digital ed.], trans. J. Ward, 10 books, New York: KōdanshaAdvanced Media.
Yano, Christine R. (2009), "Pink Globalization: Rethinking Japan's Cute/Cool Trek across the Pacific," *International House of Japan Bulletin*, 29 (2), pp. 34–46.
Yano, Christine R. (2013), *Pink Globalization: Hello Kitty's Trek across the Pacific*, Durham, NC: Duke University Press.
Yata, Midori (2011), "Yūgao," in Asuka Henshūbu (ed.), *Genji monogatari komikku ansorojii: onna hikaru genji no ikemen nikki* [*The Comics Anthology of the Tale of Genji: Ms. Shining Genji's Hottie Diary*], Tokyo: Kadokawa Shoten, pp. 27–36.
Yoda, Tomiko (2004), *Gender and National Literature: Heian Texts in the Constructions of Japanese Modernity*, Durham, NC: Duke University Press.
Yonezawa, Yoshihiro (1987), *Manga hihyō sengen* [*A Manga Commentary Declaration*], Tokyo: Aki Shobō.
Yonezawa, Yoshihiro ([1980] 2007), *Sengo shōjo manga shi* [*A History of Postwar Girls Comics*], Tokyo: Chikuma Shobō, 1980, reprinted 2007.

Yosano, Akiko, trans. (1912–13), *Shin'yaku genji monogatari* [*New Translation of The Tale of Genji*], by Murasaki Shikibu, 4 vols., Tokyo: Kanao Bun'endō.

Yosano, Akiko, trans. (1938–9), *Shin-shin'yaku genji monogatari* [*A New, New Translation of The Tale of Genji*], by Murasaki Shikibu, 6 vols., Tokyo: Kanao Bun'endō.

Yoshihiro, Kōsuke (1993), *Manga no gendai shi* [*The Modern History of Manga*], Tokyo: Maruzen Kabushiki Gaisha.

Yuki, Masaki, William Maddux, and Takahiko Masuda (2007), "Are the Windows to the Soul the Same in the East and the West?: Cultural Differences in Using the Eyes and the Mouth as Cues to Recognize Emotions in Japan and the United States," *ScienceDirect: Journal of Experimental Social Psychology*, 43, pp. 303–11 (accessed March 16, 2022).

Zanghellini, Aleardo (2009), "Underage Sex and Romance in Japanese Homoerotic *Manga* and *Anime*," *Social and Legal Studies*, 18 (2), pp. 159–77.

Zendle, David, Paul Cairns, and David Kudenko (2018), "No Priming in Video Games," *Computers in Human Behavior*, 78, pp. 113–25.

Zendle, David, David Kudenko, and Paul Cairns (2018), "Behavioral Realism and the Activation of Aggressive Concepts in Violent Games," *Entertainment Computing*, 24, pp. 21–9.

Zsila, Ágnas, Dru Pagliassotti, Róbert Urbán, Gábor Orosz, Orsalya Kiraly, and Zsoit Demetrovics (2018), "Loving the Love of Boys: Motives for Consuming Yaoi Media," *PLoS One*, 10.1371/journal.pone.0198895 (accessed February 12, 2021).

INDEX

Abe no Seimei, 64, 184 n.21
Act on Punishment of Activities Relating to Child Prostitution and Child Pornography and the Protection of Children in Japan, 6–7
adult comics label, 6
Adult Informational Manga, 141–2, 160, 161
   Marked' Women's Concerns, 142, 154–9
   Unmarked' Male Views, 142, 146–54
adult male (comics/*manga*), 5
adult-male-oriented texts, 168
"Adult women fairy tales," 104
A Fraudulent Murasaki's Bumpkin Genji. See *Bumpkin Genji* (Ryūtei Tanehiko, 1829–1842)
"A form of implicit political revisionism," 140
age- and gender-appropriate informational texts, 168
Akamatsu Ken
   Love Hina, 118
Akashi, 22, 57, 65, 69, 99, 101, 103, 114, 143, 146, 156, 157, 159
Akatsuka Fujio, 39, 117–20, 128, 136, 137, 141, 191 n.4, 191 n.6
   Akatsuka Fujio no manga koten nyūmon genji monogatari (*Akatsuka Fujio's Manga Introduction to Classical Literature: The Tale of Genji*), 118
   "high art" courtier world, 120
   mishmashing contemporary concepts, 119
Akatsuka Fujio no manga koten nyūmon genji monogatari. See *Akatsuka Fujio's Manga Introduction to Classical Literature: The Tale of Genji*
Akatsuka Fujio's Manga Introduction to Classical Literature: The Tale of Genji (Akatsuka Fujio, 1983), 39, 117–20, 128, 136, 137, 141

Akihabara, 9, 87, 169
Allison, Anne, 7–8, 13, 157, 175 n.20, 175 n.22, 192 n.11
Althusser, Louis, 12
Amagami SS, 171
amalgamation, 26
Amano Yoshitaka, 44
A Nameless Notebook, 38
Anderson, Benedict, 41
anime, 140, 141, 144, 160, 164
Aoi, 22, 23, 38, 69, 80, 96, 97, 98, 101, 103, 106, 109, 120, 143, 152
Aoyama, Tomoko, 85, 187 n.21
appropriation, 2, 6, 14, 84–8, 90, 160, 165
Article 175 of the Criminal Code, 7
Article 21 of the Customs Tariffs Law, 7
Asagao, 28, 56, 109–111, 114
Asaki yume mishi. See *Fleeting Dreams* (Yamato Waki, 1980–93)
Asuka Henshūbu 67–8, 69–71
   The Comics Anthology of the Tale of Genji: Ms. Shining Genji's Hottie Diary, 67–8
"atashi," 10
Azumanga Daioh, 89

Bachnik, Jane, 12, 176 n.29, 178 n.20
Bakhtin, Mikhail, 29–30, 177 n.10
Bandoh Iruka, 95, 104, 106–8
   Manga gurimu dōwa: kuruwa genji (*Grimm Fairy Tale Comics: Prostitute Quarters of Genji*), 95
   mitate visual puzzle, 108
   New Yoshiwara, 106, 107
   Prostitute Quarters of Genji (2010–11), 104, 106, 108
bara. See gay comics
Barazoku (magazine), 86
Bardsley, Jan, 74
Baudinette, Thomas, 87–8
Bauwens-Sugimoto, Jessica, 11, 174 n.13

beautiful men/women, 147
BE FREE! (Egawa Tatsuya, 1984), 125
bishōnen/bishōjo. See beautiful men/women
Black Lives Movement, 89
The Black Tale of Genji: So Like a Flower (Sakurada Hina, 2015–16), 63, 65–7
bōizu rabu. See Boys Love (BL)
"boku," 10
Bolter, Jay David, 2–3, 53
Bourdieu, Pierre, 30
Bowring, Richard, 31, 32
boys comics. See *Shōnen manga*/boys comics
Boys Love (BL) comics/*manga*, 2, 6, 68, 74, 75, 86, 185 n.2
　appropriation, charges of, 84–8
　BL *Genji manga*, 76–81, 167
　child porn/endangerment, charges of, 75–9
　gay culture and queering of, 84–8
　male-male sexual scenes, 169
　"rape," charges of, 80–4
　sexual tropes, 76
　shōnen-ai, yaoi, and, 74–5
　theories on, 83–4
"The Broomstick," 112
Bryce, Mio, et al., 35
Buddhist impermanence of human life, 145
Bumpkin Genji (Ryūtei Tanehiko, 1829–42), 39–40, 47, 72, 180 n.12, 180 n.13
Bunkashi manga. See literary manga
Butler, Judith, 85
Butta to shattaka butta (Pig/Buddha and the Phony, Koizumi Yoshihiro, 2003–4), 122
byōbu, 152

Caddeau, Patrick W., 40, 41, 45, 140, 180 n.13, 180 n.18, 193 n.4
Cather, Kristen, 90
chibi, 112
child porn/endangerment, charges of, 75–9
child pornography, 75, 76
Chinese Tang dynasty (618–907), 20
Chobits (CLAMP), 138
Chōbunsai Eishi (1756–1829), 39

Choisir (magazine), 84
Cinderella's Misfortune, 112
CLAMP, 138, 183 n.13
Cold War, 42
collaborative readers, 8–10, 29, 33, 94
The Comics Anthology of the Tale of Genji: Ms. Shining Genji's Hottie Diary (Asuka Henshūbu, 2011), 67–8, 69–71
context-specific selves, 10, 15, 165
Cook, Lewis, 38
Cool Japan, 42, 43, 75, 140, 160, 168, 170, 173 n.6
cosplay, 9, 10, 44, 169, 175 n.25
covert presence, 32
COVID-19 pandemic, 89
crafting selves, 10, 27
cultural capital, 3, 30, 35–47, 159, 160

Daigo (Emperor), 144
The Demon of the Heart, 112
Dengeki Daisy (Motomi Kyōsuke), 56
digital storytelling platforms, 170
dōjinshi fanzines, 74
dovetail fitting, 27

Eboshi (hat), 103, 122, 134, 135
economy of desire for images. See media literacy
Egawa Tatsuya, 13, 39, 117, 123, 124–8, 137–8, 167
　BE FREE! (1984), 125
　depiction of sexual encounters, 126
　Genji monogatari (*The Tale of Genji*), 123
　hypersexualization of *The Tale of Genji*, 127
　The Tokyo University Story (1992–2001), 125
Emmerich, Michael, 40, 44, 173 n.5, 180 n.12, 180 n.13, 180 n.14, 182 n.4
"Enacting Genji Ladies Comics," 95
　jealousy, abandonment, and unrequited love, 95–103
Equal Employment Opportunity Law (1986), 5, 93
eroge VN, 171
eromanga, 74, 75, 90, 174 n.10

eroticism, 7, 14, 59, 86, 94, 104, 159, 171, 176 n.33
Erotic Talk: The Tale of Genji Grimm Fairy Tale Comics (Hazuki Tsuyako, 2010), 65, 95, 104–5
est em, 117, 129, 133–8
  Ii ne! Hikaru genji-kun (*Twitter "Likes"! Shining Genji-kun*), 129
The Experience of Love: Special Deluxe, 104

"Fabulous Forty-Niners," 5, 52, 54
facial expressions, 76–7, 82
feminism/feminist theory, 93, 127, 170, 189 n.3
feminist movement, 5
fictional and historical *monogatari* tales, 24
Fifty Shades of Grey, 96
Fireflies, 148
First Princess, 23
Fish, Stanley, 30
Fleeting Dreams (Yamato Waki, 1980–93), 5, 40, 43, 44, 52–60, 71, 72, 151, 156, 182 n.6
  basis of modern remediations, 58–9
  female self-fulfillment, 57
  narrative conventions, 53–5, 71
  visual conventions, 53–4, 71
floating world tale, 39
"The Flute," 37
Fortnightly mimi, 54
Fowler, Edward, 42, 178 n.20
Fudanshi (rotten boys), 86, 87, 167
Fujimoto Yukari, 11, 83, 164–5, 169, 189 n.5
Fujitsubo, 22, 25, 27, 28, 55, 65, 67, 69–70, 73, 83–4, 95, 96, 97, 101, 103, 104, 105, 109, 112, 120, 122, 124, 131, 133, 143, 146, 147, 152, 155–6, 157, 158, 159
Fujiwara Kaoruko, 129, 131, 132, 133
Fujiwara no Michinaga (966–1028), 3, 19, 61, 63, 193 n.8
Fujiwara Saori, 129, 133, 136
Fujiwara no Shunzei (1114–1204), 37
Fujiwara no Teika (1162–1241), 37–8
fujoshi, 12, 86–7, 127, 167, 169

rotten girls, 127, 167, 169
fukinuki yatai. *See* open roof architectural bird's-eye view

Galbraith, Patrick W., 11, 74, 75, 83, 85–6, 87, 88, 164, 165, 174 n.13, 175 n.21, 175 n.24, 176 n.28, 176 n.30, 176 n.32, 176 n.34, 181 n.1, 185 n.6, 186 n.9, 186 n.13, 187 n.17, 188 n.7
gay comics, 87
gay culture, 84–8
geikomi. *See* gay comics
gekiga, 4, 98, 136, 137, 174 n.10, 189 n.9
  realism, 128
  slice-of-life narrative, 100
  Tatsumi Yoshihiro's *A Drifting Life*, 123, 137
Gekka no kimi. *See The Prince in the Moonlight* (Shimaki Ako, 2002–4)
gender
  and age targeting, 134
  gender flipping, 1, 13, 69, 70
  heteronormative, 69
  in-betweens, 2, 14, 81, 84, 86, 90, 127, 165, 167
  male–male, 6, 73–5, 83, 85, 87, 88
gender-based hierarchy, 20
gender chauvinism, 13
Gen/Genya, 106
Genji (eleventh-century tale, 1000–1010). *See also The Tale of Genji* (eleventh-century tale)
  BL ways of love, 76–8
  booms, 41–5, 53, 54, 170
  character (development), 26–9
  fictional world, 31
  gossip, 38
  narrative frame, 146
  paintings, 37
  plot, 25
  scrolls, 36, 37
  transpositions, 36–46, 141
  the ways of love, 76–8
Genji (protagonist), 21–4, 26, 27
  adult fare (lover), 93, 98
  apologies, 143
  in BL comics, 76–9, 80–2, 83–4
  as a cause of women's angst and unrelenting sorrow, 156

as a chestnut, 120–2
as a college student, 129–33
as a critique of patriarchy, 62, 114
empty center, 27
as an evil anti-hero, 63, 65–7
gag (hero), 118, 134
handsome, 27, 55, 60, 63, 67, 94, 104, 110, 138, 143, 145, 150, 156, 158
in *jōhō* informational comics, 139, 141, 143–4, 145, 146, 147–9, 150, 151, 152, 155–8, 159
kind, 60, 62, 64, 103, 124, 131, 143, 144, 146, 150, 168
in ladies comics, 94, 96–8, 99, 100, 101, 102, 104–5, 106–7, 108–11, 112, 113
lampooning of, 15, 128
lineage and familial connections, 28
male lust (signifier), 2, 35, 39, 47, 137, 165, 167
as a modern highschooler, 63, 64–5
as Ms. Genji, 68, 69–71
object of desire, 22, 27, 51, 54, 59, 60, 61, 69, 72, 102, 106, 110, 156, 157
paintings of, 37
parody/ing of, 15, 68, 117, 128, 131, 136, 137, 161, 165
playboy, 112, 143, 146
Rokujō's taunting of, 80–1
role model, 168
in *seinen* young men comics, 123–4, 125, 126–7, 129–30, 131–3, 134–5
in *shōjo* girls comics, 55–6, 59, 60, 61, 62, 64–5, 68, 69–70
in *shōnen* boys comics, 119, 120–1, 122
solicitous lover, 69, 133
surface depth, 28
teachable moments, 143
true love, 54, 56, 67, 72, 74, 75, 93
Genji-e paintings, 36
Genji jōhō manga, 139, 141
Genji koi monogatari. See *The Love Tale of Genji* (Sakurazawa Mai, 2001)
Genji-kun, 129, 133–6
Genji manga
 adult informational, 154–9
 BL 76–81
 category, 53–4
 children informational, 142–6

gag comics, 118–22
 informational, 141–2
 ladies-comics, 93–113
 locating/situating, 165–70
 seinen, 123–36
 shōjo, 53–71
 shōnen, 118–23
 soft porn, 13, 47, 124–8
 stage for, 1–4
Genji monogatari (*The Tale of Genji*), 95, 142. See also *The Tale of Genji*
Genji monogatari BL ansorojii: aiyoku no otoko ōchō koi emaki. See *The Tale of Genji BL Anthology: Love Scrolls of Courtly Male Desire* (Mori Yoshimasa, 2011)
Genji monogatari komikku ansorojii: onna hikaru genji no ikemen nikki. See *The Comics Anthology of The Tale of Genji: Ms. Shining Genji's Hottie Diary* (Asuka Henshūbu, 2011)
Genji monogatari manga de dokuha. See *Reading The Tale of Genji through Manga* (Variety Works, 2010)
Genji monogatari: sen'nen no nazo. See *The Tale of the Genji: The One-Thousand-Year-Old Riddle* (Miyagi Tōko, 2011)
Genji monogatari: uruwashi no karan. See *The Tale of Genji: Elegant Dissolution*) (Ide Chikae, 2008)
girlhood, 52
girls comics. See *shōjo manga*/girls comics
"good wives and wise mothers," 52, 81
Gotoh Museum, 37
Graham, Colin, 45
Grasping the Gist of The Tale of Genji, I/Chestnut (Koizumi Yoshihiro, 2002), 120–3, 137
Gravett, Paul, 4, 5, 139, 174 n.11, 174 n.12, 174 n.14, 182 n.3, 191 n.1, 192 n.1, 192 n.3
Grimm Fairy Tale Comics: Prostitute Quarters of Genji (Bandoh Iruka, 2010–11), 95, 104, 106–8
Grossman, Diane, 127
Grusin, Richard, 2–3, 53

Hagio Moto, 5
The Heart of Thomas (1974), 74

Hakubyō (white drawings), 36, 38, 46
Hanachirusato, 76–9
Hanamura Eiko, 141–2, 154, 156–8, 159, 161, 168
  Genji monogatari (The Tale of Genji), 154
  The Tale of Genji, 156
Harry Potter (Rowling, J. K.), 3
Hasegawa Hōsei, 36, 141, 142, 147, 151–4, 160, 179 n.3, 194 n.16
  Genji monogatari (The Tale of Genji), 147
  Manga Nihon no koten (Japanese Classics in Manga), 151
Hazuki Tsuyako, 65, 95, 104–5
  Erotic Talk: The Tale of Genji Grimm Fairy Tale Comics, 104
The Heart of Thomas (Hagio Moto, 1974), 74
Heian court, 36–8
Heian male-oriented sexual economy, 156
Heian no torendii dorama genji monogatari mangachō. See *The Heian Trendy Drama: The Tale of Genji Manga Notebook* (Takenaka Ranko, 1998)
Heian-period (794–1185), 8, 9, 15, 24, 30, 58, 63, 100, 123, 135, 146–7, 156, 160, 168
Heian process, 29
Heian society, 20, 114
The Heian Trendy Drama: The Tale of Genji Manga Notebook (Takenaka Ranko, 1998), 95, 104, 111–13
Hello Kitty cute, 59, 62, 63
"the hetero/homo binary," 85
heterosexuality, 2, 55–7, 68, 70, 73, 83, 86, 132, 133, 167
Hijikata Yōichi, 58, 182 n.8
hikime kagihana. See line eyes; tiny fishhook noses
Hirata Yoshinobu, 145
Hirokane Kenshi, 140
Hogwarts Legacy, 3
homosexuality, 73, 84, 86, 180 n.19
honkadori foundational poems, 28
Hori Akiko, 85
Horton, H. Mack, 26, 178 n.19
Hotaru. See Fireflies

Ichijō (Emperor), 19, 32
Ide Chikae, 95–8, 100, 179 n.3, 189 n.7, 190 n.19
  Genji monogatari: uruwashi no karan (The Tale of Genji: Elegant Dissolution), 95–6
  ladies comics, 100
Ihara Saikaku (1642–93)
  Kōshoku ichidai otoko (1682), 39, 47
  The Life of an Amorous Man, 39, 47, 108
  The Life of an Amorous Woman, 108
Ii ne! Hikaru genji-kun. See *Twitter "Likes"! Shining Genji* (est em, 2016)
Ikeda Kikan, 140
The Illustrated Tale of Genji: A Classic Japanese Romance, Japanese Edition, (Tsuboi Koh, 1989) 139, 141–2, 147–50, 160
imaginary/fantasy, 3, 7, 10, 14, 82, 87, 94–5, 108, 127, 164–7, 169
Inaba Minori, 117, 128–33, 136, 137, 138, 192 n.14
  cross-dressing, 132
  male gaze, 131, 133
  Minamoto-kun monogatari (The Tale of Minamoto-kun), 128
informational comics. See *Jōhō manga*; see also informational jōhō comics
informational *Genji manga*, 139–41, 160
informational *jōhō manga*, 139–41, 160
interpretative communities, 30
  female, 38
  transpositions, 46–7
Ishida Hitoshi, 84
Ishidori Tatsuya, 44
Ishinomori Shōtarō, 4
  Japan Inc: An Introduction to Japanese Economics in Manga (1986), 139, 151, 160
  Manga nihon no koten (The Japanese Classics in Manga), 151
  Manga nihon no rekishi (The History of Japan in Manga), 151
Ito, Kinko, 5, 95, 174 n.9, 175 n.17, 188 n.1, 188 n.2, 189 n.4, 189 n.7
Itoh, Moriyuki, 29
Iyami Genji, 118–20, 137

Jackson, Earl, Jr., 42
Japanese military-industrial complex, 140
Japanese poetry, 25, 29, 41. See also *tanka; waka*
Japanese selves, 9–10, 12, 15, 27, 164, 165
Japan Inc: An Introduction to Japanese Economics in Manga (Ishinomori Shōtarō, 1986), 139, 151, 160
Johnson, Adrienne, 74, 185 n.6, 188 n.26
jōhō manga, 15, 139, 141, 160. See also informational *jōhō manga*
jōhō remediations, 151
josei. See women comics

kabuki, 43, 45
Kagami Hiroyuki, 165, 186 n.9
Kaoru, 23, 28, 37, 42, 51, 55, 57, 144, 147, 150, 151
Kashiwagi, 23, 147, 156, 157
Kashiwagi III, 37
Kawabata Yasunari, 25, 42
Kawaguchi Kaiji, 140
kawaii, 53, 54, 98, 118, 122
Kern, Adam, 39, 174 n.9, 179 n.10
Ketterling, Jean, 83, 165, 175 n.21, 176 n.28, 176 n.31, 185 n.5, 186 n.13
Khan, Ummni, 83, 165, 175 n.21, 176 n.28, 176 n.31, 185 n.5, 186 n.13
kibyōshi, 39
Kikuchi Shū, 64–5
Kikuchi Yasuhiko, 31, 178 n.20
Kikuta Shigeo, 27, 181 n.27
Kimura Jin (later Mitsuhi), 182 n.2
Kinsella, Sharon, 4, 6, 98, 139–40, 160, 174 n.11, 181 n.1, 191 n.1
Kira, 95, 101, 102, 103
  Genji monogatari (The Tale of Genji), 95
  young ladies comics heroine, 102–3
Kiritsubo (Emperor), 55, 120, 121, 144, 147
Kiritsubo no kōi/Kiritsubo Consort/Genji's mother, 22, 68, 101, 120, 124–126, 131, 134, 147, 155, 184 n.18
Kishida Ren, 142, 146, 193 n.10, 193 n.12
  Manga genji monogatari (The Manga Tale of Genji), 142
Kitamura, Yuika, 5, 93, 180 n.20, 180 n.21, 181 n.22, 182 n.3, 182 n.6, 182 n.7, 189 n.8

Klar, Elizabeth, 128
Koizumi Yoshihiro, 37, 39, 117, 120–3, 137
  "Kiritsubo" Chapter, 120–1
  Ōzukami genji monogatari maro n? (Grasping the Gist of The Tale of Genji, I/Chestnut), 118
Kokiden (Empress), 120, 155–6, 189 n.10
Kokinwakashū, 25
Kondo, Dorinne, 10, 26, 27, 100, 127, 177 n.8, 178 n.20
Kōshoku ichidai otoko. See The Life of an Amorous Man (Ihara Saikaku, 1682)
Kristof, Nicholas, 6, 175 n.19
Kumoinokari, 23, 37, 195 n.22
The Kumon Manga Literature Classics Tale of Genji (Saeki Nao, 2004), 141, 142, 145–6
Kumon no manga koten bungakukan genji monogatari. See The Kumon Manga Literature Classics Tale of Genji (Saeki Nao, 2004)
Kunishige Hazuki, 64–5
Kure Tomofusa, 139
Kuro genji monogatari: hana to miruramu. See The Black Tale of Genji: So Like a Flower (Sakurada Hina, 2015–16)
Kuwata Jirō, 141, 142, 144–5, 193 n.5, 193 n.6, 193 n.9
  Genji monogatari (The Tale of Genji), 142
Kyoto Civilian News, 111

ladies comics, 5, 14–15, 93–4, 142, 166–8
  creation of subject positions, 94
  creators, 94
  drama features, 94, 95
  mainstream (patriarchal) society, 94
  "negative" female traits, 94
  performative space, 94
  romance/fantasy, 94, 95
  Sakurazawa Mai, 159
  sexually graphic, 94
  social and political events, 93
  types, 94
Lady Manga, 95, 111
landed (warrior) lords, 38, 141, 163
language, 21
Lebra, Takie Sugiyama, 26, 177 n.8

The Life of an Amorous Man (Ihara Saikaku, 1682), 39, 108
The Life of an Amorous Woman (Ihara Saikaku, 1686), 108
lineage, 21, 28
line eyes, 152
Lippet, Yukio, 37
literary manga, 140
"lolicon guy," 88
Lone Wolf and Cub (Koike Kazuo and Kojima Goseki, 1970–1976), 123
Love Hina (Akamatsu Ken, 1998–2000), 118
A Love of a Thousand Years: The Tale of the Shining Genji (film, 2001), 44, 61
A Love of a Thousand Years: The Tale of the Shining Genji (manga, Sasaki Misuzu, 2001), 59–62
The Love Tale of Genji (Sakurazawa Mai, 2001), 95, 104, 108–11, 159
Lunning, Frenchy, 175 n.25

MacWilliams, Mark W., 43, 61
Maison Ikkoku (Takahashi Rumiko), 129
Maki Miyako, 95, 98, 99, 100, 189 n.8, 189 n.10
    Genji monogatari, (*The Tale of Genji*), 95
    slice-of-life strategies, 100
    "warm and fuzzy," 100
male gaze, 125, 126, 128, 131, 133
male–male narratives, 74–5, 79, 83
male-oriented *Genji manga*, 136
manga, 27
    Adult Informational Manga, 141–2, 146–59
    adult male, 5, 168–69
    age- and gender targeting-categories, 13
    and *anime*, 2, 6–8, 10, 41, 75, 9
    art reproductions, 144
    audiences, 127
    Boys Love (*See* Boys Love)
    compartmentalization of selves, 164
    death scenes, 143
    in the defense of, 7–13
    drawings and text with photographs, 144
    educational tomes, 141
    female/feminine-oriented repurposings, 163
    female remediations for, 38
    history of, 4–6
    "inappropriate" fantasies, 165
    informational, 141–2, 161
    informational children, 142–6, 160
    in-group reading strategies, 29–32
    jōhō manga, 139, 141, 160, 168
    ladies comics, 93–4, 168–9
    lampoon, 167
    locating/situating, 165–70
    male–male relationships, 6
    media-rich format, 144
    modern, 4
    nooks and crannies, 163
    objections to, 89–90
    "offensive" portrayals, 7
    protocols for consumption of, 11
    pushback against harmful publications, 6–7
    remediations, 140, 169 (*See also* remedition)
    segments, 122
    seinen young men (see *seinen* young men *manga*)
    shōjo (see *shōjo manga*)
    shōnen (see *shōnen manga*)
    transpositions, 151
    twentieth-century recreation, 149
    visual literacy, 120
    young comics, 168–9
Manga genji monogatari. See *Manga Tale of Genji*
Manga gurimu dōwa: kuruwa genji. See *Grimm Fairy Tale Comics: Prostitute Quarters of Genji* (Bandoh Iruka, 2010–11)
Manga gurimu dōwa enbun genji monogatari. See *Erotic Talk: The Tale of Genji Grimm Fairy Tale Comics* (Hazuki Tsuyako, 2010)
Manga Nihon no koten (*The Japanese Classics in Manga*) (Ishinomori Shōtarō), 151
Manga nihon no rekishi (*The History of Japan in Manga*) (Ishinomori Shōtarō), 151
The Manga Tale of Genji

Kishida Ren (2002), 142, 146
Mihashi Mari (1988), 141, 142, 154, 155–6, 161, 168
Maro, 120, 122
maron, 120, 121, 122, 123
Maruyama Kei, 141, 142–4, 193 n.5, 193 n.6, 193 n.7, 193 n.8
  Genji monogatari (The Tale of Genji), 142
  Komikkusutorii watashitachi no koten (Comic Stories of Our Classics) (1998), 142
  The Masterpieces through Manga: The Tale of Genji (Sanazaki Harumo, 2010), 141, 142, 154, 159, 168
Maya Mineo, 39, 67–9
  Counterpoints, *The Tale of Genji*, 67, 69
  Patalliro genji monogatari!, 67
  Patalliro Tale of Genji!, 39, 67–8
McCormick, Melissa, 37, 38, 179 n.6
McLelland, Mark, 6, 75–6, 88–9
McNeil, Baye, 63
media literacy, 11, 53, 127, 164
medieval (1185–1600) warriors, 36–8
Meiji Restoration, 40
Meisho o manga de: genji monogatari. See *The Masterpieces through Manga: The Tale of Genji* (Sanazaki Harumo, 2010)
"mess of possibilities," 85
#MeToo Movement, 89
Mihashi Mari, 141, 142, 154, 155–6, 161, 168, 194 n.20
  Manga genji monogatari (The Manga Tale of Genji), 154
Mijuki, 76–9, 80
Miki Minoru, 45
Miller, Laura, 88, 184 n.21, 184 n.22
mimi, 54
MimiExcellent, 54
Minamoto-kun monogatari. See *The Tale of Minamoto-kun* (Inaba Minori, 2012–19)
Minamoto Terumi, 129, 130, 131–3
Miō Serina, 62, 183 n.17
  remediation, 62
  The Tale of Genji manga, 62
Mishima Yukio, 42
Miyagi Tōko, 63–4, 67

Genji monogatari: sen'nen no nazo (2011), 63
Miyake, Lynne, 30, 31, 43
Miyata Masayuki, 44
Miyazaki Tsutomu, 6
modern Japanese "translations," 40–1
moe, 85, 181 n.1
moe imagery literacy. See media literacy
monogatari storytelling, 27
Moriarty, 118
Mori Naoko, 82, 83, 187 n.18
Mori Yoshimasa, 73, 74, 76–9, 80–1, 132, 166–7
  The Tale of Genji BL Anthology: Love Scrolls of Courtly Male Desire (2011), 73
Mori Yukiko, 182 n.2
Motomi Kyōsuke, *Dengeki Daisy*, 56
Motoori Norinaga (1730–1801), 40, 43, 72, 140, 163
Ms. Genjii, 69–70
Mumyō-zōshi. See *A Nameless Notebook*
Murasaki (protagonist), 22, 24, 28, 51, 56–7, 60, 64–5, 67, 79, 83, 94, 95, 96, 99, 101, 102, 103, 109, 112, 114, 122, 143, 145, 146, 147, 149, 150, 156, 157, 158, 159, 166
Murasaki-humanoid robot, 45
Murasaki Shikibu (author, c. 978–c. 1014), 1, 19, 20, 21, 32, 33, 36, 37, 44, 51, 56, 57, 61, 63, 64, 91, 104, 111, 113, 137, 140, 144, 163, 169
Murase, Miyeko, 37, 179 n.6

Nagaike, Kazumi, 75, 79, 85, 96, 87, 185 n.6, 187 n.21
Nakamura Hikaru, 134
Nagayama Kaoru, 4, 6, 10, 11, 23, 28, 51, 52, 55, 144, 147, 150, 151
Nakao Motoko, 83
national language, 40–1
national literature, 40–1
The New Edition Tale of Genji (Kimura Jin, 1970), 182 n.2
The New Tale of Genji (Tanabe Seiko, 1978–9), 43, 180 n.21
NHK manga de yomu koten 3: genji monogatari • ise mongatari. See *NHK Reading the Classics through*

Manga 3: The Tale of Genji and The Tale of Ise (Toba Shōko, 2006)
NHK Reading the Classics through Manga 3: The Tale of Genji and The Tale of Ise (Toba Shōko, 2006), 59–60
niche-targeted *manga*, 171
ninjōbon. See sentimental fiction
Ninnaji Temple, 144
Niou, 23, 28, 51, 52, 55, 147, 150, 151
Nise murasaki inaka genji. See A Fraudulent Murasaki's Bumpkin Genji
Nishimura Tōru, 146
novelization of *The Tale of Genji*, 40–1
Nowaki, 148

Oborozukiyo, 22, 59, 60, 68, 69, 79, 86, 109, 110, 157, 159, 190 n.19, 192 n.13
Ochiba, 23, 156, 157, 195 n.22
Ogi, Fusami, 5, 94, 102–3
Ohama, 108
oiran, 107, 108
One Piece (Oda Eiichirō), 13
Ō no myōbu, 104, 105, 114
open roof architectural bird's-eye view, 152
Orbaugh, Sharlyn, 76, 79, 88, 186 n.13, 188 n.29
"ore," 10
Ōshima Yumiko, 5
Osomatsukun (*Mr. Nothing Special*, Akatsuka Fujio, 1962), 118
otaku, 12, 53
Otome Road, 87
Otome Rōdo, 169
Ōzukami genji monogatari maro n?. See Grasping the Gist of The Tale of Genji, I/Chestnut (Koizumi Yoshihiro, 2002)

Parody, 131
participatory readers, 8–10, 30–1, 33, 94
Patalliro genji monogatari! See Patalliro Tale of Genji! (Maya Mineo, 2004–8)
Patalliro Tale of Genji! (Maya Mineo, 2004–8), 39, 67–9
Penley, Constance, 83
performative readers, 2, 8–10, 31–2, 33

Perry, Matthew, 40
"phallic power," 79
"phantasy," 81
Pig/Buddha and the Phony (Butta to shattaka butta, Koizumi Yoshihiro), 122
The Pillow Book (Sei Shonagon), 20
"Pivoting Genji Ladies Comics," 95
empowering graphic sex, different genjis, and feminist critiques, 104–13
A Poem of Wind and Trees (Takemiya Keiko, 1976), 74
Pope, Alexander, 29
Pretty Guardian Sailor Moon (Takeuchi Naoko), 56
Prince Charming, 94, 114
The Prince in the Moonlight (Shimaki Ako, 2002–4), 63–5
Prostitute Quarters of Genji (Bandoh Iruka, 2010–11), 95, 104, 106, 108
Proust, Marcel, 140
Remembrance of Things Past, 140

queer, 14, 84–8, 91, 127, 128, 132, 136, 165, 167, 169
queering/queer theory, 84–8, 187 n.23

"rape," charges of, 80–4
readers/readership
collaborative readers, 8–10, 33, 94
participatory readers, 8–10, 30–1, 33, 94
performative readers, 2, 8–10, 31–2, 33
Reading The Tale of Genji through Manga (Variety Works, 2010), 141, 142, 147, 150–1, 160
rediisu komikku (redikomi). See ladies comics
Reizei, 23, 145
remediation, 2, 3, 5
Akatsuka, 118
Akatsuka and Koizumi, 128
boys-comics, 15
Egawa's, 133, 137–8
gender-flipping, 13
girls comics, 72
Hanamura's, 159
Hazuki's, 104–5
Inaba's, 132
Kira's, 102

Kishida, 146
Maki Miyako, 98
manga, 15, 38, 39, 140, 169
Maruyama's, 142, 143
Mihashi Mari, 155
Miō Serina, 59, 62
Saeki Nao, 145
Setouchi Jakuchō, 45
Tanabe Seiko, 43, 44, 52
Tomi's, 124, 129, 137
Tsuboi, 147, 149–50, 154
Yamato, 58
Remembrance of Things Past (Proust, Marcel), 140
"representational appropriation," 84–5
repurposing, 3
   remediation, 53
Rodriquez, Jorge, 88
Rokujō, 22, 28, 80–2, 94, 96, 97, 98, 99, 101, 102, 103, 107, 108, 109, 114, 124, 143, 152, 157, 158, 159
Role Playing game (RPG), 3
Rowling, J. K., *Harry Potter*, 3
RPG (Role Playing game), 3
Russo-Japanese War, 41
Ryang, Sonia, 88
ryōsai kenbo. See "good wives and wise mothers"
Ryūtei Tanehiko (1783–1842), 39–40, 47, 72, 180 n.12
   Nise murasaki inaka genji, 39

Saeki Nao, 141, 142, 145–6
   Kumon no manga koten bungakukan genji monogatari (*The Kumon Manga Literature Classics Tale of Genji*), 142
   remediation, 145
Saito, Kumiko, 74, 84, 185 n.2, 185 n.6
Sakurada Hina, 63, 65–7
   Kuro genji monogatari: hana to miruramu (2015–16), 63, 65
Sakurazawa Erica, 134
Sakurazawa Mai, 95, 104, 108–11, 159, 190 n.19
   Genji koi monogatari (*The Love Tale of Genji*), 95
Sanazaki Harumo, 141, 142, 154, 159, 168, 195 n.23

Meisho o manga de: genji monogatari (*The Masterpieces through Manga: The Tale of Genji*), 154
Santo Kyōden (1761–1816), 47
   kibyōshi, 39
Saotome Ageha, 80–2, 86
The Sarashina Diary, 51
Sarashina nikki. See *The Sarashina Diary*
Sasaki Misuzu, 59–62
   A Love of a Thousand Years (2001), 59, 61
Satō Masaki, 84
Schodt, Fredrick, 6, 8, 9, 74, 94, 174 n.9, 174 n.11, 174 n.12, 174 n.14, 174 n.17, 175 n.18, 175 n.22, 188 n.2, 191 n.1, 192 n.11
"secret weapon," 158
Section Chief Kosaku Shima, 140
Sedgwick, Eve, "mess of possibilities," 85
Seinen young men *manga*, 4, 5, 15, 167–8
   eye-candy panty shots and cherry-picking the *Genji*, 128–36
   gekiga realism and soft porn, 123–8
Sei Shōnagon (c. 966–c. 1025) 20
seme (attacker), 76, 78, 79, 82–5
Sen'nen no koi: hikaru genji monogatari. See *A Love of a Thousand Years: The Tale of the Shining Genji* (film, 2001); *A Love of a Thousand Years: The Tale of the Shining Genji* (manga, Sasaki Misuzu, 2001)
sentimental fiction, 108
Setouchi Jakuchō, 27, 43, 45, 154, 158, 159
sexual encounter, 82
sexuality, 5, 13, 14, 42, 43, 62, 81, 85, 87, 91, 114, 127, 168
Shamoon, Deborah, 174 n.14, 185 n.7
Shigematsu, Setsu, 75, 81–2, 86, 127, 175 n.19, 176 n.28, 185 n.7
Shimaki Ako, 63–5
   Gekka no kimi (2002–4), 63
Shimizu Yoshiko, 147, 154
Shin genji monogatari. See *The New Tale of Genji* (Tanabe Seiko, 1978–79)
Shining Prince, 135, 157
Shirane, Haruo, 38, 40, 41, 108, 174 n.15, 177 n.4, 178 n.11, 179 n.1, 190 n.16, 190 n.17, 190 n.18, 192 n.3
shōjo-eseque drawing style, 143, 144

shōjo manga/girls comics, 5, 14, 51, 102, 103, 114, 165–6
 challenging, 63–7
 conventions on love and romance, 54–5
 establishing *shōjo* cute, 59–63
 making, 54–9
 objects of desire, 53–72
 and *The Tale of Genji*, counterpointing, 67–71
shōnen-ai (boys love), 6, 74, 75, 185 n.6
Shōnen manga/boys-comics, 5, 8, 15, 117, 118, 136, 167
 focalizing the funny, 118–23
 inventive reworking, 120
 male-oriented *manga*, 118
 remediations, 15
Shōshi (988–1074), 19, 61–2
shunga, 7
Societal guardrails, 11–12
soft power, 2, 35, 41–6, 139–41, 160, 173 n.6
Sophomore-ish, 133
sōshiji (narrator), 30, 31
"state feminism," 93
storify.com, 170
Suetsumuhana, 22, 25, 27, 57, 66, 119, 129
suki, 143
surface depth, 28–9, 178 n.12, 191 n.8
Suter, Rebecca, 74, 83, 183 n.13, 185 n.6, 187 n.20, 187 n.22
Suzaku, 23, 144
Suzuki, Shige, 98, 123
Suzuki, Tomi, 41, 43, 140

tableau-like scenes, 152
Takahashi, Mizuki, 5
Takahashi Rumiko, reminiscent of, 129, 138
Takahashi Tomotaka, 45
Takarazuka musical review, 20, 43, 45, 47, 52, 58, 72, 181 n.22, 193 n.4
Takashima Kazusa, 69–70
Takemiya Keiko, 5
 A Poem of Wind and Trees (1976), 74
Takenaka Ranko, 95, 104, 111–13, 190 n.20
 The Heian Trendy Drama: The Tale of Genji Manga Notebook, 111

Takeuchi Naoko, *Pretty Guardian Sailor Moon*, 56
The Tale of Genji (the eleventh-century tale, 1000–1010). See also *Genji* (eleventh-century tale)
 creation of character, 27–9
 cultural DNA, 163–71
 cultural, moral, and ethical concerns, 168
 events and activities, 168
 Heian courtier, 19, 20
 hypersexualization, 127
 inception and role, 19
 in-group reading strategies, 29–32. See also readers/readership
 interpretive community, 30
 Japanese culture lay in, 140
 Millennial Anniversary Memorial Ceremony, 44, 140, 161
 millennial celebrations, 21
 modern Japanese rendering, 27
 national treasure, 168
 positionality, 140
 pushback, 169
 world's first novel, 140
The Tale of Genji (Manga)
 Egawa Tatsuya (2001–5), 13, 39, 117, 123, 124–8, 137–8, 167
 Hanamura Eiko (2013), 141, 142, 154, 156–8, 159, 161, 168
 Hasegawa Hōsei (1996–7), 36, 141, 142, 147, 151–4, 160
 Kira (2005–6), 95, 101, 102–3
 Kuwata Jirō (1993–5), 141, 142, 144–5
 Maki Miyako (1997–8), 95, 98–100
 Maruyama Kei (2009), 141, 142–4
 Miō Serina (2007–9), 62
 Mori Yukiko (1974), 182 n.2
 Tomi Shinzō (1991), 39, 117, 123–5, 137, 167
The Tale of Genji BL Anthology: Love Scrolls of Courtly Male Desire (Mori Yoshimasa, 2011), 73, 74, 76–9, 80–1, 132, 166–7
The Tale of Genji: Elegant Dissolution (Ide Chikae, 2008), 95–8, 100, 182 n.2, 182 n.9
The Tale of Genji: The Thousand-Year-Old Riddle (Miyagi Tōko, 2011), 63–4, 67

The Tale of Genji Mutated (Teradate Kazuko, 2001–2), 95, 101–2
The Tale of Minamoto-kun (Inaba Minori, 2012–19), 117, 128–33, 136, 137, 138
Tales of Yamato, 31
Tamakazura, 122, 148, 156
Tanabe Seiko, 52, 58
  Shin genji monogatari, 43
Tanaka Shigeyoshi, 26
Tanizaki Jun'ichirō, 42
tanka. *See* Japanese poetry; *waka*
Tansman, Alan, 147
Tateishi Kazuhiro, 43, 44–5, 58, 61, 176 n.35, 180 n.17, 181 n.22, 182 n.2, 182 n.8, 183 n.16
Tatsumi Yoshihiro, 98, 123, 137
Teika, 37–38. *See also* Fujiwara no Teika
Teradate Kazuko, 95, 101–2
  drawing style and narrative, 102
  evocation, 101
  The Tale of Genji Mutated, 101
Tezuka Osamu, 4
The Tale of the Genji: The One-Thousand-Year-Old Riddle (Miyagi Tōko, 2011), 63–4, 67
Third Princess, 22, 23, 103, 143, 146, 156, 157, 158, 159
Thorn, Rachel, 4, 5, 56, 74, 174 n.14, 185 n.6, 188 n.1
tiny fishhook noses, 152
Toba Shōko, 59–61, 141, 182 n.10
  Genji monogatari (*The Tale of Genji*), 59
Tokugawa Bakufu, 38
Tokugawa Reimeikai Foundation, 37
Tokyo National Museum, 37
The Tokyo University Story (Egawa Tatsuya, 1992–2001), 125
Tomi Shinzō, 39, 117, 123–5, 137, 167
  Genji monogatari (*The Tale of Genji*), 122
Tomita Isao, 45
Tō no Chūjō, 21, 23, 96, 102, 111, 114
Torii Hiroko, 145
Tosa School paintings, 36, 37
townspeople, Edo, 39, 141
traditional *emaki*-scroll-and-painting conventions, 152
translation, 35, 39
transpositions, 3
  Edo (1600–1868) explosion, 38–40
  interpretative communities, 46–7
  medieval (1185–1600) warrior Genji adaptations, 36–8
  modernization (1868 through the Second World War), 40–1
  popular soft power/cultural capital (1950–present), 41–6
Tsuboi Koh, 139, 141–2, 147–50, 160, 194 n.13
  The Illustrated Tale of Genji: A Classic Japanese Romance, English Edition, 139, 147, 148
  The Illustrated Tale of Genji: A Classic Japanese Romance, Japanese Edition, 147, 148
  single-volume *Genji*, 147
Tsuji Masaki, 144
Twitter "Likes"! Shining Genji-kun (est em, 2016), 117, 129, 133–8
2D environment/world, 87, 181 n.1
Tyler, Royall, 21, 28

uchi/soto ("inside"/"outside"), 12
uguisu (bush warbler), 25, 33
Uji princesses, 23, 122, 150, 156
uke (recipient/receiver), 76, 78, 79, 82–5
Ukifune, 23, 38, 51, 52, 57, 150, 151, 158
ukiyo-e woodblock prints, 36, 39
ukiyo zōshi. *See* floating world tale
Undoing Gender, 85
Unita Yumi, 134
unmarked male informational comics 154
US-Japan Treaty of Mutual Cooperation and Security, 4
Utagawa Kunisada (1786–1865), 36, 39
Utsusemi, 22, 66, 69, 122, 124, 158

Variety Art Works, 141, 142, 147, 150, 151, 160
  Genji monogatari manga de dokuha (*Reading The Tale of Genji Through Manga*), 147
Vernon, Victoria, 21
Vincent, Keith, 84
visual culture, 112, 176 n.8
visual novel (VN), 170, 171

waka, 25, 29, 31–2, 40, 135, 177 n.4, 191 n.8. *See also* Japanese poetry
Waley, Arthur (1889–1966), 41
Wang, Xin, 100
Washburn, Dennis, 44
"watakushi," 10
"watashi," 10
"Weird Japan," 74
Welker, James, 6, 86
Williams, Alan
   "a multitude of gender performances," 85
   "non-identitarian," 86
Williams, Linda, 78, 175 n.20, 185 n.7
women comics, 5, 142
Wood, Andrea, 73, 74, 75, 83

Yamato Waki, 5, 40, 43, 44, 52–60, 71, 72, 151, 156, 180 n.20
   Asaki yume mishi (1980–93), 52

Fleeting Dreams, 43, 56
yaoi, 6, 74, 75, 84, 85, 88, 91, 127, 134, 185 n.2
Yamamoto, Traise, 74
Yamashita, Samuel, 38
Yaoi Ronsō debate, 84–5, 88
Yin-Yang *onmyōji*, 64, 184 n.22
Yōhen genji monogatari. See *The Tale of Genji Mutated* (Teradate Kazuko, 2001–2)
"Yokobue." *See* "The Flute"
Yosano Akiko, 41, 46, 180 n.20, 189 n.7
Yūgao (Lady of the Evening Face Flower), 22, 28, 38, 96, 101, 103, 122, 143, 144, 156
yūgen, 38
Yūgiri, 22, 23, 37, 55, 101, 147, 149, 157

Zsila, Agnas, et al., 187 n.25

www.ingramcontent.com/pod-product-compliance
Lightning Source LLC
Chambersburg PA
CBHW071823300426
44116CB00009B/1412